THE
OUTSIDER

THE
OUTSIDER

*The Autobiography of One of
Britain's Most Controversial Policemen*

KEITH HELLAWELL

HarperCollins*Publishers*

HarperCollins*Publishers*
77–85 Fulham Palace Road,
Hammersmith, London W6 8JB

www.**fire**and**water**.com

Published by HarperCollins*Publishers* 2002
1 3 5 7 9 8 6 4 2

Copyright © Keith Hellawell 2002

The author asserts the moral right to
be identified as the author of this work

A catalogue record for this book
is available from the British Library

ISBN 0 00 714529 2

Set in Adobe Garamond by
Rowland Phototypesetting Ltd,
Bury St Edmunds, Suffolk

Printed and bound in Great Britain by
Clays Ltd, St Ives plc

To Bren

*To Graham, a very special nephew
who died during completion of this book*

CONTENTS

ACKNOWLEDGEMENTS

My thanks to my friend Jon Hammond, who pestered me for many years to write this book, my agent Tony Mulliken, who introduced me to HarperCollins, Michael Fishwick, who offered me sound advice and, finally, to Duff Hart-Davis, who helped me to develop as a writer.

CHAPTER ONE

ROUGH START

The telephone call came at ten past nine on the evening of Friday, 8 June 2001, the day after the general election in which Labour was returned for a second term in office with a resounding majority. My wife Brenda picked up the receiver.

'This is No. 10 Downing Street,' said a man's voice. 'Could I speak to Mr Keith Hellawell, please?'

It was Sir Richard Wilson, Permanent Secretary at the Cabinet Office. 'Keith,' he said, 'this is a courtesy call. The Prime Minister has asked me to tell you that your unit is going to the Home Office.'

So Tony Blair had decided to give the drug portfolio to David Blunkett, the newly-appointed Home Secretary. The message heralded the beginning of the end of my forty years in public service . . . but I have much to tell before then.

I was born on 18 May 1942 in Holmfirth, Yorkshire – the village in the foothills of the Pennines which has become well known from the television series *Last of the Summer Wine*. At the time of my birth my mother Ada (born Ada Alice Battye) was married to Douglas Hellawell, but I doubt that he was my father, even though his name appears on my birth certificate: apart from other considerations, he was about 5′ 7″ tall, my mother was only 5′ 2″, and I grew up to be 6′ 2″. In any case, we lived in a terrace house, one of three owned and occupied by the Hellawells, and to say that they were a mixed-up family would be an understatement.

It seems that Grandfather Hellawell was a drunkard and difficult to deal with. He had a large family, and the task of looking after it fell on the womenfolk. His eldest daughter, Evelyn, worked in the local woollen mill from the age of ten, spending the morning in school and the afternoon in the mill. When she was twelve, she went into full-time employment there. After her mother passed away she virtually brought up her brothers and sisters, and she lived in one of the cottages with her crippled bachelor brother Duke. As an adult she continued to work in the mill, but after losing her childhood sweetheart in the First World War she never married.

Our neighbours on the other side were Uncle Clarence and his Welsh wife Kate. They had no children and seemed miserable together; after she died he enjoyed the company of young women, who flattered him, and to whom he left his life savings. When I grew up I began to collect clocks, of which he had a number. He knew of my interest and once asked me if I would like to purchase one – the idea of giving me one never occurred to him. This was typical: I have never received anything from any of the Hellawells.

The other sister was Auntie Emma, who was very prim and proper. In those days she was thought to have married rather well, although it was rumoured that her union with Archibald Newbold Hector McDermott Cank Nicholls was never consummated. They adopted the son of one of the Hellawell brothers, James, the result of his previous marriage.

Apart from my 'father', there was also my Uncle Harry, an eccentric who designed quirky objects – for instance he built one house out of discarded public house signs. His marriage to Flossie was a turbulent affair. She left him several times, and lived for many years in Australia with their daughter. Eventually, in his sixties, he decided to join her, and rediscovered himself amidst nature. He bought a campervan and spent the last years of his life as a beatnik, beard unkempt, hair to his waist, surfing and living off the land. He died in his eighties, as he would have wished, surfing off the Great Barrier Reef.

My mother's background was equally unusual. Her father owned a small textile mill, and to avoid the dangers of the First World War the family emigrated to Canada, taking my mother, who was six at the time, and her eight-year-old brother, Ben. Their mother, my maternal grandmother, was a good-time girl and used to serve and sing in the clubs: she had flaming red hair, and even in her seventies wore six-inch, stiletto-heeled shoes. When the marriage was dissolved in North America, my mother and her brother were sent back to England. Grandfather never married again, but returned to this country and lived with a very sour woman who didn't like his children, neither of whom went to live with him. Instead, they were farmed out among relatives.

In Yorkshire my mother worked in the woollen mill and then followed her mother into club singing at weekends. Ben had a number of jobs, and although he was successful at none of them, he was rather a good false-pretence merchant: I believe he once sold London Bridge to some American, and received a prison sentence for his trouble.

When my maternal grandmother eventually returned to this country in her eighties, she showed me the family history, which revealed that her great-great-something grandfather had been a French nobleman, Count Dubracy. It seems, however, that he was not all he should have been, for he was a smuggler, and got caught. To avoid prosecution, he fled from France to Whalley Hall at Whalley Bridge in Lancaster (the house still exists and is in Chancery). He continued with his old tricks there, and escaped again to New Mill, near Holmfirth, where he changed his name to Debray, and his son became simply Bray – my grandmother's maiden name. So there is some quality in my background.

The other side of the coin is the name Hellawell. I have only been sent off a rugby field once, and that was by a referee called Hellawell, for a tangle with another player, also called Hellawell. When we gave the referee our names, he thought we were having him on; but once we convinced him we were not, he let us off with a caution. After the game he told us the derivation of our name. It seems that in medieval times children born out of wedlock were regarded as offspring of the devil and were drowned in the well. Later, when such practices were outlawed, those born out of wedlock were named 'Hell o' the well' or 'Hell a' the well', or 'Hell e' the well'. This developed into Hellawell – so the reader will have to determine whether I am close to nobility or a bastard.

The earliest recollection I have is of sitting in a playpen outside our house in Holmfirth. I was only a baby, but I remember it vividly. Because I was squint-eyed, I had to wear spectacles from the age of eighteen months, and I hated them. I used to tear them from my face and screw them up. Unfortunately I did the same with the glasses of others who chose to lean over my pen, and this did not endear me to the bespectacled people of the village. (I was born with strabismus, a condition which affects the muscles of the eyes, and I had a number of operations to correct it, the first when I was four. I was an in-patient at the Huddersfield Royal Infirmary, and I can still smell the chloroform they put over my mouth to send me to sleep. The pads they put over my eyes made me feel I had gone blind.)

At home, I remember screaming and screaming and being unable to move. I could hear loud noises and I was extremely frightened. Later in life Auntie Evelyn told my wife that during an air raid she had heard my cries and found me tied to the table leg in the kitchen. My mother had gone out socialising with some soldiers. I don't recall a great deal more, except that Auntie Evelyn was kind to me, and I had meals with her. I have no memory at all of my 'father' at that stage.

When we left Holmfirth we went to live with my Auntie Florence whose home was outside Huddersfield. She was my mother's sister-in-law, married to her brother Ben. Florence was a cruel woman. She had three children of her own, two daughters and a son, and I suppose she treated me as one of her own. I remember being shackled and looking up at a skylight with brown sacking over it. I was in bed with chicken pox, and to prevent me picking my spots, Florence had tied me down. Another vivid recollection is of walking in the snow to wait for a bus, without shoes, because I had been too slow putting them on. On another occasion one of the daughters and I were locked in the coal cellar for being naughty. It was dark and cold, and I was frightened. During this period I generally spent each day at the nursery in Huddersfield, being taken there by my mother on her way to work and collected on her way home.

At one point we moved to a cottage up in the hills, the home of a man who had raped my mother some fifteen years earlier: he had pestered her ever since to go and live with him, and so she went for a month, then abandoned him, to teach him a lesson. He never recovered, never married, and harassed her until the day he died.

After being packed from one house to another, we drove to 5 Bath Street in Huddersfield, a tenement building. I remember the journey because of the novelty of being in a vehicle, which someone later told me was a taxi. This place was something different. I was only four, but I can remember it vividly. We had one room on the first floor, directly next to the communal bathroom. When we arrived, the bath was full of excreta, and it stank. In due course we cleaned it out, but the only baths I had were in the big tin tub, once a week, in front of the fire. The shared kitchen was in the cellar. There were two large industrial gas cookers, which were coin-operated, and we soon learned that you had to stay with the cooker once you had paid for gas, otherwise someone would both take your food and use the gas for him or herself. The house was always noisy: people yelled at night, and there were domestic arguments throughout the day.

This was where I spent the next eight years of my childhood – and I have often been asked if that period affected my life. Clearly it did, for during it I was taught many lessons about people and the way they live.

The first stark lesson was about relationships between men and women. Our neighbours, although separated, continued to live next door to each other. They both had new partners, and constantly exchanged taunts and jibes in public. One would taunt the new man in his old partner's life about the type of sex she enjoyed and the positions he used to put her in. The new man, not surprisingly, reacted with violence. In the end the animosity got out of control, and the old flame attacked her tormentor with a coping-stone from the front wall, battering his head in. I witnessed this attack without any emotion.

My mother, meanwhile, had taken up with a self-employed plumber called Newton Heap, who had left his wife and two children to live with her. He was a cruel man who saw me as a rival. If we walked out, he made me stay across the road from my mother and him. When we travelled on a bus, they would sit upstairs so that he could smoke, and I had to sit below. In the early days I would go out with them in the evening when my mother went singing in the clubs, and I would be parked on my own in a back room, where I often fell asleep. I grew to hate the smell of smoke and alcohol, the musty, dusty atmosphere back-stage, and the raucous sound of the music. When I was older – seven or eight – I would be left at home to fend for myself.

Newton was very selfish. He had a reasonable income, and when we eventually moved into three rooms in Bath Street, he smoked Passing Cloud cigarettes and ate chocolates out of a wooden box. He would also have steak, which he cooked on the red-hot coal of the fire. (This was all in the time of rationing, when you needed coupons to purchase any sort of food or clothes.) I was not fed properly, and used to go with an old pram to the gas-works to fetch coke for people in the street, in return for food.

My mother was a good singer, with a fine mezzo voice, and although not conventionally beautiful, she had a bubbly personality and was popular in the clubs. The relationship between her and Newton was stormy. To start with we all three slept in the same bed. I remember all too clearly my mother making loud noises, and I thought he was assaulting her, but when I tried to protect her, they both laughed at me. I now realise they were having sex. For a long time I lay awake listening to the noises, and I hated it. Once Mother jumped out of bed yelling at the top of her voice, followed by Newton. A mouse had crawled into her hair, and he was as terrified of it as she was. He leapt back on to the bed, still shouting, and the poor little creature, frightened for its life, jumped clean out of the window.

Both of them regularly got drunk, and often brought other people back to our rooms. These were mostly men, and after they left there were arguments about the way my mother had cavorted with them. In all my youthful experiences of how men and women behaved, not one of them seemed to offer any support or love for the other, and certainly none for me.

It was only in later life that I began to understand how these episodes affected me. If I travelled on a bus alone, and a girl sat next to me, I would get up and move to another seat. If a girl spoke to me, I would blush and walk away. My first true feeling of love only came when I met my wife, Brenda, when I was fifteen – but more of that later.

I didn't fare much better in my relationships with brothers and sisters. My half-brother, Mellor, was born out of wedlock – the result of the rape – and is ten years my senior. I liked Mellor. He was sent into a home when he was very young and then went off to the Navy as a cadet when he was twelve. My earliest memories of Mellor are of him coming home from the Navy in his uniform, bringing presents. For breakfast he would eat a whole box of corn-flakes drenched in condensed milk, and when he bought fish-and-chips, he would order a double portion and eat the lot. In times of austerity this level of living impressed me, and I enjoyed his visits. Eventually Newton's son John came to live with us, and he and I slept together. He had diabetes and used to assault me when he went in and out of a coma. John's sister, Bronwyn, a sickly child, would stay with us occasionally and sleep in the same bed. I recall her wearing a liberty bodice and sometimes pink lint with a foul-smelling substance on it around her chest. I liked her very much as she was kind to me.

Sometimes my mother and Newton were away overnight on a singing engagement, and when I was seven or eight I was several times sexually assaulted by a young man who had access to our rooms. Because he hurt me, I fought him, and after a while he stopped. I didn't feel able to tell my mother about this, as I thought I would be chastised, and she would not welcome the trouble. Around this time our neighbour's son took me to the municipal swimming bath in Cambridge Road, where he enticed me on to the highest diving-board and pushed me off, so that I had to swim to survive.

It seems rather ironic that swimming and sport became the main enjoyment in my life. Greenhead Park, only a ten-minute walk from Bath Street, had a pool, and I would go there every day during the school holidays and at weekends, even though the pool was outdoors and unheated, and the water was dirty and litter-strewn. In winter, whenever I could afford it, I went to the indoor pool in Cambridge Road, and I became a strong, proficient swimmer at an early age.

I don't remember enrolling at Beaumont Street School, but I know I didn't like it at first. I was a big, raw-boned lad and probably looked older than I was. Two other factors worked against me: one was my squint, and the other that I had to wear clogs. My Uncle Duke, who had only one leg, was a clog-maker at a firm called Walkers in Huddersfield, and worked in a shed down an alleyway on my route to school. He gave me wooden clogs with red leather uppers, and although I had fun poked at me, being called 'Squinty' and 'Cloggy', without the clogs I would have been badly shod, as my shoes were always too small and worn through.

Because I reacted to taunts and hit out at the boys who teased me, I was often in trouble. I suppose this is why no one at home really took an interest in my schooling. Neither my mother nor Newton Heap ever asked me about it, and I never told them of my troubles. One minor consolation was that I found I was good at marbles: we called them 'alleys', and any rough piece of land was suitable for throwing them. I was thrilled when I accumulated a bag-full and became able to trade.

Beaumont Street School was a Victorian building, with a big central hall and classrooms leading from it. I was the one who climbed on to the roof to retrieve all the balls which had been thrown or hit there. I was frightened when I scrambled up the drainpipe, and with good reason, as it was probably fifty feet high, and, had I fallen, I would have injured myself severely. I think such exploits gave me some degree of acceptance at the school, and the jibes stopped – but another reason may have been that I would beat up the persons responsible.

I did have one friend of my own age – Johnny McMahon, who lived in a yard close to Bath Street. I envied his life. He had a mother and a father, who were always warm and friendly towards me. He had toys and new clothes. He later played rugby league for Fartown and captained the England Schoolboys.

By the time I was eight or nine, I had secured my place within the school community. I was tough, resourceful and strong, and I began mixing with some of the older boys who had physically assaulted me earlier. They were four or five years my senior, and previously they would either rob me of money on my way to the fish-and-chip shop at the bottom of the street or steal my chips on the way back. They once tied me to the big wooden gate of a yard where vehicles were scrapped and threw darts at me. After this incident Newton Heap beat me with a cane because he said I had got grease on my pullover.

I gave as good as I got, until eventually the assaults stopped and for a while I joined the gang. They were young criminals who went shop-lifting in Woolworths, caused damage in the neighbourhood and bullied people. I went with them, but always managed to avoid committing a crime – although I did steal a padlock from one counter and put it back on another.

The most traumatic experience I had at that time occurred on a summer's evening, when some older boys enticed a girl to go with us to a disused garage at the top of Bath Street. Against her will they stripped her naked, spread-eagled her on the floor and secured her hands and feet. Then they sexually assaulted her, as she screamed and pleaded with them to stop. I was petrified and ran away. The horror of the incident lives with me still. I reproach myself for not intervening, but I was too frightened to do so, both for her and for myself. After that, I never accompanied them again. I dared not tell my parents or anyone else what had happened, and can only hope that the trauma the girl suffered did not ruin her life.

Out of school, I spent much time on my own. Once I set the tea-table and scalded myself trying to pour boiling water from a pan into the teapot. I ran out into the street howling with pain, and was taken pity on by the man who sold the *Huddersfield Examiner* outside the George Hotel. Leaving his post, he walked me the mile or so to the Royal Infirmary so that I could be treated. Newton chastised me 'for all the trouble I had caused'.

I always felt alone, whether riding my bicycle, swimming or playing. The bike was a great joy, but almost cost me my life. Within hours of getting it for Christmas, I rode into the path of a car and was knocked off.

We lived quite close to the railway goods yard, where shire horses and carts met the trains. The final 300 yards of the approach were up a steep incline, which meant that at least two horses had to be hitched to each cart. Spare animals, with their handlers, used to wait under the railway arches on St John's Road, and I spent many hours with them, sitting on the railings, stroking the great horses, and sometimes hanging on the back of a cart as they struggled up the hill, which could be perilous for them in winter, as they would slip and fall on the icy cobbles. Over the years I saw a number of them break their legs and have to be destroyed. I cried for them, as they were my friends. This was the origin of my love of, and respect for, animals, with which I still feel more comfortable than with human beings.

Within a few hundred yards of the school gates there was a market for cattle and sheep, which I visited whenever possible so that I could stroke the animals. I used to peer into the abattoir alongside and watch the creatures being slaughtered, even though I was troubled by it. The slaughtermen would give us pigs' bladders to blow up and use as footballs, but unless we put some water in them for ballast, they were too light.

During the school holidays I might cycle the three or four miles to the mill where my mother worked. I was always there at Friday lunch-time, when we ate fish and chips from greasy newspapers.

The mill fascinated me, with its cathedral-like size, the noise of its machines, the smell of wool and grease, and the solidity of its stone staircase. I was greedy for information, and longed to know how the whole thing worked. My mother went to and from work on the bus, and I once told her that when I grew up and became rich, I would buy her a bus of her own.

On other days I would go swimming in the park, although I once had my clothes stolen when I was in the water, and, because I never took a towel with me, had to go home in my trunks, crying all the way. Then I would cycle to see my Aunt Evelyn, eight miles away. She worked in another mill, but I was never allowed beyond the gates, so I would wait by them, watching the wildlife in the river until she came.

I don't remember much about the curriculum at school. I enjoyed art, but I had little interest in the other lessons, and there was not much sport. I know we were once asked by the teacher what we would like to be when we grew up, and I was laughed at when I said I wanted to be king. Clearly I had delusions of grandeur at an early age!

Once, when I was nine, I cycled the three miles to Milnsbridge to join a boxing club I had heard about. The owner, a former professional, was grooming his eleven-year-old son for stardom, and as an introduction put me in the ring with him. He was decked out in all the best gear, but I just wore the short trousers and kicked-out shoes that I stood up in.

When the bell rang, we touched gloves and began to trade punches – although we were only tapping each other. Every blow landed by my opponent drew strong encouragement from his father and other onlookers. The first round ended, and the second started in much the same way, with both of us chintzing round each other. But because the other boy was landing more punches, and I was getting bored with it all, I hit him in the face as hard as I could. He dropped like a stone and began to cry, with blood seeping from his nose. His father jumped into the ring, bundled me through the ropes, called me a young hooligan and banned me from ever visiting the gym again.

Such was my early childhood. I now recognise that I was abused and neglected, but I didn't see this at the time, as I had nothing with which to compare my life. There was no one to turn to for help – and even if there had been, I would not have wished to enlist support, as I sought to please those who hurt me. When they told me I was a worthless nuisance, and deserved the bad things that happened to me, I believed them. But one thing I did have was spirit. Neither my family, nor anyone since, has broken that, although people have come close on occasion.

I now believe that my mother loved me. I recognise how difficult it must have been for her to show me affection when she wished to retain that of her lover, especially as he was jealous of me. I have seen many mothers in similar situations: they crave affection, and their offspring are a tiresome encumbrance. One doesn't need a great deal of imagination to see why many children, particularly boys, go wrong in such an environment.

CHAPTER TWO

THE WORM BEGINS
TO WRIGGLE

Life progressed in much the same way until, when I was eleven, my mother won £300 on the football pools – a small fortune in those days – and decided to leave Newton Heap. Then, as she put it, he saved her the trouble by dying of cancer. Their relationship had always been volatile, and there were other men in her life. On the advice of her boss at the mill, who was at that time and remained until his death her lover, she bought two cottages in the village of Kirkburton, and we went to live there.

I liked Kirkburton, where I still live, and I enjoyed my new life. I got a job scraping bread-trays at Hirstwoods bakery, and enrolled at the local Secondary Modern School. I can recall that day vividly, because when I went alone and was ushered into the headmaster's office, the head could not believe that a child could have come there on his own. With my clogs, my shock of blond hair, my squint and Harry Potter glasses, I must have looked a sorry sight.

Nevertheless, I started there and then. In the first break the other children began to taunt me, calling me 'Squinty' and 'Specky Four-Eyes'. I hit the first boy I could and knocked him down: fortunately 'Sally' Jenks was cock of the school, and by beating him I achieved instant status, which nipped any further name-calling in the bud.

I enjoyed that school. The teachers were kind to me, and for the first time I took an interest in my lessons. There was no fear at home, and I felt happier than ever before, as if I had come out from under a dark cloud into sunshine. On the sports field my physical abilities started to show through. I played for the football team, and even tried cricket, until a fast ball hit me in the mouth and cracked one of my teeth. I swam, and began to win competitions for running. Here was something I could do, and be recognised for, on my own. I would cycle to local events, don the spiked shoes that my grandfather had given me, enter every track event and win them all. After one or two clean sweeps, the parents of other children started to complain: I was very conspicuous, being big for my age and having a thick head of light blond hair with a white Mallen streak in it, and they said I was too old, or that I was cheating by having running shoes. The organisers expressed some concern, but allowed me to continue.

At home things were much better. My mother still worked and sang, but she was more relaxed with me, as her new lover didn't see me as a threat. On the contrary: he was quite kind to me, and in this atmosphere of domestic bliss, one Saturday morning when my mother was at work, I painted the doors, windows and gutters of the house green. There was more paint on the ground and on the walls than on the woodwork.

At Beaumont Street I had passed the eleven-plus exam, but after that our move had disrupted things. When the teachers at Kirkburton saw that I had some ability, they tried to secure a place for me at the local grammar school, without success. However, when I was twelve I took another exam and won a place at Dewsbury Technical College.

Travelling to and from school was difficult. I had to get a bus from Kirkburton into Huddersfield at seven a.m., change from one bus station to another and catch the eight o'clock for Dewsbury. Arriving there, I had two options: either catch a third bus, or get off outside the town and walk or run the final mile. Being unable to afford school dinners, I survived on dry bread twists from the local bakers. In the evenings I would get off the last bus and go straight to work, scraping the bread-trays. I worked five nights each week and Saturday mornings, all for the princely sum of 10 shillings – 50p in current coinage – as well as free buns and other unsold confectionery. On Friday nights our great treat was buttered-ham teacakes and cream-topped apple pies. These made a welcome addition to our normal meagre fare. We hardly ever ate meat, making do with potatoes and turnips mashed together, and Yorkshire pudding spiced with onions and herbs, covered in gravy. Chicken was a once-a-year treat, on Christmas Day.

At thirteen I got a second job during the holidays, at Carter's shovel works. This was a fascinating experience, because the staff included some ripe characters, and the bosses could have featured in a Dickens novel. When Stanley, 'Old Man' Carter, was in the factory he would sit on a raised dais and watch us working. All the time he was busy cutting the little wooden dowel pegs that were inserted through the handle and shaft of shovels to hold them together – something he could do blindfold. We were allowed to visit the toilet once before lunch-break and once after, more time being granted for the first visit of the day. If Stanley thought you had been there too long, he would come into the toilet to see what you were doing.

Men worked in the firm from leaving school until they retired or died. The conditions were appalling. I worked on a grinding machine: rotating the shovels ripped my hands to ribbons, and sparks from the metal burnt my flesh. We were issued with protective goggles, but no one wore them. One of the lads working there, Ian Thompson, still lives in the village. He used to do some odd-jobbing, and I helped him lay drives, erect garages, do gardening and the like, for extra money.

Schooling at Dewsbury was pretty uninspiring. Many of the teachers were worn out and had little interest in their work. One of my fellow pupils – although I didn't know her – was Betty Boothroyd, future Speaker of the House of Commons. There was a strong emphasis on sport, and I took part in almost every activity. I swam for the school, and represented it in the high jump, the 100 yards and cross-country events. This enthusiasm was reflected in my final report, which read, 'Keith excels at sport and little else.'

Having learned from a classmate that I was entitled to leave school on my fifteenth birthday, I did just that, departing with no qualifications whatsoever.

When I lived in Bath Street, there was a Jaguar and Rolls-Royce dealer called Rippon Brothers about 400 yards from my home. I used to look at those beautiful vehicles and dream. The company had been in existence for many years, and originally built coaches. Inside their warehouse they had old stage-coaches in various states of disrepair; I used to climb into the building through a broken window, sit in them for hours and fantasise about times gone by, imagining the fine clothes of the people who owned them. I suspect that all those beautiful vehicles were destroyed when the premises were sold as the site for a supermarket in the 1970s.

Hoping to become a mechanic, I went to Rippon Brothers in search of a job, but they laughed at me and sent me away. Then Carter's offered me full-time employment until I found a permanent job, so I took up their offer. Within months I heard that Emley Moor Colliery, which was less than two miles from my home, was looking for mechanics, and although I didn't get one of the posts, because I had no qualifications, I was offered a position on the safety staff, which I took.

Our team was responsible for implementing the safety regulations in the mine. We tested the air flows to and from the face for volume; we ensured that dust and gas levels were not too high, and that all working procedures were observed. My boss was a man called Mason Exley, and I thought the world of him. He had a dry sense of humour and was always kind to me. I suppose I regarded him as the father I never had.

He had many quaint sayings. If we were trying to line something up and were failing, he used to say, 'Tha's same as that lass thro' Flockton'. Flockton is a village close by; 'tha's' means 'you are,' and 'thro' means 'from'. If we went on fumbling, he would add, 'Tha noun anent' – 'You're not in line.' In the early days I often asked him what his sayings meant, but he would never explain. Eventually he did. It seems that one Saturday night in his youth he travelled on the last bus from Huddersfield to Kirkburton, and walked the last part of the journey with a girl from Flockton. When they were part-way home, she jumped over a wall to relieve herself. In Mason's own words, 'This was too good an opportunity to miss – just me and her with her clouts about her knees.' So he too jumped over the wall and bowled her over; but when he tried to have intercourse with her, she said, 'Mason Exley, I'll tell me mother of tha. In any event, tha noun anent.'

In the politically correct world of today, Mason would have been out of step, and you may feel he was crude. He was not. He was an extremely gentle soul, who would reserve such remarks for the pit. Later, when I told him I was courting, he asked, 'Is she pretty?'

'Yes,' I said.

'Has she a nice shape?'

'Yes.'

'Tha lucky lad. When tha gets a bit owder, tha'll judge 'em by whether they're fat or thin. When tha gets a bit owder again, tha'll judge 'em by whether they're owd or young. And when tha gets to my age, tha has to judge 'em on whether they're clean or dirty.'

Our job, as I said, was to ensure the safety of the pit. We once found a man asleep when he should have been supervising a conveyor belt. Mason poked him with his stick: the man immediately awoke and denied he had been asleep. He said he'd been resting his eyes, and added, 'If tha catches me asleep, Mason, tha can piss in me ear.' You can anticipate what happened next time we caught him: Mason deputed me to do the deed. Our colleague didn't complain, as he could have lost his job for neglect.

Mason taught me a great deal about life and people. He was firm but fair; even though he was in a position of authority, and people respected him, they also liked him. He cared for others, and through the church gave a great deal to the community.

The other member of the safety team was a single man slightly older than me. He was always talking about sex and boasting of his exploits, real or imaginary. He would wax lyrical about the pleasures of masturbation – 'T'old handgear, Mrs Fist, the five-fingered widow.' He used to say he could have any woman he chose. For a while he was besotted with fantasies about Princess

Margaret, and would tell us in graphic detail of his imaginary exploits with her. Once we were in the box-hole – the room at the bottom of the pit-shaft where we assembled before leaving. He was in full flow, telling us about his weekend, explaining that one of his female relatives had a boyfriend who used to 'warm her up' before he left her, whereupon he would meet her off the bus, take her into his house and finish the job. The only problem with this story was that the girl's father was sitting in the room with us at the time, and we were all cringing. He didn't say anything until every minute detail of the encounter had been described. Then he murmured, 'Tha's said enough now.'

The job had a serious side. We were members of the recovery team, and whenever there was a disaster, we became involved. This was the first time I had to deal with death, and I was much moved by incidents that involved loss of life and limbs. To work with people from day to day, and then have to recover their mutilated bodies after they'd been crushed by a roof-fall, was extremely distressing.

Whenever we had a collapse, the miners called the tons of rock that came down 'a little muck fall'. Once I was in the box-hole after we had recovered the body of a victim, when one of the other miners began to sound off about the dead man in a very unpleasant way. I bit back and stood up for our lost colleague.

'Well done!' whispered Mason.

'I only said what I thought,' I told him later.

'It's not what you said,' he replied. 'It's the fact that you said it which is important.'

When I pressed him, he told me I was too accommodating with people, and that it did them good to hear me bark occasionally. I came to see that this was wise counsel for people in authority: if you never show your steel, you will eventually be taken for granted and lose credibility.

Emley Moor Colliery was a shallow pit, with narrow coal seams, the thinnest of which were only eighteen inches from top to bottom. They were so low that mechanical equipment could not be used. Men worked in shifts throughout the twenty-four hours to drill and blow the seams so that the coal could be hand-loaded on to conveyor belts and taken to the surface. The daily cycle of work involved supporting the roof over the new void that this process constantly created, extending access tunnels with adequate height and laying new belts.

The faces were uncomfortable at the best of times. They were hot and full of coal-dust, and ours had the additional problem of water: quite often men lay bare-torsoed on their triangular shoulder-boards in two or three inches of water as they did their exhausting job of hand-loading twenty-two tons of coal on to the belt each day. Yet adversity brought them together as nothing else could: they were full of humour, and the bond between them was the strongest I have ever known.

As if the natural hazards weren't enough, we used to take illegal rides on the conveyor belts: rumbling along in pitch darkness was mildly sexually stimulating and strongly soporific – so much so that many miners dropped off, literally, as they were tipped into tubs at the end of the run.

In spite of the danger, ribald comments kept bubbling up. Once when a man had his arm severed above the elbow, the limb was picked from the conveyor belt as it meandered along by a colleague who passed it back down the face saying, 'I think this is thine, George.' Everyone played tricks on each other. We took our meals, known as 'snap', packed in old red Oxo tins. I always packed four slices of bread and dripping and two chocolate digestive biscuits, to be washed down with water from a hip flask. We used to hang the tins on pit-props to keep them away from rats and mice, but the miners would hide or even eat your food if they thought they could get away with it. For a new recruit, the initiation ceremony would be to replace his snap with human excreta. Incidentally, we caught vermin by putting crumbs into empty, wide-necked Ben Shaw's pop bottles: the rats and mice would crawl in, eat the food and trap themselves because of their increased girth. We would then fill the bottles with water, screw on the stoppers and drown them – cruel but effective.

Air was the most important commodity in the mine. It was

forced down to the faces by a fan on the surface through an elaborate system of airlocks and doors, and the safety team's prime responsibility was to see that each face had an adequate supply. Another critical factor was gas accumulation: methane and black damp were killers, and the cause of many explosions. We used the traditional miners' lamps to test the air: if they went out, we knew that there was insufficient oxygen, and something had to be done quickly. Mason told me that in the past he had used canaries, but had to stop because the miners became so attached to them. After a while I devised a spring-mounting for the wicks of the lamps, which avoided the flame being extinguished by the shock of being knocked or set down in a hurry – a modest invention which was never patented.

Part of our safety routine was to check the miles of roadway and workings that had become redundant over the years. I used to enjoy this job, and loved the solitude it brought. I'd turn out my lamp and lie in total darkness and silence for minutes on end. When people say they have been in absolute darkness and isolation, I do not think they know what it is like in the bowels of the earth. There is no experience like it.

Work in the mines of the 1950s was extremely hard and dangerous. The dust in the atmosphere left many men with severe chest ailments: pneumoconiosis would render them virtually incapable of breathing. It was harrowing to see their pigeon chests heaving, and hear their pain as they drew each gasping breath – yet many continued to work until they were physically incapable of standing, or until they died.

Water was sprayed in continuous attempts to suppress the dust, but it was largely ineffective: where one belt disgorged its load of coal on to another, the dust was so dense that it formed an impenetrable cloud. When it reached certain levels, we were supposed to stop production, but neither management nor miners welcomed lay-offs. As a consequence many men lost their lives without being compensated. On Saturday mornings I used to work an extra shift, spreading chalk dust, which, it was thought, would neutralise the coal dust. I would throw this stuff about with gay abandon and end the shift white all over. Only years later did we appreciate the dangers of inhaling such substances. I coughed up black dust for more than a decade after leaving the mines.

The pit had some great characters, not least Marion Rokiki, a mountain of a man from Polish or Hungarian stock, whose body was so thickly covered with hard, brittle hair, like a pig's, that at bath time it was always the duty of one of the lads to scrub him down with a yard broom, to get the coal dust off him. His colleagues in the face complained about the smell of his 'snap', which always included spicy food not part of the miners' diet in those days – but whatever else it did, it made him phenomenally strong.

Strength was part of our young men's culture then. Though I was pretty strong – I could press a blacksmith's anvil above my head a number of times without difficulty – I wasn't in Marion's league. I once saw him pick up a whole railway wagon full of coal. Part of my training was as a timber trammer – one of the young men who pushed timber props and lids to the face on trolleys or trams, because the gates – the roads leading to the face – were too low for pit ponies. If we did a good job, the miners would give us half a crown (12½p) at the end of the week, and with this incentive we would fight to get the best timber. The other miners used to say that we were 'strong in t' back and weak in yead'.

One young fellow had such an enormous appendage that it hung down to his knees even when it was at rest. The other miners were cruel: they would pull down his trousers and tie it to the rails; then they'd wait for him to scream as the tram approached, before releasing him. His reputation preceded him within the local villages, and girls queued up to discover if the rumours were true. He got married, but only for a very short time, and the talk was that 'she couldn't take it'. Mason said once, 'It's all right 'avin' a tool that size, but tha's a problem when it gets up. Tha'll have four inches 'ard at one end, four inches 'ard at t' other, and a yard a sleck in t' middle.'

The pit was my life for almost five years. But of all the things that happened during that period, by far the most important was that I met Brenda Hey.

Until that moment I had had only two perfunctory encounters with girls. One came when I was twelve, on a school trip, sitting on the back seat of a bus with some other boys and a girl, who suddenly announced that she was wearing a blue bra. Encouraged by the boys, she lifted her jumper to show us – and I was so embarrassed that I escaped to a front seat. The second occasion was on a mill trip to Blackpool with my mother. I was the only male – aged fourteen – and the rest of the company cheered me on board, asking my mother where she'd been hiding me. By the end of the visit the girls were in high spirits, and some of them tried to kiss me. I was horrified, and fought them off.

Such was my experience with young women at the time I met Brenda. One summer's evening I was near the parish church in the centre of Huddersfield, waiting for the bus home, when I heard screams and shouts and saw two girls being chased by an older man, who appeared to be drunk. I ran to their rescue, stood in his path and told him to clear off, which he did without argument. The girls were flustered, but they thanked me nicely for helping them.

I think I fell in love with Brenda at that first moment. She was of medium height – about 5′ 6″ – and in her dark skirt and white, tight jumper, which emphasised her shapely body, she looked incredibly beautiful. She had auburn hair and the loveliest green eyes I had ever seen: when she looked at me, I had to turn away, as I never faced anyone squarely because of my squint. I couldn't tell what her friend Susan was like, because for me she didn't exist.

I felt embarrassed at being so close to Brenda, and tongue-tied, yet didn't want to leave her. In thanking me, both girls remarked that they hadn't seen me before in the town, and they suggested we might all go to the pictures when I next visited. I mumbled agreement, and we fixed a time and date.

On the bus home, I felt electrified. My whole life had changed. I had spoken to a lovely girl, and I was going to meet her again. I knew she was attracted to me, and I to her. Yet when I reached home, my elation evaporated. I was certain either that the two would not turn up, or, if they did come, that they would see me for what I was, a gauche, squint-eyed boy, and they would run away.

My existence became centred round the coming meeting. I could hardly wait, yet I was frightened to go for fear of rejection. What would I say? What would I do? In spite of my anxiety, I could think of nothing but Brenda. She seemed almost surreal. I veered from peaks of excitement to depths of depression.

At last the day came, and I reached the rendezvous half an hour early, still sure they would not turn up. I wanted to run away and hide. When Brenda arrived alone, I was wildly excited, especially as she seemed friendly, and didn't look at me like I was dirt.

We walked the short distance to the Empire Cinema and sat together near the back. In a self-conscious way I put my arm round the back of her seat, but when she moved I pulled it away, thinking she didn't like it. Then she took hold of my hand – something no one had ever done before. With that single, wonderful act she showed me more love than anyone else had in my young life. Tingles went down my spine, and a feeling of well-being surged through me. I knew at that moment that this was the person with whom I would spend the rest of my life.

As we got to know each other, I found that Bren, also, had suffered in her childhood, and had been damaged by it. Her mother Dorothy, or Dot, had been born with physical and emotional problems, and when she was seventeen she had been sent away from her home outside Sheffield to live and work in a pub in Huddersfield. She lived and worked on the premises, and her pay was her keep. There Dot met Percy (known as 'Chuck'), who suffered epileptic fits. They married, and lost a number of boy children at birth. A girl, Barbara, was eventually born alive, followed by Bren ten years later.

One symptom of Dot's mental problems was that she refused to leave the house for many years; another, that she continually uttered blood-curdling screams. The house was very primitive, with only an earth closet, set apart in a little building of its own – a common arrangement in those days. Such was the environment in which Bren grew up. Bren lived in constant fear of her mother, and of what she might do to her or to her father, whom she often physically attacked.

Like me, Bren took herself to school and went on her own to get a job. At home, she was on her own for much of the time, shutting herself off from the noise and violence. Barbara married in her teens, leaving Bren alone to spend time in the field beside the house, where she tried to create a garden, cutting the grass with the household scissors. Indoors, she sought to create a homely atmosphere by arranging wild flowers and making things pretty. To add to her misery, the house was haunted – and even I, a sceptic when it comes to the supernatural, never liked being alone there, as I would feel a chill, and the hairs on my neck would stand up, when I went to the top of the stairs.

Bren always wanted to be a hairdresser, but her mother said it was unhealthy to touch other people's heads, and would not even let her wash her own hair, as this, too, was deemed unhealthy – an obsession which gave Bren a complex about herself, and left her with a fear of water which she has retained all her life. She had a similar fear of heights, which derived from falling out of a bedroom window when she was four, and, far from receiving any treatment, being chastised for it. She also suffered badly from claustrophobia, which she put down to the fact that, together with her mother, she was confined to the house for so long. Many years passed before she would travel in an aeroplane, and to this day she will enter a lift only if it is unavoidable: in hotels, when we find ourselves staying on any floor lower than the thirtieth, we walk up and down the stairs. She has never ventured on to the Underground, and we have had to get off buses when she has felt herself hemmed in.

Such was the fifteen-year-old girl with whom I fell in love. When we met, she had never seen the sea or even been on holiday. We were both damaged, both seeking someone to love, and we found that person in each other.

I was able to see her every day because I owned a little motorcycle which I had renovated – a gift from a vicar whose son had crashed it. During the week I would pick her up at six o'clock when she finished work at Whitterons bread shop in Lindley and take her home. We would have tea together, and then, if we were allowed, go for a walk until it was time for me to return home. On Saturdays, after lunch, we would meet at Manners Corner in Huddersfield and go shopping. On Sundays I would arrive in time for us to go to the local chapel together, followed by tea either at her house or at mine. We were inseparable, and have been ever since.

As we grew older I traded in the motorbike for a scooter – a red-and-white Lambretta, which became my pride and joy. During the holidays we would go on day trips to York, Harrogate and the seaside, and we thought we owned the world. We once rode all the way to Kent, to stay with Mellor, who had settled there when he left the Navy. But then one winter's evening I was knocked off the scooter by a car that shot out onto the main road and hit me square-on. I was thrown about thirty feet through the air, hit a lamppost, and was taken to hospital unconscious. The injuries I sustained led to arthritis in my spine and shoulder, and have caused me pain ever since.

I spent so much time at Bren's house that I began to regard her parents as my own. They were very kind to me, and almost took me in as part of their family. Bren's mother, who seemed to have stabilised by the time I met her, made a fuss of me, and her father used to call me 'Claud', because I wore a pair of buff-coloured gloves to ride the scooter, and that, to him, personified the gentry.

At last I had a fairly normal life, a girlfriend and a job. At the pit I developed a new interest when I started to learn first aid. Within a short time I was asked to captain a team, and we began to win first-aid competitions, which were popular with people who worked in emergency services as well as in hazardous industries, such as mining. It was my job to assess the mock situations we faced, some of them very lifelike, with gruesome make-up and elaborate sets. I also had to give the rest of the team instructions, and provide a running commentary for the judges and the audience. At one national final at the Winter Gardens in Blackpool, with an audience of hundreds, the scenario was a rail crash, and a full-sized carriage, along with some track, had been imported for verisimilitude. I was by far the youngest captain in the competition, and I enjoyed myself immensely. That was my first experience of leadership. I never believed I was better than anyone else: I was just doing something that I liked, and doing it well.

The prizes I won formed the basis of our 'Bottom Drawer' – a Yorkshire term for the collection of articles a couple makes in preparation for marriage. I won so many awards that the shop which provided them got to know Bren and me well, and they would allow us to change things, in order to build up a matching set of crockery. We have some of that service left today.

I was also progressing within the mine. One day the manager, Eric Lindley, spoke to me on the coalface, asking about my background. He suggested that I might enrol at Barnsley College of Mining, as I ''ad an 'ead on me'. I took his advice and enrolled for two evenings a week.

This was a new experience for me: I was learning because I wanted to, and the work was interesting. To my amazement, at the end of my first year I won the award for top student – a drawing set in a blue, leather-bound case. Mr Lindley, hearing of my success, allowed me a half-day of paid time every week to attend the college, and when I moved on to complete the Ordinary National Certificate in Mining Engineering, he let me have full-day release.

At the Barnsley College I met men from all over the region. There was one young fellow, slightly older than me, who had a photographic memory. I have seen people with such gifts on television, but this man was phenomenal. He could glance at the football league tables on the back of any newspaper and recite them to you – the number of games, wins, losses, and the goals for and against for every team listed. He claimed that he could read a book in a night, and once declared that he had got through *War and Peace* cover-to-cover in a single day. He was not particularly successful in his studies because he said that if he was not especially interested in a subject, his retention was short-lived. Moreover, even if he could remember something, he might not always know what it meant, as he was unable to reason with the information.

At the pit I was given a more demanding role. I learned surveying, and worked with the senior managers to get a grasp of their jobs. The under-manager, Reggie Gledhill, was only 5' 2" but as broad as he was tall, and big in heart. He used to shout out instructions in a high-pitched voice, but he gave me tremendous encouragement. As a result of my first-aid training, I was developing the ability to think on my feet and put across a logical argument, which led to my colleagues asking me to speak to management on their behalf. Through this role I was invited to National Union of Mineworkers' meetings and conferences, where I met prominent figures of the day, including Lord Robens, Chairman of the National Coal Board, and Hugh Gaitskell, leader of the Labour Party. The people with whom I worked were grooming me for management, but I didn't realise that at the time. I simply enjoyed my job and the company of my colleagues; without their support, and that of Bren, my life would have been much impoverished.

During these years my mother took up with and eventually married a retired widower, Alfred Gartrey. He was twenty years her senior, with two unmarried daughters of her age who lived in Australia. He was a kindly person, and I liked him, as he took an interest in me; yet neither he nor my mother nor any of her lovers ever came to my school, or attended sporting events to support me.

We moved into Alf's one-down and two-up house, also in Kirkburton, which had a living room and a 'cellar head', about four feet square, with a cooker and sink, a small coal cellar, a large bedroom divided into two, and a bathroom. There I had the luxury of my own bedroom until one of his daughters, Edith, came for a protracted stay. From then on I had to sleep on a bed-settee in the living room. Edith was nasty. She hated my mother, who she believed had done her out of her inheritance – the house – and she would taunt me about my eyes. She was also a freeloader, never contributing to the cost of her food and lodging, which was met by myself and my mother. After several months and much bickering, she got a job as a barmaid in a local pub, the Three Owls, but she was still after everything she could get.

I used to go and pay weekly instalments on the hire-purchase of my bed-settee, getting a card stamped to show that each payment had been made. Then Edith volunteered to take over the chore. When we began getting reminders about the payments, Edith pretended to be indignant, saying she would remonstrate with the firm for making mistakes. Eventually, when my mother went to settle the account, to save further trouble, she found that Edith had paid in nothing, pocketing the money for herself. Far worse, she had persuaded Alf to sign the deeds of the house over to her. Years later, after her return to Australia, Alf, riddled with guilt, confessed to my mother and remade his will.

On 17 July 1960, Bren's seventeenth birthday, we got engaged, and for £17.12.6, at Beaverbrooks jewellers in Huddersfield, together we chose a ring, which she still cherishes. Soon after that she told me that it shouldn't be long before we married, and that I ought to get myself a proper job.

For several years I had been planning to join the police, even though I had no relatives in the service. I had always dreamt of becoming a detective, and I had made my first effort to sign on when I was just fifteen, only to be sent packing by the large, rotund, fresh-faced officer on duty at the time, Mr Pagden, who told me I was too young and ought to go and 'get some wool on my back' by learning a trade.

When I told Mason I was planning to leave, he said he didn't want to lose me, but that the police would offer me a better career, and I would go with his blessing. He told me I would never become rich in the public service, but neither would I be poor.

I left the mines with huge regret, for the men I met there were a wonderful breed, never judgemental, never jealous of each other's achievements, and completely trustworthy. I made the right decision, but I have never again experienced the level of trust or the strength of bond between men that I found in the pit. A large number of my colleagues came to our wedding, and have kept in touch over the years. I have never forgotten the words of a fellow-miner, Paul Birt, who asked me what I would like to have written on my gravestone. When I hesitated, he said, ' "Contentment" is what tha wants. I've seen lads like thee afore. Tha'll get on in life, but tha's a little worm wriggling inside thee. If it never stops wriggling, tha'll never be content.'

CHAPTER THREE

A GOOD DECISION

One Saturday morning in August 1961 I went to the police station in Huddersfield. The Borough and County Police Forces were both in Peel Street, but as there were fewer people waiting at the counter of the County, I went there first. My heart sank when I saw that the officer in charge was Sergeant Pagden – the very man who had sent me packing six years earlier. This time, however, he was much less dismissive. When I told him I still wished to join the police, and described my years in the pit, he seemed to be impressed. He advised me that if I joined the County, I could be moved anywhere, but that if I went to the Borough, I could stay at home – so I walked across the road and completed the application form there and then.

There were the usual questions about my age, school and work histories. The form then asked about parents and relatives, and in particular, 'Has any member of your family ever been convicted of a criminal offence?' I included what I knew about my uncle, fearing that his record might bring me down at the first hurdle. Having submitted the form, I was taken down into the basement to be weighed and measured. I was 6′ 2″ inches tall, and 215 lbs. Height was significant in those days: you had to be at least six feet tall to join the Borough, and I learned later that the recruiting staff got up to all sorts of tricks to drag candidates through. One was to hang them on the wall-bars in the gym with weights attached to their legs and measure them in this stretched position.

I was told that someone would be in touch. I doubted it – but four weeks later I received a letter telling me to attend the police station at 9 a.m. on a day in September, 'to sit the entrance examinations'. Together with a number of other candidates I took a three-hour written exam in mathematics, English and general knowledge, and afterwards we were all asked to wait while the papers were marked. Soon, we learnt who had passed and failed. Then the successful candidates were told that we were to have an immediate interview with the Chief Constable. This came as a shock to me, as I was neither dressed nor prepared for a formal meeting. I expressed my concerns, but was told, 'It's now or never.'

Minutes later I was ushered in front of the Chief Constable, David Bradley. He sat behind a large oak desk which looked too big for him, as he was relatively short, bull-necked and grey-haired. With a pronounced Yorkshire accent he barked at me to stand to attention on the other side of the desk, facing him, and then demanded, 'Who gave you the answers?'

I told him I didn't know what he was talking about. He repeated the question, and got the same retort.

'No one gets 100 per cent in my maths test,' he said irritably. (I later learned that before joining the police he had been a school-teacher, and he was proud of the high standard he set for the entrance exams, which in those days were at the discretion of each force.) He then wrote out an equation on a piece of paper and tossed it across the desk, saying, 'Do that.'

I did it with ease, which appeared to make matters worse – whereupon he repeated the exercise, with the same result. He seemed to be getting more and more angry, but calmed down a little when I could not solve his third problem.

At last the interrogation turned into an interview. He asked me if I chewed my nails, brushed my teeth, had any savings. Was I courting? Did I intend to get married? What did Bren do? He made some sour comments on my clothes, my shoes, which were long, pointed winkle-pickers, and my hair, which I had set in two coils at the front and a duck's-arse at the rear, in the style of many pop stars at the time. I conceded that if I was accepted as a police officer, I would have to change.

He also asked if I felt uncomfortable looking at people, because of my eyes. I told him I did – and when he asked if I thought people would feel uncomfortable looking at *me*, I agreed they would. I explained that over the years I had had several operations on my eyes, and that if I joined the police, I would have them done again. He then asked if there was anything I would like to ask *him*. Stupidly, I wrote an equation on a piece of paper and said, 'You do this, Sir.' I knew this was foolish, but I was aggrieved at being accused of cheating. I have always felt this: if I have done something wrong, so be it, but if the charge is unjustified, I think I have to respond.

The Chief was taken aback. In the moment's silence that followed, the sergeant who had been standing behind me stepped back one pace – and he was wise. Mr Bradley jumped up from his chair, gesticulated with both hands towards the door, and shouted '*Get out!*' Then he yelled at the officer, '*Get this man out of my sight!*'

I took no time at all to leave. Outside, the sergeant asked, 'What the hell did you do that for? You were all right until then.' He said I was the first person ever to get all the maths correct, and this had made the Chief suspicious. He reckoned Mr Bradley had been impressed when I completed the first two equations, but said that no one had ever challenged him as I had, and I had certainly blown it.

After about twenty minutes I was taken back in front of the Chief, who gave me a dressing-down, told me I lacked manners and said I should respect my elders and betters. Much against his own judgement, he went on, he would let me in, but he would be watching my every move, and, if I gave him any excuse at all, he would sack me.

Welcome to the British police service! I was elated at my success, but one more obstacle cropped up between the interview and my appointment: I was stopped for speeding in my blue Minivan, doing 40 mph in a 30 mph limit. I shall never forget the feelings of despair I suffered, believing that one stupid mistake could cost me my career.

I started work on 4 January 1962. The force handbook I was given to learn now makes amusing reading, for it reveals how amazingly bureaucratic and parochial the police were then:

> No member of this police force will marry without written permission of the Chief Constable . . . No member of this police force will leave the Borough whilst on or off duty without written permission of the Chief Constable . . . No spouse of a serving member of this police force shall take up any employment without the member having first obtained written permission from the Chief Constable . . . No member of this police force shall reside outside the Borough of Huddersfield, nor in premises which have not been inspected and approved by the Chief Constable. Moreover, the Chief Constable, or a person of not less than the rank of inspector, will visit and inspect the house of an officer on an annual basis to satisfy the Chief Constable that it is kept in fit and proper condition for an officer of this force.

I could go on. This is a far cry from the conditions under which an officer joins today, and although the housing and spouse-employment rules still apply, they are rarely enforced. In fact there was some sense in the housing restrictions, since they forced officers to live in the heart of the communities they policed. Today they tend to live in the leafy suburbs and are totally dissociated from their work.

I was issued with my uniform just before Christmas. There was no question of measuring: we were simply given the choice of two sizes to see which fitted best. There were two sets of uniform – one for day, with silver buttons, and a night set with black furniture. Handcuffs, a truncheon and a whistle on a chain were also provided, and a raincoat, a heavy overcoat and a cape completed the ensemble. I felt ungainly when I first put on my helmet, but I came to love it.

It was to Pannal Ash Police District Training Centre in Harrogate that I went on a cold winter day in January 1962 to begin my first residential course of thirteen weeks. The centre was based in a Victorian public school, and the culture of the place was somewhere between that of the army and prison. Each of us was allocated a dormitory bed and shown how to make up a 'bed-pack', with sheets and blankets folded into a neat square, and the pillow placed on top – a construction we had to produce every morning for inspection.

Training began each day with reveille at 07.00, in pitch darkness, followed by morning assembly outside on the parade ground, which required us to form up in squads of three ranks, tallest on the right, shortest on the left. We were brought to attention by a Drill Sergeant and inspected by the Commandant. We had to bull our boots – bring them to a mirror shine with spit and polish – an easy task for the many former military personnel, but difficult for an ex-miner. At meal times we had to wait outside the mess hall until the bell rang and we were ushered in. We were allocated specific places at table and a list of our duties – fetching food, collecting plates and so on. There was no choice of menu: we were told that vegetarians and 'people like that' were not men, and had no place in the police.

Our introductory talk was given by the officer entitled the Course Inspector, who in reality was a sergeant, acting up in rank. He was a slight man, small in stature, with a weasel face and a bald pate. His first words were, 'There are some bastards in this world, but I'm the biggest one you'll ever meet. My job is to make your lives misery. If any of you are happy here, I'll be failing my duty.' He explained the punishments for bed-wetting, being late for parade and returning late to 'Camp', as he described it. He talked about namby-pamby boys missing their mothers, and warned us that we would wish we had never left home. The punishments varied from having to write down some definition a number of times and being tested on it, to an extra shift on Definition Doorway – the entrance to the centre which each of us had to cover as a watch-guard at least once within the course. The most serious punishment was to be sent back to force, which would effectively end your career.

The inspector spent the next thirteen weeks trying to live up to his own high standards, and he made many enemies. 'His arse is too close to the ground,' said one wag. 'He keeps dragging it in the gravel, and that's why he's such a pillock.' I was appalled that anyone in authority would carry on as he did, but I soon saw that it was only his position which enabled him to behave like that. He hid behind his job and rank, without which he was nothing. Most bullies have themselves been bullied in the past: I have seen any number of police officers, trained in this way, acting out their power over the public when they were on the streets, just because of their status.

I quickly settled into my new environment. I enjoyed learning about policing, and found I had a knack for taking in new information and recalling it in examinations. I enjoyed the practical exercises, which involved a great deal of role-playing and leadership – and here my first-aid experience came in useful. There was also much emphasis on physical fitness, which suited me fine. In class the methods of teaching were Victorian: all lessons were barked at us, and we had to recite definitions of different laws and powers of arrest when pointed at by the tutor. Not being a drinker, I had little interest in socializing, so in the evenings I worked hard and long.

The only difficulty I encountered was with the drill. I felt uncomfortable marching, saluting on the move and going through other quasi-military manoeuvres. I have soft skin, and marching in boots caused me huge blisters, which burst and bled. The centre had a surgery and nursing staff, but visits were considered non-macho and were not encouraged. I was further inhibited by the fear that, if I declared my problem, I might be sent back to the force and lose my job – so I kept quiet.

As the days went on, we began marching to music. One drill sergeant, a very artistic, humane individual who didn't seem comfortable with his role, would walk among us with his pace stick, shouting orders. All this work led to a final parade of marching and inter-marching. I also felt a berk when practising the signals we would need to control traffic: we did this by numbers, and no doubt it was amusing for outsiders to watch a group of young men waving their arms about in unison.

In spite of the difficulties, I enjoyed the overall experience of initial training. I found it challenging and totally engaging – the kind of environment in which I feel most at home. Yet the final sporting event of the course, a boxing competition, proved anything but comfortable. I was matched with a former army champion, as we were of similar build, and he gave me the biggest hiding of my life. Due to my squint I didn't look at him, so he used me as a virtual punch bag: in the course of three rounds he knocked me down over twenty times, burst my nose, chipped a number of teeth and cut me in several places. I refused to give in, and was awarded the prize for best loser, but it ought to have been for the most stupid.

I won other prizes on that course – for best academic student, for gaining most marks in the examination, for life-saving, first aid and sport. Years later I again came across our bully instructor. By that time he was junior in rank to me, yet he was pleased to tell me that when the Commandant suggested that I deserved the rarely awarded Victor Ludorum trophy for my achievements, he personally had managed to quash the idea.

How childish some people are! I have always felt that unless I can say something good about someone, I would rather not say anything. My inclination is always to try and help rather than hinder. I have met any number of people who work in the opposite way. If they can't do something themselves, or have it themselves, they don't want others to do or have it, apparently believing that they will be viewed in a better light if they undermine all perceived competition.

I shared the journey to and from Harrogate with a former cadet called Tony. Unfortunately, his career didn't last long, as he was summarily dismissed by the Chief Constable – allegedly for chewing gum in uniform, but in fact (we thought) for a momentary lapse in concentration. At that time one of the principal duties of a police officer was controlling traffic. Each morning and evening at peak times the traffic lights were turned off, and constables manned road junctions. The main crossings in Huddersfield were outside the George Hotel – the birthplace of Rugby League, a hundred yards from Bath Street – and the top of Chapel Hill. Chapel Hill required the greater skill, but the George was the most important, as the Chief Constable drove through the crossing on his way to and from work. When you were on that point, you had to look out for him approaching in either his silver Bentley or his red MG-TF, so that you could stop other traffic and give him precedence. One morning Tony failed to do this, and we all believed that was the true reason he was sacked. In distress, he joined the fire service, where he served for thirty years with distinction.

I returned to Huddersfield to take up my duties in April 1962. I had been allocated the collar number 150, and thenceforth that was how I was addressed, by number, not by name. If an officer wanted me, he would call out not 'Hellawell', but 'One-fifty'. We were entitled to one and a half days off each week, and while theoretically there was a limit to the number of hours we worked each shift, this was at the discretion of our senior officer, so that in fact there was no finite number. Nor was there any compensation for working excessive hours, either by way of time off or overtime, and no one dared challenge any request, for fear of being dismissed. Each officer had to work a two-year probationary period, during which the Chief Constable could dispense with your services at will.

Our first six weeks were spent on night duty, learning the beats. We had to parade thirty minutes before the start of each shift. There were neither lockers nor showers in the police station, as we were encouraged to go to and from work in uniform – the idea being that the sight of uniformed police on the streets was a deterrent to criminals, even if the officers were off duty. It was a disciplinary offence to wear half uniform.

In the parade room we lined up, standing to attention, for the duty inspector and the shift sergeants. We had to hold our truncheon in our right hand at right angles to our bodies, with our whistle and chain draped over it and our handcuffs in our left hand. We placed our torch on the floor in front of us between our feet. Our hair, uniforms, boots and equipment were inspected. If anything was not up to standard, we would have to rectify the problem, and the time it took us to do so would be added to the end of our shift.

Once approved, we would be allocated a particular beat, told in which order to go round it, and briefed with details of anything unusual known to be occurring or needing attention on that patch. These would be entered on a card, which we had to complete at the end of the shift. With our briefing completed, we would march out of the station in a crocodile, and in beat order. The officers coming off duty would stand waiting for us at pre-arranged points, and each one would join the back of the marching line as his relief dropped off at the front. By this means we avoided any beat being unmanned at any time. We provided a much better service in those days.

As this was long before the advent of personal radios, we had to make fixed points – for instance outside the Rose and Crown, or in front of Lloyds bank – every thirty minutes at night and every fifteen during the day. We might have to return some property which had been found in the town centre, or check the security of a house whose owners were away on holiday – a call which would occasionally necessitate feeding their cat. We held the keys to yards, chambers and vulnerable premises, all of which we would search. In winter, premises with furnaces were particularly attractive, as we could go in and get warm. Toilet facilities were naturally few and far between, but I managed to collect a number of keys which gave me access to some comfortable hideaways.

We were treated not as human beings – merely as numbers, to be dealt with however the senior officers decided. One night, when I was working Nos. 9 and 10 beats, one of my points was at a Dr Who-type box. To my surprise, I found another police officer there when I arrived. There had clearly been some mistake, as we were never allowed to meet a colleague on the beat, and it was a disciplinary offence even speak to each other when we passed on opposite sides of the road. We quickly established that the other man was in the wrong, but before he had a chance to leave, a sergeant came into the box. Without seeking any explanation, he hit my colleague with the back of his hand, ordered him to get out, and warned him that if he caught him again he'd be up before the Chief.

Those early days were exciting: learning about the town, its streets, its yards and its chambers. We were instructed to make ourselves conspicuous in the day, by walking on the outside of the pavement, and invisible at night, by keeping close to the wall. The first time I worked nights on my own, I was spooked. I had been told that I would find all sounds threatening, and that was certainly true. Cats jumping out of a dustbin in a back yard catch you by surprise and make the hair on the back of your neck stand up. People are less frightening, because at least you can see and hear them approaching.

The first nocturnal stop I made was of a man walking up the centre of the road in the early hours of the morning. Summoning up my courage, I moved out of the shadows into his path and challenged him, 'Where are you going at this time of night?'

I must have sounded apprehensive, as he asked me if it was my first stop. When I told him it was, he said I needn't be nervous, as people were frightened of police uniform, and disconcerted by the surprise of seeing it unexpectedly. He turned out to be an army sergeant, coming home on leave, and the incident taught me a great deal. I realised afterwards that if he had been up to no good, he would not have come marching up the centre of the road, cracking his steel-tipped heels into the tarmac. Whatever the level of training or simulation, nothing can replace real experience.

We were paid weekly in cash, lining up on the pay parade and saluting as we were given our packets. With our pay we received our duties for the following week. We had to work the shifts we were allocated, however difficult that might have been for our social life, and officers were frequently refused permission to take leave, change shifts or have days off for important family occasions. Your life was not your own: it belonged to the police. When I submitted a written request to marry Bren and live at Zions Hill, a lane in Kirkburton, two things happened in quick succession. My request to live 'out of the Borough' was refused point-blank, and I was instructed that my girlfriend had to appear before my superintendent, for him to decide if she was a suitable person to marry a police officer.

There were three superintendents in the force – the Deputy Chief, and one for each of the geographical areas into which the force was divided. Both these latter were called Fred, and they were distinguished by their build. Mine was Fat Fred, the other Thin. Before he joined the police Fat Fred had been a plumber, and he once visited our police house to assess what work was required on our toilet system when it broke down.

Bren was naturally nervous before her interview, not knowing what might be asked, but conscious of the occasion's importance. When Fat Fred offered her a toffee to put her at ease, she luckily did not know that normally, when he did this, it meant that an officer was in trouble. He asked her why she wished to marry me; if she would be able to put up with the hours and the trauma of the job; if she was prepared to sacrifice her life in order that I could do my work. Afterwards, Fred told me she had passed the test, and we could marry, adding, 'You've got a cracker there.' But just imagine any employer trying that tack today.

The two Freds shared a single office and desk, and on the wall facing each of them was a map of their part of the Borough. Every two or three years they exchanged responsibility for divisions, but instead of swapping the maps over, they emptied their drawers and moved to the other side of the desk. Years later, when I asked Fat Fred why they didn't just move the maps around, he said that they 'liked a change of scenery'. Their lives were so simple.

The police service in those days was far different from that of modern times. It was a great deal more violent and corrupt – yet the image created by the media did not reflect this. *Dixon of Dock Green*, a favourite television series, portrayed the police as a kind, caring and benevolent organization – but this was far from the truth. It was brutal, authoritarian and corrupt. People arrested for street disorder would be physically assaulted on arrival at a police station if they spoke out of turn, and their injuries would be attributed to them 'falling'. If they complained, no action would be taken. Those arrested for crime would, if necessary, be beaten into confessing: they had no right of access to a solicitor, and would be detained until they had signed a confession.

The police did not act in this way without public consent. We were supported in what we did, the belief then being that the end justified the means. Local governments had the power to make their own laws, and these reflected the mood of the time: 'A person may be arrested by a police officer in uniform for: acting in a disorderly manner; failing to obey a lawful order; failing to open his pack for inspection; failing to move when directed so to do; swearing, insulting or lewd behaviour; urinating in the street'. The list went on.

Those arrested would be kept in the cells until the next available court sitting, and there was little bail. The courts had the power to pass sentence summarily. For repeated minor offences they would impose a term of imprisonment, and by these means the streets were kept relatively peaceful.

I am not suggesting that every prisoner was assaulted or had confessions beaten out of him: merely that this was an accepted course of action if it seemed necessary.

Since those days there have – quite rightly – been significant changes, but the consequence has been that the police have lost control of the streets. Initiatives to outlaw vigorous police action have allowed the yob and hooligan culture to flourish. The police are now largely powerless to act, and the public have lost confidence in them. Moreover, officers have lost confidence in themselves. Politicians, unduly influenced by small but vociferous pressure groups, have not helped by increasingly criticising the police for the consequences of their own actions, and by legislating for the exception rather than the rule. They talk the strong talk by introducing headline-grabbing but largely ineffective powers, and bring the police service more and more under their control. Society has moved on, and the balance has shifted firmly towards the freedom of the individual – but I hear very little about the individual responsibility which should go with it.

In the old days Chief Constables set their own standards for recruitment, and promoted whomever they wished. Nepotism was rife. One officer, ineligible even to join, had a remarkable rise through the ranks because of a family connection with the Chief

Constable of the day. There was also a strong Masonic influence: our Deputy Chief Constable was an active Mason, and ambitious officers were signed up in droves. I was approached more than once, but always declined, as I have little interest in Freemasonry, although I have nothing against it.

There were other ways in which senior officers controlled our lives, operating a regime of fear and favour which is difficult to comprehend today. If you wanted to be posted into a particular department, particularly the CID, and remain there, you had to do exactly what you were told. Often this meant playing cricket, golf, snooker or just buying the boss a few drinks. You learned never to win. One promising officer was stupid enough to beat the Deputy Chief Constable in a snooker competition. The room fell silent. The Deputy threw his cue across the table, glared at the constable and said, 'That's your f—ing career finished.' The man was never promoted.

Later, the Deputy came into the CID one evening when I was relatively new there, and complimented me on the way my sports car handled. Before I could reply he let on that he had asked 'Traffic' to start the vehicle by hot-wiring it, so that he could take it for a spin. A year or so afterwards, when we had changed the car for a saloon, he asked me for the keys, telling me that he needed the vehicle for a 'special purpose'. I handed them over without question, as I didn't wish to cause offence. The special purpose, I later learnt, was to take out a female acquaintance, in a vehicle that would not be recognized.

Efficiency was by no means improved by the fact that we didn't have telephones in our homes, and if anyone was needed in a hurry, a car had to be sent to fetch him. We used to work this deficiency to our social advantage: if someone wanted a night out to celebrate a promotion or a retirement, and was afraid to ask his wife for leave of absence, he would arrange for the duty officer to come out at a set time to tell him that one of his prisoners had been arrested, and he was required at the station immediately. He would ensure that he was in the bath or the garden when the car arrived, so that he could complain to his wife about the inconvenience.

On day shifts, we worked patrols. The town centre was split into a number of streets, and it was our duty to walk 'at a measured pace' up one side and down the other for the three or four hours before and after meal break. To relieve the boredom I would help the drivers of articulated vehicles manoeuvre into tight places and talk to the street cleaners and shopkeepers as they were opening up. Patrolling the fruit and vegetable market was a much sought-after duty, usually reserved for those long in service, as you generally came away with some vegetables or a bag of fruit.

New recruits were often allocated the breakfast patrol, which entailed visiting one particular butcher and purchasing about twenty breakfast rations. For the price of an old shilling (5p), each would include several rashers of bacon, three sausages, two eggs and often liver or kidneys. The main duty of the man on this patrol was to cook breakfast for all his colleagues and for the prisoners. Since I have always enjoyed cooking, this was no hardship to me, but my culinary career came to an abrupt end when the inspector discovered some grit on his fried eggs. Little did he know that I had let them slip off his plate on to the floor of the kitchen, picked them up and dusted them off before serving them up to him. Dominoes was played at all meals for pennies and halfpennies: for some this was a serious matter, and cheating took place. One of the sergeants, dubbed 'Honest John', was notorious in this respect.

Partly to break the boredom, I took to stopping motorists and seeking production of their documents. Besides discovering a substantial number of motoring offences, I was fortunate in detecting several more serious crimes of document forgery. My other speciality was reporting people whose cars had faulty bodywork. In those days vehicles were not built to last, and owners didn't have the money to maintain them. I took pride in submitting detailed drawings of the faults on any offending vehicle. My work necessitated frequent court attendances and brought me to the notice of senior officers. My peers used to say I was 'jammy' for discovering so many offences, but I was merely working hard. The force pioneered a scheme whereby motorists could avoid prosecution by rectifying faults within a set time, and this initiative was adopted by the whole service some twenty years later.

I was always looking for new things, and once reported someone for an offence under the Merchandise Marks Act, because he had a number of chewing-gum dispensing machines which misrepresented the type of gum inside. When I brought this to the notice of the owner, a prominent local businessman, he told me he didn't intend to do anything about it. I suspected that Masonic influence was at work, but I managed to have him prosecuted, even though one of the inspectors tried to dissuade me, on the grounds that the shopkeeper was 'a good chap'.

There were many occasions on which senior officers tried to intervene because of their relationships with individual members of the public. I once found a man sprawled out on the street in a drunken state, and when he reached the police station he was recognized as a local doctor. The duty inspector said that we should take him home without charge 'because of who he is'. I was annoyed at this, because we always took drunks before the court, and I said so. The inspector insisted. I resisted, saying that I was not against taking people home in principle, but would he do it if the drunk was a miner or a plumber? He told me not to be silly.

Years later, when I became an inspector, the same officer tried to intervene and have a young drunk driver released on the grounds that he was the son of a local solicitor. When I refused, my colleague told me that the lad's father was 'in the lodge' with him, and we ought to do him a favour. I still ignored the request. The young man was charged and convicted – and afterwards, ironically, I was visited by him and his father, who both apologised and thanked us for taking action, as the boy had been 'running wild'.

My first arrest for crime had a touch of farce about it. I was patrolling the vegetable market when I heard the cry, 'Stop thief!' I gave chase and rugby-tackled the fleeing villain, who dropped the box of radishes he had stolen, having thought in his drunken state that they were strawberries. He appeared before court the next day and was sentenced to two months' imprisonment, due to his previous criminal history.

Once I was confronted by Mary, a well-known prostitute, who was waiting to appear before the court. She stood in my path and lifted her skirt above her head, displaying her all and saying that, as I was new, she would like to introduce herself. 'Put it away,' I told her, 'or it may get cold.' I had already arrested one woman for prostitution, but the charge had been refused, and when I asked why, I was told that there were no prostitutes in Huddersfield. When I repeated my observation, the charge sergeant repeated, 'There are no prostitutes in Huddersfield,' adding, 'because the Chief Constable says so.' That was how history was written.

Other fictions were maintained. Crimes were rarely recorded until detected, and by this means we kept the number of recorded crimes artificially low, achieving an almost 100 per cent detection rate. This changed when resources were allocated in accordance with the number of crimes reported. Within a year the recorded crime rate in Huddersfield soared and the detection rate plummeted. So much for the validity of statistics.

We attended many domestic disputes, largely caused by men assaulting their wives after drunken binges when they had drawn their wages. I felt sorry for those women, and for their children, because I had shared their hell. When the men were arrested, spent the night in the cells and appeared before court the next day, their wives would drag the children along to plead for their husbands, as it was not in their interest for their men to be imprisoned, or to receive another hiding for reporting them. It was only in the 1970s that we began to address this issue – and it will probably never be resolved. Tens of thousands of women, and some men, live in constant fear of their partners, and more attention needs to be devoted to alleviating their misery.

I used to do what little I could to help – but the sight of those children standing on earth floors, in houses which stank, dressed only in vests, blue from cold, bruised all over, feeding themselves with the cold baked beans they scooped from a jagged can, will live with me for ever. Seeing how badly they were abused and neglected, I wanted to take them away, clean and feed them, show them love. That is why I am driven to do what I do. My compassion, born out of my own experience, didn't go unnoticed by my colleagues, who regarded me as a bit of a bleeding heart, or by families within these poor neighbourhoods, who would entrust me with their confidences.

My own life was good. I enjoyed my work, I was playing rugby with the force team, competing in the swimming team and captaining the force's first-aid team. Bren and I were planning the details of our wedding. Compared with the complexity and pace of today, our existence was very simple. Our pleasure was in each other, walking, talking and visiting places in my Minivan.

When my shifts allowed, I would collect Bren from work and go on to the school where her mother cleaned, to take her home as well. It was on the empty playground – an ideal place for lessons – that I taught Bren to drive: we argued constantly about what she was or wasn't doing right, and she did have a dozen lessons from a professional, but she passed her test at the first attempt, so it was worth the struggle.

In Huddersfield we spent the last three months of our two-year probation attached to different departments, first Traffic, then the CID. I revelled in the duties of the detectives, and liked the officers I worked with. They all seemed to be as large as I was, and I felt at home in plain clothes, which included mandatory brown suede shoes and a trilby hat.

At Christmas 1963, immediately after my attachment, I was summoned to see the Chief Constable. I approached the meeting with much trepidation, for a number of reasons: first, I had never forgotten his warning at my initial interview, when he said he had the power to sack me; and second, I had recently come across him in the garage one day when I was there to pick up a stray collie pup which I had bought. The animal had peed all over the Chief's shoes, and he had gone off in a huff.

My fears proved unfounded. Not only had I passed my probation: even better, I was to become a detective. For the second time the Chief said that he was promoting me against his better judgement, but I had done a surprisingly good job, and he would give me a try. He added his usual caveat – that he would be watching me closely, and one false move would put me out.

I was overcome. No officer had ever gone into the CID with less than eight years' service. Unfortunately the force was not ready for such an innovation, and I experienced the full weight of many colleagues' jealousy.

The year 1963 was also a milestone in my private life, because on 2 February, amid one of the worst snowfalls for many years, Bren and I got married at Lindley Methodist Church. Bren wore a beautiful white dress, which she still owns, and I wore top hat and tails, in which I felt most conspicuous and uncomfortable. The reception was held at a local banqueting suite, to which all our relatives were invited. We had to pay for the whole event ourselves as Bren's parents had very little money. My father, who by then owned a number of bakers' shops, had been persuaded by Auntie Evelyn to provide the cake, which he duly did, but he ran true to form by sending Bren's father the bill.

After the wedding Bren and I were driven to our new home, a police house on Yews Hill Road in Lockwood. Our intention had been to change and set off on our honeymoon to Cornwall; but due to the atrocious weather, and the fact that I had spent the remainder of our savings on changing the Minivan for an Austin Healey sports car, we decided to stay at home. When we consummated our love on the sheepskin rug in front of the gas fire, we felt warm, secure and happy.

My relationship with my father had always been tenuous. When I was seventeen, I went to a cousin's wedding, and as I stood in the queue for food, my father asked his brother Jimmy, my uncle, 'Who's that blond-haired young lad in front of us?' To which my uncle replied, 'That's your son.' The information did not seem to impress him, as he ignored me, and went on talking to his brother.

Years later the duty inspector from Bradford rang me at home to say that a man had been arrested for drink-driving, and had asked the police to call me, claiming that he was my father. I confirmed that he was, and told them to continue with the normal procedure. On two occasions he turned up at our home, each time drunk and with a different woman in tow, telling me how much he loved me and promising me all that he had when he died. We were hospitable, but his visit was unsettling for our children. When he died at the age of sixty-three, he left his worldly goods to the woman he was living with at the time.

CHAPTER FOUR

ENDS AND MEANS: THE CID

I began work as a detective in January, 1964. The CID was a different world: all the petty restrictions were lifted, we could travel out of the Borough, visit pubs and cafés, and I was allowed to drive the CID car, a grey Ford Anglia estate. The work was much more interesting, as we were dealing with real criminals, and the cases were brought to us. When I made some remark about having to wear a trilby hat, I was told I was lucky, because until the 1950s detectives had been obliged to wear bowlers.

I only had one suit, and was told I must buy another in order to look good when giving evidence at Quarter Sessions and Assizes. Not having any cash to spare, I got my 'sessions suit' on hire-purchase from March the Tailor in Huddersfield.

Our working pattern was much different from that of the uni-formed branch. Except when we took our turn with a Traffic officer in the immediate-response car, we worked either days, from 9 a.m. to 5 p.m., or nights, from 5 p.m. to 1 a.m. In reality this meant that we often also worked between shifts: if we were on late, we would give evidence in court during the morning, and when we were on days, we visited local pubs and clubs in the evening.

Drinking played a large part in our activities. I was teamed up with an officer much senior to me, but as he and I played in the pack at rugby together, we trusted each other. Within my first week we started doing our daily round of the local pubs where the criminal fraternity would congregate. We would always order two halves of bitter and hand over some money, usually receiving change equal to the amount we had offered. By this means the licensees showed they were pleased we were there, without opening themselves to ridicule and perhaps violence from the remainder of their clientele.

Most evenings we would drink seven or eight pints of Tetley's bitter, staying until the pubs closed at half past ten. If we were working evenings, we would go back to the station with fish and chips, deal with any drunks and offenders who had been arrested, and then go to night clubs in the town. It was no surprise that our wives were vetted before we got married: we were wedded to the job, and they had a lot to put up with. Looking back, I don't know how I got away with it, or why I enjoyed it so much, but I did.

One afternoon we went into a public house at the bottom end of Huddersfield. Some particularly unsavoury characters, whom I didn't know, were sitting in the bar eyeing us up. My colleague exchanged some banter with them, and then asked me if I was ready, so I drank off and expected to leave. Not so: we went into the toilets, followed by the three men. I was told to take my coat off, which I did, and we had a stand-up fight with the trio. We beat them soundly – not without difficulty or bumps and bruises – put our coats back on, and left them on the floor in the urinals, nursing their wounds. We then said goodbye to the licensee and left.

My partner made an entry in the 'Griff Book', a general message and information book left open on the office desk, which read, 'X, Y and Z have been sorted out in the Ramsden's Arms today and they won't cause us any trouble for a while.' I am still not sure whether this was a test for me, and the whole thing had been set up. Whatever the truth, it was a strange baptism in the detective ranks. There were no complaints, and when I later saw the same men again, they made no reference to what had occurred between us.

We were an exclusive bunch in the CID, there being only seventeen of us in all, and we occupied five interconnecting offices off the main entrance hall. The constables' room was no more than twelve feet square, with a fireplace, a bookcase and two desks. We conducted all our business there, keeping books and records, and typing our reports. I had taught myself to touch-type, and became popular with my colleagues, as I would do some of their work; more important, I would type statements from their witnesses, and in doing so learnt a great deal about how their minds worked. Once crimes had been reported, we made an entry in the Crime Complaint Book (CCB), or the lost-property register. We had to report progress in writing on our investigations after seven, fourteen, and twenty-eight days, after which, if we were lucky, we reported no more.

Villains knew what to expect from the police in those days. They knew that there was no point in telling the court if they had been mistreated, as the police could deny it – and in any event the magistrates would not believe them.

I felt uncomfortable with some of the things we did, but I didn't want to lose my job, so to satisfy my colleagues and achieve the same results, I would slowly and theatrically remove my jacket in front of a prisoner, asking him, 'Which way do you want it – easy or hard?' I am not proud of what I did: by failing to blow the whistle, I was as guilty of mistreatment as anyone else, because I used violence by implication.

In the early sixties attempts were being made to outlaw such behaviour. We were all told to be more careful. Having said that, we were still expected to obtain confessions. During my early days I had to interview a man who had thrown another person through a plate-glass window, causing him serious injuries. He was under the influence of drink, and aggressive. The interview took its normal course. I began quietly and smoothly, gradually increasing the volume. I had just reached the point of seeking an admission when a detective sergeant came into the room from the next office, called me aside and told me to 'keep it down', as he didn't want any trouble. Soon afterwards this happened again, and when the sergeant appeared for the third time, the prisoner said, 'Who the f—ing hell is that chap who keeps coming in?'

The sergeant, now dead, had one of the wildest tempers I have ever known, and ran across the room at him shouting, 'Don't you dare talk to me like that!'

'I'll talk to you how I f—ing want,' the prisoner answered – whereupon the sergeant punched him in the mouth and knocked him off his chair. In another interview, when a prisoner told this same officer that he dare not hit him because he wore glasses, the sergeant gently removed the spectacles and smacked him.

Another time, one of my colleagues dressed up in a white coat and posed as a doctor, so that he could visit a difficult prisoner 'to deal with his injuries'. In the course of treatment he persuaded the man that it was in his own interest to confess. Unfortunately for 'the doctor', he appeared in court for another case at the same time as this prisoner, who, when asked if he wished to say anything, looked in the direction of my friend and said that he wanted to thank 'Doctor —', giving his real name. 'Ah yes, Doctor —,' said the magistrate, immediately spotting the subterfuge. The man went to prison, and no mention was made of the officer's action.

Other ingenious methods were used: policemen even posed as lawyers, probation officers and priests. Once during the early hours of the morning some of us set up a courtroom, in which we tried and sentenced an SAS trainee who had broken into the Post Office sorting room and confessed, under interrogation, that as part of an exercise, he'd been required to frank a letter without being caught. The poor man was convinced that he was going to have to serve the two-year sentence imposed on him, and he spent four hours in the cells before we put him out of his misery.

All the parties in the criminal justice system either condoned or ignored police actions. I once arrested a man for stealing his friend's coat. The prisoner's excuse was that the coat-owner had 'pulled a bird, and he wouldn't take me home'. He told the court that he intended to return the coat, and this undermined the charge of theft, which would have required him to 'intend to permanently deprive the owner of it'.

Acting completely outside court procedure, the police officer prosecuting stood up and began to question the prisoner. He asked if there had been any cigarettes in the pocket of the coat.

'Yes,' was the answer.

'Did you smoke them?'

'Yes.'

The prosecutor sat down. Without commenting on this un-authorised intervention, the magistrates declared the man guilty as charged and imposed a fine, rather than imprisonment, as he had no previous convictions.

Some of our actions were more unorthodox. The police station used to house fire engines, as in earlier days it was combined with the fire service, officers being known as 'fire bobbies'. The huge vehicle inspection pits were still in place in the garage, and on some occasions this forbidding place was used to interview difficult prisoners.

We relied very little on scientific evidence, other than finger-prints, and even when these had been found at the scene of a crime, we would have to obtain a written confession, one of the reasons being that we didn't trust forensic evidence.

We used to make up the names of people we had 'interviewed' in connection with our inquiries and wrote down a list of relevant places we had 'visited'. In reality, except for the more serious crimes, we did nothing but interview at length all the people who were arrested for other offences, many of whom were quite amenable to admitting crimes they had not committed, just to keep in our good books. Only if a person did confess to a crime would it be recorded; by these means we achieved the magnificent detection rate of over 90 per cent.

We never made any meaningful pocket-book entries at the time, so we were vulnerable if called on to produce our pocket-books in court. To avoid embarrassment, we drew a new book for each court appearance, and back-dated entries in the middle pages, leaving blank ones on either side. To avoid the blanks being discovered, we taped them together and, if asked, explained they contained information sensitive to the state and could not be examined (we did undertake the duties of Special Branch in those days).

One case nearly backfired on the officers involved. A man had been found dead in a one-up, one-down house on the outskirts of the town. He had sustained multiple injuries, which the detectives managed to convince the Coroner's Court were self-inflicted. This was no mean feat, as he had been strangled, hit over the head, stabbed several times and then gassed. My colleagues claimed to have deduced that he was desperate to kill himself – reason unknown – and had tried to strangle himself with the flex from the hanging light-bulb at the top of the stairs. After he had been suspended for some time (the detectives claimed), his weight tore the fitting from the ceiling – a task undertaken, in fact, by the investigating officer – and he fell down the stairs, sustaining his head injuries. He survived the fall, and so, still determined, he crawled to a drawer, from which he pulled out a knife and stabbed himself. Unfortunately the knife had mysteriously disappeared from the scene, so one had to be provided for authenticity. In the end, still alive, he put his head in the gas oven and turned on the gas – by which means he finally achieved his task. There was a great deal of embarrassment when a man gave himself up and confessed to the murder, which even they dared not try to talk him out of. He served life imprisonment.

One night we raided a shebeen, or unlicensed drinking den, in a cellar at the top end of Huddersfield, run by an Afro-Caribbean male. I weighed nearly nineteen stone at the time, so I was sent in to break down the locked door. My shoulder-charge was so successful the door, together with its frame, was knocked completely away from the wall and crashed into the room, to the surprise and annoyance of the company gathered there for a quiet drink. Unfortunately, with the door came the masonry above it, part of the cellar ceiling and the floor of the room above. My boss suggested that I make a hasty retreat, as it 'might inflame the situation if you stay'.

Many other incidents enlivened our working days. One officer used to hold the supply of condoms, for which he would be called upon day or night if any of us was in urgent need. The wife of another colleague would leave a bowl of cornflakes on the kitchen surface if she wanted sex, and if he discovered this when he came home late at night, he would drive to the source. At our supplier's house, if knocking failed, he would throw stones at the bedroom window to awake him. This was naturally not to the liking of his wife, who would tell us so in no uncertain terms: if she was in a reasonable mood, she would just shout to her husband, 'They've come for Johnnies.'

That marriage was stormy in any event. The lady of the house once blew up the television set by pouring the contents of a vase of flowers into it, to prevent her husband watching rugby. He retaliated by picking up the coal bucket and dumping its contents onto the settee which she had just been cleaning. Another day, when I called to collect him for work, she said, 'You'll have to wait – he's having a shit.' The marriage eventually broke down. One day this officer came into work livid, because he had found his daughter 'in bed with a bloody soldier'. 'I wouldn't have minded,' he added, 'but he'd kept his boots on.'

Another officer used to pretend that he was mad. Maybe he was, a bit: he would peer at people through a tube of rolled-up paper, and shout down it in public. When we visited a mill, in the foyer of which there was a large ship's bell, we were told that it was the fire alarm and must be used only in emergencies. Needless to say, when we were leaving, our colleague rang it as loud as he could. He used to tell us that at Christmas he could not afford a turkey, so he would put up photographs of the birds in strategic positions about the house, and large signs with the name written on them. On the day, he said, his family had to put up with gravy made from Bisto.

The only mustachioed detective in the office had his life threatened by one of the town's most violent criminals: the man didn't know his name, but referred to him as 'the one with the tash'. Our colleague acquired a hand-gun illegally and shaved his whiskers off so that he wouldn't stand out, and the rest of the office riposted by growing moustaches. That officer was seriously hot-headed. Long after retirement he could not get the builder of his new house to repair a leak in the bathroom: after badgering him without success, he solved the problem by visiting the builder during the night, putting a hosepipe through his letter box, and letting it run until it was discovered in the morning. His repairs were completed expeditiously.

There were many embarrassing moments, like the time I was out with a Traffic officer nicknamed Jet, who was exceptionally tactless, and we stopped at some traffic lights behind a female learner-driver. When the lights changed to green, she crunched the gears but did not move, and as the signals went through a second cycle she stalled her engine – harassed, I feel sure, by the fact that there was a police car behind her. My colleague then drove alongside and asked me to wind down my window. When the woman did the same, he called, 'What's matter wi' thee, lass? In't there a colour to suit thee?' When answering a criticism that he had sworn at a motorist, this same officer replied to the Deputy Chief Constable, 'I didn't swear, Sir. I only told him that if he spoke back to me, he'd measure his length in shit.' This, he thought, was a perfectly acceptable expression to use to a member of the public.

One day when I was helping him deal with a road accident caused by snow on the ground, a passing doctor stopped his Rover and gave us a hand, not only with the injured person, but also in pushing the vehicles off the road. As the doctor was walking off, my colleague said, 'Hey – just a minute. Is that thy car?'

'Yes,' said the doctor.

'Can I see the licence, then?'

That was too much. I stepped in, apologised and thanked our good Samaritan for his help.

One Christmas morning we were called to a mill-owner's house because the place had been burgled. The house was beautifully appointed, but we could see that there had been a party the night before. When the lady of the house apologised for 'the mess', my colleague replied, 'Never mind, lass. Our house is always a shit-hole on a morning.' I just didn't know where to put myself.

Another officer – a big, powerful man – would occasionally hurry into the fire or ambulance station at breakfast time and tell the crews that they were needed immediately to attend an incident, which he had invented. The moment they were out of the station, with sirens blaring, he fell on their breakfast – a trick that did nothing for inter-service co-operation.

All these reprehensible actions were fuelled by a strong belief that the end justified the means. This was the law of the streets: it was dog eat dog, but the police and the system had the more powerful bite. Police officers gained nothing personally: they even knew they were putting themselves at risk. They acted as they did because they wished to remain detectives, they wanted to rid the town of criminals, and were expected to come up with results.

There was a desperate need for change, but it took the exposure of some high-profile cases to make an impact. After a while I began to feel very uneasy in this environment, and similar views were held by officers in the surrounding forces. When my partner and I visited one of them to interview two prisoners, all the local staff insisted that they leave before we could start, so that they would not be tainted by what they thought we were about to do. All we did, in fact, was to give the detainees a piece of paper and a pencil. We told them we knew what they had done; *they* knew what they had done, and we would leave them for half an hour to prove to us that they were telling the truth by writing their offences down on the paper. They did, and they both received long prison sentences.

As for what the criminal fraternity thought of police methods – they accepted them. If they were sent down on the strength of a statement made under duress or falsified evidence, they generally held no grudge. Many would say, 'What goes round, comes round.' Innocent people had no fear of the system: in fact they were comforted by it, because they knew there was a very high likelihood that a crime would be solved and someone sentenced. In the majority of cases innocent people did not go to court, but there were the tragic exceptions. One of the officers I worked with was involved in the imprisonment of a man who received a life sentence for murder, the main evidence for which was a semen match that was later proved to be impossible. Broken by the experience, the man died shortly after his release.

The kind of actions in which we indulged have no place in

modern police practice. If they are detected, they are brought to notice, and the offending officer is firmly dealt with. The ironic result is that the police today are generally less respected, and subject to more scepticism from the public and the media, than they were in the sixties – and this is entirely wrong. One of the penalties of a democracy is that, without draconian methods, we will never be able to control the criminal elements in society.

In the autumn of 1964 I began my initial detective training course at Bishopgarth, in Wakefield, along with officers from all over the world, who acquainted me with some very interesting interview techniques. An African colleague, for instance, said the best way to obtain confessions was to place a loaded rifle vertically on the ground, barrel upwards, and make the prisoner place his forehead on the muzzle and his finger on the trigger, and then shuffle round and round, bent over, as fast as he could, until he either shot himself or confessed. An Arab was appalled by such barbaric practices. In *his* country, he said, the police were much more gentlemanly. He would invite the prisoner to sit, offer him a cigarette and a drink, and then ask him, in a polite manner, if he had committed the crime. 'If he confesses,' he said, 'I tell my staff to take him out and shoot him. If he denies it, I tell my staff to take him out and shoot him.' By the end of the course, our own methods seemed rather tame.

Before I went off to Bishopgarth, my Chief had given me his usual warning about my future. But when I came back, he was over the moon. 'You're first lad we've 'ad to get top marks,' he said, 'but don't let it go to your 'ead.' He suggested that I might be a contender for the Special Course – a top-level, accelerated-promotion course for serving officers, derived from a scheme set up by Marshal of the RAF Lord Trenchard, when he was Commissioner of the Metropolitan Police during the 1930s.

At this stage of my career I became eligible to take my exam for promotion to the rank of sergeant – a national examination attempted annually by over 11,000 constables, of whom the top sixty became eligible to compete for the twelve-month, residential Special Course.

I had many doubts about spending so long away from home. I was still learning my trade as a detective, and we were trying for a family. But when I passed the exam with high marks in January 1965, Bren encouraged me to have a go. We did not understand at that time the difference this result would make to our lives.

To obtain a place on the Special Course, one had to compete in a series of interviews, the first of which took place in Fetter Lane, off Fleet Street, in London. I drove down from Yorkshire wearing a white shirt with detachable starched collars. On arrival I washed my hands and face, brushed my 'sessions suit' and changed my collar in a public toilet. Ready for action, I walked into the interview with my adrenalin high.

In a small, drab room four people sat behind a desk. They were the Chief Constable of Rochdale Borough; a member of the Superintendents' Association; one representative from the Police Federation;* and a civil servant. They began by asking me about my job. The civil servant wished to know which crime was I dealing with at the time. I explained indignantly that only radio and tele-vision detectives dealt with one case at a time, whereas I had thirty on the go. My questioner was not amused and said, 'All right,' (I'm sure he would have liked to have added 'Clever sod') 'what are they, then?' I explained that they ranged from the theft of a milk bottle to a rape. When he inquired sarcastically which I regarded as the most serious, I retorted, 'It depends whether you've been raped or had your milk stolen.' The police officers sniggered, and he had no further questions. (It helps to make people laugh during an interview, but one is skating on thin ice if the joke is at the expense of a member of the panel.) Anyway, I survived and went forward to the next stage.

This took place over three days at a residential college in the south of England. The only advice I had received in advance was that I should read *The Times* newspaper, as that would impress my

* The body representing all ranks up to and including chief inspector. Police officers are forbidden to be members of any political party or trades union. Superintendents have their own Association, and senior officers belong to the Association of Chief Police Officers (ACPO).

interviewers – so I did. When I arrived, late on a Sunday evening, I was shown to my room, and then met the other candidates. With naive confidence I announced myself as 'Hellawell from Huddersfield Borough' – a title which stuck with me for some time afterwards.

That night I met three basic types of individual. There were former public-school boys, one of whom arrived in a vintage car, telling us that he was related to some of the most senior police officers in the country, and it was a foregone conclusion that he would be selected (he wasn't). The second minority group, of which I was a member, I would describe as the 'rags and tags' – officers from poor social backgrounds, who had had other work experience. The third and by far the largest group were the grammar-school boys, many of whom had gone straight into the police cadet service.

The three days of interviews and exercises were modelled on the civil service-cum-military pattern. I found them demanding and difficult – and I understood why when I learned of the amount of preparation my colleagues had undertaken.

My first interview was with a civilian. I entered the room to find him sitting on a chair with his feet on the desk, looking away from me in the direction of the window. Without turning, he bade me sit down, then theatrically swung his chair round, took his feet off the desk, looked directly at me and said, 'Do you think you are a handsome man?'

I was taken aback, but confidently replied, 'I haven't thought about it, but I believe I'm a lot better looking than you.'

This seemed to please him, as he muttered, 'A good start,' and began to write furiously. His questioning continued in this odd manner.

'Who are your heroes?'

I told him I had none, but this did not seem to satisfy him and he offered up John Wayne and other screen stars. I was resolute, explaining that I had always had to look after myself, so that his question was not relevant.

'Did you masturbate as a boy?'

I told him it was nothing to do with him, adding that I was prepared to answer reasonable questions, but not ones of such a personal nature. He didn't push me. After many other queries he signalled that the interview was at an end, and asked if I had any questions for him. I said I would like to know the result. When he said he was not supposed to tell me, as that was part of the assessment process, the detective in me took over – and within a minute he gave in, suggesting I would have nothing to worry about on that score.

In another interview, with senior police officers, I was cautioned for my attitude. 'You answer like a detective in the witness box, being cross-examined by a barrister,' one of them told me. 'You go over, round and under when you answer, and it's very frustrating.' At the time I took this as a compliment, since I was practising the tools of my trade, but afterwards I realised that it was not a wise way to carry on. Interviews should not be seen as a battle: the closer you blend with your interrogators, the better your chance of success. Any attempt to be clever will work against you. Incidentally, my *Times* reading did come in handy, as I was asked about topics of the day and had ready responses.

On the last day I was summoned for an additional interview with the Commissioner of the City of London Police. I was told not to worry, as he wished to see 'a random sample to assess the standard of the intake'. The Commissioner was very pleasant with me, and seemed interested in the way I had approached the other interviews. He said that I had displayed 'high skills in interviewing his colleagues', and that had rankled with some of them: he suggested I adopt a more open approach in future. In spite of this mild censure, I left feeling that I had performed reasonably well, and that the panel had seen me as I was. But was I what they were looking for?

Several weeks passed before I was summoned from home, on a Saturday morning, to see the Chief straight away. Fearing I had committed some misdemeanour, I entered his office with trepidation and stood in front of his desk.

'Well then,' he said, 'what do you think?'

'I'm sorry, Sir,' I replied. 'I don't know what you are talking about.'

'Call yourself a detective, and you don't know why you're here?'

At last he told me that he had received the results, and then paused, waiting for me to say something.

'Did I get through?' I asked.

'Call yourself a detective?' he repeated. 'You should know what goes on in this place before I do.' He began to berate me for being so ignorant. Afterwards I realised he was only playing with me, but at the time it was most uncomfortable. In the end he told me that I had been successful, and would attend the fourth Special Course, which began in October 1965.

I was almost airborne with elation, but dared not show it, believing that the Chief had the power to prevent me going. I thanked him very much, but was shaken by what he said next: that my success was nothing to do with him, and if he had had a hand in my future, I wouldn't be going. He went on to explain that as I was the fourth person to gain a place on this course, the force would not be able to support us all, and we would upset the equilibrium of his promotion plan. 'You'll be n' good for us,' he said, 'and we'll be n' good for you. Now get out.'

He was not joking, and added insult to injury by informing me that on the day I started the course I would be transferred, on paper, to the Road Traffic Department, so that he could stop my £2.10s per week detective allowance.

Despite his ambivalent attitude, I was over the moon and went straight home to share my news with Bren. We celebrated with a Chinese takeaway meal, which for us was a treat. It was only over the weekend that the consequences of our good fortune began to sink in. Bren was pregnant and due to give birth at about the time I was to leave home for twelve months. We had little or no money, and our financial situation would worsen when I lost my allowance. Bren's wages would go when she gave up her job, and we anticipated there would be substantial expense attached to the course. Yet, whatever the cost, we knew that this was too good an opportunity to miss, and we were determined to get through.

Our misgivings soon proved well-founded. We were too poor to buy the essential clothes and equipment listed in the pre-course information pack, so again I resorted to hire-purchase at March the Tailor. We were also faced by the expense of my travelling to and from the Police College at Bramshill in Hampshire – a 200-mile journey in each direction – and a weekly subscription which I would have to pay during my stay. We worried about how we would meet these demands – and meanwhile Bren was having a difficult pregnancy. More and more I wondered if I ought to pull out – and without Bren's strong support, I would have done so.

Our first daughter, Samantha Louise, was born on 26 September 1965, eight days before I left home, and our joy was tinged with sadness at the prospect of my departing. In those days women were confined in hospital far longer than they are today, and I kissed mother and baby goodbye in hospital on Sunday, 3 October, knowing that I would not see them again for a month. I left with a leaden heart, but Bren was so stoical that years passed before I learned how badly she suffered, returning to an empty home with little money and virtually no support. The modern conveniences of washing machines, televisions, dishwashers, central heating and fitted carpets were at that time the province of 'the better-off', and having no telephone, we were forced to rely on our daily letters to each other. I can never repay the sacrifice my love made for me in those days.

CHAPTER FIVE

SOMETHING SPECIAL

It was with much pain that I began my new adventure. There were no motorways in those days, and the journey to the Police College took six hours. I shared the drive with two colleagues from another force: fortunately for me they had been to Bramshill before, and told me something of its history and the regime. The core of the college is a beautiful Jacobean manor house, once the property of the Brocket family, some of whom were Nazi sympathisers, and it is said that members of the High Command of the Third Reich visited the place.

We arrived late in the evening and were allocated quarters, along with a set of printed rules which mirrored those I had met on initial training. My spartan room was ten feet by eight, with grey walls and a single light-bulb hanging from the ceiling. It had a bed, a chair, a desk, a set of drawers and a wardrobe. Feeling lonely, I wrote a long letter home before I retired to bed.

The first morning did not inspire me. We assembled on the parade ground, tallest on the right, shortest on the left, for inspection by a number of senior officers, who told us how important they were and how insignificant we were. Each day was to begin with a parade and an inspection, before breakfast at eight. Any transgression would result in return to force, as would failure in one of the many examinations. Even if we had not already misbehaved or botched an examination, we could still fail on the final course assessment. We would work for a minimum of ten hours a day for five days each week, and go in for compulsory sport on Saturday afternoons. We were not allowed to return home for the first four weeks of the course. Welcome to higher police training in the mid-sixties!

Thirty-eight men and six women began the course. We came from police forces all over the country, and were a broad mix. I was the youngest, the most senior being thirteen years my elder. I was also the heaviest, at 260 pounds, eighty of which I shed during the course by hard work. I had the shortest period of service, and was one of only a handful who had left school at fifteen with no qualifications. Our number included an ex-naval officer who had bred bulls until his prize stud died. There was also a member of the landed gentry who had 'Bart' after his name, and another was a close relative of the Lord Lieutenant of a major English county. He once sounded off about the lack of quality on the course, rating only two others as worthwhile (besides himself, naturally). I was reassured to know that I was one of them.

This fellow was proud of the private plates on his car, which, though only a Morris Oxford, bore his initials and the number 1. One night some wag took the plates off and attached them to a child's pram, which he parked on the parade ground for us to discover next morning. The owner was highly embarrassed, but he removed the offending vehicle with a degree of dignity and without comment. He repaid those who he thought were the culprits by secreting items of women's clothing in their cars, for their wives to discover.

Once I got into the swing of my new environment, I liked most of my colleagues. I found the law work easy, and consistently achieved a high place in the examinations. I struggled, however, in the general studies, where my lack of formal education showed. My general studies tutor, Peter English, often confronted me with my inability to spell. In order to help, he gave me the task of learning a number of words each week, and to this day I am grateful for his kindness. I scraped through the monthly examinations by the skin of my teeth.

I enjoyed the sport and was determined to bring myself back to peak fitness. To do this, I had to work off the effects of the seven or so pints of bitter I had drunk each night in the course of my detective duties. Together with two officers from London, I began the Canadian Air Force fitness regime, with miraculous results. By the course end I had competed for the college at cross-country, rugby, football and athletics with some success.

At the end of the fourth week I went home to Bren and Samantha, leaving on Saturday evening, and returning in time for Monday morning's parade. The baby was chubby and had her mother's eyes, but I was worried about Bren, who looked drawn and sickly. She tried to allay my fears by saying that she was just recovering from childbirth. I was not convinced, but there was little I could do in the short time I was at home. In those days we were loath to call a doctor, because we did not want to intrude on someone whom we regarded as socially a cut above ourselves.

I dreaded leaving my little family, but I had no alternative. Although Bren put on a brave face, I was distressed by the strain I could see she was suffering.

The following Wednesday evening, I was sent for by one of the course tutors, who told me he had received a message from our family doctor, saying that Bren was ill. I told him I must go home straight away. He refused me permission, and said I would have to wait until next morning, when he would speak to an officer of higher rank. I told him how concerned I was about my wife, and said I intended to go straight away. He threatened me, saying that, if I left, I might not be allowed back, as I would be going without permission. He added that the Special Course was a chance of a lifetime, and urged me not to throw it away.

I could not believe what I was hearing. I told him that our doctor was of the old school, and would not have called unless the trouble was serious. Fortunately I had used my own car to return to the college: I took off in a blizzard without further ado, and drove all the way north in heavy snow. I arrived home during the early hours of the morning, to learn that my beloved Bren had suffered a pulmonary embolism. She was at home in bed, on her own, with Samantha by her side, and the room was lit only by the glow of the gas fire set in the wall. When I appeared, she was overwhelmed, as she hadn't expected to see me, having told the doctor not to worry me, as I had enough on my plate. Thank goodness, she recovered, although with some lasting damage to her chest.

I returned to the college the following Sunday evening to face the music. On parade next morning my colleagues looked on with hushed anticipation as I was told to present myself immediately to the Deputy Commandant, Philip (now Lord) Knights. In his room I found the officer who had tried to stop me leaving. When asked why I had absented myself without permission, I explained, and on hearing the story Mr Knights quickly became sympathetic. He reassured me that I had done the right thing, and that no action would be taken against me. He then asked his colleague to stay behind, and I can imagine what was said – but as far as I was concerned, that was the end of the matter.

I generally feel uncomfortable living in communal surroundings, as I am too fond of my home. Yet the course was good fun, and sufficiently challenging for me to accept the parts of it that annoyed me. Apart from anything else, it helped me enormously with my public speaking. I still looked down rather than into the eyes of the person I was speaking to, but I gained enough confidence to face my audience directly, even though they were probably not sure who I was looking at. I also learned a great deal about history, geography, politics and economics from books and projects. I was impressed by the visiting speakers, in particular military leaders: I liked their crispness of dress, their clipped accents and war stories.

We students went out on several visits, the last of which was to a number of police forces. On a trip to the north-east of the country, I suggested that my group might like to go down the mine where I used to work, and they jumped at the chance. On the day, they were like children, eager with anticipation, and when we reached one of the coal faces, they were very excited: each of them took a piece of coal as a memento, and they all admitted it was an experience they would never forget.

After we had bathed we went to the miners' pub, where we joined a group of my former colleagues. The drink flowed and stories were exchanged. The miners were most interested in hearing about my friend's prize bull. When the evening ended, this officer, who had been plying the miners with drink, remarked, 'What a charming group of chaps they are!' A moment later one of the miners called me back and demanded, 'Who the bloody 'ell's 'e?' When I explained, he remarked, 'He's a pillock.' Both parties were satisfied, for utterly different reasons.

The rest of that visit was extremely informative. We went into the clubs in Newcastle which the Kray twins had tried to infiltrate, but from which they had been literally thrown out by the local criminals. We were welcomed in one rural force as if we were royalty, since the Chief Constable there was a relative of one of my colleagues. Not so in Scarborough, where the senior officer had us parade before him. His desk was barren except for the Bible and the Discipline Handbook, and he only thawed when we started to talk football. When I asked him which of the books he used most, he said the one for discipline: the Bible was there only to make a good impression, and because it was 'heavy enough to throw at people'. I was surprised to find that we were viewed with deep suspicion by senior officers, as if the Special Course label was a curse. I had much more of this to face on my return to the force.

As our training developed, we began to bond together as a team. Despite the competition between us, we all rallied round when a member was sent down for failure or transgression. I also felt that we descended into some very childish behaviour. I have found the same thing on other residential courses, and I wonder if it is inevitable when people work and live so closely together. Or, in this particular case, was it due to the way we were treated?

Each Thursday evening we had to attend a mess night, to which senior officers and other luminaries were invited. Our duty was to greet and escort guests, many of whom were less than courteous, treating us like dirt. The idea of this charade was that it would develop our social skills. We had been taught how to handle a knife and fork, what to say when greeting a lady, and how to respond to the loyal toast. We were briefed before each event, about getting drunk, high spiritedness, singing, being sick or wetting the bed, the consequence of which would be return to force. As a matter of principle we would disobey some of the orders, and towards the end of the course we took our tutors to task over the way we were being addressed.

After-dinner entertainment was provided. The music society, of which I was a member, wrote and performed a version of *Oliver*. I enjoyed singing: as a child I had been involved in stage performances at my chapel; later I learned the rudiments of guitar, formed a skiffle group known as the 'Spiders', and busked around the local pubs. Other events included debates organised by the debating society, and 'balloon' debates, in which the audience had to decide whom to throw out of the basket, depending on their pleas. On other occasions we had speakers and solo performers.

Every student had his or her idiosyncrasies. Some were there to do nothing but study, and were tagged for this: one was known as 'the Q-Block Hermit', as we never saw him outside lessons (he became Professor of Law at Durham University). In order to wake him up a bit, one night some of my colleagues took his bed from his room and hung it in a tree by the lake.

Towards the end of the course we were told that a number of university places were available for us, and asked if we wished our names to be put forward. I would have liked to attend, but felt it was out of the question because I wanted to get home to my new family. Almost half our number went directly to university; most graduated with firsts or upper seconds, but then left the police service for other careers – a sad waste of talent.

Other course members didn't seem to care whether they passed or failed, and were there only to enjoy themselves. I envied those who lived within travelling distance, as they could go home whenever they wished. I suppose I was middle-of-the-road: I played sport, participated in the social life of the college and worked reasonably hard.

The final examinations put pressure on us all. Whatever we had achieved during the twelve months of the course would be thrown away by failure in one of the twelve or so papers. The tension was so high that it made some officers ill, and we all became quite fractious. To keep us occupied during the marking period we were sent away for a week to Sunningdales Training Centre for a War Duties course, and then on to other attachments.

At my last tutorial with the course director, I was pleasantly surprised to find that I had achieved good grades in the final examinations, and the staff thought well of my performance. I was told that my overall assessment would be sent directly to my Chief Constable.

The final dinner was a joyous affair. We were allowed to bring our respective partners, so Bren came down – the first time she had been parted from Samantha, who was looked after by her mother – and, as she was not allowed to share my room, I broke course rules by staying with her in a boarding house. Our course provided the after-dinner entertainment – a 35 mm film in which we had all been involved, and which sent up the College and its staff. It was greeted with great enthusiasm by students and guests, but with some reserve by the staff. The next day was tinged with sadness: I was thrilled to be returning home with Bren, but knew I would miss my many friends.

I did not realize it at the time, but the Special Course had an enormous influence on me. It opened up my perspective on life, developed my self-confidence and changed my appearance, as I had lost so much weight. But most of all, it put police work into context. I knew I would have to change, and that I must influence others to do the same.

CHAPTER SIX

BACK TO IT

I began work back on the streets of Huddersfield in September 1966 as the youngest sergeant in Britain, and I soon realised how badly out of practice I was. My colleagues regarded me with so much suspicion that I might have been working with strangers. There had been jealousies when I was posted to the CID, but this was much worse: whenever I tried to discuss a situation, I got the retort: 'You're the sergeant. You sort it out.'

My former detective colleagues expressed concern because I was so much thinner and, as they described it, I 'talked posh'. I had not consciously changed my accent, but exposure to a broader group of people, as well as speaking in public, had obviously had its effect. I got some stick for this, as my mates felt I had changed from 'the old Keith'.

The Chief, David Bradley, welcomed me back and made no reference to his last words of warning. On the contrary, he said he was proud of me, because I had gained the highest grade on the course, which he said was rarely awarded. Then, typically, he told me I would have to get my feet back on the ground, and work as a uniformed sergeant in the town centre, which suited me, as I knew it well.

I made some mistakes during those first weeks, but luckily they were not significant. I knew the law, which meant I couldn't go far wrong. Many of my friends thought I had lost my edge, because I began to work by the book and expected them to do the same.

Within a few months I was posted to an out-station at Milnsbridge, some four miles from the town centre, where I was more my own boss and could do things my way. This was my first command. I had my own team of officers, and set about making a difference.

During this period I passed my promotion examination for the rank of inspector, and on the anniversary of my graduation from the Special Course a sergeant from personnel spoke to me off the record. Police regulations had changed, he said, and I was entitled to be promoted to inspector. This was a complete surprise, as I could not have expected promotion for several years, and my scepticism was reinforced when weeks passed without any further development. I began to believe I was being wound up. Then in October the call came to see the Chief Constable.

As I stood before him, he seemed to be in his usual foul temper. He ranted and raved about the regulations which made my promotion mandatory. He said that he had done everything in his power to stop it at the Home Office: he had even taken legal advice, to no avail. He added that, had I not passed the promotion exam, he might have had some ground for delay, but I had 'taken even that' away from him. He added that he had managed to delay the day, which was some consolation to him, and I would not be promoted until 13 October 1967. (This turned out to be the second blessing of that year, as our daughter Alexandra Jane was born on 18 May, my birthday.)

I thanked the Chief for being so frank with me. He repeated his advice that I should seek employment elsewhere. At the time I felt hurt at the way I was dealt with, but in retrospect I can understand his misgivings. Sergeants were not normally promoted until they had at least fifteen years' service, and the force had only a handful of inspectors. I was twenty-five years old, with five years' service. The rule-book had been ripped up and thrown away, and I was seen as the cause of it. In fact, the new regulations meant that a successful Special Course candidate did not need to pass the promotion exam, so all my colleagues who passed the course, including those who failed the exam, were promoted, much to their embarrassment.

Other clouds were looming over our force, for changes in local government boundaries had heralded our end as an independent organization. Along with the other small borough forces within the region, we were to be amalgamated with our neighbouring county force in the autumn of 1968. It is difficult to explain how deeply affected we all were. We had intense pride in our organization, and even though others might judge us harshly, we felt we were providing the public with an adequate service. Everything was to change, and there was a huge amount of trepidation.

The Chief Constable called everyone to a meeting, to tell us about the proposals, and he opened by saying, 'This is a black day for the force.' He explained that he, along with the Chiefs of the other small forces, would become an Assistant Chief Constable (ACC) in the new West Yorkshire force. He remonstrated with those who had congratulated him, saying that he liked 'being a big fish in a little pond'.

His scepticism was soon justified. Our uniforms, helmets, badges, report forms, procedures and processes were all to be jettisoned in favour of those of the 'Riding', our nickname for the West Riding, for which we had little respect, regarding it as a bureaucratic organization.

At the final meeting of our force, David Bradley recounted its proud tradition of public service. We had opened clubs and workshops aimed at diverting young men from crime; we had pioneered the fast-tracking of cases to court, and the free use of public telephones for police officers for emergency calls; we had geared shift systems to demand, and modified schemes for dealing with vehicle defects – all innovations well ahead of their time. The Chief was clearly moved by the thought of the impending changes, and I could understand why: to lose command of something about which you feel so passionate must be very difficult, especially when the change has been brought about by powers beyond your control.

On amalgamation day, in October 1968, I was the night-duty

inspector, and because we had taken an obstructive stance, little had been done to facilitate the changeover. On the stroke of midnight we were invaded by officers from the 'Riding', who brought a van full of forms which we were instructed to take into use. Noticing that these did not carry the name of the new combined force, but were their old stock, I gave an instruction that we should not use them: for the time being we would continue to use our own. This was probably the first act of disobedience by our force, and it lasted for years.

Some senior officers from the small forces took the opportunity to retire, but others soldiered on for many years and, quite frankly, became a liability. Our old Chief was a broken man and seemed to fade into oblivion. Just before he retired we had a long and moving conversation, during which he revealed that he had always liked me, and was proud of the way I had overcome my physical disability.

He told me that he had given me a hard time for my own good, as he wished to teach me humility, 'which is a rare commodity in successful people'. He went on to express concern about the way the police service was going: he feared that unless someone made a stand, it would soon be run by politicians and administrators – a comment I found very interesting. He wished me success in my future, and the meeting ended quite emotionally with a hug from him, which seemed most out of character but probably was not. I learned at that moment that many people in command have to do and say things which do not come naturally to them. Sadly, David Bradley died shortly after he retired.

I had difficulty coming to terms with the procrastination of the new regime. For example, I was called to account for marking up a file with only the word 'Prosecute' scribbled on it. I was told that I should have included more information about the case, and possibly some legal argument. When I asked the point of this, my critic replied that it would 'impress his superior officers'. I thought this a total waste of time, and told him so, refusing to become involved in such a farce. He said that I had disappointed him, and I was making a big mistake, adding that many a career had been launched and built upon 'this type of window dressing'. I replied that if such was the case, I was destined to fail.

I enjoyed my new responsibilities as an inspector, because when on duty, I was virtually in charge of the force. All operational decisions were mine, as were the fate of prisoners and all files submitted by my officers. The protocol was that one cleared all outstanding issues before going off duty, but the inspectors I relieved consistently failed to do this, and I will never know if they were testing me or were just plain lazy. I didn't complain, as I welcomed the challenge and was eager to learn.

One bit of unfinished business concerned a gypsy's horse, which had broken its tether and mounted a prize pony in a nearby field. When the owner sought advice from the police, one of my colleagues found the case too difficult to deal with and filed it away, remarking that it was one of those situations in which 'you take your helmet off and join the crowd'.

My position allowed me to go anywhere and visit anyone I pleased within the force. I was not welcome in the CID: my former colleagues made it clear that as a uniformed officer I ought to keep away. Being shunned made it easier for me to take a stand against some of their methods, which had become even more repugnant to me. One night when I visited the cells my way was partially blocked by a detective who asked me to come back later, adding, 'It's a bit of a blood-bath in there.' I carried on, examined a particular prisoner's injuries, and then called the officers present to account for their actions. They all denied any wrongdoing, and I could not take the matter further, as the prisoner corroborated their story that he injured himself falling down. The mere fact that I had pursued the matter sent reverberations through the building, but it was many years before I had the power to make a real impact on this incestuous culture – and then not without personal cost.

During this period of my service I first became aware of the need to increase opportunities for women in the police. Traditionally, they had separate conditions of service, their own rank-structure and duties being largely restricted to dealing with women and children. Some female recruits were eager for change, but they met opposition from their long-serving colleagues, who wished things to remain as they were. I could see why some women wanted to retain the status quo. They worked shorter hours than the men, retired after serving fewer years, and were assured of promotion if they passed their examinations. Male officers opposed any major extension of their responsibilities, as they thought women would not be able to undertake all duties, and would be vulnerable if 'let out on their own'.

I supported the new recruits, as I believed they had the right to choose. I allocated women a broader range of duties, determined by skill and ability, not gender. I met some resistance from the head of the women's department, who told me in no uncertain terms to stop interfering. My superintendent said he didn't mind, providing 'you don't go too far. They'll be running the bloody place if we're not careful.'

Ever since those days, I have striven for consistency of approach to issues of race, gender and sexual inclination, both within and without the police service. Adaptation has proved to be a long, hurtful and frustrating process. I do believe, however, that the police deserve credit for addressing these problems earlier than many other public bodies.

One tragic incident I had to deal with was the death of three small children killed in a house fire. The suspect, a woman, was an aggrieved lover of the occupant. This was my first lengthy crime interview with a woman, and I found it quite taxing, as she went through an array of antics which I have since seen during other such confrontations: first she flaunted her sexuality, then she switched to vulnerability and finally to aggression. However, she did not confess, and there was no physical evidence against her, so she was not charged. I will never forget cradling those charred little bodies in my arms as I carried them out of the bedroom. Feeling vulnerable myself, I rushed home to hold my baby girls.

There were many lighter moments. Having decided that bicycles might help crime detection, and increase the speed at which foot officers could reach incidents, I asked the night shift for volunteer cyclists, and a number put themselves forward. When I visited one of them towards the end of his shift, and found him pushing the cycle up a steep hill on his way back to the station, I remarked that it was much easier going downhill – whereupon he replied that it was all much the same for him, as he couldn't ride a bike anyway.

One sunny afternoon I was walking out with this same officer, and we stopped to talk to a lady leaning on her gate. When we left her, he asked me if I had been setting a bad example, since he regarded chit-chat as idling and gossiping. I told him that this was just practical police work: we had made a contact, and if we ever needed information in that area, he could ask the lady, who would not regard him with suspicion. We then came upon a large number of people waiting for a bus. My colleague, seeking to put my advice into practice, stopped, faced them and said, 'Good afternoon, everyone.' I hope his common sense improved, because he was promoted to a supervisory rank.

I have outlined some of the down-side of amalgamation, but the larger unit did create new opportunities: within months I was invited to become the inspector at Holmfirth, my place of birth. I was to be the only inspector in the station, working directly to the superintendent. The post also involved prosecuting, which I enjoyed, and would give me experience of rural policing.

My first morning was a baptism of fire, as the superintendent shouted at all the staff. Nothing was good enough for him. They were not up to the task. I was appalled, and when he asked for my comments, I told him so. 'That's what I expected you to say,' he retorted. 'But if you keep 'em frightened, you'll keep 'em in line.' I realised that he ruled by fear, and felt as if I was back in training school. It was awful to see a person using his authority to treat others like dogs, knowing they could not answer back because he had power over their livelihoods. To me, this was the worst form of bullying, and I am sad to say that many managers continue to operate in this way today.

Court was held in the afternoon once every other week in the Civic Centre. Before my first appearance in front of the magistrates, I was invited to speak to them about my local background and family connections, and they showed quite some interest. I was then asked about the cases I was to prosecute. This made me uncomfortable, as the defendants were not present, and at Huddersfield I had been taught that it was inappropriate even to be seen speaking to magistrates, as any contact might be misconstrued.

I avoided the issue by making some excuse about having to prepare for the court. They seemed to accept this, and when the first case came up – which involved a road traffic accident – I merely read the statement of facts to the court and then sat down.

'Is that it?' the chairman of the bench inquired.

'Yes,' I replied.

The chairman said they were used to getting more information, and another magistrate piped up, 'Look, lad: this is our day out, and we like to make the most of it. Tell us some more about the offence.'

I searched the papers again, and to indulge them I added the colour of the car and the destination of the bus involved, then sat down. They were clearly displeased, because after they had made their judgement they called upon a local authority representative to prosecute the warrants for non-payment of rates – a long-winded administrative procedure which was normally taken after the criminal cases. As my punishment for not humouring the bench, I had to wait a full hour before I could continue.

My main area included a number of rural stations which straddled the Pennines, where Myra Hindley and Ian Brady, the Moors Murderers, had buried the bodies of their child victims. I was impressed with the calibre of the officers there, who had to operate alone across huge tracts of land, and deal with a much broader range of incidents and offences than the average city police officer.

During the Special Course I had presented a paper on the drugs problem in the United States, in which I suggested that the British police should seriously consider this growing menace. On my return to the force I pursued the idea with senior officers, who, when I had been at Holmfirth for six months, asked me to form a small squad. I was told that it was unlikely that drugs alone would fully engage us, so we would have to deal also with 'toms and queers' – prostitutes and homosexuals – to justify the initiative.

This was one of the first drug squads formed in the United Kingdom. We were a young team; the male officers grew their hair and went unshaven, in the hope that this would allow us to blend in with our clientele. This was the Flower Power era, and, as usual, young intellectuals were embracing the latest forms of civil disobedience. Concentrating on clubs and pubs where students congregated, we began arresting people for possession of cannabis and occasionally LSD. It didn't matter to us how small the amount – we would prosecute every offender. We gave little thought to what we were doing, and we had no perception of the problem the community would face in later years. As homosexuality was an offence in those days, we spent time in public toilets – where men frequently met to have sex – acting as *agents provocateurs*.

Prostitution was another matter. During my detective days the women of the streets had provided a valuable source of information, and I had built up a rapport with them. They knew who had money – so that a punter who paid them with a large number of small coins, for instance, would be arrested and questioned about crimes of theft from coin-boxes. They generally knew where a particular criminal could be found, and they overheard 'villains'' conversations with each other. They lived their lives in fear of disease and violence from both clients and pimps, who were mainly of West Indian origin.

I had a great deal of sympathy with them, particularly those who prostituted themselves to support their children. Their minders expected them to perform whatever their condition: whether they had been hurt by a client, were recovering from childbirth, or in the middle of menstruation – they had no excuse, and would be beaten if they failed to comply. Sometimes, at their request, I would arrest them, as they preferred an occasional period of imprisonment to the treatment they received on the streets, and they regarded a spell inside as rest and recuperation. Not that every gaol was a rest cure for them: they sometimes had to ward off the advances of frustrated women who came at them with condoms loaded with mashed potato or cold rice pudding.

One year after amalgamation, Ronald Gregory was appointed Chief Constable of our force. Former Borough officers like myself saw this as a positive development, as he had served in boroughs himself, and was young and open to new ideas. I first saw him during the annual inspection by Her Majesty's Inspector of Constabulary. All officers had to assemble in the local drill hall for questioning (detectives would always try to absent themselves on spurious pretexts to avoid the inquisition). I was there with my little squad, and when the HMI asked for the senior detective on duty to stand up, I did. I must have looked extremely young, as he tried to wave me down, repeating, 'I said the *senior* detective.' When I assured him that I was his man, he asked about my rank and length of service before questioning me about crime.

Next morning I was called to force headquarters to see the Chief Constable. I had never been to 'the Kremlin' before, and did not look forward to the experience, because of previous encounters with my old Chief. Ronald Gregory was a complete contrast: he was young, good-looking, athletic and tanned, and instead of making me stand in front of his desk, he invited me to sit down. He told me he had been impressed with my bearing the previous day and wished to know more about me.

He asked what I considered to be the duties of a staff officer. This took me by surprise, and my knee-jerk reaction was, 'To be discreet, and to recognise that he is not the boss.'

Gregory said, 'That's good enough for me. The HMI says I need a staff officer, and he thinks you fit the bill. *I'm* not sure I need anyone, but I'll give it a try if you will.'

Without hesitation I accepted the job, inquiring if it would mean promotion. He told me not to push my luck.

When I told Bren the news, she was very excited, even though my new post would entail moving the family to Wakefield. We had enjoyed living in Yews Hill Road, and took with us many happy memories of the place and people. Our girls used to walk the twenty yards to the corner shop, and for some reason Samantha (who had been born with the same eye condition as myself) always took off her spectacles before she left. In the end the shopkeeper told Bren that a packet had once fallen off the counter and dislodged Sam's glasses and he had never seen her wearing them since.

I have always enjoyed gardening, and the girls once picked the heads off all the tulips. Bren was horrified and told them that I would be furious. If I ever had to chastise them, I made them hold out one hand for me to smack. When I came home that day they were both in the kitchen, looking very penitent. Unprompted, they had put socks on their hands, anticipating what I would do. I was overcome by love for them, and could do nothing but smile.

Bren was also the cause of some merriment. Being unfamiliar with the controls of a new car, she drove it straight through the back wall of our wooden garage. It took the help of several bulky detectives to lift it out, and she never lived the incident down. That particular car, a blue-and-white, two-door Ford Cortina, became the common property of the CID: I loaned it out to colleagues for special occasions, stopping only when one of them returned it empty of fuel, informing me that I would have to fill it up. Give people an inch, and they really will take a mile.

My first day in headquarters was a big culture shock. The buildings form a quadrangle, with the car park in the centre, and I parked in an unmarked bay. Mid-morning I received a telephone call from a woman who asked me to move my car immediately, as it was parked 'in the detective chief superintendent's place'. After being told by a colleague that she must be wrong, as that officer had his own bay inside the senior officers' garage, I ignored her request; and when she called again at lunch-time, I told her she must be mistaken. She admitted as much, but claimed that her 'boss' might wish to park in the yard, and if he did, he would use that space. She added, 'He always allows me to park there, because I can move out at any time.' The truth was out: she had designated her own parking place. I said I didn't wish to be difficult, but there were plenty of other spaces in the yard.

At three o'clock I answered the phone to a most obnoxious-sounding man who said, 'Who the f—k do you think you are? Get your arse down here immediately,' and slammed down the receiver. I took no action, but within an hour I was visited by an old colleague who told me that, if I knew what was good for me, I should go across to the caller's office straight away. After being kept waiting for about ten minutes, I went in to face the wrath of an officer who had dismissed me for taking notes of his comments when he had tried to interview me about an incident years earlier.

He was sitting behind his desk, with his deputy lounging against a table to his right. He turned to him and said, 'Can you smell something?'

'It's like something the cat's dragged in,' his colleague replied.

I was so angry that I turned to leave. For the first time the principal looked at me, saying, 'I'll have no "Borough" tactics here. You've got no David Bradley to protect you now.' Both sniggered. He then ordered me to move my car, and report back to him when it was done. I refused, added that I would not be spoken to in that manner by anyone, turned heel and left.

I did not remove the car, and heard nothing more about the incident. Within a week I had organised my own reserved parking bay – in the disputed place. But I had made a powerful enemy . . . who changed into a friend when I became his boss.

I quickly learned of the tricks these bullies put over on their subordinates. Some people dared not even leave their offices if they thought the boss was still around and might call them. In order to keep them guessing, the bosses would leave their office lights on and either walk home or get a lift from someone else, purely to keep these poor souls from their families. The penalty for disobedience would be a 'tall hat' – return to uniform. At functions these thugs would be surrounded by their sycophants, speaking in riddles out of the sides of their mouths, looking down on the rest of us as if we were dirt.

I shared my office with the Research and Development staff, who were an unusual bunch of characters. Our Assistant Chief Constable was the former chief of one of the small boroughs: a charming man, large in stature and of military bearing, with a thick white moustache. He had little to do, so he used to busy himself with reading the newspapers for an hour in the toilet each morning, and would lock himself in his cigar-smoke-filled office for the duration of Test matches, which he listened to on his radio. (He kept this secreted in the bottom of his filing cabinet, so that he could kick the drawer shut if anyone came in.) His deputy was a former head of the CID, a bitter man who felt that he had been wrongly deposed by Gregory for the way he dealt with a particular murder inquiry.

The bureaucratic nature of the system was exposed when the Chief told me to get a carpet for my office because of the poor condition of the old oil-cloth. The officer in charge of buildings refused to supply one, claiming that my rank did not entitle me to a carpet. I told him that the instruction had come from the Chief Constable.

'No it didn't,' he said. 'I'm quoting from Chief Constable's orders.' He then produced the said orders, which were thirty years old. Gregory told him to tear them up, and my carpet appeared. These petty rules were the props on which a substantial number of headquarters inhabitants relied.

I enjoyed working for Ronald Gregory. My principal role was to prepare, accompany and report on his visits to all the stations within the force. Travelling with him was a challenge, as he would ask me questions about the places we were to visit, which in the early days I could not always answer. Queries about crime and accident rates were predictable, but others about the percentage of officers in police accommodation, the age-range of female officers and the annual cost of heating, were not. In trying to keep ahead of him I became extremely knowledgeable about the force, and noticed that his questions ended when he knew I could answer them.

I used to pre-brief each station commander about the Chief's interests, his likes and dislikes. This information was usually well received, but one officer was affronted by my call, and told me, 'If I want to speak to the organ-grinder, I'll call him.' The result was that he did not get a briefing. During our visit this individual fawned all over the Chief: for example, he promised some of his wife's home-made apple pie at lunch-time. My boss was unimpressed, and when things began to go badly wrong, his demeanour darkened.

When visiting control rooms, he always asked the staff to test their systems. In this case he suggested that a particular burglar alarm had been set off in an office block, and asked them how they intended to respond. The sergeant told him that they would activate the plan they held for the premises involved. Gregory asked them to go ahead. To everyone's acute embarrassment, they could not find the plan, and when they opened a large filing cabinet, its contents spilled on to the floor. The station commander suggested that we resume our tour. Gregory refused, and we waited more than an hour while the flustered staff scraped around on hands and knees, trying to locate the plan. We left them still looking. Gregory was fuming, and in front of everyone instructed me to return at a later date, to satisfy him that the procedure was in order. The station commander was crestfallen, and when I returned, he was extremely obsequious towards me. This gave me some satisfaction, as he was the man who had described me as 'something the cat's dragged in'.

At the debriefing, Gregory tore me off a strip, saying that if I wished to remain with him, such a situation must never occur again, and I must ensure that the divisions were properly prepared for him. I ensured that things did not go wrong again.

We enjoyed working together – when we visited the stables in Harrogate, the Chief was lobbied by the staff for an extension to the building. On the way back he asked me what I thought. I told him I reckoned the demand was excessive, as there was plenty of room for the number of horses we had. The staff, I said, were seeking sufficient room for the horses to lie down and stretch out, which was unnecessary, as the animals slept perfectly well standing up.

'Is that really true?' the Chief asked.

'Absolutely,' I assured him. 'They're like birds. Have you ever seen a bird asleep, lying down with its feet stretched out?'

He agreed he had not, and I said, 'Well, it's the same with horses.'

A day or two later, when I met him on the steps to his office, he blocked my path and said, 'Sleep standing up! You'll pay for that, Hellawell,' and laughed.

Another time we encountered a drunken motorist. Neither the Chief nor his driver had dealt with an offence of this nature, and to our embarrassment, we had no breathalyser kit with us. To exacerbate things further, we were in a poor communication area, and our radio would not work – so the two drove off to seek help, leaving me to deal with the offender.

There were two other people in the car besides the driver – a former police officer and, in the back, a woman who was naked and unconscious from drink. I was afraid for her well-being, so I covered her up, roused her and turned her into a three-quarters prone position. I thought there was something suspicious about the manner of the former police officer, in contrast with the driver, who was quite relaxed. I therefore took the keys out of the ignition and was about to open the boot when, by chance, another police car arrived carrying an ACC. Recognising his rank, the former police officer complained about me, and, although he was not the owner of the car, objected vociferously to my opening the boot. The ACC ordered me to stop and took the keys from me – something I was not happy about.

Within a moment a Road Traffic car screeched to a halt, and the crew breathalysed the driver, who was arrested for being over the legal limit. I accompanied him to the nearest police station, where he was charged and placed in the cells for refusing to provide a sample of blood or urine. When the ACC arrived, he ordered me to wait until he visited the prisoner. He asked the man to make a complaint against me, but his request was declined. The ACC told me that he was unhappy with my conduct, and would pursue the matter with the Chief Constable. The upshot of all this was that the driver was convicted, the ACC got a roasting from my Chief for interfering, and the unsavoury former policeman got off scot-free. I never discovered what he was protecting in the boot of the car.

One other major responsibility of mine was to compile the Chief Constable's annual report, a document which is prepared for the Home Secretary and the Police Authority.* The report outlines the performance of each force over the past twelve months. Since ours included the Chief's view on trends and issues, I expected him to write this part himself. Not so: I had to do it – and in my first year it took some soul-searching. After that, he trusted me to such an extent that he read only the final version. We worked the same way on his speeches: at first he made a detailed scrutiny of my drafts, but then took to delivering speeches without prior reading. I saw this as a compliment, and felt pride in my work.

As the months went by I came to respect Ronald Gregory more and more, for he developed West Yorkshire into one of the leading forces in the country – and did so against a weight of resistance. He told me that on his first day in office he arrived for work at eight in the morning and found an array of bell-pushes on his desk. He rang the first, designated 'chief superintendent', and got no reply. He did the same for the superintendent: no reply. Nor was there any response from the chief inspector or the inspector. The first reaction came from the sergeant, who told the Chief that the others didn't normally arrive before half past nine. When the chief superintendent eventually appeared, at about 10 a.m., he was in plain clothes, and explained that this was his normal start time, as he liked to help his wife open her millinery shop before coming in. Gregory instructed him to appear in his office, in full uniform, at eight the next morning.

By forcing his staff to change their habits, he engendered deep resentment, which was stored against him to be used later. No one should ever underestimate the power of hate, or its longevity.

Its first manifestation came within two years. The house allocated to Gregory needed refurbishing, and until the work was completed, he travelled home each weekend to Devon. He used various means

* This uniquely constituted body, made up of local politicians, business people and magistrates, has a statutory responsibility to oversee the running of each police force on behalf of the community it serves.

of transport, including a Triumph 2.5 petrol-injection police car. He was entitled to recompense for any cost he incurred on these journeys, and relied on headquarters staff to complete the necessary forms for him to sign. One weekend they completed a claim for a return rail journey, which he signed, when in fact he had used the police car. Another time, he was taken ill, and his doctor, believing the problem was serious, suggested that he visit a specialist in London, which he did in his staff car.

These two incidents, and others, were leaked to the local Press in an attempt to discredit him. To clear his name, Gregory persuaded the Police Authority to appoint a QC to take evidence. He was cleared of all charges, the only negative comment being that he was too trusting of others, particularly those who had reason to dislike him. Yet, even though the case had a positive outcome, the negative publicity came at a bad time, as the Government of the day had decided to reduce the number of police forces still further.

Leeds and Bradford were to amalgamate with us, and we had to surrender the majority of our rural area to other forces. The protocol on this occasion was that a Chief Constable from one of the three constituent forces would be appointed head of the new combined unit. Clearly there was going to be competition for the job, and Gregory's opponents used the case to undermine his credibility. The day was saved for him by the death of a tramp who was found drowned in a river in Leeds. Suspicion fell on the police there, and the subsequent criticism reflected badly on the Leeds force, with the result that our Chief got the job.

In the spring of 1970, out of the blue, Gregory asked me if I would like to go to Cambridge University for the summer, as the force had been offered a place on a senior course at the Institute of Criminology, and I jumped at the chance. When I arrived, I found a middle-aged lady struggling to unload her car, so I gave her a hand. She offered me a drink in recompense and asked me to accompany her to the course reception later that day.

At the party I was surprised by the way people greeted her: there was much bowing and scraping, and they were all addressing her as 'My Lady' or 'Your Ladyship'. When I asked her about this, she told me that she was Lady Elizabeth Cavendish, sister of the Duke of Devonshire, and besides other things a lady-in-waiting to Princess Margaret. She was not at all what I expected an aristocrat to be: she was down-to-earth and very good company. I was fascinated by the stories of her family, and her accounts of the Kennedys, whom she knew, as her elder brother had married into that clan.

A third course member, Brother Wilfred, a Roman Catholic priest, joined us, to form an inseparable trio; but the combination of his office, and mine as a police inspector, proved of little use in vouching for Elizabeth at the bank, when she tried to cash a cheque without means of identification. It was outside this establishment that I fell in love with a Jaguar E-Type convertible, carmine-red with wire wheels. I vowed that I would have one – and did, within twelve months.

During the course we examined every aspect of the criminal justice system, and our studies were enriched by contributions from magistrates, judges, prison governors, probation officers, academics and other police officers. I enjoyed the environment, and found the work, the staff (which included many outstanding academics) and the other course members stimulating. I was exercising my mind in a way I had not done before.

During the course Elizabeth announced that we were to have dinner with one of her special friends – but she would not tell us who, until, one balmy evening we went by punt to the Master's Lodge at Trinity College to dine with the Master, Rab Butler, a former Cabinet Minister. Our host was most charming and gracious in his welcome – and lived in the lap of luxury. Until then I had only ever seen liveried staff in period films, and had never set eyes on such wonderful furniture, soft furnishings and paintings. Our meal, and the way it was served, seemed to come from a different world, and I was hugely impressed.

When we were relaxing over a glass of port, Rab said, 'I hear you have a fine mind.' This was the last thing I had expected to hear, and, feeling uncomfortable, I made some inadequate response. Rab went on to say that Leon Radzinowicz, the head of the Criminology Department, had told him that I showed much promise, and he asked if I would be interested in taking a degree course. I was taken aback, and told him I didn't possess the necessary qualifications. 'Let me worry about that,' he said, and he went on to tell me that, as Master, he held a number of 'preference places' at Trinity, and he was prepared to offer me one of them, as he thought I was a deserving case. I was almost speechless, and could only respond by saying I was greatly flattered, but would have to consult my wife and my Chief Constable.

In fact, I was elated by the offer, and longed to take it up; but Gregory was not amused. 'I sent you to Cambridge for six weeks, not three bloody years,' he said. 'If you want to go, you'll have to leave the job.'

I loved the police service. Moreover, we had a new addition to the family – our son Charles, born on 17 May, only weeks before the course had started – and it would have been difficult to move our growing family. I told Leon Radzinowicz that, with great regret, I would have to decline the offer. He said I was making a big mistake, as the opportunity I had been offered only occurred once in a lifetime. He predicted that a university degree would be a prerequisite for future leaders of the police service, and that, however bright I was, I would need that qualification. He advised me to try for an external degree when I returned to the force.

I took his advice – and I am pleased that I did, as his predictions came true. Within three years of talking to him I obtained an external law degree from London University. I went on to study successfully for an external master's degree in science, and in later years I was awarded three honorary doctorate degrees for my contribution to public life.

After that stimulating, six-week break in Cambridge, I threw myself back into work, and was much involved with preparations for the coming amalgamation. I learned a good deal about the methods of policing in Leeds and Bradford, and made acquaintance with many of the officers there. We were all determined to avoid the mistakes of the past, and implement new systems which were acceptable to us all.

Luckily for me, Bren loved being at home and looking after our three children – which was just as well, since I contributed very little to their upbringing during the early years of their lives. I was at work for at least ten hours each day, in the course of which I would either run or play squash. When I left the office I would retire for two or three hours to our caravan parked at the bottom of our street, and in the period leading up to my final degree examinations, I took it to a remote spot, to study, accompanied by one of our dogs. This was the only way I could get through the necessary work, as there were too many distractions at home. There was another price to pay, as well: family holidays had to be forfeited. In the end the sacrifice paid dividends, as I was one of only a handful of external students from London University who graduated within three years. I found law fascinating and relatively easy to understand, although I had difficulty teaching myself enough Latin to complete the Roman Law paper.

My first degree was presented to me by Her Majesty the late Queen Mother at the Royal Albert Hall in London on a foggy winter's day which was almost my and Bren's last, as on our way south we were involved in a motorway pile-up which killed several people and injured many others. In an instant I drove from bright morning sunlight into dense black fog, to be confronted by an articulated lorry which had jack-knifed across my path. Instinctively I swerved to the left, on to the grass verge at the side of the carriageway, and kept going, with vehicles piling up behind me. We shot past scenes of horrible carnage – people screaming, metal being torn and glass being smashed. It was a glimpse of hell.

We were incredibly fortunate, because within a few hundred yards there was an exit road. I stopped the moment I could, and got out shaking. The driver of a Rover who had followed me also stumbled out and hugged me in relief. Almost immediately the emergency service vehicles were on the scene, gaining access to the motorway via the slip road down which we had escaped.

At home in Sandal, on the edge of Wakefield, our children gave us much pleasure and some worry, as both girls had inherited my maladjusted eyes (luckily Charles was all right). We had endless

trips to the hospital for different consultations and eventually operations, for, like me, they were not cured at the first attempt. Charles
was a very poor sleeper and created each bedtime and throughout
the night. Bren, with her endless patience, took the lion's share in
caring for him.

We enjoyed our house and garden, of which I became particularly
proud. I could always lose myself planting, tending and watching
things grow throughout the seasons – so much so that our neighbours nicknamed me Percy Thrower, after the famous gardener of
the time. However, we had always dreamed of buying our own
home and we decided that, with a growing family, this was the
time.

We very much liked a new house being built in the yard of
the disused railway station in the village of Kirkburton, south of
Huddersfield, but the price was a problem: £6,650 was a third
more than we would have had to pay for a new, four-bedroomed
estate house in Wakefield. My salary at that time was about £2,000,
and I knew that funding would be difficult.

Nevertheless, I sought written permission to open negotiations,
only to be told that I was prohibited from purchasing any house
until I had served at least twenty-two years. When I challenged
this, I was told that it was the Chief Constable's directive, the
aim being to keep police-owned houses occupied. I knew this was
inconsistent with the view of Ronald Gregory, who wished to dis-
pose of these properties, as they were a financial liability. When I
raised the issue with him, he withdrew the restriction – a move
very well received by the force. (A police officer still requires permission from the Chief Constable to live in a house of his own,
and it is a disciplinary offence to fail to obey his or her ruling.)

One unforeseen hurdle had been removed, but there was still
the matter of money – we were helped to come to a decision by
events I wish had never occurred. One Friday lunch-time I had
fish and chips in the mess with two of the force's other high fliers:
Barry Taylor, who worked in uniformed operations, and Tony
Davies, who was attached to the training school. We were discussing
our future, and Barry suggested that he ought to come in out of

the cold and take my job. Tony said he would like to go back to operations, and that I should take *his* job.

Our conversation was no more than three young men musing. But within days Barry had been murdered by a man he disturbed robbing a mill safe: having already killed the night watchman, the criminal turned his shotgun on my friend. When I heard about the incident on the news, I went cold, and like hundreds of my colleagues reported for duty to see what I could do. A man was subsequently sentenced to imprisonment for life for the offences. Shortly afterwards Tony also died, in mysterious circumstances. He awoke in the night and complained to his wife that he was hot. She asked him if she could get him a glass of water, but he chose to fetch his own. She found him dead beside her in the morning. The pathologist could only liken his demise to the cot-death of a child: there appeared to be nothing wrong with him, and there was no explanation of the tragedy. Both men were in their early thirties.

The sudden loss of these friends had a profound effect on me: I realised how fragile life was, and that I could have gone the way they had. The shock made me even more determined to buy the house and create a secure base for my family. I had always been careful with money and invested a percentage of every wage-rise in unit trusts, which I intended to accumulate over my lifetime. By 1972 these were valued at £4,000, and I cashed them in, put down half as a deposit on the house, and used the remainder to buy carpets, a second car, and other luxuries like the telephone and freezer that we had never had.

We watched the final stages of our house's construction with much joy. I lovingly touched the stone and wood, as this was our first home to do with as we wished, and not subject to the indignity of annual inspections by a senior officer. Soon after we had taken possession, Bren and I were in the middle of decorating when a couple touring the site offered us £1,000 more than we had paid. Although it was tempting at the time, in retrospect the offer was not particularly generous, as houses similar to ours sold for £8,500 on the builders' next site. Over the thirteen years we lived in that house we improved and extended both the building and the garden, and had no difficulty in selling it for over £70,000.

After six years as an inspector, I was becoming disillusioned at work. For the past three years I had been graded 'Outstanding' on my appraisal, and the rules stated that the few officers achieving this grade would be promoted to the next rank within one year. This had not happened in my case, and I confronted the architect of the system, Ronald Gregory.

Clearly taken aback, he asked me how old I was, and when I told him I was twenty-nine, he retorted that at my age he had only been a sergeant – and the youngest in the force at that. I pointed out that he hadn't done badly since. I had the nerve to tell him that age was immaterial, and I reminded him that he had introduced the new system to bring fresh blood to the ranks.

He was not a man who liked to be challenged, and my head-on approach could have worked against me. Luckily it didn't. Within a week he sent for me and told me I was being transferred to the Detective Training School as a chief inspector. I was delighted, not only to be back as a detective, but also to be able to put my legal knowledge to good effect. The Chief could see my elation, and punctured it by saying that I was not going to train detectives: he needed me to take over as head of Cadet Training. I must have shown my disappointment, because he went on to convince me that this was a job in which he needed someone he could trust. These young men and women were the future of the service, he said, and I would enjoy working with them.

I was lucky that Gregory liked me. Others didn't fare as well, especially if they showed hesitation or indecisiveness in front of him. When one officer said that he would have to consult his wife before he made a decision on a posting, he was told that he would not be promoted. Another time, the Chief asked a colleague if he was prepared to move for promotion; the man replied, 'Depends where to, Sir' – and he was not promoted either, even though the job in prospect did not require a move. On the other hand, when one of my former Borough colleagues went to see Gregory for promotion, the Chief congratulated him for a particularly good piece of detective work, and then told him that he was moving him back into uniform, 'to sort them out'. My colleague was much put out, since he saw this as demotion; but as he was leaving, the Chief said, 'Oh, by the way – it's on promotion,' which drew the response of, 'You pillock!' Gregory would have gone spare with most officers, but he took this in good part.

CHAPTER SEVEN

SWEET AND SOUR

I knew nothing about the cadet force, so I visited the man I was to succeed. He was regarded as a national expert, having held his job for more than ten years, and he commended it to me on the grounds that it would allow me to pursue my own thing. He was pleased to tell me that, while in the post, he had obtained a teaching degree, which he intended to use when he left the service. He added that he had been put into the job because he had depression, and he was told that work with cadets would pull him out of it – which, he said, it had.

I thought this very strange. Young men and women need someone with stability and strength to guide them, and I did not consider it their responsibility to provide a prop for a lame boss. My predecessor went on to say there was not a great deal he could tell me in the way of briefing: all he did was open the top drawer of his desk, to reveal three tin boxes, each containing a substantial sum of money. One, he explained, held the proceeds of the fines he had imposed on the cadets. The second contained money due to the cadets, but not paid, for expenses they had incurred; and the third held proceeds from the sale of ties and scarves.

He then opened a bottom drawer, took out a number of red folders containing sheaves of papers, and suggested I look through them, as they were outstanding discipline cases which he had found 'difficult to deal with'.

I started in the job some days later, and began by visiting a classroom where cadets were being taught. My new deputy was conducting the lesson, and it was a fiasco: the cadets were talking among themselves and completely ignoring what he was saying. One young woman was sitting on the knee of a male colleague, who appeared to be whispering sweet nothings in her ear. After asking my deputy to see me at break, I walked out. When we met, without my saying anything he began to apologise for his class. 'You probably think they're an unruly mob,' he said, 'but they're good kids really.' He told me he liked to give them a free rein, so that they could express themselves: that was how he got the best out of them.

During my research for the post I had noticed that the GCE O- and A-level pass-rate of our 240 cadets had declined over the years, and concern had been expressed by the local polytechnic where they studied. My deputy argued that results were not everything, and that we were training the cadets for life. I disagreed. I said I believed our job was to prepare them for the police service, and while they were in our care we had a duty to them and their parents to see that they achieved their best. He was not happy, and said we must 'agree to disagree'. I made it clear that so long as I was responsible for these young people, we would work towards *my* objectives. He did not respond.

I then changed the subject to money. I told him that we must account for the money in the boxes, as it was not ours: I suggested he hand over to the cadets that which was theirs and bank the rest. This would be difficult, he said, as no one really knew who the money belonged to. In that case, I told him, he had better open bank accounts to hold the funds and put them on a proper footing. This he did, but within a week he told me that he was applying to transfer out of the department, as he could not support my new regime. I wished him well and made no attempt to stop him.

The red files made interesting reading. One described how a drunken cadet had boarded a bus in possession of a stolen beer glass; another report concerned a cadet shooting air pellets from the hostel window at a local resident's washing, and causing damage. These and other incidents were months old, and nothing had been done. The appraisal reports on the alleged offenders made it obvious that they were difficult young men. I saw them one by one, and when I asked each of them for an explanation, I was met with insolence and, in one case, verbal abuse. I sensed that they believed they could get away with anything.

I didn't know if I had the power to do so, but I dismissed each of them on the spot. The first one was shell-shocked. 'You can't do this to me!' he exclaimed. 'My father's a police officer, and he said you couldn't touch me.' I ordered him to leave my office, and waited for any repercussions – but there were none.

After the showdown I called the staff and cadets together, to explain what I had done and why. I told them that I had their interests at heart, but that I intended to change things radically, and looked for their support. I wanted 100 per cent of their effort, and pledged the same of mine. I recognised that we had different strengths and weaknesses, but suggested that we must make the best of what we'd got. If they didn't want to participate in this new environment, I would quite understand, and anyone who wished could quit there and then. No one did.

I put some of the responsibility for raising standards, including the power to impose minor punishments, into the hands of the cadets themselves. I was surprised how co-operative they became. In due course I recognised that the majority were there to learn, and had disliked the lax regime. They were fed up with being kept awake at night by the bawdy behaviour of a few, and found the classroom atmosphere inimical to their studies. They had been reluctant to speak up, however, because they thought the boss liked things the way they were.

The junior members of staff asked me if they could 'put some life' into the course, as they considered the bad behaviour had been partly due to boredom. They likened the course to a glorified school when the cadets were at study, and to cheap labour when they were posted to divisions, and had to perform odd jobs, running errands and making the tea.

With the help of the senior cadets we developed a new pro-gramme of activities. When in divisions, they had to be attached to departments for set periods of time and experience the full range of police duties. We introduced a work book in which their supervisors had to log the activities prescribed for them. These included dealing with a crime, a road traffic accident and a sudden death, working in the cells and being present at interviews, besides visiting social services, the coroner's officer and the probation service. The cadets' performance was taken into account in deciding whether to accept them into the service proper, or not.

I had helped pioneer these activities after the Cambridge course, working with a senior probation officer from the West Riding, who was as keen as I that we share experiences. I continued the theme throughout my police career, developing exchanges at senior officer level with the various agencies. Later in Humberside with British Aerospace, and in Cleveland with ICI, we developed assessment criteria for exchanges with industry.

I was very fit at this time, running at least ten miles each day, playing competitive squash and competing in half and full marathons – so I was pleased to develop the physical side of the cadets' activities. I arranged for us to take on surrounding forces in all sports, and because of the harsh regime my cadets were subject to – a three-mile cross-country run at 6 a.m. for any minor infringement – we usually won with relative ease. I could see the pride developing in these young people: they were on winning teams, and respect for them grew within the force.

A further fillip came from a most unexpected source – George Lane-Fox, the owner of a stately home who was trying to increase his income. He decided to start up a three-day equestrian event in the grounds of Bramham Park, and asked me if the cadets would run the communications. I jumped at the chance, for I knew they would enjoy the experience, and it would be good operational training. My cadets took on that task successfully for a number of years, and my friendship with George gave me an insight into the problems the aristocracy face in their struggle to survive and retain our national treasures.

One year George wished to raise the profile of the event and invited Princess Anne as his star guest. He and his wife Victoria ran the house on a shoe-string, and had only a Spanish couple to help out. For the royal visit, therefore, he brought in a maid, and decided he would need a butler to orchestrate the 'staff'. He told me what trials and tribulations he had in hiring one. Some butlers were so snobbish that they would not contemplate working in a house with such a small number of servants. Others would do the job providing he met their own stringent conditions. In the end one grudgingly took the job, only because royalty would be present.

The man was condescending, and made it clear that he had come as a favour to the owner. On the first night of the Princess's stay the company had a meal and repaired to the study for coffee and an after-dinner drink. When Princess Anne said she would like a brandy and soda, the butler handed her a glass of brandy, but then squirted the soda water all over her. The room went silent. George thought he would end up in the Tower of London, and with him all his dreams. The Princess was shocked – not for long. In a moment she recovered enough to say, 'Do you mind? That's gone all over my t—s.' This broke the ice in a way that very few things could have done. The butler was put in his place, the relationship between host and Princess blossomed, and the event was a huge success.

Back at the training school I advertised for a replacement drill sergeant, and I was given the name Thomas Butler, a former army sergeant major who my colleagues felt would meet the criteria. I arranged for him to come and see me.

My office was on the first floor of the old Bishop's Palace in Wakefield, at the top of a rickety wooden staircase. One morning I heard loud footsteps drumming up the stairs, followed by a brisk knock on my door.

'Come in!' I shouted, and in marched the most military-looking man I had ever seen. He crashed to attention and threw up an exaggerated salute. The peak of his police hat had been slashed to such an extent that it was resting on his nose. His boots had large and bulbous toe-caps, bulled to a mirror finish, and his trouser legs and jacket arms were pressed to a razor's edge.

'Butler reporting for duty, *SIR!*' he yelled.

I was taken aback. I hadn't realised that such characters existed in the service. Standing to attention, and politely refusing my offer of a seat, he told me of his background and what he thought he could bring to the job. He was working in an administrative role in criminal records, and clearly didn't like it, although he said, 'Whatever duty I'm given, *Sir*, I'll do it to the best of my ability.'

I warmed to the man at once. He was exactly what I was looking for, and I offered him the job there and then. He was moved by the offer, saying it would give him a new lease of life, as he felt he had been written off. I asked when he could start, and he answered, 'Now, *SIR*.' This was at 09.30 in the morning: he told me he was on nights, and should be working that night, but that he was prepared to start straight away. I asked him what time he had last finished duty, and the answer was 06.30 hours that morning. I told him to start the following Monday and sent him home to bed.

Tom Butler was one of the best appointments I have ever made. Over the years he brought something special to the lives of thousands of young men and women, and was subsequently honoured by the Queen for his contribution. However, when he started, he brought culture shock to the cadets, for he shouted at them, made them run everywhere rather than walk, and insisted that they all have regulation haircuts, which smartened up their appearance beyond recognition. I cannot recall all his sayings, but they were in the best traditions of a drill sergeant, yet he never swore: he could wither a cadet or even a senior officer by just a stare.

At his suggestion we introduced a drum-and-pipe band and started musical drill. I must confess I was sceptical at first, but the cadets loved it. We had the only such band in the country, and it was invited to perform elsewhere. Within a short time the cadets loved and respected Tom. He was their father and mentor, and he worked round the clock, as he was devoted to them and the job. Other courses would look on and marvel as he barked instructions at his young charges. He would never tolerate anyone, of whatever rank, taking the mickey out of his cadets. Our annual parade became an event which attracted hundreds of people. Parents could not believe the improvement in the manners, physical shape and deportment of their children – a sharp contrast with the number of letters complaining about lack of progress I had inherited on my arrival. The grades in examinations improved immeasurably.

One cadet suggested that it be a good idea to visit a Common Market country, to gain a better understanding of the changes taking place in Europe. I immediately thought that the Côte d'Azur in France, which I knew well, would be an ideal location, so I sought permission from the Chief. He, too, thought it a novel idea, but put it to the Police Authority. I wrote a long and detailed report, and readied myself to appear before them. The Chief Superintendent, Administration, asked if I was serious about the request, as 'it will never get through in this form'. Instead, he prepared a one-line submission – 'Approval of Cadets' visit to a Common Market Country' – which he cunningly placed in the middle of a long list of recommendations for disposal of domestic appliances from police houses, and which was accepted without comment.

This taught me a valuable lesson about how to manipulate the political process. I saw the same trick pulled years later, when the Chief Constable of Devon and Cornwall placed a request to purchase millions of pounds worth of computers between tenders for tyres for police vehicles. The committee spent most of its time in heated debate about the increased cost of prisoners' meals – a subject which was widely reported in the local Press.

For our trip to France we chose the eight most worthy cadets, selecting them on performance, potential and the quality of their project proposals. I decided to go myself, as I knew the region, and chose our PT instructor as the second member of staff, since fitness was an integral part of the programme. We set off in two Ford Transit vans so heavily loaded that the mud-flaps were trailing on the ground and had to be cut short. Our catering staff packed large joints of every conceivable type of cooked meat, and parents had loaded their children with food and provisions, believing they were going to the outback.

After one overnight stay we arrived at a camp-site I knew and set out our tents in a circle, in the centre of which we created a communal area. Rosters were made out for food preparation and site cleaning. Every morning, after a five-mile run and breakfast, cadets were dropped-off at locations appropriate for their projects, which included housing, transport, policing, culture and the economy. They were collected in the late afternoon and reported progress over dinner. The end-product of their work was a comprehensive presentation to their colleagues and staff.

I had agreed that during our month's stay the cadets could have free weekends, and there was a general request to visit a particular nudist beach. Teasing them, I said, 'Look – when you've seen one naked woman, you've seen them all.' A big, raw-boned lad, who ended up a professional rugby league player, put his hand up and said, 'Please, Sir, I haven't seen one yet.' An enterprising cadet who was studying housing asked one morning if he could be dropped off at a heliport, explaining that he'd posed as the son of a rich buyer, and arranged for the agents to fly him to see an exclusive coastal villa. (Surprisingly, with that level of initiative, he never achieved senior rank.) I was proud of the way the cadets conducted themselves, and I know they benefited by the experience.

At home, they had to complete at least one course at our outdoor centre at Buckden, in the heart of the Yorkshire Dales. Before my arrival this phase of their training had degenerated into little more than a romp in the countryside, and I was determined that it should become a real test of endurance and courage. The change met strong resistance. Some cadets refused to participate when they learnt that they were expected to bivouac overnight in snow, to complete the three-peaks run, and tackle an obstacle course which entailed climbing over and under Land Rovers and fording streams. When I made it a rule that failure to complete meant automatic dismissal, even my staff objected, but I held my ground, and I am pleased I did, because more often than not the cadets declared that the course was the most influential experience in their lives, and it prepared them for any eventuality. My blood boils when I read of the diverse reasons police officers give for absenteeism or early retirement. 'Stress' is the modern excuse for everything, including laziness.

I continued to work long hours, to study and run, and it caught up with me. I was too preoccupied to eat the packed meals Bren prepared for me, surviving only on a light snack late at night. One lunch-time I collapsed in the shower, where I was found unconscious. A senior officer was called, because my breath smelled of acetate, which the stomach produces when empty, and my colleagues believed I was drunk.

It turned out that I had hypoglycaemia, and after one week's recuperation, during which I was greatly chastised by my doctor for starving myself, I returned to a normal diet. Apart from giving me a salutary fright, the episode highlighted the difference in people. The senior officer who was called to see me when I collapsed wished to discipline me for being drunk, whereas Ronald Gregory was only concerned about my welfare, and supported my wife.

During my period with the cadets I formed a close working relationship with the Head of Training, Colin Sampson, who was to have a major influence on my career. A slim Yorkshireman of military bearing, about 5′ 10″, with looks reminiscent of the actor David Niven, he was always immaculately turned out, and wore a gold fob watch. Whenever we drove together to visit Buckden, at his request we would engage in mock interviews, to help him prepare for the Senior Command Course – which he completed with distinction. I found our exchanges stimulating and instructive.

CHAPTER EIGHT

LAISTERDYKE

In the summer of 1974, immediately after the amalgamation with Leeds and Bradford, I was posted to Laisterdyke, a small station on the outskirts of Bradford. We were housed in a conglomeration of temporary buildings, permeated by the smell of lanolin from the surrounding woollen mills, in one of the busiest ethnic areas of the city.

Even though the facilities were wholly inadequate, I joined a very committed team of officers, who worked so hard that they rarely had time for meal-breaks, and would of their own volition change their days-off or work extended hours to get a job done. I created a bit of a stir on the first day, arriving in my E-Type Jaguar, and it was typical of my colleagues that they cleared out one of the storerooms so that it would not have to stand in the open. The difficult conditions created a common bond, which we lost when we moved to better premises.

Laisterdyke was an interesting district. On my meal-break runs I regularly passed the house of a notorious murderer, later dubbed 'The Black Panther', whose identity we did not know at that time. One has to wonder why the same city bred him and the Yorkshire Ripper – two of the most sadistic killers in recent history.

I enjoyed the opportunity of building relationships with the Asian community. Life was very hard for some of those families, and I detected early signs of tension and frustration at the injustice they faced.

I experienced evil, manifest in two nine-year-old boys who preyed on younger children, besides other things making them eat excreta. There was little we could do, as they were below the age of criminal responsibility. In another disturbing case a number of thirteen- to fifteen-year-old children terrorised an old man who befriended them: they took him to collect his pension, which they then stole, together with valuables from his house. When his meagre savings were exhausted, 'for something to do' they tortured and killed him by stabbing him a number of times. I never stopped asking myself the question, 'Why?' Children are not born this way. What do we do, as parents or as a society, to allow this to happen? A worrying aspect of this case was the lack of action by care workers, who knew what was happening but were afraid to intervene, as 'it would have breached our professional confidentiality'. I have seen many more tragedies occur, particularly to children, because of this rigid code of conduct.

This was also the first time I had in-depth contact with the media. Trevor Philpott, a respected film maker who won acclaim for his documentary series *The Philpott File*, turned his attention to the police. He planned to make a three-part series on the service, the first being focused on new recruits, the second on future leaders, and the final part on current leaders. Ronald Gregory decided that I should feature in the middle programme, while he and Lawrence Byford, who was later knighted and elevated to the position of Her Majesty's Chief Inspector of Constabulary, were to be filmed as the current leaders.

I found the procedure tedious: shooting the same sequences over and over again became embarrassing when we were at the scene of an incident and the crew kept asking offenders and victims for repeat performances. The end-product was disappointing – one general film about the service, with no more than brief comment and snippets of our work.

One of the advantages of working in Bradford was that it gave easy access to the newly opened supermarket owned by a friend,

Kenneth (now Sir Kenneth) Morrison. I used to do our shopping, and I could tell you the cost of any item of food or household commodity. Because there was a shortage of sugar, police officers were tipped off whenever a consignment arrived. I enjoyed shopping at that time, but confess my interest has since waned.

It was here that I had my first experience as senior officer in charge of a strike. This particular stoppage was the national bread strike, in which it became apparent that the genuine workers were being incited by extremist elements who had no connection with the industry. We tried to isolate the trouble-makers and reassure the bona-fide workers that we would not intervene with their right to strike. The policy worked: we arrested the rent-a-mob and maintained public order.

I was well practised in this area of police operations, as I had helped train the force in public-order techniques during the miners' strike of 1972. In a hangar at the Leeds/Bradford airport we drilled thousands of officers in crowd-control and riot duties. My cadets acted as a hostile crowd, which tested the young men's resolution and that of their regular colleagues. My lads, being the fitter, normally came out best.

I will never forget the violence and hatred expressed towards the police during that strike. I took a contingent to a pit in Doncaster, where we were met with jeers, foul language, flour and more noxious substances flung at us by miners' wives. The roar from the thousands of miners, all with arms linked, blocking our path, was frightening. Our job was to break this line, to allow non-strikers through. The strikers were determined to stop us at all costs, and they acted as if their lives, not their livelihood, depended on it. I was torn between my duty as a police officer and loyalty to my former colleagues. I had taught 'Meet aggression with aggression', but recognised that this would only inflame the situation, and would be unlikely to resolve it, as we were outnumbered thirty to one.

We approached the line, and, attempting to shout above the noise, I asked the strikers to give way. Their response was caustic. Then I tickled a man in the line who seemed to be their spokesman. He squirmed, wriggled, called me a bastard and let go of his colleagues on either side. Their cordon soon reformed, and we failed to breach it, but I learned that unusual tactics could pay off.

Over the years the British police service has had to develop more sophisticated techniques to deal with public disorder on our streets. These include the provision of clothing and equipment like that worn and used in the most violent cities in the world. What a sad, sad reflection on our society.

On one of my visits to headquarters in Wakefield I had a chance meeting with Colin Sampson, who was by then an ACC. He told me he knew I was there, as 'Only you would have the audacity to drive an E-Type Jag.' He said he longed to have a sports car, but feared he would never get one, because of the image it created. He offered to rescue me from Bradford, and had found me a better posting. I told him I was enjoying the work at Laisterdyke, but he insisted, and within a month I was posted to Halifax.

This was closer to home, and I also played rugby for a local team. Halifax housed the local Quarter Sessions, which I had attended in earlier days to give evidence, and – equally important – enjoy our Chinese set lunches. On one such occasion a colleague – a noted trencherman – asked for an additional ice cream, only to find, when the bill came, he had been charged for a second complete meal. Even with convincing argument, the waiters would not bend: they said he had ordered part of a meal, and therefore he must pay for the whole of it. He agreed, insisting that they give him courses one and two, which he ate, on top of everything else. I served with this officer at another station in later years when he was on a slimming regime. One Friday he asked for his 'usual salad', which impressed us – until it came with an enormous helping of fried fish and chips on top.

During my relatively short stay in Halifax I was more often than not acting as the sub-divisional commander, since the incumbent was wholly engaged in setting up a new police station in Bradford. This worked to my advantage, as I liked being in charge and felt very comfortable, especially as my former partner in the Huddersfield CID was the chief detective.

The year 1975 saw the first recorded crime of the man who

became known as 'the Yorkshire Ripper'. The victim of his second assault – one of the few women who survived – lived on our patch, and the attack caused us a great deal of heart-searching. There were similarities between the two crimes, and we tormented ourselves with the question, 'Do we have a serial killer on our hands?' Although we had no way of knowing it, this was the beginning of the largest murder inquiry the country had ever faced, and one with which I would become deeply involved.

I was surprised by the level of public disorder and violence in the centre of Halifax, where young men from surrounding areas gathered to binge-drink. My first Saturday night on the streets showed how the police had lost control. Not many years before in Huddersfield the night-duty inspector would have cleared the streets after the last bus had gone, and anyone who refused to go would have been arrested. I tried to resurrect these tactics – but the results included more than twenty arrests, injuries to some of my officers, and a word in my ear from the magistrates' clerk, saying that the exercise had proved a burden on his court.

By then a more formal procedure had been introduced for regis-tering complaints about police actions, and many of our arrestees made their dissatisfaction known. It was clear that gentler forms of persuasion had to be used. Since then police officers on the streets have had to take even more steps backwards in dealing with unruly behaviour – a change that has led politicians to blame them, wrongly, for the breakdown in public order, and given members of the Government the latitude to introduce headline-grabbing measures which will have little or no effect.

Even within the constraints which existed at that time, I was determined to do something about the anti-social behaviour I experienced when I attended my first football match at Halifax Town. The racial chanting and foul language which players, officials and supporters (including women and children) had to endure were totally unacceptable. I took hold of the public-address microphone and told the crowd that I was new in Halifax, that I was bitterly disappointed to find that fans could behave in this way, that they showed no respect for those present who were trying to watch the game in peace, and that they were giving a terrible impression of the town.

This seemed to stun the most vociferous trouble-makers, and although I got some cat-calls, they toned their language down. Afterwards, the club withdrew membership and season tickets from the worst offenders. My officers worked hard work at pre-match searching and expulsion during games, and with support from the local newspaper, we virtually outlawed rowdy behaviour. I am sorry to say that it took the disaster at Hillsborough, more than a decade later, to trigger more serious consideration of this problem.

CHAPTER NINE

HOME OFFICE AND NORTHERN IRELAND

Towards the end of 1975 I saw an advertisement in the *Police Review* for a superintendent in the Home Office, to advise the Home Secretary and the police service on technology. Although I had no skills in that area, the notice attracted my interest, because I thought that new technology and computers, in particular, were a coming issue. Colin Sampson tried to talk me out of applying, saying that he knew the Chief, Ronald Gregory, intended to promote me in force. Gregory confirmed this, but said I would learn more in two years at national level than I would during ten in the force – and so, after making a few inquiries, I applied for the job.

This was the only occasion on which I had ever taken such a step without first consulting Bren. I knew that any mention of it would unsettle her, as she would not relish either our moving to London, where the job was based, or me being away from home. I thought that if I was not considered for the short list, that would be the end of it, and I need not cause her concern by mentioning it. If, as happened, I was short-listed, I would face her then.

She was far from pleased, not so much because of the threatened disruption of our domestic life, but by the fact that until then we had shared everything, and now I had gone ahead without consulting her. Nevertheless, after much discussion, she gave me her blessing to apply.

The interview took place in London. The panel consisted of a senior civil servant, an Inspector of Constabulary (HMI) and the head of the unit I was applying to join. I find that it puts me at ease if I speak to other people while I am waiting to go in – a tactic that enables me to hit the ground running. I therefore chatted with the person who received me – the director's personal assistant, who unbeknown to me had been asked to give her assessment of the candidates. This is common practice – although such individuals cannot have a decisive influence, they are often asked how they feel about the candidates, and whether they could work with them, so that speaking to such persons can be beneficial in more ways than one.

I was the last candidate. When asked about my lack of knowledge of computers, I told the panel that if they wanted a computer expert, they should not choose me, but if they wanted a police expert, I believed I was their man. They chose me – in preference to more than 100 other applicants.

I embarked on a new lease of my professional life in December 1975. I was thirty-three years old, one of the youngest superintendents in the country. The Home Office was a totally new experience to me, and I found it disconcertingly impersonal: there were so many disciplines that didn't blend together and lacked any common aim.

The offices of the building in Horseferry House all looked the same: the corridors were much alike, and so bland that you could easily get lost. When I arrived, there was no one to meet me, and I had to inquire at the desk to learn where my office was. It turned out to be in a quite pleasant position on the fourth floor, overlooking Lambeth Bridge. The room contained nothing but a desk, a chair, a table and an in-box full of brown paper envelopes with my name and room number printed on the outside.

I wondered what I had done, leaving the security of the police service, an environment I knew so well. I spent my first morning in splendid isolation. No one visited me, and when I looked into the next-door offices to see if they housed police officers or anyone I could recognise, they were either empty or contained unfriendly-looking folk. At lunch-time I went for a walk, returning to find a man from the Establishments Division. He apologised for the sparse furnishing of the office, and said that when they had looked up the civil service equivalent of my rank, they had found I was entitled to a bookcase, a mat (not a fitted carpet) and a desk lamp. He told me that if I spoke to him nicely he could also get hold of a coat-rack. I talked to him nicely.

I said I would probably import a few things to make the office look more like home, but this seemed to confuse him. He said it would be difficult, as extra objects would need to be on the inventory, and I might need to seek approval from the Head of Department. (I ignored this idiocy, and was never brought to task for my misdemeanour of putting family photographs on my desk and personal paintings on the wall.) After the man had left, I continued to go through the brown envelopes, which contained circulars of little or no relevance to me. Nevertheless I paid great attention to them, as I had nothing else to do.

Leaving the office, I walked back to my new temporary home in the Barbican, in the City of London, where I met the first friendly face. A rotund man with a pleasing countenance and wisps of fair hair combed over the top of his head in Bobby Charlton style came bouncing into my flat. He said his name was Brian Morgan. Welsh by birth, he had a roguish grin, and his tactile manner, which usually I find difficult to handle, made me immediately at ease. He was my boss. There was one man above him, but Brian was the one to whom I reported. Another product of the Special Course, he was on secondment from the West Midlands Police, and had risen to this position via the Metropolitan Police. He apologised for not meeting me earlier, as he had been out of town.

After I had showered we went out for a drink and a bite to eat to a pub in St Katharine's Dock. He dismissed all civil servants as 'wankers', and said that we policemen had to stick together (there were only five of us in the Home Office at the time). He told me that I would be responsible for advising police forces in the north-east and south-west, and that he would give me a fuller brief with the papers in the office next morning.

We had a most enjoyable evening. Brian was extremely good

company: he seemed to know everyone wherever we went, and had bags of confidence. I, being quite a reserved person, found his approach novel. Next day I met him again, along with the other colleagues with whom I was to work. One officer from Liverpool was large in stature and had hands like shovels, but his prizefighter looks belied his sharpness of intellect. My other new colleague was from Lancashire. He was quiet but knowledgeable and later proved to have very sound judgement. I was then taken in to see the top man – a Metropolitan officer who was clearly introverted, just the opposite of Brian. He was very pleasant, and he welcomed me to the unit.

I enjoyed my second day better than my first, and in the evening the four of us decided to eat in and make spaghetti Bolognese. We bought the raw materials during our lunch hour, including copious supplies of red wine, and prepared supper in the sketchily equipped kitchen of my flat. We had to crush the garlic by hitting it with the bottom of a saucepan on the worktop, an exercise which contaminated everything that rested on that surface for the next month or so, but we much enjoyed the first of many celebratory meals, this one being in honour of my arrival.

One morning when I went down for breakfast in the section house I was joined by a young male officer from the City of London force who called me Guv'nor, with a pronounced Cockney accent. I asked him how long he had been in the job, and he replied, 'Free years, Guv'nor.' Where did he come from? 'Barnsley, Guv'nor.' How quickly they can become typecast! Brian used to call the City of London officers 'the Vatican Guard', and he maintained that *The Sweeney* was their training programme. It is certainly true the thousand or so of them had little to do in the square mile of the City of London, and many of them mimicked the fictional detectives by carrying bunches of keys on rings suspended from their belts, said they would 'give you a bell' – meaning make a telephone call – and used the word 'Guv'nor' all the time.

I was allocated the forces of Dorset, Northumbria and Strathclyde, my job being to advise them on their command and control needs. Each force was in a different stage of development.

Strathclyde had a computer in place, and was refining its software – in those days everything was bespoke – and training the staff how to use it. Dorset was still drawing up its specification for a system, and had not completed a needs assessment. The people in Northumbria were at an even earlier stage, as they hadn't fully decided whether they needed a computer or not. My work with these forces was fascinating, as I learned a great deal about the different way in which each set about dealing with its problems, and enjoyed being able to share the experience with others.

I spent all my time away from home travelling, at first mainly in Dorset, where I took rooms in the Cecil Hotel, a small, family-run establishment with a good holiday trade and an excellent chef. I would fly down from Leeds on a Monday morning and return home on Friday evening. On my visits to Glasgow I would stay in the Central Hotel above the railway station, where I learned to insist on a room above the second floor, to avoid the noise of the trains. Some of the bedrooms were without facilities, and I was embarrassed more than once before I packed a dressing gown. The rooms with bathrooms had baths so big you could almost have swum in them. In Northumbria I had no set base, so I stayed in various hotels up and down the county.

Living in the Cecil Hotel at that time was an enigmatic man who every day wore cavalry twill trousers, a blazer, white shirt, with either a loud cravat or a bow tie, and a straw hat to protect him from the sun. He had rooms on the top floor next to mine, and although he would pass the time of day, for many weeks he was reluctant to engage in any other conversation. The staff told me he was a former Indian Army officer who had lost his wife.

He took his meals at the same table at precisely the same time each day. One summer morning he asked me to join him for breakfast, and I gladly accepted. I believe he thought I was a spy, because after the formalities he asked, 'Do you work for Her Majesty?' I told him I did.

'Thought so,' he said. 'I can tell by the cut of you.'

The fact that I had joined him for a meal was causing some interest among the other guests, especially as he spoke in such a loud voice that they couldn't help but overhear what he was saying.

'I knew some of your fellows in India,' he said. Then he asked abruptly, 'Do you like the ladies?' When I told him I was married, he went on, 'Your chaps liked the ladies, and marriage didn't seem to quell their appetite.'

I acknowledged this fact – and by this time there was more than faint interest from the other occupants of the dining room. Leaning towards me in an attempt to be secretive, but in a stage whisper which could be heard in the kitchen, he roared, 'One of them, one of them . . . *fraternised with the natives*.' At this all the other guests downed knives and forks and stopped eating to listen. 'Ruined him, ruined him, you know,' he said. I made some appropriate gesture of surprise. There followed a few seconds' silence, after which he shouted, 'Socially, I mean.' I don't know how I stopped myself laughing. The remainder of his audience didn't, but he seemed oblivious of them.

'Married, you say?' he barked. 'What does your wife look like?'

I showed him a photograph of Bren I carried in my wallet. He said he had been married for many years, then stopped, pondered and said in his stage whisper, 'Damned fine filly! Damned fine filly when we married.' He paused, looking pensive, and added, 'She's knackered now, of course.'

That was too much. I burst out laughing, along with everyone else. He took it in good spirit and laughed with us. It seemed that his wife believed she was blind, even though she had sight. He told me that when the telephone rang, he would refuse to answer it in order to encourage the poor creature to react. He said that this policy was fraught with danger, as she would fall over any obstruction between her and the phone. She was in a home on the Isle of Wight, which he visited every week.

In time, as I got to know him better, I realised how lonely he was: he really missed his wife, and had moved into the Cecil so that he would be looked after. We enjoyed each other's company and had many a meal together.

My job was all-engaging, but I missed my family and quickly realised how lonely my own life was. I don't require much sleep, so I would run by the side of the sea at six o'clock in the morning to maintain my fitness, but after dinner I faced solitary evenings in my room.

After about six months we were told that there was a huge increase in demand for our services from the police forces of the United Kingdom, and we would have to change our pattern of work. The boss told us that he could no longer afford the luxury of an officer being virtually resident in a force: instead, we would have to act more like consultants, and advise and train local officers to do the detailed work. As the newest member of the team, I was told that I would be trained as a consultant because I had the longest time to repay the investment.

I received some of this training within Government, but the bulk came from private industry. I was attached to a large American computer company, and the technological arm of a big consultancy firm.

One of my course tutors at the computer firm was a charismatic, evangelistic type who oozed confidence and inspired others. I confess I find most such people to be little more than showmen, and sure enough, on our first morning he told us that we could be anything we wanted, could go anywhere we wanted and do anything we wanted. He said silly things like, 'You have the power to get any woman you wish into bed. If that's what you want, that's what I'll teach you to do.' The only constraints, he told us, were in our minds. He promised to show us how to overcome any limitations we might have in order to unlock our 'full potential'. I found him amusing, and said as much. Unfortunately he was deadly serious, and in one of our hand-holding sessions he revealed my scepticism to the other members of the group, inviting them to comment on my perceptions. This was my first experience of the touchy-feely type of programmes which were vogue in the USA at the time. This one was run badly, and I saw how destructive it was for the less secure people in the group, who simply couldn't cope when they became the focus of discussion. Those who dropped out were dismissed by our leader as 'having no bottle'.

The consultancy company adopted more traditional methods of

training, part of which was an attachment to one of their customers' businesses, to work through a real problem. Mine was to advise on the rerouting of a production process in a company that manufactured doors. My most lasting recollection is of the long-term nature of the planners' cycle, as, in order to plant the right kinds of trees today, they had to predict the type of wood that would be required for doors far into the future.

Much of what I learned was common sense, but I believe there is a place in industry for consultants, who can perform a function which organisations and individuals cannot always carry out for themselves, as people are often too close to their problems to find effective solutions on their own. What I have against many consultants is that they have no real experience of management, charge ridiculous fees and their knowledge is more theoretical than practical.

With my newly formed skills I was launched on the police. At one stage I worked with more than a dozen forces – which was an even more valuable experience. I was able to set my own agenda, and got right to the heart of their business. I developed a pro forma to assess the level and effectiveness of each of their operations, and followed this up by interviewing all ranks, from constable to the Chief. By this simple device I could assess the workings of the organisation and see, both from my own experience and by comparison with others, what needed to be done. I would then present my findings and recommendations for change to the senior managers, and, on occasions, to their Police Authorities. There was a general misconception at that time that all problems would be solved by the introduction of a computer, whereas often changes in management practices were all that was necessary. I wrote an article to this effect for a national computer magazine entitled 'Management Push or Technology Pull?'

If my recommendations were accepted, I prepared a programme of work and helped train staff to implement it. My role thereafter was to keep a watching brief, assisting each force to achieve its targets. In short, I was helping to shape the future of the police.

There were marked differences in the way the forces were

managed, and in the demands they faced. Each officer on one north-eastern force dealt with the same number of incidents in a single shift as officers faced each week in a Midlands force – yet both thought they were under pressure.

One morning, out of the blue, I was called in to see Her Majesty's Chief Inspector of Constabulary – an old-type copper who told me that he had just been to visit the Royal Ulster Constabulary, and they needed help. He said that the Chief Constable, Sir James Flanagan, was ready for retirement, and that Ken Newman had been sent there as his deputy, to learn the ropes before replacing him. He asked me to go across, look at what they were doing and help them.

This was 1976. They were extremely difficult times in Northern Ireland, as the Troubles were at their height, and I felt privileged to be asked to make a contribution. On my first visit I was introduced to the Chief Constable, to the General Officer Commanding, to Merlyn Rees (the Northern Ireland Secretary of State) and to other police and military officers who were to look after me. It was exciting stuff. I was right at the heart of the most difficult policing problem in the world. On that reconnaissance trip I travelled with a former army colonel who worked for the Home Office as a technical adviser, and on our return flight he said, 'I've set it up. Now you can f—k it up.' This was my first real experience of military humour, but not my last.

Back in London, I discussed the work that had to be done with my colleagues, one of whom was to accompany me on the visits. Next time over, I met and was briefed by other major players whom I had not previously seen, the first being the new Chief Constable in waiting, Kenneth (later Sir Kenneth) Newman. He was small in stature, thin and gaunt, always with a serious countenance, which hid a very warm and caring person. He told me of his hopes and aspirations for the police force and the community it served. He was a deep-thinking man and asked me to leave the programme I had prepared with him, so that he could give it more careful consideration. He later expressed his satisfaction with it, and asked that he be kept informed of progress.

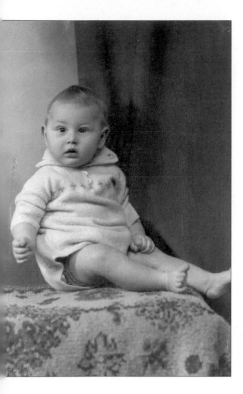

LEFT: Keith Hellawell, 1942, Holmfirth, Yorkshire.

BELOW: Aged two, with glasses to correct strabismus, a condition that required six eye operations throughout my life.

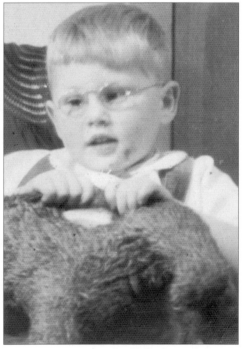

LEFT: With my dog, Whiskey, at age sixteen – a year after I quit school and began working as a safety inspector at a Yorkshire mine.

LEFT: On my Lambretta
motorcycle, 1960.

BELOW: In my first car,
an Austin Sprite.

LEFT: Sporting a trilby
hat off-duty in 1963,
a year after I joined
the police force.

RIGHT: Marrying Brenda F
at the Lindley Metho
Church, Huddersfield, 19

ABOVE: With colleagues at the Police College at Bramshill in Hampshire circa 1966 (second row, third from left).

BELOW: With the Halifax rugby team (second row, third from right).

ABOVE: With officers on the Teacher Training Course (back row, second from left).

As an Inspector in Huddersfield, 1967.

Brenda Hellawell, 1973.

ABOVE: Bren with our children – Alexandra, Charles and Samantha – in 1971.

LEFT: With son, Charles, at the Ellaad carnival, 1972.

ʀɪɢʜᴛ: With a friend
at my master's degree
ceremony, June 1982.

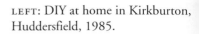

LEFT: DIY at home in Kirkburton, Huddersfield, 1985.

BELOW: With Charles.

BELOW: Bren and I greet Princess Diana at Leeds Bradford Airport.

The next person I met was the Lieutenant Colonel responsible for the SAS detachment. On our way to the glorified Portakabin in which he worked we passed through a series of elaborate security measures, including two sets of steel-barred gates. On our way I noticed a soldier, in full battle fatigues and armed with a rifle, standing in front of a steel filing cabinet which I was told was protected for twenty-four hours a day as it housed encrypted NATO material.

As I entered the Lieutenant Colonel's office, he came from behind his desk to greet me. We shook hands, and in a loud voice he said, 'Damn you, you've got a grip!' I didn't make any reply, but I thought this a strange introduction. I have always had a firm hand-shake, and at that time I was at the peak of physical fitness. I can't stand those who hold out their hands to shake yours as if they were hanging out a wet kipper to dry. Nor do I feel comfortable with the Freemason handshake; I am always amused when I am tested to see if I am a member. As I rose through the ranks I had to shake a large number of hands. I found that many people were nervous, and their palms perspired. I would try not to let them see, but would always try to dry my hand before I shook the next person's, lest he or she should think that the transferred dampness was mine.

The army officer bade me sit down while he briefed me on the situation in Northern Ireland. What followed was vintage James Bond. When he pressed some contraption on his desk, the lights went down and a young female soldier entered the room. He pressed another button and on the wall appeared an image from a projector secreted in the desk – a map of Northern Ireland. In his clipped accent he said, 'This is a map of the Province. We are here.'

He then said he intended to show me what contribution the military was making. As he pointed out a particular spot, the young officer held the tip of her stick over the right place on the screen. When she got left behind by the frantic pace at which he was narrating, he would shout, 'Hurry up, gal! Keep going!' At one point he yelled, 'Come on, gal! You're losing the bloody war!'

This pantomime went on for about twenty minutes, but was most instructive. The last slide was of two lions copulating. As the image came up on to the screen, the Lieutenant Colonel concluded, 'This is just to show you that we have the lions' share' – which he immediately followed with 'Cover your eyes, gal. This is not for you'. She left the room in a scurry.

I was enthralled. Clearly the whole show was stage-managed, even though it looked quite casual. Presentations by the military are usually rehearsed to the last detail, and for a time I copied their methods.

That officer proved to be great fun. I worked closely with him throughout my time in Northern Ireland, and once, in London, he called to ask if I would like to go for a drink after work. When I said I would, he asked if it should be at his club or mine. I explained that police officers from the north didn't have clubs. All right, he said, it should be his. He then asked if I was in for a 'jolly or a thrash' – a few drinks or getting ratted. I said I would see how it went.

He told me the address and I arrived at the time stipulated. I thought I had come to the wrong place, because all I could see was a very beautiful house; but after I had rung the bell and given my name, I was ushered up an elegant staircase into a first-floor bar. It was a summer's evening, and the French windows were open on to balconies. My friend greeted me with gusto, introduced me to the group of friends he was drinking with, and got me a glass.

They were all army chums: one asked if my friend had heard about a colleague – let's call him Smith. My friend said he had not. 'What a bastard!' was the response. My friend asked why. 'He's the worst bastard I've ever worked with,' said the other. 'I can't stand him.' My friend then said, 'Well, when I served with him in so-and-so, I found him all right. He might have the odd strange habit, but one could live with him.'

The response of the first officer amazed me. 'Well, perhaps I've been too hasty. Maybe I've only seen one side of him. No – thinking about it, he's a damned fine fellow.'

I couldn't believe my ears – such a complete turn-around within the space of a few moments – but nobody commented on the volte-face.

Other guests joined us, some for pre-dinner drinks. One was a very attractive woman, in long evening dress, with a choker necklace around her throat. My friend asked her why she was wearing 'that confounded thing', as it made her 'look like a Zulu'. This also went without adverse comment.

Another officer joined our circle. He was bronzed and lean: it seems he had just been on a mission overseas. Let's call him Dicky. He drank a whisky, then another and another: he was clearly unwinding. After an hour or so he said, 'I'm going,' and a few moments later he repeated his announcement. He then collapsed on to the floor, whereupon my friend remarked, 'He's gone.' No one seemed concerned: the staff just lifted him into a chair at the top of the staircase.

When the night was ending and my car arrived, I asked what would become of Dicky. The staff told me he would be all right – either he would sleep it off where he was, or they would put him to bed. I told them I had a car and a driver and would be more than happy to give him a lift home, so they accepted and gave me his address.

He lived in a beautiful Regency terrace house a few minutes away. When I rang the bell, a woman leaned out of the second-floor window and called, 'Yes?'

'Is that Mrs X?' I asked.

'Yes.'

'I've got your husband here.'

'Is he drunk?'

'Yes.'

'Leave him on the step, then.'

Which I did. I thought this a most bizarre way to carry on – but I was learning fast.

In Northern Ireland my brief was simple: to look at the operations of the Royal Ulster Constabulary and advise how they could be improved by the introduction of computer technology. This could not be achieved without taking into account the work of other organizations, which was inextricably linked with that of the RUC, and that was why I had been briefed so widely. The command and control systems had to take account of this combined effort, and the information upon which they depended needed to be brought together to avoid duplication. This was a substantial task, as the organizations all had different backgrounds, access to unique information sources, and mistrust of each other.

Senior police officers were uncomfortable with the role the military were taking as quasi-peacekeepers on 'their' streets. The military were frustrated that they could not operate in the way they had been trained, and 'take on the enemy'. They were also suspicious of the armed police, whom they considered less professional than themselves. In the middle, the politicians were trying to keep the peace between these two and other interested elements of the establishment. The civilian community was caught up in the bitter guerrilla war being fought in the streets.

I went on operations with the military and the police, some of which were quite sensitive, others very moving. In the aftermath of a terrorist bomb at a restaurant, I saw the devastation the explosion had caused to human life. The body parts littering the pavement brought home the full horror of the moment. I sat in checkpoints with the army, listening to their conversations with irate motorists, who described them as occupying forces. I went on military sorties to rout out terrorists, one of which was aborted because the army had clearly been set up with false information, and I flew in helicopters over the border areas and in the vicinity of The Maze Prison. I was present when suspected terrorists were interviewed. Some – fresh-faced and only in their teens – were accused of planting the bombs which killed, steeped in the belief that they were just 'following the cause'.

The helicopters we used had thermal cameras on board which allowed us to identify different heat sources, and thus establish if there was someone in a building, or if the ground had been disturbed – an important capability in anti-terrorist activity. On one occasion this equipment – then secret – was brought across to England to show to the minister. Brian, myself and the RAF pilots went out for the evening and in an inebriated mood decided to fly the helicopter under the bridges of the Thames. Only the stern rebuff of a Royal Air Force sergeant saved us from the potentially disastrous consequences.

Due to the nature of my work, I had an armed contingent with me wherever I went, and this put a particular strain on the whole experience. I stayed in different places, more than once being moved at short notice for my own safety. Another elaborate exercise I went through – in case I ever needed to get out in a hurry – was a rapid departure by military jet. At the airfield I was introduced to my pilot, who looked about sixteen years old, and asked me if I had flown in such an aircraft before. When I said 'No,' he went on, 'All right, Sir, I'll drive.' He then took me through the safety procedures.

'The most difficult times are when we are taking off and landing.'

'Yes,' I said.

'When we set off, I'll open the throttle and our speed will increase. If anything goes wrong, I'll call "Emergency! Emergency!" You will put your hands over your head and pull the red lever behind you, whereupon you will forcibly be ejected into the air and titter down to the ground. Do you understand?'

'Yes,' I replied.

'Do you have a gas cooker?'

'A what?'

'A gas cooker?'

'Yes.'

'Good! When we come into land, I will gradually take my foot off the gas. If I take it off too far, the flame will go *poof!*, and we will fall out of the sky. I will call "Emergency! Emergency!" You will put your hands over your head and pull the red lever – but it won't really matter, because you will be dead. Now get in, Sir.'

With that, we took off, skimmed out over the sea and hurtled across the Scottish lowlands before returning. The speed was exhilarating, the landscape just a blur. I understood why the military needs individuals in the peak of physical and mental condition to fly such aircraft. Thankfully I never had to use that form of transport again, but I was glad to have had an experience which I will never forget.

* * *

I discussed my emerging thoughts with Kenneth Newman, who by then was Chief Constable and affectionately known by his troops as 'the wee man'. I recall vividly walking around the heavily fortified compound at Castlereagh, where he had quarters, in the early hours of the morning, talking through some of the issues. He always visited the family of any officer who was killed, and called on any injured officer. He worked tirelessly, to the detriment of his own health, and cared deeply. I learned a great deal from him, and came to admire and respect him enormously. After Northern Ireland he became Commissioner of the Metropolitan Police, on which he had a profound influence, and later headed police training at the Staff College. No other officer has ever served in all these posts, the most senior in the police service, and I suspect no one ever will. He is a very special man.

One of the key issues in the Province concerned the use of information. The military, the police, the Special Branch and the security services each put different weightings on the information they received. They were also very reluctant to share their sources with other potential users. This led to disharmony, particularly when one organisation would refuse to act on the information from another unless it knew its source or was able to verify it by its own means.

This was a crucial issue, as misinformation is a tool frequently used by terrorists to wrong-foot the opposition. In one case a military source reported that a wanted terrorist would be at a particular location at a particular time. The information was false, and we discovered that a group of old people was due to meet in the building at the given hour. Had we acted, the result would have been valuable propaganda for the terrorists, and certain death for their informant, who had purposely been fed the phoney information to test him.

After much discussion with all the agencies, we agreed a formula which equated authenticity of information to action. This became the basis of the computerised operational system in Northern Ireland which still exists today. Our proposals were accepted by all the different organisational heads and the politicians, and I spent much of the remainder of my secondment helping them implement the new scheme.

In Dorset, after a while I moved out of the Cecil Hotel and into a detached house, in a quiet cul-de-sac on the outskirts of Poole – an ideal base to use when working in England, and an escape from Northern Ireland. I made myself known to the family next door, and explained that I would only be visiting the house occasionally as I worked for the Government. The lady of the house said that she would look out for me, and get me in some milk and bread if I let her know when I was coming. She clearly got the wrong impression, as she left me notes headed 'Dear James' and signed them 'Moneypenny'.

That house was convenient for the family, and Bren and the children stayed during many school holidays. I like the sea, and when I was there for short periods on my own I would walk on the beach, collecting cockles to eat. On one of these excursions I was approached by a young woman, whom I tried to avoid, as I wished to be alone. She thought I was foreign because my skin was tanned and my hair bleached blond by the sun, and when she asked where I came from, I merely nodded. She then proceeded to tell me that she was married, but was having an affair with the Chief Executive of her county council, who was attending a conference in Poole. She had used some excuse to be away from her husband, but now she was having second thoughts about the tryst. As she poured her heart out to me, I just nodded and smiled, reflecting on how odd it is that people open up to strangers.

The two years I spent in and out of Northern Ireland involved me in many distressing and moving events. The stress was such that I several times experienced irregular, heavy beating of my heart, and once, at a scene of violence in the outskirts of Belfast, the palpitation became so bad that it could plainly be seen through my clothes. Luckily a doctor was present. She noticed my discomfort, took me away and examined me. She told me that I was suffering extreme stress and needed to do something about it.

My colleagues in that force suffered the same every day of their lives. My driver was often nervous, and although he would never say anything, I saw the beads of perspiration on his forehead and hands when we went through points particularly vulnerable to ambush. His fears proved justified, as he was later shot in the stomach, but luckily survived.

Not so Stan Hannah, the chief inspector who looked out for me all the time I was in the Province. We drank together, laughed together, cried together. Through him I experienced the difficulties he and his family were facing: the fear they felt when his pay-slip, addressing him by his rank, was inadvertently sent to his home, and the precautions they all had to take in their everyday lives. Only someone who has lived in those conditions can ever really understand the sacrifices people make on behalf of others. Imagine the bigotry of a headmaster and a bank manager who both declined to stay in our company, when we were having a drink in a safe place, because I refused to agree that all Catholics ought to be exterminated.

Some years later Stan, then a superintendent, was killed by a terrorist bomb planted in a milk churn by the side of the road – the most senior police officer murdered in the Troubles. I still grieve for him and his family, and the hundreds of others who lost their lives in the struggle.

I returned to base in 1978, after nearly three years away, to 'Welcome Home' banners strewn around the house. In my absence my children had grown, and I had missed some of the most important years of their development, which I will always regret. Bren had supported me loyally, and had never told me what trials and tribulations she had faced. At the outset she had said that she didn't want me to go to Northern Ireland, but that if I was sure I ought to, she would not try to stop me – and she added something which really moved me: 'You must remember that there are many police officers just as well qualified as you to go and do that job, but there's no one else who can fill your shoes here.' At the time I just felt it was my duty to carry on with what I was doing, but in retrospect I realise I didn't fully consider the consequences for my family.

It was only when I returned that I saw what pain Bren had suffered – how she had dreaded any item on the news about a killing in Ireland, immediately thinking that I was the victim, until reassured by my telephone call or return home. Charles used to wait for hours by the window, asking when Daddy was coming home, and, as the months went by, why his father never came home at nights, as others did. My long absence had a profound effect on him, and I lost something precious, for which I will always mourn.

Successful people are often looked on with envy by others, who believe that high achievers have been given everything without having either to work or to pay for it. In my experience this is rarely true. Some sacrifice has to be made. In my case it was that magical time spent with young children. I vowed not to miss the opportunity with my grandchildren, if it ever came. In all, at the time of writing this book, I have spent almost fifteen years of our married life away from home. If I had my time over, I would make sure that did not happen again.

CHAPTER TEN

BRADFORD

I was delighted to be given a command in the centre of Bradford, one of the busiest stations in the force. Bradford is second only to Leeds as the major city in West Yorkshire, and besides commanding 200 officers, the post carried a number of additional responsibilities, among which was a bridewell, which charged and housed prisoners for the whole of the surrounding area and serviced the Crown Court. In addition, this station housed a prosecution department and the command centre for the region.

Being housed in a prestigious building in the centre of the city, we suffered from a lack of parking, and this led to problems, as officers had to park in the streets, where their cars were regularly vandalised. Across the road was a national insurance company, which had an underground car park with twenty-four-hour security staff, and I soon negotiated permission for my officers to use it after normal business hours – a move well received by my staff.

Another innovation which proved popular was my determination to walk out frequently on the streets with my officers. I wanted to get a feel for the job first hand, and this was what I had joined the service for and what stimulated me the most. In my absence there had been many changes, the greatest being the officers' increased reliance on radio handsets. They would no longer face a group of unruly young men, as we had in the past: they would either try to avoid them, which undermined the public's confidence, or they would call for 'back-up' – other police to help them. More often than not, a stronger turn-out only exacerbated the situation and resulted in arrests.

Drawing on my experience in Northern Ireland, I encouraged officers to join me in resolving confrontations without recourse to back-up. I walked with them into the middle of groups of young men and talked to them in a normal manner. I cannot claim that this had more than limited success, but we did defuse a number of potentially difficult situations, in which the public could quickly have shifted from a position of support for the police to one of antagonism. By getting in among groups of youths, we generally forestalled the cat-calling that a stand-off provokes, and whenever we managed it with the right tone, we encouraged better relationships between the police and young people.

The late seventies saw the re-emergence of the National Front, which was extremely active in Bradford because of the large Asian community. Before my arrival, police strategy had been to contain possible trouble by providing a large presence along the route of any march, in order to keep the marchers and those demonstrating against it apart. We often failed, with the result that violence broke out between the groups and the police.

I changed to the system used in Northern Ireland, where the police did much work in advance of a march or demonstration, either to try and prevent it occurring, or to lay down strict conditions under which it could take place. I insisted that we begin to speak to the organisers before the event – something we had been reluctant to do with the more extreme organisations – and we threatened to ban the march if they didn't agree to our conditions. (In reality this was an empty threat, as only the local authority had power to impose a ban, and it was very reluctant to act.)

We changed our tactics to providing a light police presence, with substantial reserves to act quickly if we anticipated trouble. We left the organisers in no doubt that, should things go wrong, they would be severely dealt with. To the surprise of us all, the organisers welcomed this dialogue with us, saying that at least they knew where they stood, and accepted their responsibility to marshal themselves and rout out rogue elements.

We altered the criteria by which we judged our success during these marches from the number of arrests made to the lack of trouble, assaults, injuries and complaints against us. When we began to reduce the disorder on the streets of Bradford, the sceptics were convinced – although my ACC remarked on my first appraisal, 'It's a pity it hasn't been as bad as last year, because you haven't really been tested in the thick of it.' I told him why – we had prevented trouble, rather than reacted to it – and to his credit he said, 'I'm out of touch, lad. I'm a gas-light policeman in a technological age.' He went on to serve another eight years. My mettle had been tested, but I like to think I used my brains not my brawn.

At home we began to settle into normal family life. The children were happy with my return, the garden was getting back into shape and we were extending our home. We did consider moving to a larger house, and visited several, including an old manor which had been completely restored by the vendor, a very wealthy man. The price was at the limit of what we could afford, but we had always stretched ourselves in this way since the death of my friends. We were told we were in competition with another seriously interested party who wished to remain anonymous – but who we later learned was Arthur Scargill. We eventually decided against it.

Running the police service in the heart of one of our major cities is a joy. You are an integral part of the community, and if you do your job reasonably well, you are respected by many sections of it, including business leaders, who give you their support and trust. Local politicians are also very interested in what you do. In cities like Bradford, which until its amalgamation with the larger forces of Leeds and West Yorkshire in 1974, had its own police force, there was lingering resentment over the change in which locals felt they had lost not only 'their' Chief Constable, but also their power and influence over the police. It was a delicate task to keep them involved and establish a new relationship. On the whole they were resigned to the changes, but their frustration became evident in times of crisis.

Another factor was the Press. Local papers have a substantial interest in what the police do, and are only too willing to criticise when occasion arises. The objective of the police service at that time was to keep the media at arm's length. 'They need us more than we need them,' was the phrase used – my philosophy was different. I would rather engage with them – an attitude my colleagues found surprising. At least, in that way, we were assured of getting our point across. The papers didn't always use what we said, but at least they knew what we were thinking.

During the early days of my office a man was found dead in the markets area. His body had been there for some time, and the papers criticised us for not discovering it sooner. Our natural reaction would have been a defensive, 'We have no comment to make, but we will inquire into the circumstances.' I took a different line. I said I was sorry for the death of the man, and offered my condolences to his family. I said I didn't know why his body had not been found, but if it was shown to be due to the neglect of the police service, I would take action against the officers concerned. There was no more criticism about the incident.

Such cases show that people expect the police to be ever-present, which is impracticable. This places you in a dilemma. Do you openly admit that you have insufficient resources to do the job, and thereby reduce public confidence? Or do you put a brave front on it and face the consequences when you cannot meet the public's needs? This is a far cry from the situation today, when police leaders engage in open public debate about lack of resources in order to deflect criticism and persuade politicians to give them more resources. I am not sure that this politicising of the police is by any means a good thing.

Openness with the media has been a hallmark of my career, and has been criticized by my colleagues, who have seen it as a desire on my behalf to 'get on the box', or get my name in the papers. I have never had the slightest interest in such exposure from a personal point of view – and in fact a high profile is more of a burden than a blessing in public life. I believe, however, that organisations like the police need to be more visible: they should answer for their actions, and comment on matters of public concern.

Not that every incident need be exposed. I was at my desk one day when an official from City Hall asked if he could come and see me on a delicate matter. He had received a call from one of the local solicitors who had been given an extremely sensitive mission by one of his clients. The client had stolen the mayoral chain and couldn't 'fence' it, but was prepared to sell it back to the council for a reasonable sum.

The official sought my advice. I asked him which solicitor it was, but he couldn't tell me, as the man had to remain anonymous. I asked him how badly they needed the chain returning, and he said they were desperate, as it was irreplaceable, and the embarrassment factor would be high if the news got out. I asked him how much he was prepared to pay for its return, and he said, 'Any reasonable sum, because it's priceless.' I gave him the following advice: 'As a police officer, I could never countenance paying a criminal. As a commonsense person, pay him.' The transaction took place and the chain was returned. I was never told how much they had to pay for it, and the story never reached the newspapers.

After I had been in Bradford for eighteen months, I applied for the Senior Command Course, hoping that my varied experience in the ranks would make up for my relatively short service. The first hurdle was to gain the support of my Chief, who had to agree to candidates going forward for central selection. He backed me, but warned me that I would have a more difficult time convincing the interview panel.

In those days the interview was in two parts. My regional interview took place in the library at Pannal Ash, where the year-book photographs showed me how much I had aged in the years since my first visit for my initial training. I had also changed my hairstyle and grown a moustache, to try and look older than my thirty-seven years, as on one embarrassing occasion, when I visited a Lancashire police station, I had been taken for a new recruit.

In this reflective mood I faced the interviewers. They included Lawrence Byford, who besides later becoming Chief HMI was elected President and Chairman of Yorkshire County Cricket Club.

The interview lasted no more than thirty minutes, and I felt I had acquitted myself adequately; however, when I got up to leave, Mr Byford bade me remain.

He announced that he was going to do something that he should not do, but he was doing it for a reason. He told me I had been successful, and would go forward to the next stage of the interview process. But then he asked, 'What's happened to you?' He remembered me as a robust detective in Huddersfield Borough, during the early sixties, when he commended me for helping to detect a substantial theft of cloth from a mill in Halifax. My openness and honesty had impressed him on that occasion, and he detected a 'charm and cheek' about me, which I seemed to have lost. He said he had no criticism of my interview skills, but thought I seemed a bit synthetic. He told me that my personality was what marked me out from other people, and without it I was just one of the crowd. 'Let them see the cheeky Hellawell again,' he said – and it turned out to be sound advice.

The second stage of the selection process, held in Eastbourne, was similar in format to that for the Special Course. They tested problem-solving skills, but the major part of the competition was, as before, the interviews. My panel, chaired by Sir Philip Knights, confronted me with a very detailed account of my career: they produced early appraisals, course reports, feedback from my Chief Constable, the Home Office and Northern Ireland.

The chairman's opening gambit completely threw me. He held up this sheaf of papers and said, 'This is a perfect CV. You've worked in every department. You've excelled on all the courses and attachments you have attended. You have a good degree – so I have nothing to ask you about your career.' Throwing the papers theatrically on one side, he leaned forward and said, 'What I really need to find out is about *you*. What is the man behind the reports really like? Can he hack it? Is he as good as these papers suggest?'

He said this in a combative way, and in the same vein he followed with, 'Why should we put you on this course? You're one of the youngest candidates [I was ten years below the average age], and it's your first time. Tell me why we should put you ahead of others more senior and experienced than you.'

I told him that age was not always a criterion for experience. What I had done at the Home Office, and particularly in Northern Ireland, had given me rare experience, and was worth many years in a normal role.

He didn't seem to think much of this. He said that was the answer he expected, and he was not impressed. His aggressive manner was beginning to make me feel uncomfortable. He then asked one or two other questions, and my answers prompted the same sharp or dismissive response.

I reacted. I said I didn't like his manner. I understood my career was on the line, but there was no justification for conducting the interview in this way. That did not go down well. He said I should realise what power he had – that he could break or make my career at that moment.

'I'm aware of that,' I told him. 'But I won't be spoken to in this way. At best it's discourteous, and at worst it's downright rude.'

The colour rose in his face. He said, sounding excessively polite, 'Answer me this, then. What's the thing you most fear when you go into the office at 9 a.m. on a morning?'

'First,' I said, 'by 9 a.m. I've been in the office for nearly two hours, if I'm working in the daytime. But I often work in the evening and overnight.'

Looking even less pleased, he responded, 'All right. What's the thing you most hope won't happen when you go into the office, whatever time that might be?'

'I don't think like that,' I told him. 'I look at the possibilities and opportunities for the day. I know something may go wrong, but I reckon it's part of my job to anticipate that and prevent it happening, rather than worry about it.'

By then he was visibly cross, and he said with some venom, 'You're either very confident, or you're very foolish, and I'm going to find out which. If you'd turn your mind to the things which could go wrong, I'm sure I and my colleagues would be only too pleased to know.'

I said cheekily, 'The first thing I would fear in this mythical situation is that I may drop dead of a heart attack.'

He waved his hand dismissively.

'Then, as we're on the flight-path into Leeds Bradford airport, I hope that a plane doesn't crash.'

He seemed more satisfied with this.

I then said I would hope that there had been no riots, that none of my officers had been injured. I went through a list of lesser things that may happen in the day of a police officer. He could recognise that I was sending him up. I judged from his body language that I was not doing myself any good, so I switched tack (in any interview it is important to read the panel-members' movements – they're only human).

I said that the things we all must fear were those against which we could not legislate or manage. I mentioned the policeman who was on the take, the over-exuberant officer who assaulted a prisoner, the neglect of a prisoner which resulted in a serious injury being missed and a cell death. I explained that as a senior officer you should be aware of such hazards, and by foresight and leadership attempt to reduce the risk of them happening, but there was little more you could do. 'But this,' I added, 'is something an officer has to take in his stride. I think I'd go mad if these were the main issues which preyed on my mind.'

He seemed more satisfied with my answer, although his demeanour remained aloof. He continued, 'Let us presume you're a Chief Constable hearing a disciplinary case. The circumstances are these. During the night a serious incident requires the attendance of the shift inspector, who cannot be found. After repeated calls to his personal radio, the staff become worried, and begin to search for him. He is eventually found in a dishevelled state with a woman of low repute. He refuses to comment about his behaviour, either on the spot, or during the disciplinary investigation, or at the hearing you are conducting. What penalty would you impose?'

He added that one of the officers was badly assaulted at the first incident, which could have been avoided had the inspector answered the radio call.

I questioned him. Was the shift inspector married? Was there a history between him and this or other women? Had there been a medical report on him?

My interviewer seemed unimpressed, because although he partially answered my questions, he was still dismissive. When I began to ask another, he stopped me in mid-track. 'Why won't you make a decision? I've told you the circumstances. Just get on with it.'

I retorted that a man's career was at stake here, and I felt it was important that I knew all the attendant circumstances before I made a judgement. He said, 'You've had your questions. Now make your decision.'

I said, 'I would require him to resign.'

He sat back as if he had achieved a victory, but glanced at his colleagues with a look which said, 'That took some doing.'

The interview had gone long beyond its scheduled time. He looked at the clock and asked his colleagues if they wished to ask any questions. Unusually, they declined. He told me I could go, but as I reached the door he stopped me and said, 'Mr Hellawell, if you fail this interview, and you have to come back before a panel again, will either your answers or your attitude be different?'

'Sir,' I said, 'if the questions were the same and addressed to me in the manner in which they have been today, my attitude and answers would be just the same.'

'Thank you,' he said – and I left the room.

I was deflated, certain I had failed the interview, and would have to wait at least a year before becoming eligible to make another attempt. I thought it was just my bad luck to get Knights on a bad day. However, I reconciled myself by thinking that I had reacted in the only way possible.

Discussing it with my colleagues didn't help. They all told me I'd blown it. They said Knights had been reasonable with them, and I must have rubbed him up the wrong way. I consoled myself with the thought that he just didn't like me.

Weeks later, when I had put the disappointment behind me, Ron Gregory called me to tell me that I had succeeded and would be going on the course. I was dumbfounded, and asked if he was sure there had been no mistake. No, he said – he had it in writing: I had passed. I was over the moon. Bren and the children were thrilled for me, as they knew that successful completion of this course was the gateway to the most senior ranks in the service, even though it meant another six months away from home.

So, together with sixteen other police officers from the United Kingdom and half a dozen from abroad, I attended the 1979 Senior Command Course at Bramshill. On our first evening, at a reception given by those who had selected us, Philip Knights singled me out and said, 'Ah yes, my coal miner from the north!' He put his arm around my shoulder and told me that my interview was one of the best he had ever experienced. He said that he had always wanted to take someone to the limits, explaining that this was possible only when he was satisfied that it wouldn't destroy the candidate. He said that he kept pushing me and pushing me, and had been exhilarated when I didn't crack. When he asked that last question as I was about to leave the room, he said he hoped against hope that I would stick to my principles. That episode taught me a lesson I have never forgotten: things are not always as they seem.

I enjoyed the Senior Command Course and found it stimulating. As one of the youngest members, I was looked after by some of the more mature officers, among them a man called Alan Smith, who eventually became Chief Constable of Derbyshire amid much controversy as he was appointed as the last act of an outgoing Authority against the wishes of the new. I had the greatest regard for this man, who, besides being a policeman's policeman, was a talented artist and an archer of some renown, having competed for this country. Sadly, he died shortly after retiring. Even he was affected by rank. At the beginning of the course he was an ACC, and told me that although it would be convenient for us to travel together, it would be inappropriate because of the difference in our ranks. This awkwardness was soon resolved, as I was promoted to the rank of chief superintendent, the one below his.

The day of my promotion became quite traumatic. Ron Gregory and his wife came to dinner at the college and invited Alan and myself to join them for pre-dinner drinks, where he shook my hand

and told me he was promoting me. I was elated – until I began to talk to his wife, whom I had scarcely spoken to before. When I asked if she had been pleased with the boat we had named after her, she seemed nonplussed, but told me to go on. I explained that when I had been in charge of the cadets we had purchased a new sailing boat, and I had asked the Chief Constable if we could name it after his wife, and he had agreed.

'What name did he give you?' she asked.

'Grace,' I replied.

'But my name's not Grace. I'm called Betty.'

My heart sank, and I was sure I would lose my promotion. I didn't know where to put myself, and dreaded the Chief's return. When he arrived, she confronted him with what I had told her, and the animated conversation that followed was acutely embarrassing to all three of us. It turned out, however, her real name *was* Grace, but she didn't like it, claiming that there was nothing graceful about her. I had survived, but what a close shave!

Our programme was similar to that of the Special Course, but more advanced. The emphasis had changed from leadership to management. Instead of high-ranking military officers, who told us of their exploits, we were fed a diet of business leaders and management gurus telling us how to do our job, and we were not particularly impressed. The police service is unique, and although it should obviously adopt business principles and be managed in a professional manner, it will always require strong leadership in order to deal with the incidents which modern society throws up.

Another of the officers on the course was John Stalker, who is very good company. We shared an interest in sport and keeping fit, and spent time running and in the gym together. When I asked him how he got the scar on his face, he replied that he would normally never say, as he liked people to surmise that he had obtained it in the course of duty. In fact, he revealed, it was an old football injury. It certainly made him look tough, but that was misleading, as I discovered when we ran past the lake at the college during the mating season of the Canada geese that live there. As they advanced on us aggressively to protect their territory, John sprinted the other way as fast as he could, calling out that he was frightened to death of them.

During our six-month stay there were many visits and attachments, one of which was to the United States. We were hosted by the FBI and lodged at their Academy at Quantico, Washington DC, which adjoins the Marine Corps training school and shares some of their facilities,

After we had successfully completed the initiation ceremony of drinking a bottle of tequila, including the worm in the bottom, we were shown to our quarters. We had nothing like them in the United Kingdom. Each of us was given a personalised smart card, which opened the doors and gave access to the dining room, the swimming pool, and – most impressive of all – the computer system.

I already had an interest in computer technology, but the FBI system, designed in-house, was far in advance of anything I had seen, and there is still nothing approaching it in this country. At lessons each of us placed our smart cards in the computer terminals in the desks, and we answered questions by pushing the relevant buttons on the screen. This allowed the tutor to see who got the answers right, and enabled him to rerun part of a course if the class scored poorly on it. At night our room monitor gave us our scores for the day, and advised on remedial programmes for us to catch up. With the aid of this equipment, assessments and appraisals were very objective.

There are 17,000 police forces in the United States, and most are tiny, averaging only seventeen officers each. Most towns and cities have their own; some are scarcely more than a man with a badge and a gun, and the rest of the country is policed by Sheriff's Departments, in much the same way as county forces policed this country forty years ago. There are no common standards of entry, and except in the larger organisations, very little training. Many thousands of American police officers are literally taken off the street, sworn in, and given a badge and a gun. Some of the abuses of power and unprofessional conduct one sees portrayed on the television are all too true. To raise standards, the FBI ran a six-month course for police chiefs.

Quantico was only our base. We visited the FBI headquarters

in the heart of Washington and had the usual photograph taken with the Director. We had a tour of their facility, and again their level of technology impressed me. Their forensic laboratories were state-of-the-art – but they needed to be, as they provided services for many police forces who couldn't afford their own. It surprised me to learn that those which lacked facilities would try to investigate crimes, including murders, without the aid of forensics, which is almost impossible.

We also visited the numerous police forces within the locality of Washington, and were surprised how little contact they had with each other. Indeed, one officer bragged about rolling a body over the boundary to avoid dealing with it.

One night we were taken for dinner to the Gaslight Club, opposite the Russian Embassy. The premises had been used as a speakeasy during the time of Prohibition, and they had retained some of its character. All the guests, men and women, entered the bar via the male urinals. When our host stood in one of the stalls and flushed the handle, a flap opened in the wall behind him, and with the right password the whole urinal rotated to give us entry to a smoke-filled room, pulsating with people and live jazz.

One of our number was a German officer, whom I complimented on his English. He admitted that he had found things difficult when he started the course, adding, 'Ven I came I had to translate every word from English to German and then back to English. Now I even dream in English!' His skills were tested when a man collapsed on the floor of the bar, the worse for drink. Hans knelt by his side and ordered everyone else back, including a man who said he was a doctor. Against all advice he insisted that an ambulance be called. We humoured him by helping carry the drunk downstairs, and waited until a siren wailed up outside the door. A large red fire engine arrived at breakneck speed and hit a fire hydrant, which didn't begin to disgorge its water, but put a huge dent in the vehicle's mudguard. The driver got out, looked at the damage, threw off his helmet and shouted, 'Shit!' His displeasure was not reduced by having this German citizen insist that the drunk leaning against him ought to go to hospital.

That was not the last time we heard such an expletive from a public servant. At five one morning, in the glow of a summer dawn in Washington, our secret service driver knocked a motorcyclist off his vehicle. Bike and rider slid across the wide road in slow motion. Our driver stopped, cupped his head in his hands and also cried, 'Shit!' It seemed that to cause an accident was a sacking offence and could result in huge penalties from the court. We waited tensely as the motorcyclist retrieved his bike and a white box he had been carrying on his knee, which he opened and examined carefully. As he came towards us, without speaking, he displayed the box's precious contents – a cake, which was miraculously undamaged. Then he said, 'Shit, that was close! If you'd squashed that, we'd both have been f—d.' Without another word he left.

Our White House tour was fascinating. We were shown the private rooms and the collection of crockery donated by successive presidents on their departure. Our guide made derogatory comments about the paucity of some of the gifts, indicating that some donors were careful with their money. In the gallery of portraits of former presidents we discovered President Nixon's on the floor, leaned against the wall. We were told that people hadn't decided what to do with him, as he had caused so much embarrassment (on a later visit I saw that his picture was hanging with the others).

Jimmy Carter was in office at that time, and our guides told us he was a workaholic, who started very early in the morning, so that we might bump into him. We did. He was holding a meeting in a basement room, separated from us only by baize-covered room-dividers, and he passed the time of day with us as we walked through, which greatly impressed us.

This was the occasion of my first meeting with a new group of FBI officers who were assembling personality profiles to help solve serial killings, and I continued my relationship with this team for many years to follow. At one stage they even suggested that I might like to join the FBI.

I learned an enormous amount during my first visit to America, and over the six months at the College which benefited me for the rest of my service.

On return to the force I was given charge of the Research and Technology Department, which was a posting I didn't particularly like, as I preferred to be more operational, and I was impatient to move on. My chance came within months, when my colleague in charge of the Discipline and Complaints Department decided to leave. I was assigned to this coveted position by Colin Sampson, who by then had become our Deputy Chief Constable; my appointment sent ripples through the force, as many officers senior to myself had been considered.

The job posed a tremendous challenge. It involved running a team of senior detectives who conducted internal investigations into the criminal activities of police officers, in both our own and other police forces, and dealt with complaints made against the police by members of the public. Some of these complaints do not really deserve the attention that legislation determines they are given, but others are serious and have the potential to undermine public confidence. However, it is reassuring that most of the information about police corruption or criminal activity comes from fellow officers.

One amusing incident involved an officer who was less than five feet tall. He was ribbed mercilessly by his fellow officers, the public and the criminal fraternity. He could not be seen above the traditionally high cell counter, and the canteen staff cruelly offered him a buffet to stand on in order to be able to see the food on offer in the hot containers.

I never met this officer, who had been appointed at a time when political correctness was coming into vogue, and those who were vertically challenged were not excluded from anything. There is an unkind saying in Yorkshire that small people are nasty because 'their arse is too close to the ground and they keep getting gravel in it'. I am not sure if that was true of this individual: however, when he showed his warrant card to try and get into a night club without paying, he was arrested for impersonating a police officer.

Despite his protestations, he was taken into custody, and it was some time before he was able to prove his bona fides. His actions should have been the subject of a disciplinary charge, but he was let go with a warning and a great deal of leg-pulling.

The incident taught me that such a situation should not have been allowed to occur. It was unfair to subject the individual to such barracking, and brought the police service into ridicule. I later reversed some of the most pedantic politically correct policies.

Complaints made against the police by the general public are taken extremely seriously. Investigations are carried out by a high-ranking officer, supervised by the independent Police Complaints Authority – and if the allegation is of a criminal nature, the Director of Public Prosecutions. The process is cumbersome and time-consuming, and yet it has never satisfied those who believe that all investigations ought to be undertaken by an outside agency, rather than by the police service itself. I disagree, as I believe that to bring in outsiders would achieve nothing and lose a great deal. Police investigators arc fcared by their colleagues, as they are trained detectives, have access to all the files and records, and can determine the future of careers. Outsiders would pose much less of a threat, and those countries which employ them do not achieve half the success in routing out the bad apples that we do.

One example from my own experience will help illustrate this point. A small team that I led uncovered institutionalised corruption within a major force within this country. It all began with a disparaging remark made by a detective sergeant to a solicitor, who complained about it. I interviewed the officer, who openly confessed to his indiscretion. When we were done, he asked me when I would return to see him with 'my statement'. I told him I didn't know what he was talking about, to which he replied, 'Oh – we tell our investigators everything. Then they go away and prepare a statement for us, which gets us off the hook.' The colour drained from his face when I told him that I didn't operate that way, and that his confession would be submitted to his Deputy Chief Constable. He was subsequently disciplined for his indiscretion.

One consequence of my actions was a telephone call from a

solicitor on a winter's evening, inviting me to meet him at a motor-way service station. At the rendezvous he handed over two large boxes of documents which he said contained evidence of criminal actions by members of a squad of senior detectives over a number of years. He asked me to deal with them as best I could, since he believed I was 'an honest copper'. Those documents contained information which took twelve people years to investigate and uncovered a long trail of unlawful police activity, much of which had already been the subject of scrutiny by other officers.

The tactics I employed to preserve evidence and obtain con-fessions were at the edge of what was acceptable in those days, and would have not been practised by an outside agency. These included dawn raids on a number of police stations, and threats to arrest officers when I did not have the power to do so. My conclusions from that investigation fundamentally changed the rules of engage-ment between the police and their informants and the tenure of officers on crime squads.

Another interesting case involved a young man and woman from the north-east who had visited Leeds to shop-lift. He had been caught in the act, and the police were called. When the couple were taken to the police station, the detective brought in to supervise the case drew the young woman to one side: he said he fancied her, and that if she was cooperative with him, he would make sure the charges against her boyfriend were dropped. Because she was frightened, she agreed to see him at the time and place he suggested, but she then went home and visited her solicitor, who rang me and told me what had happened.

We met her in York, and gave her a comprehensive briefing about what she should and should not say, to avoid any suggestion of entrapment. We then wired her up with a miniature tape-recorder and radio, and went to the rendezvous to watch. We could hear the girl when she spoke, but we had no means of communicating with her.

The detective arrived on time, and told her to leave her car, as they would go in his to a local country inn. We had told her not to sit next to the door, the bar, the fruit-machine or the juke box.

She chose reasonably well, but we did get some sound interference. After the pleasantries, the officer turned the conversation to the criminal acts of her boyfriend, and asked if she had thought over his earlier offer.

She asked him to remind her of what he had said, and he did, basically saying that he would let the boy off if she would allow him to sleep with her. She procrastinated, asking how she could be sure he would keep his word, and asking if he had the power to do what he promised. He then went on to outline police procedures in detail, breaching the Official Secrets Act more than once.

We waited for them to leave the inn, then confronted him. We showed him our listening and recording device, and she took the microphone out of her handbag for him to see. To give him his due, he didn't attempt to hide his guilt. He was prosecuted for attempting to pervert the course of justice, received a sentence of imprisonment and lost his job. That day – 21 July 1981 – will live in my memory for ever, as it was the one when Ian Botham won the Test Match for England almost single-handed.

In addition to actually conducting investigations, my task was to administer the system and ensure efficiency within the office. I have a passion for reorganising, and simplified the complaints reporting system, more than halving the time officers spent on paperwork. I was the first officer in the service to introduce tape-recorders into general use, years before this became an acceptable practice.

CHAPTER ELEVEN

THE YORKSHIRE RIPPER

By the early 1980s the saga of the criminal known as the Yorkshire Ripper had gripped the entire country. Beginning in 1975, a series of murders in and around Yorkshire had been attributed to the same man: interest in the case was international, attracting journalists and, believe it or not, tourists, from all over the world.

In Yorkshire ordinary citizens were wrapped in fear, not knowing when or where the murderer would strike again. It is difficult to imagine the degree of apprehension that he aroused: the mere fact that he was at large affected the behaviour of the whole community, and it was as if the county were under siege. Secure transport was provided by universities and employers to ferry their people about, and although there was no evidence to suggest that the Ripper had ever attacked a man, even we, the police, were wary when venturing out at night.

The case had engaged all the detectives and many of the uniformed staff within the force, and everyone was desperate to make a breakthrough. The murderer was so-called because of the method he used to kill his victims. He first hit them over the head with a round-headed hammer: we could tell from pathology reports that the same weapon was used on more than one occasion. His next action was to disturb their clothes, uncovering their torsos. Then followed a ritual which grew progressively more violent. In the earliest-known cases he left scratch marks on the body, which we believed were inflicted with either a screwdriver or some form of knife. In the later crimes he mutilated the women's private parts, in one case viciously and violently ramming a large Phillips screwdriver in and out of a young girl's vagina and stabbing her in the breasts twenty-one times. There were obvious similarities with the work of the Victorian murderer Jack the Ripper on the streets of London.

In most murder cases there is some connection between the killer and his victim, the most common being family. This link gives the detective a start-point from which to operate. By identifying a person's relatives, friends and associates, tracing his or her last movements, finding a motive and using the constantly improving techniques of forensic science available, a police officer can normally identify the offender. But murders committed at random, without any of these reference points, are very difficult to solve. There is a myth – perhaps orchestrated by the investigators themselves – about the ability of individuals to solve crimes. Sherlock Holmes does not exist, and never has existed, in the police service. It is the painstaking work of gathering and sifting information which solves crimes.

If all the usual lines of inquiry have been exhausted, you have to broaden your net and look for others. For instance, during a 'normal' murder inquiry you would not contemplate trying to trace the source of the money the victim had in his or her possession; but in the Ripper case this was one line of inquiry which engaged dozens of detectives full-time. In normal circumstances you could not afford to deploy over 200 uniformed officers daily to stop and check every motorist who entered a particular area – but this is what we did during the investigation.

Perversely, when more than one random crime is committed by the same person – and this is not always easy to establish, as killers don't always use the same methods (the Ripper garrotted one of his victims) – your chances of detection increase. We knew early on what kinds of weapons were being used. Tyre marks at the scene of some of the murders helped us identify the type of vehicle the killer had been driving. Witnesses and surviving victims gave us a description of him – bearded and dark-haired. Teeth-marks left on victims' breasts added to his idiosyncrasies.

It may sound as though we had enough information to solve the crime, and by the late seventies we were subjected to enormous criticism for not having made a breakthrough. In reality, we were looking for a needle in a haystack. There were several million tyres of the same type on the roads, and thousands of models of the same vehicle. We had no option but to set about the laborious task of tracing them all. We published a photo-fit description of our suspect on television, on posters, in newspapers, in schools and in factories. We were satisfied that everyone in this country knew roughly what the Ripper looked like, and we followed up every lead brought by this initiative.

Some of the killer's victims were prostitutes, who would have been paid, as such women always seek their money in advance. Few, however, were found with money on their bodies, so we believed that he relieved them of whatever cash they had. Once, when disturbed in the act of murdering a Manchester prostitute, he failed to get her money, and as there had been no report of the crime in the newspapers, he returned to the scene a day or two later to recover the £5 note he had given her. When he couldn't find it, he flew into a rage, took a piece of glass from the window of a disused greenhouse and slashed at her body. With her stomach opened, he pulled out her intestines and rolled her over and over until they coiled round her like a rope.

We found the £5 note secreted in the pocket of her handbag, and set about tracing it. This single line of investigation was the largest of its type ever undertaken in the world. The Bank of England could tell in which run of tens of millions of pounds the note was produced. Their records showed how the run was split into batches and distributed to banks throughout the country. So we knew, for example, that certain banks had received 100,000 of these £5 notes not long before. We directed our attention to banks within the Ripper's hunting ground of Yorkshire and Lancashire and focused on large sums paid out for wages by transport and engineering companies, as by this time we believed – from the oil and grease traces found on victims' bodies – that our man had some connection with those industries. We visited each of these companies and through their records identified the individuals who may have had one of these £5 notes in their wage packets. Then we set about interviewing each employee. Sutcliffe was one of those interviewed; our painstaking work had succeeded, but we didn't know it at the time.

Until the killer was caught, we had no means of knowing whether any murder or assault was one of the series: the criminal might have changed his modus operandi, he might have bought a new vehicle, he might have shaved off his beard, he might have had false teeth made – and someone else might have started to copy his actions. So each attack had to be investigated as an individual crime and either linked or not with the others. The pressure to link became intense, because the media hailed every reported killing of a female as another in the Ripper series. Senior investigating officers found themselves in the position of having to defend not doing what the media told them to do.

Every murder inquiry is co-ordinated by a senior detective, known as the Senior Investigating Officer (SIO), whose responsibility is to set up a murder room, determine lines of inquiry, and direct actions. He or she oversees the evidence collected and decides whether or not to take any further action. If, for example, a body is found in the street, house-to-house inquiries will immediately be made to ascertain if anyone saw the crime, or knew or had any connection with the victim, and to collect any other information which may help. As a matter of course the police establish who was in every house at the time of the murder, who normally resided there, who lived there in the past and who visited the premises, including tradesmen.

The SIO decides how many of these people should be interviewed for elimination. A window-cleaner with convictions for assault would obviously be questioned, and a ninety-year-old, wheelchair-bound woman would not. Resources and common sense shape the SIO's judgement as the web of people connected with a single street may extend to thousands. However, if it subsequently turns out that the murderer had a connection with that street, however tenuous, and the police have not interviewed him, they will be criticised.

In the early days of the Ripper inquiry each murder had its own SIO, with its own murder room and team. As numbers grew, more than one murder would be clustered under an SIO, which complicated matters, as each team tended to be insular, and there was no effective means of cross-referencing information. In 1978 I was tasked with a small team to see if computers could help this process. At that time only IBM were prepared even to consider the task, and then on their own terms. They judged that converting our database to electronic form would take many years and cost millions of dollars. We had to soldier on with our paper-based systems. Today, we all take technology for granted, but what we were asking of the industry twenty-five years ago was cutting-edge. Nowadays I casually use word search on my laptop; in 1978 our investigators had to try and identify patterns and link tiny snippets of information from hundreds of thousands of pieces of paper, taken over a number of years and located in different premises. The task was impossible.

We reorganised ourselves as best we could within these constraints. The ACC Crime, George Oldfield, was appointed in overall command. The murder teams and their files were brought together under one roof, and the massive task of assimilating the information from all the murders into one filing system began manually. We knew this work would never be completed, but we made it a rule that all new information from whatever source should be filed on a common basis and read by a group of senior detectives who, in conjunction with George, would direct action.

After the killer had finally been arrested, it was these officers who bore the brunt of criticism, and to me this was an outrage. The stress killed George, and severely damaged the health of the others. These officers worked eighteen hours a day for months on end. They did not take leave, for fear of missing some crucial piece of information. They became human databases. Yes, they made mistakes – anyone would have – but they were some of the finest detectives I have ever worked with, and should have been recognised as such.

As a force we had tried everything we could possibly think of to help. Under political pressure, the Chief Constable enlisted the support of the murder squad from the Metropolitan Police. This rankled the SIOs, who between them had far more experience than their southern colleagues. Their scepticism was heightened when the London team acted like prima donnas, apparently more interested in the size and quality of their accommodation, and in acquiring lengths of local cloth for suits, than in reviewing the murders. We employed psychiatrists, astrologers, voice and handwriting experts. The latter two became crucial to a line of inquiry which proved to be our downfall.

In the late seventies George began receiving handwritten letters which criticised him for not solving the Ripper case. They chided him for missing a clue, or not including the murder of a particular woman in the series. The author signed himself 'Jack'. In the first instance the letters were thought to be the work of a crank, but they were taken seriously when they started to contain information that was not in the public domain. When they began to include predictions about crimes, which loosely matched later murders in the series, the writer had to be taken seriously.

To ignore him would have been folly, particularly when he started to send tape-recordings of himself talking, toying with George as a cat would with a mouse. After much deliberation, we made a decision to publish most of the tapes and letters. Copies of the letters were placed in national newspapers, and the tapes played on radio and television. 'Jack' had a distinctive type of handwriting, and a Geordie accent which experts placed in a small area of the north-east of England. Teams of officers were dispatched to interview the male population there, and recordings were made of local voices for matching with the voice on the tapes. All suspects brought into the investigation by any other means were screened for voice and handwriting.

This proved our downfall, as the real killer was interviewed and eliminated more than once because of these criteria. In one of these cases an interviewing officer, Andrew Laptew, was so sure that his suspect was the Ripper that he made a special plea to arrest him, but his appeal was ruled out on the ground that the man did not have a Geordie accent.

By then the investigation had grown to colossal proportions. It was, and remains, the largest murder inquiry ever undertaken by a British police force. Hundreds of thousands of people featured in one line of inquiry or another, from having purchased a particular tyre or having been logged entering one of the murder zones. To interview each and every one of them was impossible, so we used certain standards to rule some out. 'Jack's' accent was so easily recognisable that this became the first criterion for retaining or discarding candidates. We could not be half-hearted about this: either we believed that our man was a Geordie, or we did not – and we had to believe that he was. (In the end it turned out that 'Jack' may have been an accomplice of the murderer, but this was never confirmed.)

At the start of January 1981, with exasperation growing all round, I asked the Chief if he would allow me and my team of detectives to take an independent look at the investigation. He was 'giving it some thought' when at last the arrest came. Next morning, when Ron Gregory told a small band of us that a man had been held, there was jubilation in the Oak Room (his office). 'There's only one problem,' he said. 'He doesn't have a Geordie accent.' I jokingly suggested that perhaps we should give him elocution lessons.

Peter William Sutcliffe, a thirty-four-year-old lorry driver from Bradford was arrested in Sheffield on the evening of 4 January 1981 by police officers who were patrolling an area to which prostitutes take their clients. They found him in the company of a prostitute, and noticed that his vehicle tax-disc did not match the numberplate of the Rover in which he and the woman were sitting. After being allowed to relieve himself in the bushes, he was arrested and taken to a Sheffield police station. It later transpired that he had used the need to have a pee as an excuse to dump the ball-peen hammer, secreted up his coat sleeve, with which he intended to kill the girl. When he was allowed to go to the toilet in the police station, he hid his other murder weapons in the system's water-tank. Officers later retrieved them, and forensic examination linked him to the murders. Sutcliffe was subsequently convicted of murdering thirteen women and attempting to murder seven others, and received twenty life sentences in May 1981.

His wife Sonia then made a number of complaints about the way the case had been handled, and in particular about the damage caused to her home and garage in Garden Lane, Bradford. Colin Sampson asked me to conduct an inquiry.

I first saw Sonia, by appointment, at her parents' house in Bradford. Mr and Mrs Szerma, of eastern European stock, were devastated by the arrest of their son-in-law, and had been treated abominably by the media, who had besieged them. One reporter had entered their home by pushing past them, and had stolen family photographs.

The couple received me most courteously, and I struck up such a positive relationship with Mr Szerma – a very gentle person who liked gardening. Sonia came into the room wearing a blue, loose-fitting terry towelling dressing gown, fastened only at the waist with a belt of similar material. She was naked underneath, and her body was partly exposed through the gaping garment. I was embarrassed, and when I told her so, she folded the gown and tightened the belt. I do not think she did this to be provocative: rather, she was so upset that she hardly knew what she was doing.

I found Sonia an articulate woman, and she outlined her complaints against us with some precision. Set against the magnitude of her husband's crimes her grumbles seemed relatively trivial, but I reassured her I would investigate myself.

I never really fathomed Sonia. My later meetings with her took place in her own home. At first we went into the kitchen, where we would sit on buffets in front of the lighted gas cooker with its door open – the only source of heat in the house. I later graduated to the front room, where she would make a great fuss of me, on one occasion asking me if I would accompany her to the cinema. More than once she sat on the floor by my side leaning her arm on my knee. There was never anything untoward between us, and she always addressed me as 'Mr Hellawell'. I believe she just needed someone to trust and confide in. She wrote letters and cards to me for many years, congratulating me on my promotions or seeking help, which I tried to supply. You may believe I cultivated this relationship for an ulterior motive, but that is not true. I had my job to do, but I felt compassion for her and her parents. Partners of criminals are very often unfairly ostracised, and in a case as horrifying as this, the public can be very cruel.

The house in Garden Lane had three storeys. The whole living area was immaculately cared for, even though much of the furniture was threadbare. Sonia was pedantic about order and cleanliness: the contents of drawers and cupboards were set out with military precision, even the worn tea towels were neatly folded.

After Sutcliffe's conviction, other police forces with outstanding murders of young women approached us to ask if they could interview him about their crimes. Colin Sampson, smarting from the criticism we had received at the hands of the media, and conscious that (due largely to political pressure) we had interviewed Sutcliffe for only a short time, and would be embarrassed if he admitted further crimes to someone from elsewhere, asked me to take on this responsibility. 'Make sure that if he admits any further crimes, he admits them to you alone,' Colin instructed me. So began one of the most interesting and challenging experiences of my professional career.

I pulled together a small team of experienced officers who had worked on the inquiry, including Detective Inspector John Boyle, one of Sutcliffe's interviewers.

There were seventy-eight unsolved murders and attempted murders potentially committed by Sutcliffe. By a process of elimination we reduced the number to twenty-two possible offences, twelve within our force area, the remainder outside. To reduce the number still further, we examined each of these in more detail and exercised our professional judgement. Did the place, the time or the type of assault match our man? The ten which did were singled out as probables and reinvestigated, the most likely first.

Tracey Ann Brown was a fourteen-year-old schoolgirl who was savagely attacked at Silsden near Keighley during the evening of 27 August 1975. Miraculously, she survived and was willing to help me. I walked with her over the route she had taken before her assault, from a friend's house to her home. On the way she had been hit over the head a number of times with a ball-peen hammer, which resulted in a fractured skull and caused a depressed bone to touch the dura, the outer membrane of the brain. Tracey told me a man – she was by then certain it was Sutcliffe – had walked up beside her and asked, 'How far have you got to go?' She replied, 'About a mile.'

'That seems a long way to go,' he said. 'Do you have to do it every night?'

He asked her name, and when she told him, said, 'That's nice.' Tracey said he seemed pleasant, and she was not afraid. She described his Yorkshire accent and fairly high-pitched voice. The girl told me that he stopped more than once to kneel down to tie his shoelace, making some excuse, and several times took a handkerchief from his pocket to dry his nose. When she remarked about that, he retorted, 'I'm getting a summer cold.' She remembered nothing more until being roused on some grass and taken to hospital.

The second probable, on 2 March 1979, was an attempt on a twenty-two-year-old student. When I interviewed her in her rooms, she was very nervous and frightened. It was clear that she wished to put the whole matter behind her, and it took some persuading to get her to relive the experience. Her fellow students were willing to help, and I gleaned more information than we had on file.

This girl had been attacked from behind while walking in the grounds of her college, and received three blows to her skull, which caused a compound depressed fracture. The description of the man who assaulted her partially fitted Sutcliffe: the weapon was a hammer with a round head, one inch in diameter. Witnesses also described seeing a dark-coloured Sunbeam Rapier, the type of vehicle owned by Sutcliffe at that time.

The third assault was on a twenty-one-year-old newspaper reporter, who was attacked from behind a few hundred yards from her rural village home on 11 October 1979 (she wishes to preserve her anonymity). Her assailant had neither beard nor moustache, but otherwise matched Sutcliffe. Her injuries included a compound depressed fracture of the skull and four scratch marks to the abdomen. She recalled the attack with great reluctance.

Two of these three crimes were at the top of my list because they were so recent that witnesses would have a clearer recollection. In the other, the conversation closely matched that which Sutcliffe had with surviving victims of offences he had admitted. Other surviving victims added detail, and some of the modus operandi fitted perfectly.

I do not underestimate the trauma these women had suffered, or the pain caused by going back over their terrible experiences. All three had tried to erase the episodes from their minds and just wanted to get on with life. Yet a common feature among the survivors was guilt. It was as if they all thought that they were somehow to blame for what happened to them. Even though none had any reason to feel this, it was something in the back of their minds which came to the surface during our discussions. I thank them again for their courage and fortitude in helping me.

I completed my investigation of the other seven crimes. Parents of the young women who had died were able to add little. These were very distressing meetings as the parents were understandably full of grief. They insisted that I saw their daughters' rooms, which had been left as if the children were still alive, and would one day return. Some were angry with me for not catching Sutcliffe sooner, blaming their daughters' deaths on our omissions. In some ways they were right, and I felt guilty.

In the course of my career I have seen much grief, and I don't think I will ever fully come to terms with it. People say that a policeman must detach himself and grow a hard skin, but I have never been able to do this. I have always felt empathy with sufferers, and shared their grief with them. This has been a burden I have had to carry, and on occasions I have felt unable to take any more.

Bren has borne the consequences, and it has caused friction between us. She worries for me, and has often said that there is little left of me emotionally when I come home from work. I think every police officer faces this likelihood. Most of us can come to terms with losing someone to a terminal illness, but when death is caused by a crime or an avoidable accident, it almost impossible to be reconciled to.

I told Sonia I had been given the task of investigating other crimes which the police thought her husband might have committed. I explained that officers from other forces were anxious to see him, but that I could keep them away. Sonia was most unhappy, saying, 'Peter has *not* done nothing else. He's told the police all he knows.' I stressed he would have to answer questions about these further matters, and suggested that, as she trusted me, it would be best if *I* asked them. She agreed. 'You'll be wasting your time,' she assured me, 'but I'd rather Peter saw you than anyone else. I've already told him about you, and I'll tell him to expect you.'

The scene was set for me to interview one of the most notorious killers in criminal history. He was housed in Parkhurst Prison on the Isle of Wight, which necessitated a long drive to Southampton and a ferry crossing. I travelled with Detective Inspector John Boyle, who had already interviewed Sutcliffe, and our mood was sombre when we approached the gaol for the first time. It was a cold, grey, dark winter's morning, and the Victorian entrance gate looked like Bleak House. We were received by the Governor, who was extremely pleasant, and told us that Sutcliffe was not under any medication, and had been trouble-free. We would conduct our interviews in the Roman Catholic priest's office: it was away from the hub of the prison, and Sutcliffe felt comfortable in the room, where he had many times visited the priest.

The nondescript room, lit by a two-foot-square, barred window five feet from the floor, was small and drab. It was poorly furnished, with an old wooden desk, a filing cabinet and three metal chairs, and there was little on the walls to give a clue about the occupation of its user.

I felt some apprehension as I waited. When Sutcliffe arrived, I saw that he was about 5′ 9″ tall, shorter than I had imagined and fuller in body than photographs suggested. He wore a standard-issue blue, open-necked shirt and denim trousers, with heavy black industrial shoes. He was obviously nervous. I held out my hand to him, which took him aback: he was slow to respond, and when he did, his palm was sweaty but his grip firm. He looked directly at me with his dark, hooded eyes, and I felt fear, hate and revulsion, which I knew I must not show.

I introduced myself and John, whom he didn't seem to recognise at first. 'Sonia's told me about you,' he began. 'She says you're all right.' His voice – higher-pitched and with a more pronounced Yorkshire accent than I expected – cracked when he spoke, and he continually cleared his throat.

I told him we were there to question him about a number of outstanding murders and attempted murders. He responded by saying, 'Look – I know Sonia's told you. I've told you everything. There's nothing else to say, but I'll listen for her sake.'

I beckoned him to sit down, which he did, on the left-hand side of the desk as we faced it. John sat on the right, and I took the chair on Sutcliffe's right. When I offered him one of the mints I always carried with me, he smiled and accepted. I asked him what he found amusing, and he said, 'Is this a bribe? If so, it won't work.' He reckoned I had done my homework, as those mints were his favourite brand of sweets. In fact I didn't know about his penchant for mints, but I shrugged and took the credit.

He thanked me for supporting Sonia 'through her troubles', and seemed quite happy to continue a conversation about his wife, claiming all the time that he had told us everything. I asked him how he could be so sure, as some of the incidents had taken place nearly five years ago. I said jokingly that *I* couldn't remember what happened to me two or three weeks ago – so how could he be confident in his memory?

He changed the subject to myself. Was I married? How long had I been in the service? Was I ambitious? Where did I live, and where had I served? He was fascinated to hear I had worked in

Bradford at the time he was 'active'. He joked that I might have bumped into him when he was killing. When we discussed general matters, he was open, bright and engaging. If I hadn't known of the ghastly crimes he had committed, I would have thought I was talking to an ordinary, reasonable human being.

I asked him what had made him confess when he did, as he had many earlier opportunities. 'God told me,' he said. 'My mission was over.' (At his trial he had tried to use his 'mission from God', to rid the world of prostitutes, as mitigation.) I mocked him gently, pointing out that it seemed strange that the instruction came after he had been caught and his murder weapons had been seized, with human blood and hair traces found on them. He denied that the timing had any significance, repeating that God spoke to him when he was sitting in the police station in Sheffield, but that it might have happened anywhere.

Our first meeting lasted the scheduled hour and went largely as I had anticipated. Each time I approached the subject of other crimes, he clammed up, so I took him into areas where he felt more comfortable. The purpose of the visit was to make contact and build confidence – which we achieved.

We left on good terms with another handshake. His palm was still moist with sweat, but his manner was more confident. When I reached the open air, I felt a huge surge of relief. I didn't sense it while inside, but the meeting had drained me; John felt the same. We went back to our lodgings to plan our next visit. We needed something to get Sutcliffe talking about his actions, and decided to grill him again about the crimes to which he had confessed.

In preparing for the first interview I had acquainted myself with all the medical evidence on the man. There was disagreement between the specialists who had examined him. I read the limited number of publications on 'criminal madness', and these were confusing. The simplest explanation was given me by a psychiatrist, who said that the conduct of serial killers was so far off the scale of normal behaviour that it must be classed as madness. This analysis was consistent with the advice I received over all the years I saw Sutcliffe. Until relatively recently he received no medication: I had to be satisfied that he had full control of his mind, and was fit to plead. I was also interested to know if anything I said to him was causing his health to deteriorate, but I was told not.

Our next meeting began in the same cordial manner, including the handing-over of mints. I told him I was not satisfied with the precision of his memory, and intended to take him through his previously admitted crimes. He was visibly shaken, protesting, 'I've told you everything. I don't want to go over it again.' I insisted, and asked him to recall his earliest crime. His account came almost in the form of bragging. He had been arrested in the early seventies for going equipped to steal. 'Little did they know,' he preened, 'I was going equipped to kill.'

Over the many hours and days of our subsequent meetings I took him laboriously through each confessed crime, often having to remind him of details, and by this means I opened him up to questioning about other matters. The exercise threw up a number of disparities. In one case he said he negotiated 'business' with a prostitute for a sum of £5. In evidence he had earlier claimed that he gave her a £10 note, and that she went into the local pub to change it but never returned. He waited a while, and then followed her in to retrieve his money, but retreated when he met cat-calls and derision. These angered him, and fuelled his hatred of all prostitutes. I discovered that £10 notes had not been issued at the time, and when I told him, he remarked flippantly, 'It just shows – you always have to check.'

He told me he had no sexual feelings for any of the women, and became very disturbed when I confronted him with the admission that he had had intercourse with one woman as she lay moaning and dying. This was during the murder of Helen Rytka in Huddersfield on Tuesday 31 January 1978, when, after hitting her over the head, he stripped her of her clothes, had intercourse and stabbed her five or six times before rolling her body under an asbestos sheet. He also stood astride Patricia 'Tina' Atkinson, and masturbated as she lay dying from the injuries he had inflicted.

It was only when I called into question 'God's mission' of ridding the world of prostitutes that I began to get through to him. The case which first moved him was the murder of Josephine Ann Whitaker, a nineteen-year-old clerk, in Saville Park, Halifax on 4 April 1979. I asked him to justify this as being God's will, and when he didn't reply, I pressed him.

'You shouldn't ask me about her,' he said.

'I must,' I told him. 'If you're so confident, prove it to me.'

He held his head in his hands and said, 'She was the worst. I told God not to make me do it.'

I became authoritative, and positively instructed him to tell me more. He began to talk, as if in a trance.

'She was a nice girl . . . I asked her why she was walking home that late at night, when the Ripper was about, and she confided in me. It was her birthday. She'd fallen out with her mother and been to her gran's. When it struck midnight, she showed me a watch her mother had bought her, and said it was lovely. She was so sorry she'd walked out. She'd make it up to her later.

'I thought she was a mistake and kept my hammer up my sleeve. God and I began to argue about whether she was a prostitute or not. I was having this conversation with God while I was walking. God was telling me to kill her. I was telling God He was wrong. God told me I oughtn't to question His wisdom. He said I'd be struck down.

'I hit her on the head, and she fell down. She cried out and whimpered, "Please, please don't hurt me." I had the hammer ready to hit her again, but I couldn't do it. God was screaming at me, "*Kill her! Kill her!*" I was shouting out loud at God that I couldn't.'

As he told the story, Sutcliffe became very animated and distressed, frequently looking upwards, as if to heaven, and downwards, as if at a body. After a pause for breath he went on:

'I was yelling, "Don't make me do it!"

God shouted, "*Are you questioning my authority?*"

"I can't kill her. She's a nice girl."

"She's the worst. She's the Devil. This is the Devil at work! He's there with you! He's testing you! He's making you doubt that this is My will. This is your biggest test. Either you believe me, or you live with the Devil."'

It was then, said Sutcliffe, that he struck the fatal blow. When the girl was dead, he mutilated her body, causing unspeakable damage to the sexual organs. He said this was due to his anger. He just drove the screwdriver and other weapons he used in and out of her. He said he was out of control, and just kept on and on, shouting at God, and crying with rage.

The effort of reliving that dreadful crime, and the ordeal he had inflicted on the child, left Sutcliffe drained. We listeners felt the same: merely to listen to that outburst was a horrifying experience. But I told the prisoner that his judgement had been right. The girl was innocent, and he had taken away her life in a most savage manner. He broke down, sobbing out that if she was not a prostitute, he was a monster, and he had not done God's work, but that of the Devil.

I ended the interview session there and then, partly so that I could escape, but mainly to let the horror play on Sutcliffe's mind. Evidently it did: he did not sleep for many nights, and cried out to God more than once, 'You made me do it!'

He was never relaxed with me again, always fearful that I would ask him more about Josephine Ann Whitaker. I alluded to her, but put pressure on him by making him relive some of his other repugnant acts.

How could he justify stabbing a long screwdriver into the eye of Jacqueline Hill, a university student in Leeds, in November 1980? I asked him. He was visibly shocked and replied, 'Because I couldn't stand her looking at me. I was surprised how easy it was until it reached the back of her skull. There was no blood – only pus.'

I felt sick, as I often did in his company. Sometimes he showed anger rather than remorse – as when he justified virtually drawing and quartering Vera Evelyn Millward on some waste ground in Manchester one evening in May 1978. 'The filthy bitch, she deserved it,' was all he said. Evil permeated his whole body.

During his low points I introduced my priority cases one by one. 'I know what you're doing,' he would say, 'there are no more.'

After some time he cleverly moved position. 'Look, Mr Hellawell,' he wheedled. 'I trust you. If you say I've done some more, I must have, and I'll admit what you want. I just don't remember.'

This was clearly unacceptable, and he knew it. I was searching for the truth, not concessions. I questioned him over and over about Tracey Brown, asking him to explain why she was convinced that he was her assailant. After hours of pressure he confessed that he had tried to murder her.

Once I had achieved this breakthrough, he recalled the incident with remarkable clarity: he told me where he parked his car, he remembered what Tracey had been wearing, and remarked on her ample breasts. He said he had a cold and kept wiping his nose; he bent down to tie his shoes as a guise to remove his hammer from his sleeve, and he explained how, believing she was dead, he threw her over a fence, which he could describe in detail, on to the grass where she was found.

His recollection was no less clear after his admission of the second probable on my list, the attempted murder of the student. He had used the car which witnesses described, and joked that he had tried to escape down a dead-end street, and had to turn round and retrace his route. He showed no remorse at all for either of these crimes, adopting a very matter-of-fact approach. He even tried – for my benefit – to recreate the sound made when a hammer strikes a skull. 'It's impossible when they're standing up. I tried that at first, but it won't kill them. You've got to get their head on the ground to smash it.'

The subject obviously fascinated him. 'It surprised me how different skulls are. The black ones are much thicker, and I knew I had to hit them with all my strength. I hit that one in Leeds [Marcella Claxton, in May 1976] on the head eight times with a hammer, and she just turned and asked me, "What was that?"'

He told me that he had intended to kill a woman for a long time before he actually did. He said that it took a lot of bottle. He joked that once he used a bag of stones to strike a woman, and it had no effect. He said he hit her hard, and couldn't understand why she hadn't dropped. It was after this incident that he decided to use a hammer. He was adamant that he didn't wish to cause the women pain, and that is why he killed them before mutilating their bodies. He carried out the mutilations as a warning to other women not to become prostitutes.

He said he grew in confidence each time he was stopped or interviewed by the police and they took no action. That was why he was convinced that God was on his side – but he agreed that if he had *not* been undertaking God's mission, he was evil, and ought to be put to death for what he had done.

He denied any knowledge of the author of the 'Jack' letters and tapes. We believed that on at least one of the killings he had an accomplice, but he would never admit this. A lady who ran a transport café in the north-east told us she was certain that Sutcliffe frequented her premises in the company of a man with a Geordie accent, who we thought may have been the accomplice. But Sutcliffe denied ever being in the café, and we tried unsuccessfully to trace the second man.

Try as I might, and certain as I was that Sutcliffe had committed other crimes, he clammed up. He told me that after his two further confessions Sonia remonstrated with him for not telling *her*. She said he had betrayed her trust.

After a number of years he was moved to Broadmoor Hospital, where I visited him one Christmas. Before I left he gave me a Christmas card. I had a number of official West Yorkshire Police cards in my briefcase, so I wrote 'Best Wishes' on one and signed my name. The card was spotted by an unscrupulous nursing officer, who sold the story to a local newspaper man, who in turn sold it on to a national. Chester Stern, a former police officer, was the journalist who received it, and he asked me if it was true. The story made the front page headline 'Police Chief Sends Ripper Christmas Card', which inflamed the public. To be fair to Chester, he did accurately reflect my reason for handing the card over.

I continued to see Sutcliffe until I retired from the police service, but I did not expect any further confessions. One final ploy I used in trying to break his silence was to participate in a television documentary about his surviving victims. This angered him, because of his paranoia about the media, to which he believed I would never speak. I hoped the programme would provoke him into confessing to a police officer from another force, purely to show me up as inept – but no such luck.

Some women are fascinated by notorious criminals. Sutcliffe bragged about the number of women who wrote to him in prison, sent him presents, visited him and offered to marry him. He clearly basked in their attention, showing me photographs of each latest admirer. I used one of these women to keep me informed of his moods and his thoughts. She showed me copies of his letters, relayed conversations she had with him, and introduced to him ideas I had fed her – but all to little avail. Whenever I mentioned Sonia, his mood would turn serious, and even after they were divorced her name would bring him up with a start.

Few people have the opportunity to get close to a serial killer, and perhaps the majority of us would not wish to. 'What's it like?' I am often asked. The answer is, 'It's different.' You look into the eyes of a multiple murderer who places no value on human life. You cringe at some of the things he tells you, and could cry out at others. Yet you must not show your emotions, as you need him to trust you implicitly, trust you in such a way that he will tell you his innermost secrets, knowing the consequences will be a lifetime behind bars. To achieve this trust, you cannot be false or superficial. He must be certain you will act upon what you say, and deliver what you promise (in my case, a degree of support for his wife). A bond develops between you – not a brotherly one, but a unique one, between a person who is sworn to uphold the law and one who has broken it.

CHAPTER TWELVE

LEEDS

In the spring of 1981 I was invited to become Divisional Commander in Leeds. I had enjoyed my work in the Discipline and Complaints Department, but pride at taking over the premier division in the force meant that I had no regret leaving.

Leeds considers itself to be the second city in England, and at that time it had a dynamic leader of the council who was determined that the importance of the place should be recognised. He attracted pop concerts, beer festivals, sporting and other events, and created a twenty-four-hour city, which meant many challenges for policing beyond the norm. I also worked more closely with local politicians than I had before, and sometimes I had to rein in their aspirations because I knew we could not cope – for instance when they planned two major events in the city on the day of a Leeds United home game.

At this time we took the controversial step of charging the council for the additional cost of policing commercial events. We decided to do this when we learned that the council charged organisers for their services: if they exacted fees for, say, street cleaning or erecting barriers, why should policing be free?

Public order was a major issue in Leeds at that time. Marauding and drunken football fans would invade the city after matches and cause havoc. This provoked large-scale disorder, causing fear and anxiety for ordinary citizens, many of whom would even boycott the town. Local newspapers were highly critical of the police for allowing this to happen – and I found this frustrating.

I have always enjoyed being out on the streets with my officers, and began working Friday and Saturday evenings to become more involved. I usually returned to work at about 8 p.m., visited the control room to get a flavour of the number and type of incidents we were handling; walked across the city to the cells, under the town hall – which bore the hallmarks of a Victorian prison – to check what prisoners were housed there, and then returned to Millgarth to parade with the night-duty officers at 10 p.m., after which I would ask if any officer would volunteer to walk out with me.

Fortune shone on me on my first night out, when I was able to get my hands dirty by arresting a man for throwing a brick through a plate-glass shop window and running off with a violin and a mouth organ. It was pure theatre. My colleague and I heard the sound of breaking glass and ran to the area, where we found the shattered window and a trail of blood, which led us to the hapless criminal who subsequently received a suspended prison sentence for his trouble. My participation went down well in the division, as it was rare for the boss to become so involved.

Another night I arrested a man for throwing a beer glass into a group of young people. Fortunately it smashed on the ground without causing serious injury, but the young man, who was the worse for drink, became extremely abusive, swearing and prodding me as he tried to evade arrest. When I got hold of his arm to restrain him, he punched me in the chest. I pushed him into a shop doorway, grasped his throat with one hand and told him that if he didn't stop, I would drop him where he stood. That was the way we used to deal with this type of person in the Borough days, but things had changed. When the duty inspector arrived on the scene to find me man-handling the youth, he whispered, 'We can't do that now, Sir. Leave him to me.' The man was arrested and charged, and we heard nothing more about him – but I could have been the subject of a public complaint, which would have caused amusement back in my old department.

I was the only ACPO (Association of Chief Police Officers) officer on duty one early afternoon when the control room inspector notified me that a police officer had been shot in the centre of Leeds. For the moment that was all he knew, having received a call from a member of the public. The tragic details then began to filter through as other police officers arrived at the scene of the crime, directly opposite Leeds Parish Church.

John Speed, one of my officers, had been shot dead. Another, John Anthony Thorpe, had been shot and wounded so seriously that he never really recovered from his injuries. The gunman had made his escape on foot, firing further shots at another police constable, who gave chase.

I visited the scene of the murder and spoke to the officers there, who gave me more details. They said there was no apparent reason for the man's actions: there had been other people in the street, and John Speed and his partner were on foot when the man suddenly started shooting at them. John fell first. Then his colleague went down, and when he tried to crawl into cover, the gunman came up to him to finish him off. It sounded horrific – just like a gang-land shooting on the streets of Chicago, only this was Leeds. I went to the hospital where the two officers had been taken. Even though John Thorpe's condition was critical, the doctors told me that he had a reasonable chance of recovery, but I could not see him because he was still being operated upon. I met his relatives, who drew some comfort from knowing he was still alive.

I then met Judith Speed, who was completely distraught. Later in the day I went to her home to offer her more support. It is very strange what grief and shock can do. She was ironing some of her husband's police shirts, at the same time as preparing fish fingers, peas and chips for her two children, who were only just old enough to realise that Daddy was not coming home. I felt intensely sad, especially when she showed me their bedroom, where, on the pillow of John's side of the bed, lay the cards which the youngsters had painted for their father, for his birthday the next day.

The murder investigation lasted a number of years, without success. All suspects were eliminated, and inquiries among informants drew a blank. Then in the nineties, a man named David Grisewith was shot dead in a gunfight when police tried to stop him in his motor car. Ballistics matched his weapon with the one which killed John. He was a mechanic with no previous convictions. To all intents and purposes he was a law-abiding citizen, but in fact he was a cold-blooded killer whose previously unblemished record showed how skilfully he had evaded the law.

There were also some comical moments. One lunch-time I was asked to visit the bar to see one of my male officers who was reported to be 'acting strange'. I arrived to find him decked in a flowery gown, with high-heeled shoes and a handbag. He approached me and said, 'I know you will understand, Sir.'

'I like the dress,' I told him, 'but the bag and shoes don't match.' This clearly offended him, as he ran out of the room without another word. I thought the matter closed until we received a telephone call from the French police telling us that the officer, still in the same attire, was at Orly airport in Paris, refusing to pay for the breakfast he had just eaten, on the grounds that 'God doesn't pay'. He was treated for his illness – or was he? Years later I confronted him, dressed in hot pants, in Leeds market, where he told me he was 'blending into the crowd', as he was on pick-pocket patrol.

At that time I had dealings with another male officer, who was arrested for stealing women's clothes. When he told me he was a cross-dresser, I asked him why he didn't use his wife's garments, and he replied, 'She has no taste, Sir.' A third male officer was discovered, accompanied by another man, in full evening gown in the front seat of a Rolls-Royce, being driven down Park Lane in the heart of London. There was little we could do about his activities, as he was off duty and breaking neither the law nor the discipline code.

One holiday while we were living in Leeds, Samantha surprised us by saying she wished to join the police cadets. We encouraged her to stay on at school to complete her degree and qualify as a lawyer, her aspiration from the age of twelve. She told us that her mind was made up and she would do as I had done, and take her degree in her own time, which she later did.

*　　*　　*

For years all else had taken second place to the Ripper inquiry. More than a third of our officers had been engaged on the investigation, and many of them had been obliged to live away from home. Once the case was over, they had to be reintegrated into the normal pattern of work. This became a major issue for the force, and I don't think we realised the magnitude of the task. One trouble was loss of earnings. People had lived up to the overtime payments they were receiving: some constables had been taking home more pay than their superintendents, and when the extra money dried up, several officers found themselves in financial difficulties. Some, in very bad taste, had named their house extensions after one of the Ripper's victims.

Claims that we had bungled the four-year inquiry affected us all. People give a police officer a hard time after a report of some indiscretion, but this condemnation was much more widespread, as public fear had been so strong. Almost everything we did met with criticism, and officers had to bear snide and cruel comments, which added to their burden.

The Ripper inquiry also acted to my personal detriment, for the Home Secretary announced that he would ensure there were no internal promotions to the highest ranks within the force. This precluded me from applying for a vacancy of Assistant Chief Constable, and caused a blazing row between my Police Authority and the Home Office. The chairman of the Authority apologised to me, and promised they would make amends as soon as they could.

An ACC was appointed from another force: he proved himself perfectly capable of doing the job, and went on to become a Deputy Chief Constable (DCC) elsewhere. Nevertheless, I was upset at not having been allowed to compete. I would never complain if I was beaten in a fair fight, but to be excluded for political reasons was galling.

My disappointment didn't last for long. Within a year I was approached by two senior members of the Police Authority who said that the post of DCC was to become vacant and they would like me to apply for the job. I was flattered, but told them that I didn't think the Home Office would allow them to advertise for other than substantive ACC. They said they would try as they wished to make amends. Within days they came back to me and apologised for failing at the first hurdle. My Chief Constable, Colin Sampson, would not support me, as he wished them to promote Peter Nobes, an existing ACC, and would block any attempt they made to put me forward. I told them that I thought Peter was far better qualified for the job than I was. He was duly appointed, and ironically I got the vacancy he created, through a proper interview procedure.

The Ripper case did provide me with one benefit. During a visit to the FBI Academy in Quantico to lecture on serial killers, I was approached by a senior officer of the Los Angeles Police Department (LAPD) to ask if I would be interested in an exchange with him. For several months during 1981 my whole family exchanged homes – and jobs – with the District Commander of North Hollywood.

Our temporary home was in Wortser Avenue, Studio City, where all the major film studios are located. We took some time to acclimatise to the intense heat – well over 100 degrees – and to the house, which was an open-plan bungalow. We discovered that many of our neighbours were recognisable film stars, which surprised us, as we thought they all lived in mansions protected by guards and high walls. Several of my police staff acted, as, unlike in Britain, they were allowed to pursue other employment. My millionaire deputy had a number of law practices, and one street officer was flown to work each day from his fruit farm 200 miles north of the city.

Policing is by and large the same all over the world, the main difference in LAPD being the excessive number of murders and sexual assaults, which in Los Angeles alone annually exceeded the number for the whole of the United Kingdom. Hollywood had more than its fair share, as it was populated by budding starlets, some of whom were extremely vulnerable when, to make ends meet, they became involved in porno movies and the escort business.

When I arrived, LAPD rank-and-file officers were holding a 'blue out' – a work-to-rule, their dissatisfaction being largely over pay and having to provide their own guns and body armour. I was invited by the local Teamsters' Union leader, who represented them, to a presentation prepared by a public relations company outlining their case against the Mayor. We were shown a fifty-second film of death and carnage, with a sickly American male voice dubbed on to it which said, 'When you're in trouble, who do you turn to? The LAPD! When the chips are down, who can you rely on? The LAPD! When you need a friend, who's always there? The LAPD! Now we need your help: we need a friend – but those people who are not prepared to support us, go f—k yourselves!' The long-legged PR woman then said, 'Now I'll show you guys the right one.' She certainly gained our attention.

The film actors' union was also picketing the studios for improved conditions, and it was a great pleasure to visit the lines on a morning and speak with some of the most famous actors in the world. During our stay we paid social visits to some of them, including John Travolta and James Garner.

Other memories of Los Angeles include eating out, as people rarely prepare their own food; cycling most places; qualifying on firearms and pursuit driving; appearing on a day-time television programme where both female and male callers inquired about my marital status; the joy of our children. We all liked our stay but not one of us would wish to live that life.

CHAPTER THIRTEEN

ASSISTANT CHIEF CONSTABLE

Assistant Chief Constable (ACC) is the first Chief Constable rank, and an appointee is not an 'assistant' to the Chief Constable: this may seem to be splitting hairs, but it has some significance. The Chief Constable may have many assistants, but for appointments, promotions and discipline ACCs are in exactly the same position as he is.

Colin Sampson congratulated me immediately after my appointment and gave me a clear brief of what was expected of me. His first priority was to rebuild the image of the force and shed the negative impression the Ripper inquiry had caused. He gave me a portfolio that included Complaints and Discipline, which I knew well, and a new role of Public, Community and Media Relations. He announced this at the next Police Authority meeting, and added that he had asked me to improve the image of the force. The Press, picking this up, quickly dubbed me 'the image man'.

I felt uncomfortable with this title for a very personal reason – my eyes. Although I had undergone a number of operations to redress the squint, none had been fully successful, and I was still very self-conscious. I felt confident in small groups but did not wish to appear in front of the media. I therefore booked an appointment with an ophthalmic surgeon and had the sixth operation on my eyes, which fortunately righted the squint and increased my self-confidence immeasurably.

Within days of my eye operation I had a health scare. I experienced severe pain in my left hand, which I favour for most activities, writing included. When I reached the stage at which I could no longer hold a pen, I visited a specialist, who insisted that he should operate on me within twenty-four hours, as he had found a worrying growth on my ligaments. Thankfully the operation was successful and I have had no further trouble.

My office, close to that of the Chief, was rather grand. I had my own parking-bay in the garage, my car was washed daily, and I had use of the executive toilet. I replaced the modern furniture in my room with some in keeping with the style of the building, which was completed in 1914, and borrowed a few beautiful paintings from the local art gallery, for which I thank them. I like to be comfortable with my surroundings.

I was extremely fit and trained daily with two dear friends, Peter Nobes, the DCC, and another ACC, John Domaille. Peter is now sadly dead, and John's athletic career was curtailed by heart attacks in later life – but at that stage we were all still highly competitive. The three of us would run at lunch-times; Peter was overweight, but had enormous courage and would battle for three miles or so before we left him to carry on for another seven. John and I were both competing in half and full marathons at the time.

At the end of Peter's stint there was one particularly steep hill which used to tax him severely. There we would ask him for decisions on all manner of things, knowing that he didn't have the breath to ask us his usual searching questions. He soon got wise to us, and told us he would answer no questions on the hill. After our run John and I would work out in the gym for half an hour or so; my routine included three sets of twenty sit-ups on an inclined board, three sets of twenty press-ups, and some weights. Peter would often cycle on the machine, and he always said, 'There's more of me left on the floor of the gym than I carry about.' I do miss him.

My period as an ACC was also productive for Bren, in that a business she had created in the 1970s was booming. It had begun on holiday in France, when a person we met through our children playing together said that his ability to expand was limited by the size of his factory. Jumping in, I volunteered Bren as the person to help him out. She, justifiably, gave me a withering look, as we had not discussed the subject at all; but after our holiday the friend rang to ask if she really would like to take on some of his work. We had talked the idea over in the meantime, and she had warmed to it, so she told him she would have a go.

The job was assembling printed circuit boards for the security industry, and Bren recruited her first employee through the local newspaper. She was overjoyed with her first weekly wage of £5, but over the years her earnings rose to a level far above my salary as an ACC, and her income afforded us a lifestyle not available to others in my position. With it came envy, particularly over the trappings of wealth such as Porsches and house extensions.

Neither Bren nor I have ever been envious of others' wealth or achievements. We have both worked hard: we have never frittered away our money on meals, cigarettes or drink, and we have spent modestly on holidays, camping and caravanning for the most part. We put our money into our house and family. A friend says that envy is 'the national disease', and we know what he means. Bren was wiped off the road in the mid-eighties by a lorry in her Porsche, and we have never owned such a vehicle since, but that image of us is still perpetuated by the media today. I believe that all is possible in life, providing you are prepared to go out there and work for it. Our society offers more equal opportunity than most in the world, and we ought to be proud of that and those who toil to take advantage of it.

The role of an ACC is radically different from that of a divisional commander. I left behind the operational work which I enjoyed so much, and became more involved in shaping the long-term policy of the force. The days were extremely full, but their end didn't bring the satisfaction which I had felt in Bradford and Leeds.

Our day began at about eight when we received by phone – the Internet hadn't been conceived then – a round-up of the previous twenty-four hours' activity from our staff. We had on average a murder a week, and my colleagues would need to know the stage of the inquiry and its cost on a daily basis. I would be updated on complaints and the progress of internal investigations. I read all the Press cuttings, organised any response where policy was involved, and undertook interviews and media briefings when necessary. It was clear to me that journalists had their own agenda, for they would print half-truths or inaccurate stories without justification. I worked hard with editors and reporters to build trust in order to get our point across, and lessened their negative impact. Good relationships are essential and clear lines of communication necessary between a large public-sector organisation and the media, but neither can be in the other's pocket.

All the information on the day's stories was brought to the table of the Chief Constable's morning meeting, held at 9 a.m. in the Oak Room, which was part of the Chief's office. These gatherings were often testy affairs, as the Chief would blame me for any adverse criticism, repeating, 'I *told* you to Bobby the Press, so get on with it.' During my time in Leeds I had built up a solid relationship with editors and journalists through informal lunches held under Chatham House rules – whereby conversations are not repeated – and they never let me down. In my new role I drew upon these contacts, who several times paid me back by consulting me before running a story, and then publishing my response faithfully.

Reporters will always have their sources. Often information comes from inside an organisation, leaked by people who hold a grudge against it. Colin used to get really cross about this, and whenever the Press reported something which clearly came from inside, he instructed me to 'find the mole'. This became a bit of a joke, and people would accuse others of being the mole – so when I found a dead one in the road outside my house, I had it stuffed and displayed it on my desk, with an engraved plaque proclaiming, 'The West Yorkshire Mole'. The Chief Constable saw it, but didn't appreciate my sense of humour.

Nor was he amused when I entered the morning meeting with a ten-foot pole under my arm, as a reaction to his previous day's announcement that we should all carry silver-topped walking canes, since these befitted the high office we held. 'But,' he had warned us, 'don't waste any of your money on one yet. I'm going to buy one and try it out.' He did the same with other items of clothing and equipment, including a silver whistle, a Belcher chain, and brown instead of regulation black gloves. In reality he intended that only he should sport these affectations, but he sought to pacify his conscience by pretending that we would too.

When Colin was an ACC, he was described as the 'First Assistant', and when he was made Deputy, he recreated this title for Peter. I too was honoured with the role, part of which was to stand in for the DCC, but within a short time it became clear that I was no longer in favour. One of my colleagues, recognising Colin's need to be needed, stepped into the void I had created. I never played up in such games, but this man would pretend to support Colin in whatever he did: he would even go and seek his advice on a subject he had already mastered, to 'keep in his good books'. If he had ever overheard the derogatory way in which the sycophant talked about him, and realised the contempt in which he held him, he would surely have treated the man quite differently. His behaviour taught me a salutary lesson: be aware of your own weaknesses as well as those of others, and recognise when someone is exploiting them.

The media were always at the forefront of my mind, but discipline and complaints and community relations took up most of my time. To improve the latter, we pioneered courses and ad hoc sessions aimed at bringing the police into closer contact with people from ethnic backgrounds and minority groups. The meetings were often highly charged, but overall beneficial. Britain was dealing with the aftermath of the Brixton Riots, when mistrust between the police and the community in London was at its height, and the tensions spilled over into the worst disorder we had seen for decades.

Almost all of us recognised that we had to change, but many officers were racist through and through. A former Borough colleague always said that he hated 'the black bastards' and boasted of a close relationship with the National Front. One of our trainers was disciplined for describing an equal-opportunities lesson as a 'be-kind-to-Pakis' session; but we persevered in the classroom and on the streets. I knew the complaints system through and through, and continued with the reform I had previously set in train. In the short time I did this job we increased productivity and reduced our overheads. We were seen as a leading force in this regard, and as a guest lecturer at the Police College I began to teach investigators from all other forces in the country.

The Chief also set up a new committee to better acquaint the Police Authority with complaints and the procedure for dealing with them. This was pioneering work, objected to by other Chief Constables, who felt we were telling the Authority too much, but it soon became common practice in all forces.

I felt part of a good team, and we generally gelled together well under Colin's leadership. We began to make a difference in the force, and with experience I became more confident in interviews. I was thrown in at the deep end quite early when I had to face a battle-hardened solicitor on television about the number of injuries caused when mounted officers had ridden into a crowd of disorderly young men after a football match. I just said what had happened, and it seemed to work, because afterwards she commented, 'At least you told the truth, and that was difficult to contradict.'

As my confidence grew, I felt able to joke with the film crews, one of whom did a *Vox Pop* on bad language on the streets of Wakefield. In a pre-recorded interview in my office I was asked, 'What are your views of the bad language which seems to be commonplace on our streets?', and I replied, 'I think it's f—ing awful.' Until they realised I was joking, the crew didn't know how to react (needless to say, that sentence was not broadcast, except to themselves in their Christmas 'out-takes'). My riposte broke the ice and helped us reach a better understanding, which paid dividends when I was under the spotlight over more serious issues.

CHAPTER FOURTEEN

THE MINERS' STRIKE

Our reforms virtually came to a full stop with the Miners' Strike of 1984. During their previous stoppage in 1972 the miners had forced the Government to back down, and the police had devoted much time and money to ensuring that this could not happen again. Twelve years on, we were prepared for virtually anything. Gone were the dustbin lids and home-made shields we had used to ward off missiles; in were flame-proof overalls, steel-capped boots, long and short shields, support teams of police-trained medics and fire fighters. Also in place was a national mobilisation scheme to which each force committed 10 per cent of its resources – over 12,500 officers – and a centre in London to command them.

Suitable premises were identified in schools, public buildings and drill halls to house this substantial mobile force, with stockpiled rations to feed them. Furthermore, we had developed a national intelligence network, using Special Branch and the intelligence agencies to gather evidence on dissidents. The Government knew of our plans, and the Prime Minister, Margaret Thatcher, was determined to use our capability to smash the strike when it came. The miners were lambs to the slaughter.

As on the previous occasion when I had been involved in such a conflict, I had mixed emotions. Most of the miners were honest people who were worried about the future of their industry, and they were about to come up against a force whose power they could not really imagine.

We were fortunate in that we were not the first region to be targeted, and could learn from the mistakes of others. This also gave us time to build up closer relationships within our mining communities. We put more constables out into those areas, organised sporting events through schools, and – of all things – church services on road safety. This was the first occasion I spoke from the pulpit, and Bren said I missed my vocation – I ought to have been a vicar.

When our turn came, we were prepared. We had convinced the miners that they had nothing to fear from us if they abided by the rules of engagement. We had cautioned them against a small group of vicious activists who would try to use the strike for their own ends, and we had sought their help in weeding out the professional troublemakers, as they would only damage the legitimate cause.

We decided to exclude officers from the Metropolitan Police from our area as they had, deservedly or not, an appalling reputation on the ground. There were stories of them burning £10 notes in front of the impoverished miners, urging them to 'stay out' in order to be able to 'burn more of this'. Our officers were only too willing to share the contents of their 'doggy bags' with the miners, but food had to be left, rather than handed over, so as not to hurt their pride. At Christmas we sent our force band on to the picket lines, and presents were left under the makeshift trees for the miners to collect for their children. Through these and many other initiatives we avoided some of the carnage which occurred elsewhere.

I do not wish to romanticise the event. Many police officers and miners were injured both physically and mentally by their experiences. Some poor souls who decided to break the strike lost everything: they were bombarded by menacing telephone calls, severely beaten and had their homes burnt to the ground. The anarchists succeeded in pelting the police with potatoes in which razor blades had been embedded, and throwing nails and petrol bombs into the path of police vehicles, ambulances and fire tenders to halt their progress. Our tactics of encouraging the miners and the police to have pushing matches, partly to relieve tension on both sides, backfired: we were lucky that no one was crushed to death, as the power of hundreds of strong men pushing each other in a reverse tug of war is awesome.

The strike threw up some interesting constitutional issues. It confirmed the power of a Chief Constable to deploy his resources wherever he chose – in this case outside the area of his own force – on activities which were against the wishes of his Police Authority. It confirmed the statement by the House of Lords, in a case brought by a man called Blackburn against the Commissioner of the Metropolitan Police many years previously, which said, 'A Chief Constable is answerable to the law and God' – pretty heady stuff, which has always got up the noses of politicians who would like to control the police. Having said that, local politicians were not best pleased with us, and we also managed to offend the Prime Minister by politely refusing her request to visit our command centre in London. This was a brave stand to take against Margaret Thatcher, who was used to getting her own way. She made her displeasure known, but the Chief Constable in charge held his resolve because he considered that such a visit would seen as partiality towards her government, and might upset the delicate balance we try to maintain in such situations.

I was later told by one of Mrs Thatcher's Cabinet colleagues that she was livid, demanding, 'Who do these Chief Constables think they are?' She suggested that she should bring in her generals to run the police, but luckily this was impossible. My colleague was punished by not receiving the knighthood which in normal circumstances would have been his. Police independence in this country sets us apart from all other similar forces throughout the world, which ultimately have to act on behalf of their governments. Successive Home Secretaries have been frustrated by their inability to direct the police, but they will lose more than they gain if they take away its operational freedom.

No one gained from the strike. The miners had to capitulate, and their livelihood was taken away from them for ever as one coalfield after another closed down. Families were split beyond reconciliation, brother hated brother, fathers despised sons. The relationship between the police and the mining communities was damaged for generations. The way in which the police had to operate was inconsistent with a community-based organisation: we tried to be fair and equal, but we operated with all the power and might of a military force.

Sitting in a hard-skinned Range Rover on the top of a pit heap at dawn, commanding a massed army of police officers in riot gear, facing the 'enemy', talking about 'sterile zones' and 'winning ground' was anathema to me. Equally, separation from the public, and an ability to win by sheer might of numbers, affected the attitude of the police officers involved. 'Waiting to engage the enemy' and being ready and eager to 'break a few heads' are concepts against all the ethics of the British police, and not the type of experience I would have wished on them. Many young officers were so influenced by their experience that it affected the way they dealt with other people.

The media were anxious to gain inside knowledge of the way we organised ourselves for this major event, but they were frustrated by the service, whose consensus was to refuse them any access and brief them post-event. This led to the media taking a negative attitude to the police and siding with the strikers, who were only too happy to engage with them.

After a while I convinced my Chief that there was benefit in giving the media better access, even though there was a potential risk. He agreed, and many television companies bid for the opportunity. Granada TV won the contract, even though it was regarded as an enemy of the police because of less than flattering previous documentaries. I thought if Granada came out in our favour, a report would have more influence than one from a team who generally backed the police. I therefore briefed reporters and cameramen about our strategy and the problems we were facing. I asked them to film the strike from a police perspective and gave them all the access they required, with the proviso that they gained approval from each officer before filming him.

Our strategy was simply to uphold the law, supporting those

who wished to work and allowing those who wanted to strike to do so within the bounds of the law. This policy brought us into conflict with each side, as the Government wished us to smash the strike and lock the strikers up, whereas the unions wanted us to support the strike and arrest the 'scabs' who broke their ranks.

The miners' unions were well organised, and operated on a cell network, individuals being briefed on a need-to-know basis only. Information about targets and tactics was passed down the chain of command using secret codes. Different rendezvous would be chosen each night for large groups of miners to assemble, and from the collection-points they would be transported to the chosen pits, individuals never knowing which these were until they arrived. The organisation was very professional and difficult to infiltrate, and in the early days we were often caught unawares. However, as we turned informers within the union ranks, and developed a network of spotters at strategic points throughout the country, we were able to anticipate the strikers' actions and mobilise our forces in advance.

The police were divided into self-contained operational units of twelve, each with a driver, a first-aid officer and a team leader. Every team had its own identification number and call-sign, as well as a uniquely numbered personnel-carrier, which could be identified from air or ground. Teams would be moved to forward posts during the night, and then to their final locations when we learned where they were needed. The officers occupied their long waiting hours in many ways: we introduced training and quiz programmes, but many of them slept, read or played games to stave off the boredom.

When the Granada crew invited me to the first private viewing of their film, I was shocked. They had sequences of rowdy officers watching porno movies, others using foul and abusive language towards groups of miners. Police were caught making extremely politically incorrect statements and telling blue jokes. One officer had been filmed wearing a ridiculous hat, sporting a large cockerel on top, which he had named 'Arthur', after Arthur Scargill, the National Union of Mineworkers leader. The bird was used like a ventriloquist's dummy, and although amusing was highly embarrassing.

Altogether, the Granada footage reflected anything but the moderate, dispassionate approach we were trying to achieve. My heart sank, and I expressed severe reservations about the film being broadcast. To my intense relief, the producer told me that he had shown me the out-takes, and that he had no wish to hurt us, as he appreciated the access we had given him.

The public showing of the film proved a watershed for our force. Political commentators praised us for the way in which we dealt with the strike, in contrast to others, whom they heavily criticised. This created a certain amount of acrimony in other forces, but our gamble had paid off.

CHAPTER FIFTEEN

DCC

By the early eighties Bren and I had made a decision to send our children to private school – not out of snobbery, but from concern that the local schools would not get the best out of them. This proved to be a huge financial burden over the coming years, but the investment has been worthwhile.

I had been an ACC for eighteen months when promotion fever entered the arena again. Alan Smith had secured the Deputy's job in Derbyshire, and Peter Nobes had been head-hunted for the Chief's job in North Yorkshire; so when a vacancy occurred for the Deputy in Humberside, I discussed things with the family before applying for it. This was an important decision for us, as, if I got the job, it would mean moving as a family for the first time, and we were very happy where we were, although we were looking for a larger house. I don't care how often people apply for jobs – it is always unsettling to put yourself on offer.

I attended for interview at the town hall in Beverley on a spring morning in 1985. We were asked to wear uniform, so when my turn came I entered the committee room wearing my cap, and saluted the Police Authority. I could see that the panel liked my gesture, and it got me off to a good start. The chairman introduced his colleagues and the Chief Constable, and then each member asked questions, some of which were very technical. One, about rural policing, I found easy to answer because of my previous experience, but when I was asked how I would deal with a terrorist incident on an offshore platform, I hadn't a clue, and said as much. Notwithstanding this, I was offered an appointment, starting in a month's time.

I had mixed feelings about leaving West Yorkshire, and reservations about the domestic consequences, but I was generally pleased with my success – until Colin Sampson told me at my farewell lunch that he considered Humberside a backwater: no senior officer had ever been promoted from there, and I would end my days in that county. This was extremely depressing, and I was determined to prove him wrong.

David Hall, the Chief Constable of Humberside – a smart, slim man in his late fifties, dapper and relatively short – was one of the longest-serving Chiefs in the country. He was a past President of Association of Chief Police Officers, and well respected by many of his colleagues. He was, however, in dispute with the Police Authority. Although a close friend of the leader of the Conservatives, who at one stage had chaired the Authority, he was at loggerheads with the Labour element, who, among other things, felt he was too close to the rival party.

Within days of my arrival he told me not to have any direct dealings with members of the Authority – an instruction in complete contrast to the philosophy of the force I had left. He laid down that telephone calls and conversations with politicians were to be recorded and immediately fed back to him. This proved difficult, as various Authority members singled me out, on the fringes of meetings and in informal gatherings, to offer their help and support, and the leaders of all three parties intimated that they had chosen me to succeed my boss when the time came. Some asked if they could confide in me, as they found it difficult to talk to the Chief.

As luck would have it, the first local election after my arrival created a hung council: neither Labour nor the Conservatives had an overall majority. The Liberal group held the balance, and although it was only small, it could decide which of the major parties to support, and therefore had power beyond the electorate's wishes.

The consequences for the Authority were that the chair would rotate between Labour and Conservative. The latter took it for the first year, which pleased the Chief, as he knew that any aggravation would be limited. The chairman, his friend, was invited in for lunch, and there was a great deal of bonhomie.

Hall's staff car was an old Jaguar saloon which had seen better days: it was costing a fortune in maintenance, but he had been unwilling to change it, as he knew the previous, Labour-controlled Authority would only have supported its replacement by a vehicle of lesser status. His friend gave him the green light to buy a new Jaguar, providing he could get it within the price-range of the top Rover model.

I arranged the purchase through my contacts at Jaguar. Hall offered me its use for official duties – a concession he had never granted to any previous deputy and one which didn't particularly impress me, as I have a weakness for cars and already owned a Porsche, an E-Type Jaguar, a Mercedes saloon, a 4 × 4 off-road vehicle, and one or two others used by Bren in her business.

There were a number of apocryphal stories about my cars. In one I was refused entry to police headquarters in my black Porsche by an officer who asked me, 'Who do you think you are, Knight Rider?' This was pure fiction, but the tag stuck with me for years. Strangely enough, a true story was never repeated. A friend who owned a garage was trying to sell me a tomato-red Ferrari, and as a lure loaned me the car for a weekend. On the Saturday, together with Bren, I drove it along the M62 on our way to a private function. I was travelling well above the permitted speed when the rear engine cowl sprang loose of its mountings and almost detached itself from the body.

I stopped to repair it on the hard shoulder, where I was abruptly joined by two Road Traffic officers in their patrol car. They got out of their vehicle and with that slow, stomach-sickening gait they came towards me. Without a word one of them walked slowly around the Ferrari, while the other stared at Bren and me. The walker then said, 'I knew these bloody things could go, but I never knew they needed an air-drogue to slow them down.' We all laughed, and they let me off with a caution: all they were really interested in was the sports car.

By the time I did come to use the Chief's Jaguar, the relationship between us had soured. When he was away on annual leave, I took it to Manchester University, where I was speaking to a two-day course on community relations. During the late morning of the first day I was called out of my lecture to take an 'urgent' telephone call from my office. On the line was the Chief's secretary, who said that her boss wished to talk to me, but that she wanted to forewarn me that he was furious about my using his car.

Hall came on the line, clearly in a great rage, demanding to know by whose authority was I using the vehicle. I reminded him of his offer and told him that it had been convenient for me to take the car, as he was on leave. He responded by saying he needed it that moment, as he was putting himself 'back on duty' (which he was entitled to do), and I must return it immediately. I explained how inconvenient it would be for me to come back prematurely. He then *ordered* me to return the car. I said I would only do so when I had completed my commitment.

That evening I arrived home to find his staff officer sitting outside my house. He was very apologetic, telling me that the Chief had instructed him. I apologised for putting him in such a difficult position, and gave him the keys to the Jaguar. When I returned to work next day, the Chief said nothing about the incident, as if it had never occurred. I did not pursue the matter, believing he had thought better of his actions.

Things changed radically when Labour took over the chair of the Authority. The new chairman, Charlie Brady, was a man in his mid-sixties – a moderate type, with whom I got on well. Having held the office before, he now sought an informal meeting with the Chief. Hall agreed to see him, but directed that he should not be allowed to park his car in the police yard. He further stipulated that I should be present at the meeting, 'to corroborate all he says, in case we need to use it later'.

I was surprised at the chairman's conciliatory tone. He admitted that he and the Chief had had their differences in the past, but now he wished them to work closely together, in the interests of the force. He was complimentary about the way in which the Chief had 'pulled the force together over the years' and brought about improvements in policing.

Hall received these comments in silence, and his body language gave nothing away. The chairman went on to say that some of the new, younger members of his party were out to make a name for themselves and were out for his – the Chief's – blood.

The chairman said he was not particularly bothered about this: if they worked together, he would keep his fractious members under control. The Chief asked what 'working together' would entail. The chairman said he would like to know when Hall was away from the force, on holiday or duty. This lack of awareness of what the Chief was up to at a particular time appeared to be the main problem.

The Chief made no comment, merely indicating that the meeting was at an end; but as soon as the chairman left he became very agitated. When he asked for my views, I told him I had been agreeably surprised by the attitude of the chairman, who was clearly holding out an olive branch. The Chief dismissed the idea and said, 'I'll show you what *I* think about it,' and instructed his secretary to get Her Majesty's Inspector of Constabulary (HMI) on the phone.

He said that the chairman was trying to undermine his independence by controlling his movements, and that he needed the protection of the Home Office. I was amazed. I just could not see how he could take this view given what the chairman had said. But I made no comment.

Even my brief summary of the meeting seemed to have put my loyalty under suspicion, as he told me that I should not accept telephone calls from the chairman, that I must put down in writing any remark he might make to me, and that I must no longer attend Authority meetings. Naturally the members noticed my absence, and I got a number of messages from them telling me that they understood what was going on, and recognised the difficult position I was in.

Relationships between the Chief and the Authority deteriorated still further as he tried to deploy the Home Office against them. One day he was called to County Hall for an unscheduled meeting with some of the members, and, unusually, he asked me to go with him. There present was the county solicitor, the county's Chief Executive, and the leaders of the three parties on the Authority (including Hall's Conservative friend).

The solicitor indicated that he was speaking for them all when he told Hall that they intended to suspend him from duty, and were putting him on notice as a matter of courtesy. The Chief made little comment, except to say, 'I will reserve my position,' which was one of his favourite utterances.

He set about dealing with the threat to his position by briefing the HMI and arranging a meeting with the Home Secretary, Douglas Hurd, to which he insisted I accompany him. In the event I was not allowed in with him to see the Home Secretary, but was waiting when he came out. He was rather contrite. Hurd had told him that the issue had to be resolved locally, and that he, the Home Secretary, had no power to dismiss a Police Authority. To my mind these words were telling, as the Home Secretary does have powers over the process which leads to the dismissal of a Chief Constable.

As a result of this conversation with Hurd, in my opinion, he was at the end of the line. He needed the support of the Home Office and once he had lost that he had lost everything.

From that time on our relationship was very difficult, and it was exacerbated by other incidents. I endured five-and-a-half years under this man's leadership – the most unhappy time of my career. I developed severe stomach ulcers, which required hospital treatment, and lost a substantial amount of weight, as well as much of my self-confidence.

Things were not too happy on the domestic front either. When I got the Humberside job, we put our house on the market, and it sold within days to a family who required immediate possession. This meant that we had to fall back on a small-holding which we owned on the side of a hill above Kirkburton – a few fields and a collection of derelict farm buildings, which we intended to make our retirement home. So, with the prospect of moving to Humberside in a short while, we bought two large mobile homes, to live on our land as a temporary expedient.

It was summer, and at first everything seemed idyllic. We installed a septic tank, had the old lead water supply plumbed into the vans, and hooked up electricity from the farm buildings. We engaged an architect to make the cottage part of the buildings habitable. Our dogs and cats loved their new environment, and our eldest daughter brought her horse home from livery. At first it seemed very much like the good life, although the friends who visited us thought we were out of our minds.

While this was happening, we were seeking a new home in Humberside, and virtually settled on one in Bishop Burton, a lovely East Yorkshire village. Unfortunately, or fortunately, we were warned off this house, coincidentally by the Chief's Conservative friend, who was an estate agent: he knew the house and told us that it suffered from flooding. We began searching again, but the process was laboured, as we lost one house to gazumpers, and another deal fell through just before completion because the vendors, an estranged couple, decided to get back together again.

As winter approached, our euphoria at living on the land became a nightmare. The 1985–6 winter was fierce. The water froze, and many mornings I had to break the ice on the animals' trough to get a bucket full. The gas heaters we used in the vans caused severe condensation, and all our clothes were mildewed and the beds damp. The lane to our house became an impassable mud track, with water often more than a foot deep, and we were thankful that our neighbours at the bottom allowed us to park our cars in their yard. Plastic pipes burst, spilling water and effluent all over the floor of the caravans.

Tempers became frayed, and Bren was generally left on her own to deal with the mess, as I was away at work for at least twelve hours a day. She had to put up with the builders and contractors not meeting agreed deadlines; she had to carry heavy shopping the quarter of a mile from the road uphill to our front door, and ferry the children to and from their many commitments. No wonder she begged me to find her 'somewhere decent to live'.

On top of all this David Hall was putting pressure on me to move into the county. He tried to enlist help from members of the Police Authority, who told me what he had done, but said they would back me whatever I wished to do. He also solicited assistance from my previous Chief, Colin Sampson, who telephoned me and said, 'David Hall has had a word with me and I think it would be in your own interest to leave the county, old boy.'

I learned the hard way that any conversion takes twice the estimated time to complete, and costs three times the amount predicted. I reached a stage at which I could not really afford to complete the rebuilding of the farm *and* purchase another house. Because I found the hour's travel to work and back each day quite easy, I asked Hall if I might abandon the idea of moving into the county. He flatly refused, and told me that if I could not buy a house, I would have to move into police premises.

This I did in the early part of 1986. Our police house was in a pleasant village on the western approach to Hull; it had the usual facilities, three bedrooms and a small garden. We purchased new carpets and curtains, and furnished it to a reasonable standard. Bren and the children had no incentive to move there, especially as by that time part of the farm complex was available for occupation, and we were continuing with work on the rest of the house, with capital we had set aside for a Humberside home. I took the police house merely to satisfy the Chief Constable, and continued to travel as before, using my official residence only on the rare occasions that it was more convenient to stay overnight, usually after some social event with a late finish.

The Chief was very unhappy with this, telling me that the house must not be a 'curtained cottage', and that I should use it as my main home. I argued that I had met all his requirements – and at some personal cost, since besides the expense of furnishing and running the house, by occupying it I had lost my rent allowance – a tax-free, inflation-proof allowance equal to 12 per cent of salary paid to police owner-occupiers. Hall was unimpressed, saying that it was the principle which was at stake: I needed to be seen to be living in the county, and the Authority was not happy with the situation, as it showed a 'lack of commitment' on my part.

I did not believe him, and went to see the chairman, who said that he had been perfectly satisfied with my old arrangements, and added that he was surprised I had taken a police house in the first place, as his members were quite happy with me travelling. I conveyed this information back to the Chief, who said – surprise, surprise – that he would reserve his position.

The political make-up of the Authority changed at the next local government election, when Labour returned a majority. The old chairman was set aside, partly because he had not delivered the Chief's head, and he was replaced by a very young, left-wing, unorthodox career politician, Stephen Bayes.

The new broom and the Chief were never going to see eye to eye on anything and eventually the feud between them became very acrimonious. The chairman criticised the Chief's use of vehicles and the Chief let it be known that he wouldn't mind the chairman being caught 'up to no good' – a cryptic reference to the fact that he was gay. The chairman later told me that he knew what was going on, and made a point of telling police officers of his movements. I know most of them liked him, because he was so open and quite amusing.

Notwithstanding his attitude, I felt that he was vulnerable, not having openly declared his sexual orientation, and I suggested that he should 'come out'. He took a little persuading, but eventually agreed and spoke openly to the *Police Review*, the largest in-house magazine. This featured a sympathetic article about his life, the fact that he was gay and the youngest Police Authority chairman in history. The piece attracted some media interest for a week or so, and that was the end of it.

CHAPTER SIXTEEN

A TASTE OF POLITICS

Some of my most interesting assignments came during this period of my professional life. As I held the drugs brief for the Association of Chief Police Officers, which entailed leading on the subject on behalf of the service, I was invited to join the Trevi Group, which comprised European Ministers of the Interior (including the British Home Secretary, Douglas Hurd) and officials, who met to discuss matters of terrorism and crime.

I was bored by the formal meetings, at which most of the time was devoted to protocol and technical matters. All these had been thrashed out during prior negotiations by the bureaucrats, who had prepared carefully drafted notes for their politicians to deliver. Ministers knew little of the subject, and I saw at first hand how much they were influenced and controlled by their civil servants.

Beneath the top level we, the practitioners, created our own fringe groups, in which we would discuss the real subject matter and, through mutual agreement, make things happen. The civil servants were suspicious of our activities and protective of their ministers. They hated the access we often had, as it undermined their power. I had a number of interesting conversations with Mr Hurd, who complained about the independence of British police chiefs. Whenever his overseas colleagues left a meeting, he said, they had the power to instruct their police service to implement their decisions. 'In Britain,' he complained, 'I have to persuade forty-three Chief Constables, who make the decisions'.

I explained that things were not that simple, as European police forces lacked consistency. Many countries have more than one national force, and rarely does one minister control them all, so that inter-ministerial negotiations have to be held before any action can be taken. I added that most European countries also have a local tier of policing, controlled by the mayor, who has the power to frustrate national initiatives. In our country, we have a single tier, and if the argument is persuasive enough, we can act much quicker than any police service in the world. Hurd thanked me for these observations, and said that he hadn't looked at it in that way. In later years he told me that I was right: even with its failings, he found our system more flexible and dynamic than those on the Continent.

Part of my work was to prepare issue-papers – documents about specific law-enforcement topics – on the consequences that an open-border policy might have for crime in this country. The matter was complicated by the fact that different countries had different criminal justice and data protection systems, but I addressed this and other problems. Among these were the hot pursuit of criminals across national boundaries; barriers to successful cross-border prosecutions; access to information; the lack of a corporate approach to border controls; corruption; the difficulties associated with 'informal' police networks; the lack of technology; cross-border carrying of firearms by law-enforcement agencies; and many more. My papers became the basis for inter-governmental discussions, but although some progress has been made, many of these problems have still not been resolved.

One area where we did make substantial progress was that of drugs. The National Drugs Intelligence Unit, created in this country in the early 1980s, was the first of its type in Europe. Through our contribution to Trevi, each of our European partners copied the institution, and then combined their resources to create the European Drugs Intelligence Unit (EDIU), which was hijacked by Chancellor Kohl of Germany in his desire to create a European Police Agency. Europol's much-heralded, much-publicised launch was nothing more than a renaming of EDIU – but that's politics.

Another bizarre feature of this episode was the length of the negotiations between countries as to which of them should house the new institution. The logical place would have been within Interpol, at its new headquarters in Lyon, France; but for political reasons that was unacceptable, so millions of Euros were spent on refurbishing the old Gestapo headquarters in the Hague. The 'Schengen' agreement between the majority of mainland European countries also unduly complicated the way in which we co-operate with each other, and, more than a decade on, practical and technical differences still frustrate progress.

Away from such heady stuff, as DCC in Humberside I was deeply involved in helping run a medium-sized force, with all the problems that entailed. Discipline was a key responsibility of mine, and I had a number of particularly difficult situations to deal with. Two involved the deaths of prisoners in custody, which are always difficult to explain.

The first casualty was a man who, when being taken in for questioning about his involvement in a particularly distasteful child pornography ring, asked if he could get out of the police car because he felt unwell. He collapsed by the side of the vehicle and died before he reached hospital. In such circumstances the police are open to much suspicion. Was he assaulted? Did the police officer bang his head against the vehicle? Such questions are difficult to answer to the satisfaction of the public.

We deal with this kind of event as if it were a murder. The scene is secured for forensic scientists to examine, the vehicle is compounded and subjected to similar scrutiny, as are any officers concerned. Witnesses are sought and questioned, all under the supervision of the Police Complaints Authority and the Director of Public Prosecutions. In this particular case, the postmortem revealed a natural cause of death, and that was the resulting verdict of the Coroner's Court.

The second case was less easily concluded, as a man died within hours of being released from police custody, in which he had been held for more than twelve hours. His postmortem discovered that the base of his skull was fractured, and there was strong evidence that the injury could not have been inflicted after his release. To add to our difficulties, the man had been medically examined in the cells by a police surgeon and pronounced healthy.

All the initial evidence pointed to an assault by police officers, but detailed investigation uncovered a different story. The man had fallen and cracked the back of his head after a four-hour drinking spree in which he had consumed the equivalent of fourteen pints of lager and six or seven whiskies. His fall had been witnessed, and an ambulance called, but the crew refused to take him to hospital because of his drunken state. The police had little alternative but to take him into custody for his own protection. Under examination in court, the police surgeon admitted that he might have missed the head injury, and the jury cleared the police of any suspicion.

It is difficult to describe the effect these cases have on individual officers and the force as a whole: everyone is tainted with the incident, and the papers, ever keen for sensationalism, always put the worst construction on events.

There were other serious operational matters to deal with. One involved Anthony Edward Pulling, a twenty-two-year-old who barricaded himself in his parents' house and discharged a shotgun at us and the neighbours. His problems, we discovered, derived from the trauma he had experienced early in life. His mother had been subjected to brutal and sadistic treatment by his father, and the boy saw her kill him by discharging both barrels of a shotgun into him while he was sleeping in their marital bed. Anthony had taken to drink, which the mother ignored as her way of pacifying him. When she remarried, his behaviour grew more extreme, culminating in his final desperate challenge. I commanded the siege, which lasted for seventy hours and ended in tragedy, as Anthony turned the gun on himself and blew part of his head off. Incredibly, his mother retained the bed on which both father and son met their violent ends.

Another casualty was an unknown young woman whose naked body was found one Christmas Eve in a ditch behind a lay-by used by thousands of truckers each week on the A180 in Humberside. It was clear she had been there for about twelve hours, as the rats had already eaten her eyes and were beginning to disfigure her other orifices. (These are often the circumstances the police face in a murder case.)

Our first task was to identify her – she could have been foreign – then trace her movements, relatives and associates. Luckily for us identification proved easy, as she was a local girl who had been reported missing from home. Her killer was arrested within a few days and subsequently convicted before court.

An exercise can be equally as taxing. We were responsible for the security of a large number of offshore gas platforms in the North Sea, and because of their vulnerability to terrorist attacks, we launched a real-life exercise involving the military, under the direction of the Prime Minister. Actors, playing the part of terrorists, kidnapped a minister while he was visiting one of the platforms and threatened to kill him unless we agreed to their demands. We ran the operation from our control centre in Hull, where we employed negotiators, a Press bureau, members of the Special Boat Services (SBS) and RAF Nimrod surveillance aircraft.

We all operated as if the incident was real – with almost disastrous consequences. One of the SBS team, deployed to gain access to the platform, was washed away by tumultuous seas. His colleagues had to abort their mission, and it took many hours to rescue him, but fortunately he soon recovered from the hypothermia which had set in.

This was by no means the last occasion on which I came into contact with the Special Forces: all senior police officers train with them, as we have to work closely together in terrorist situations. I attended the Special Air Service's training school in Hereford more than once, to my discomfort. I will not take away the dubious pleasure of others – suffice to say it's not for the faint-hearted.

I have many happy memories of Humberside and its people. It was there that I first met Princess Diana, when she visited the county with her husband. During the morning's visits, the Chief went with Prince Charles, and I, in plain clothes, as requested by the Palace, accompanied the young Diana.

One of our lengthy stops was at a Barnardo's home for children, where the two of us spent time with a number of different families in private rooms. In the first was a young couple and a little child. The man wore a T-shirt exposing his arms, which were completely covered with tattooed women's names. When Diana touched him and asked, 'Who are all these?' he replied, 'My girlfriends!' She then asked his partner, 'Where's your name?', to which the woman replied, 'I'm not there. There's no room for me.' The couple were icing a cake for their child's birthday, which seemed most incongruous. When we left the group, Diana said, 'I'll get in trouble for that, because I'm not supposed to touch anybody without gloves.' 'Don't worry,' I replied, 'I won't tell anyone.'

The second family group was much more moving, as they were all deaf and dumb. Neither Diana nor I could sign (she later learned), and understanding them was extremely difficult. Yet I was much impressed by the way she handled the encounter: she was so gentle, and had such warmth and intuition, that she brought the family to tears – and I was close to crying myself. When we left their company, she was visibly upset at her own inadequacy, and said she wished she could have done more for them. I told her she had done everything possible – but when she asked, 'Why do people have to suffer in that way?', I had no answer.

Before lunch, at which the two royal parties were due to unite, we had a walkabout on the streets of Hull. The crowds were out in their thousands, as for many it was their first opportunity to see the young Princess. It was an extremely joyous occasion, and Diana soon got into the spirit of it, holding longer conversations and spending more time with groups and individuals than any other celebrity or royal I had ever accompanied before. Soon I had to remind her that we were running behind schedule, and protocol determined that we must reach our lunch rendezvous before the Prince. On my third warning, she said, 'Mr Hellawell, do you do everything your wife expects of you?'

'Unfortunately not Ma'am,' I replied

'Neither do I,' she said, with a twinkle in her eye.

Needless to say, we were late. Lunch, in Trinity House, Hull, was one of those affairs at which the guests visit the specially prepared royal loo (which will probably never be used again, but will be preserved 'for historical reasons') and then are received by the highest in rank of the local worthies. With that formality over, leaders of the community are strategically placed in different parts of a large hall so that the royals can wander among them with food collected from the finger buffet, which they rarely eat, but push around their plates.

Bren had joined me, and we were both pleasantly surprised when Diana approached us. 'It's so good to meet you,' she said to Bren. 'Your husband's told me all about you. Can I thank you for the fact that he's dressed in a suit?'

Bren acknowledged the praise, and asked if she was enjoying the visit.

'Very much,' she said. 'Have you met my husband?'

We said we had in the past, but not that day.

'Then I must get him for you,' she replied, and good as her word, brought Prince Charles across to us by the arm. I think he was probably as embarrassed as we were, but we had some small talk before the organisers steered them both away. I reckon I am a good judge of character, and I can say without any hesitation that on that day Diana was a very happy, warm and caring young woman. I received a personal letter of thanks from her for my part in the visit, and a telling-off from the Chief for not getting her to lunch on time.

The Princess Royal was a frequent visitor to the county, as she had horsey friends in the Beverley area. The Duchess of York also came, and brought some colour to the community; but it was a visit by Princess Alexandra and her husband, Sir Angus Ogilvy, which proved to have lasting consequences for me. When Bren and I were introduced in the line formed to greet them, the Princess looked at me for a moment and asked if we had met before. Remembering the time she had come to Huddersfield, I replied, 'Many years ago, Ma'am.' Later in the day I was sitting immediately behind her at the Scunthorpe Football Club, which she was about to open formally, when she turned round and said, 'I know! You were my gallant young inspector.'

She had visited Huddersfield on a cold, rainy day in the mid-1960s. The reception party, including David Bradley, was waiting on the steps of the Town Hall to receive her, and I was the duty inspector, standing in the street, helping keep the crowds back when she arrived. As her car drew up, she emerged immediately in front of me, so I held the door open for her and instinctively remarked, 'I think you've got out of the wrong side, love.' As I guided her round the back of the car, she smiled and said 'Thank you.' Now, twenty years later, she remembered that tiny incident. What recall! Sir Angus and I later took up a closer friendship, as he gave me his support in my work against drugs.

Over the five-and-a-half years I served in Humberside I suffered substantial ill health, and lost a great deal of personal confidence. I even became nervous about delivering talks, which was abnormal for me. This notwithstanding, Bren and I forged many lasting friendships in that part of the world, which offered a senior police officer numerous challenges. I would have liked to become the Chief Constable, but it was not meant to be.

It was a great pity that the relationship between the Chief and myself was strained for most of the time we worked together, because I admired many things about him. I learned from him the importance of looking after officers who were injured or sick. He would visit each injured man, and, with his wife, would spend his Christmas Day calling on staff who were ill – which was highly commendable.

He was always smart and correct, and was a mine of information about the police service and our force. He was respected by the community, and impressed those he met outside the job. He was devoted to his dear wife Molly and his two sons. I wish them both much health and happiness in their retirement.

CHAPTER SEVENTEEN

A FATHER'S TRIBULATIONS

One of the most troublesome episodes in the life of our family happened at this time. Our son Charles had joined the police cadets in West Yorkshire, where he distinguished himself in many ways. Bren and I were proud that he and his sister, Samantha, had both chosen to follow in their father's footsteps. He excelled in written examinations, won all the physical fitness competitions and received commendations from people in the voluntary sector, where he had been working on community attachments.

His achievements were such that he was among a small number of cadets chosen nationally to work on a prized assignment at Bramshill Police College, from where he returned home on leave a few days before his eighteenth birthday in May 1988. One Saturday lunch-time he set off to go shopping in Huddersfield with a male friend, before a night out with a girl, slightly older than him, whom he had been dating from the village. He called us in the middle of the afternoon to say that his mate had invited him to stay overnight, and not to expect him home until the following morning. This was not unusual, as both he and the girls were very popular and often had their friends sleep over at our house, as they did at theirs.

Telephone calls in the middle of the night are unsettling for parents, as you always think the worst. This one came at ten minutes past two, and haunted us for years. The caller had a pronounced

Yorkshire accent, accentuated by a rude, brusque manner. He announced that our son was in the police cells in Huddersfield, having been arrested earlier that evening for being drunk and disorderly and assaulting a man.

Shocked beyond belief, because Charles seldom touched alcohol, I asked if I could visit him. I was told it was unnecessary. 'He's had a skinful,' said the aggressive voice. 'He's sleeping it off, and he doesn't want to see you.' On reflection, perhaps I should have insisted on going in, but I felt helpless. We didn't sleep another wink that night, or for many nights to come. The whole thing was completely out of character. Charles drank sparingly, and used up his physical energy on the sports field. At that moment we realised how one of my bosses had felt when I rang to tell him his son had been arrested for stealing. He refused my offer of help, and I now understand why: you have to bear these problems as a family.

I collected Charles from the police station first thing the following morning, and was shocked by his physical condition, as he was bruised and battered all over his body. He was very contrite, believing I would be angry with him, but nothing was further from my mind: I just wanted to hold him and keep him safe in my arms.

We sat in the car and he told me his story. His girlfriend had ended their relationship, because in his absence she had found someone else. The new man, a butcher ten years her senior, worked on a stall in Huddersfield Market Hall. Out of interest Charles and his mate had gone to see what he looked like. The man recognised Charles and began gloating over his triumph in 'taking a cop's girl'.

Charles was upset and decided to join his friend in a drink to drown his sorrows. He knew he was a few days below the age at which he could legally purchase alcohol, but his friend was over eighteen. After a few beers he decided to stay over at his friend's house, as he knew that if he came home, we would smell alcohol on his breath and chastise him.

Later in the day, the butcher, accompanied by two other men in their late twenties, came into the bar where Charles was drinking. There were heated exchanges, which resulted in the five of them going outside on to the street 'to sort it out'. I am certain that this would never have occurred had Charles not been fuelled by drink, as all his training both at home and in the police service had been to defuse tense situations, not to inflame them.

A street fight began between the three men and our son – his friend did not wish to become involved. Charles was and still is extremely powerful, and against the odds gained the upper hand. Two of his combatants accepted they were beaten and had just stepped back bloodied when two inexperienced constables arrived on the scene. Charles and the butcher were still sparring, but the fight was virtually over, and even the small crowd which had gathered to watch had lost interest and left.

The young men were told to go on their way, but before they left the female constable inquired about the butcher's injuries. He complained that he had lost part of a tooth, but said, 'It were fair feyt.' Charles was not asked about his injuries, which must have been very apparent: he was just ordered to go. He ambled around the centre of Huddersfield in search of his friend, and returned to the scene of the fight twenty minutes or so later.

He was surprised to find the police deep in conversation with his adversaries, as they too had been instructed to leave. He gained the impression that the butcher was chatting up the female officer. Charles was ordered brusquely to go away, which he did. Some twenty minutes later he ran into the same two police officers once again. This time without warning the male officer grabbed him by the throat, pushed him into a shop doorway and said, 'I don't care a f—k who your father is. You're nicked.' There was real venom in his voice and aggression in his eyes, his ferocious expression exaggerated by his heavily disfigured face – he had a hare lip. It is well to remember that Charles worked at the same station as this officer, who was effectively arresting one of his own colleagues.

Charles was taken to the police station, where he was placed in a cell and fell asleep. He was awoken during the early hours of the morning by a detective sergeant named Bedford, who interviewed him in his somnolent state.

Many of the codes of practice under the Police and Criminal

Evidence Act were violated at that moment. In the eyes of the law Charles was a juvenile, and so should not have been interviewed without a parent or guardian present. A person of any age should not be interviewed while under the influence of drink, and other than in the most extreme circumstances, prisoners should not be interviewed in the middle of the night.

Charles was prepared to comply, however, and answered Bedford's questions, even though they were aggressively put and peppered with obscenities. When asked if he had caused injury to the butcher's mouth, he said that he had. When asked if he had caused the minor injuries to the other two men, he agreed that he had. He was charged with assault occasioning actual bodily harm and put back into his cell.

I was struck by other abnormalities of police action in this case. First, fights between young men are so common that they rarely result in arrest. Second, when arrests are made it is usually because one or other of the parties refuses to desist when told. Third, it is rare for an officer of the rank of detective sergeant to become involved in such a case. Fourth, any person charged with an assault should automatically be medically examined, to prevent him or her bringing a counter-charge of assault.

My immediate concern was the state of my son's health, so – as the police had not had him medically examined – I took him to the home of our family doctor. His examination, within half an hour of Charles's release from custody, discovered more than 100 cuts and bruises on his body, the most severe being about his buttocks and testicles. He later testified that his injuries were 'consistent with a severe beating by being kicked about the body on numerous occasions'. The doctor added that his condition was so bad that he might have suffered internal injuries and ought to have received medical attention at the time of his arrest. He added that had it not been for Charles's outstanding physical condition, he would have been hospitalised.

The family had gathered to receive Charles home, and the reunion made me realise what a close clan we are. We all hugged, as football players do when they score a goal – only in our case there was deep emotion caused by the harm done to the team's youngest member.

I had a belief in the system which I had worked so many years to improve, and I convinced myself that the Crown Prosecution Service (CPS) would take the matter no further. I was wrong. A detective superintendent was appointed to prepare the case against Charles – even though officers of this rank normally deal with nothing less than attempted murder. After an exhaustive inquiry, the senior detective recommended that no further action should be taken. Most unusually, the CPS over-rode this recommendation, and decided to prosecute. I was incensed at the injustice of this decision and determined to fight it all the way.

When Chris Darnton, the solicitor I appointed for Charles, read the case papers supplied by the CPS, he expressed his concern: being a part-time prosecutor for the agency, he could see no case to answer. He pressed them for a reason and when badgered, they admitted that the case was a 'thin one', which they intended to prosecute because of 'his father's position'. This seemed incredibly unfair. Why should my son be victimised because of who or what I was? I was furious.

We opted for a trial by jury, believing that a magistrates' court might treat the case as a trivial matter and not recognise the possible consequences for the defendant. The CPS were very unhappy about this, as I am sure they didn't relish being exposed before a judge.

Charles was suspended from duty – and in a most unsympathetic way. A superintendent was dispatched to our home to strip him of his identification card and uniform. This was very hurtful to Charles, who said that his life 'was taken away at that moment'. As with many other crises, Bren had to deal with this one on her own, because I was at work in Hull.

During his long wait for the trial, Charles became a physical wreck. He could not sleep, developed psoriasis over every part of his body, and lost three stone in weight. He looked desperately ill: he had lost his purpose in life, and we were reluctant to leave him alone, fearing what he might do to himself.

The law took its usual leisurely course, and it was months before the trial began at Wakefield Crown Court. During the interval I had been told by the ACC, Personnel, that, were Charles acquitted, which he believed he would be, he would be reinstated as a constable, not as a cadet, which was some consolation.

I took leave, as did the rest of the family, so that we could attend the trial. Each day our sad little band trudged to the court with heavy hearts and took up position on the front row of the balcony in the ornate Victorian building (which has now been turned into a night club). In an attempt to raise our morale, we likened ourselves to *Bread*, the television sitcom involving a large Liverpool family who always stuck together.

The choice of people for the jury was of special interest to us, and we tried to weigh up whether they would give our son a fair chance. When your child is under threat, everything is important. Our barrister, Paul Worsley, considered that the case was 'full of inconsistencies'. He was at a loss to understand why a seventeen-year-old boy was being prosecuted for fighting with three men ten years his senior, especially when he had received more injuries than they.

The prosecution opened the case and called their first witness, the butcher, who strolled into the box and leant nonchalantly on the edge of it. He remained in this posture when answering the questions put to him, which annoyed the judge, His Honour Geoffrey Baker, who interrupted proceedings to comment, 'You seem completely disinterested in the whole affair.'

The butcher's reply startled the court. 'I never wanted to be here in first place,' he said. With encouragement from the judge and frowns from the prosecution, he added, 'Police brow-beat me into giving evidence. I told them it were fair feyt. Charles got better of us, and that was end of it.'

When asked to elaborate, he said, 'That police woman kept badgering me. She wouldn't leave me alone. But I wouldn't give a statement, as it were a fair feyt.' (During cross-examination he told the court that the woman police officer had asked him twelve or thirteen times if he wished to prosecute, and added, 'I think she fancied me.') The judge asked why and when he had changed his mind, if he had no wish to prosecute. He said that Detective Sergeant Bedford had pestered him at home to make a statement; he had refused, but Bedford had 'come back again', so he had given in. The judge made no comment, but shot a telling look at the jury and the prosecuting barrister, who was clearly shaken.

The next person to give evidence was the female police officer. She was very nervous, and extremely uncomfortable when asked why she kept badgering the witness to give a statement against his wishes. She had no logical explanation: she was embarrassed by having to admit that she had not examined Charles's injuries, and could offer no reason for her oversight. She took no comfort in having to agree that, whatever the nature of the fracas, it was over when she arrived, and she had difficulty justifying the fact that Charles was arrested half an hour after the event. The jury were patently unimpressed by the prosecution's evidence.

Our barrister insisted the jury hear the tape-recording of Bedford's interview with Charles. The prosecution objected, but the judge decided in his favour. Speakers were specially installed – for the first time in a Crown Court, we believed, as taped interviews were in their infancy. The sound of Bedford's dull voice, his use of bad language, his bullying manner, his flip remarks – all had a visible effect on everyone in that room. Charles sounded sleepy, and his responses were slow; but he addressed Bedford as 'Sir' and answered all his questions in a very courteous way. The judge looked incredulously at the machine, as if he could not believe what he was hearing. The prosecuting barrister squirmed in his chair, whispering aggressively to his instructing solicitor from the CPS. Our barrister sat tall, with a look on his face resembling a cat with a bowl of cream. The jury, plainly shocked, looked at each other, recognising the significance of the moment.

The prosecution evidence concluded and the defence began. Our family doctor outlined the injuries our son had sustained and was firm in his views of how they were caused.

Charles elected to take the stand and give evidence under oath, which meant he would be cross-examined by the prosecution. He looked a sad, lonely figure in the box. The only advice I had given him was to tell the truth and seek clarification if he didn't understand any of the questions. He told his story in exactly the same matter-of-fact manner that he had used on the tape, including the earlier confrontation in the market hall. He admitted that he caused the injuries to the complainant. He was cross-examined for two hours and acquitted himself with distinction. He later told us he was so nervous that his knees knocked and he thought he might pass out, but it didn't show.

Our barrister was full of confidence in his summation. He highlighted the inconsistencies and lack of clarity in the prosecution's case, which he destroyed with precision. Judge Baker summed up in favour of a not guilty verdict. He praised the way in which Charles had given evidence, and was derogatory about the prosecution witnesses.

Even so, we were not confident of the outcome. Juries can make perverse decisions, and we were almost convinced that this would be our fate. Our fears were unfounded. Within minutes of retiring, they returned a not guilty verdict. Judge Baker told Charles he was free to go and wished him well with his future. We hugged each other with joy. The nightmare was over, justice had finally been done, and we could get on with our lives – or so we thought.

We celebrated that evening with a family meal, encouraging Charles to put the whole saga behind him. I told him that the experience would be useful to him as a police officer, as he was unlikely to receive such a grilling again.

The following Monday morning, as directed, he reported for duty to Personnel in Police Headquarters in Wakefield. He was told he would be employed there on a temporary basis until a place could be arranged for him on the initial training course for constables. He was instructed in the rudiments of the personnel system, shown how to access information quickly, and advised about the type of queries he was likely to receive from people within the force. The staff suggested that he should familiarise himself with one or two personnel files, 'to get used to them', and gave him full access to the system. Among other papers, he pulled out his sister's record, to study as an easy starter.

When we welcomed him home at the end of this first day, he was not very happy, although he put on a brave face for his mother. We used to play a great deal of snooker together at that time, and we retired for a game after dinner. When I asked him why he was troubled, he said things didn't feel right. He couldn't give me any concrete evidence for his misgivings, merely saying, 'It's just a feeling I have.' I reminded him that he had been through a highly disturbing experience: his confidence was at rock bottom, and he might be sensing things which did not exist. This pacified him in some degree, but we both retired to bed troubled.

He arrived in the office next following morning to be met by the chief inspector from the Personnel Department, together with a detective inspector and a sergeant from Discipline and Complaints. He was ushered into a private office, cautioned under the provisions of the criminal code and questioned as if he were a criminal. He was asked if he had accessed his sister's record the previous day, which he confirmed. Had he been given explicit permission to do so? 'No,' he replied – but added that he had been given free access to all the records. The short interview concluded with him being told that the circumstances would be reported to Paul Whitehouse, the Deputy Chief Constable. In the meantime, he was allowed to continue his work, but instructed not to access Samantha's file again.

At home that evening it was obvious that this latest incident had destroyed what little confidence he had regained after the trial. I reassured him as best I could. He was close to handing in his notice. He said the attitude and behaviour of his fellow officers had destroyed his respect for them and the police service, which had been his life. I persuaded him to carry on, convinced that nothing more could happen.

Next morning I spoke to the head of West Yorkshire's Personnel Department, to ask what was going on. He distanced himself from the previous day's events, admitting that he was at a loss to know why and how what had happened did happen. He confessed that he didn't like it any more than I did. He agreed that the speed and nature of recourse to the Discipline and Complaints Department was without precedent. He reassured me that he had Charles's interests at heart: he was confident that there would be no follow-up, and gave me a possible date for Charles's induction course into the service.

A few days later this same officer telephoned me, full of apologies, to say that he had been instructed that Charles would not be processed in the normal way for a cadet: instead, he would face the full assessment procedure undertaken by applicants from outside the service, most of whom were seven years Charles's senior.

I was crestfallen. Nevertheless, I tried to boost Charles's confidence in the three weeks or so he waited to attend the two-day selection programme.

On completion, he considered he had done reasonably well in the tests, exercises and formal interviews, and felt that even in his poor state of health he was as fit as the other candidates; but he was slightly unhappy at the attitude shown towards him by one of the assessors. We were on tenterhooks waiting for the results. Neither Bren nor I had had any proper sleep for months, and we were back walking the bedroom floor during the early hours of the morning.

I was driving in my own force area the next afternoon when I received a telephone call from Paul Whitehouse. I pulled off the road into a lay-by so that I could concentrate fully. I should emphasise that I had known the man since the mid-1970s, when he was responsible for the development of technology in his force in the north-east, and I had once even stayed overnight with him and his wife Elizabeth at their home in Durham.

Now Paul told me that Charles had failed the entrance examination: he had done well on the exercises: but he had come across as sexist. When I asked how this had manifested itself, he said that on one of the exercises candidates had to use tyres and other equipment to cross an imaginary stream. Charles had elected to go first, and had then returned to help the female members of the team across.

I waited, expecting more, but that was it. 'How was that sexist?' I asked. 'It seems to me he was displaying both leadership and team-building qualities.' Paul disagreed, claiming that Charles's actions had intimated that the women could not have done it on their own, and thus portrayed male dominance.

I thought this was utter nonsense, and said so, inquiring if the female candidates had complained. Apparently they had not – 'but one of the female assessors considered they would have been justified in doing so'.

I regarded myself as being well tuned to political correctness, but had never heard of it being taken to such lengths. If this was the gauge, any act of courtesy or offer of assistance by a male to a female could be interpreted as sexism.

I was very upset, but took the opportunity of asking Paul why he had changed the selection procedure. He replied that the system had to change sometime. He added that anyway all was not lost: he told me that he had the power to accept Charles on his performance and he would review all his record and assessments as a cadet, and take that into account in making his final decision. I was slightly encouraged by this, as the records and reports were outstanding. Despite this he still rejected Charles.

Paul sent for him to tell him of his decision, after which he said, 'It's all right. You can cry if you want to.' By the time he got the call, Charles was resigned to his fate, and the last thing he felt like doing was crying. He handled the encounter with dignity, and left the room to get on with his life.

I reproach myself for not intervening more, although my rank made it difficult to act as a normal father, and Charles was against my doing anything which might question his ability to survive alone. Years later, the leader of the Police Federation for West Yorkshire told me he thought the way Charles had been dealt with was 'appalling'.

It is strange how, after a saga of that kind, fate seems to even the score. Charles went into the private sector and is extremely successful in his work, having become one of the youngest managers in a multinational corporation. He is talented at music, holds Black Belts in two Martial Arts disciplines, and is British champion at all-in fighting. He is very happily married with twin boys.

CHAPTER EIGHTEEN

MUSICAL CHAIRS

I was at home one Friday evening when I received a telephone call from a friend, who told me he had heard on the grapevine that Colin Sampson was to be made an Inspector of Constabulary, and that the chairman of the West Yorkshire Police Authority had suggested that I ought to apply for his job, as I was 'one of their favourite sons'. While being flattered, I was quite surprised by this last remark, since I had been away from West Yorkshire for more than four years. Other than at the crime committee meetings, my only conversation with Colin had been when he telephoned to suggest that I sell the farm at Kirkburton, as retaining it 'would do me no good'.

Bren and I both thought this was the break we had been waiting for – an end to all the trouble with my Chief, and a return to the county I loved. It was not to be. The first obstacle was David Hall, who told me that *he* might apply for the job. 'If I do,' he said, 'it would be inappropriate for you to do the same.' I told him he could make his own choice, and so would I. He had competed on the previous occasion when Colin got the post, and I realised that it would hurt his pride if his deputy were to beat him now. I also anticipated that he would do all in his power to obstruct me.

What I didn't anticipate was that other forces would also be at work. I was told in confidence by a member of the West Yorkshire

Police Authority that they wanted me, but it would be difficult, as Colin wished his close friend Peter Nobes to succeed him. 'But,' they said, 'Colin wants too much of his own way, and we intend to teach him a lesson.' They failed. I did not receive Home Office approval to go on the short-list, and Peter got the job – even though he had previously told me that he was very happy as Chief of North Yorkshire, and was not sure he wanted to move.

The Home Secretary's approval is crucial for any candidate wishing to achieve Chief Officer rank. The actual selection is done by Police Authorities, but they cannot make an appointment unless the Home Secretary agrees. In the 1990s there was much criticism of this process, which was abused by Chief Constables and HMIs so that they could control access to senior ranks. Selection was secret, the Home Office never giving a reason for rejecting a candidate. As I learned when I became a Chief, decisions were made during a single telephone conversation, in which a person's career could be blighted for ever. Members of Police Authorities were even prohibited from telling a candidate why he had not been called for interview.

In my case, they believed that the Home Office had been manipulated, and considered sending a delegation to London, to see if they could change the mind of the Home Secretary – but they were advised this would do no good. (The process was successfully challenged years later by Alison Halford, a senior officer in Merseyside, who contended that such back-door tactics had blighted her career. Her case was settled out of court, but fear of exposure ensured change, and the system is now much more open.)

I was devastated – not because I hadn't got the job, but because I knew I had been cheated out of competing for it. I took the unusual step of seeking an interview with my HMI, whom I considered to be an honourable man. He surprised me by saying that he was as disgusted as I, and went on to reveal that he had recommended me for interview, but had, for the first time ever, been over-ruled by the Chief HMI, a close friend of David Hall. Then he allowed me to read his submission, which was glowing. He promised to put the wrong right.

Within months of this incident, vacancies for Chief Constables occurred in Lincolnshire, Norfolk, Cleveland, Derbyshire and South Yorkshire, and I was encouraged to apply by Colin Sampson. I was particularly interested in South Yorkshire, as it was close to home and I had worked and studied there. I was advised, however, that I would have to throw my hat in the ring for more than one job, so against my better judgement, I did.

From a candidate's point of view, most of the forces on the list had some drawback. South Yorkshire Police Authority had been at loggerheads with their two previous Chief Constables, and the Home Office had been obliged to step in to support them. Derbyshire had been in open warfare with the Home Office, as they had been refused permission to appoint their own Deputy Chief. Norfolk had also gone through a selection process and rejected all the candidates, including some of the same people – and no one knew why. Lincolnshire alone seemed all right. I was short-listed for them all.

My first interview was in Derbyshire County Hall, a forbidding grey stone building like a Victorian mill perched on a hill. Things started badly when I was refused entry to the car park by the attendant, who said he had been instructed to tell the 'Chief Constables' to park in the street. After hearing my mining credentials, he did allow me in, provided that I didn't 'tell them'. The main receptionist was less than helpful: after satisfying himself that I was on the list, he ushered me into the members' lounge, where I was glad to be recognised by a local MP, who offered me coffee. When I told him I was there for the Chief's job, he shrugged his shoulders and said 'Best of luck'. Spotting another candidate, I went to sit beside him. He informed me that he had been involved in the previous set of interviews, after which he had been told by the committee that he was second choice, and that if the job was re-advertised, he should apply again. 'But,' he added darkly, 'anything could happen here.'

Attending the interview proved to be a complete waste of time. The Derbyshire interview committee appointed the deputy, even though they knew their decision would not receive Home Office support.

I withdrew from Norfolk, as I didn't really want to live or work there, but my notification was badly received. The Chief Executive of the county telephoned me to say that no one had ever withdrawn from their short-list, and he was displeased. I apologised for any inconvenience but confirmed my decision. He wouldn't accept this and told me that he had spoken to members of the selection committee, who had said they were likely to give me the job. I thought this smacked of Derbyshire, and told him I was flattered, but would not change my mind. He became quite unpleasant, insinuating that I would damage my career if I withdrew. By then I didn't really care, as I had become disillusioned with the whole process.

In Lincoln the venue for interviews was the Judge's Lodgings, where we were all treated with the utmost courtesy. The process began with pre-dinner drinks, at which most contenders stuck to water, to impress the committee with their sobriety. Then came musical-chairs at dinner, during which we changed seats after each course in order to talk to as many members of the selection committee as possible.

For the first course I was on the right of the chairman of the Authority, who, uniquely among his peers, was a Canadian businessman. He suggested that I had a very good chance of getting the job, as, being the youngest, I would be able to serve the longest. This filled me with dread, and I told him so, for it has always been my belief that a spell of five to eight years was long enough for anyone to be at the head of an organisation.

I sensed this was an inappropriate answer, as he moved on to small talk – and clearly he passed on my remark, for after dinner Colin Sampson asked me if I had really said what he'd heard, as he believed that 'it was in the bag'. I told the truth, explaining that I would feel uncomfortable if I misled the panel, as it was important that they knew what they were getting. During the next day's interviews and tests I tried my best, and I believe performed quite well, but the position was offered to a man who told them that he could serve for ten years . . . and retired after three.

Next in line, and for me the most important, was South Yorkshire, the selection for which took place in Barnsley over the Easter

holiday. Proceedings began with dinner, followed by a day of interviews designed to reduce the number of candidates, the survivors
of whom were to go forward for a final interview on the third day.
Although the accents differed, the dinner was similar to the one in
Lincoln. I felt at ease with the politicians, but sensed that the
magistrate members found me unimpressive.

A chance conversation with a politician member was most illumi-
nating: he said that the magistrates had little to do with the selection,
which would be made by 'elected members'. The boroughs of
Barnsley, Rotherham and Doncaster, he said, would vote together
against Sheffield as a matter of principle, and 'You'll get our vote.'
Feeling cynical about the whole system, I thanked him for his
confidence but suggested that there was a long way to go.

The next day's programme comprised group exercises, tests and
discussions, after which, of the eight who began, only three remained: Paul Whitehouse, Richard Wells from the Met and myself.
Richard was surprised at having got so far, as he believed that the
panel would not touch a Met officer, due to the way the London
officers had behaved during the miners' strike.

In speculating about who the successful candidate might be, the
local media had made little comment about Paul, but they had
ruled out Richard on the grounds that he came from the south of
England, and described me as an ex-miner who drove a black
Porsche – untrue at that time, as my car was white. I was last of the
three to be interviewed. I was relaxed, and enjoyed the forty-minute
experience. We waited nervously together for about half an hour,
until someone came and asked Richard to rejoin the committee,
who offered him the job. He was delighted, but also incredulous,
responding to our congratulations with, 'I'm sure they've made a
mistake.'

The journey home from such a disappointment is long and
lonely: your confidence is at rock bottom, you search your soul for
what went wrong, you conclude that you were just not good enough
– and that's the end of it. Given time, you realise that this is not
true, and that the panel just decided to chose someone other than
yourself – but it is difficult to be logical when you feel rejected.

Bren was there to help me; the weather was very cold, with snow in the air, and we walked for miles contemplating my future in the police. We came to the conclusion that I should abandon my promotion chase and retire as soon as I had my requisite service in.

Three nights later Colin Sampson, who had been the presiding HMI at the interviews, telephoned me at home to ask what had gone wrong. He was baffled, since he had considered my performance in the final interview flawless, and he was amazed when the Authority announced its decision.

The truth, which emerged over the next few months, reflected no credit on those who conveyed it to me. I learned that I had fallen victim to internecine jealousies between Sheffield and the three boroughs. It sounds incredible, but the borough politicians withdrew their vote in my favour simply because they refused to agree with Sheffield, which had been the first to declare for me.

I tried to put the disappointment behind me and get on with my job. However, on my first day back in Humberside David Hall sent for me. He was gloating, and couldn't wait to tell me that he had been in contact with the chairman of the selection board the weekend before the interviews, insinuating that his object had been to undermine my application. I was fascinated see that, in order to frustrate me, he had been obliged to overcome his normal political prejudices and had toadied with the Labour chair of the Authority.

Summer arrived early in 1989, and I was taking leave at home when the whole rigmarole began again. One of my senior officers rang to say that Cleveland had advertised for a Chief Constable, and they'd had a call in Hull from the HMI's office suggesting that I should apply. In an uninterested way I replied, 'Put me in for it,' and rang off. I mentioned the call to Bren, but didn't consider the matter further until I received notification of an interview date. My colleague had taken me at my word, used his initiative, copied one of my other applications and submitted it under my copied signature. The result was that I got the job.

CHAPTER NINETEEN

MADE IT!

This was a time of joy. My family and friends were thrilled, and I received close on 100 letters of congratulation. The media response was positive, for at the age of forty-eight I was about to become one of the youngest Chief Constables in Britain. Bren knew *she* had made it when another Chief Constable from the region greeted her at a social function with the words, 'What does it feel like to become the first lady in Cleveland?' The sad thing is that he wasn't joking – he believed what he said.

When I left Humberside the papers carried the headline, 'Knight Rider Roars Away', and Cleveland picked up the theme with 'Knight Rider Arrives'. I began work in Cleveland on 1 August 1990, and the atmosphere was electric, as this was the first change at the top for eighteen years. In the entrance hall of headquarters in Ladgate Lane, Middlesbrough, my name had been painted on a banner, beneath which there was a huge caricature portrait of me, with the words, 'Under New Management'. Our headquarters was a very modern, angular building which had previously been used as a laboratory and sold to us at a knockdown price. My office was on the south-west corner, with a pleasant view over the lawns which surrounded us.

My predecessor, Christopher Payne, was proud to be a fourth-generation police officer, and all his forebears had reached senior rank (his daughter later joined to make the fifth). On his desk was a photograph of his grandfather in uniform, standing beside an early police charabanc. A colleague, pointing at the picture, remarked that the old man would have been proud of him for reaching the rank of Chief Constable, 'particularly as he was a bus conductor' – whereas in fact he too had been a Chief Constable. The same colleague remarked about his/my desk, 'Some people try and make MFI furniture look like the real thing. You've managed to do it the other way around' – which was rude, but a response to being told of its cost.

My new patch was relatively compact, comprising the towns of Middlesbrough, Hartlepool and Stockton (the place where the safety-match was invented, boasting the widest main street in Britain), all set in a tract of the North Yorkshire moors named the Cleveland Hills and flanked by a stretch of dramatic coast. It is a region of huge contrasts: I described the approach to the edge of Middlesbrough as 'Gotham City', for the chemical and steel plants belched out plumes of flame and smoke from their smelly processes, and at night their flares could be seen for miles around. From the windows of our penthouse apartment in Saltburn, however, there was nothing in sight but the rolling Cleveland Hills and the sea crashing onto the craggy shoreline. We had put the farm up for sale as it was our intention to buy a house in France with the proceeds. Fortunately for us, as it later turned out, there was little interest and it was never sold. I would spend most of my week alone in Cleveland, going home to the family at weekends. This had one advantage – I could work long hours without incurring Bren's wrath. On the other hand, it was a very lonely existence, returning to empty rooms late at night to eat a take-away meal or a microwaved jacket potato with cheese. Bren would come and stay some weekends and on any occasion she was required for a social function. One national newspaper carried a photograph of the whole of the apartment block, and a critical story about how public funds were being used to pay for my 'millionaire lifestyle'. If only they knew! I lost tens of thousands of pounds when I came to sell that flat.

The Cleveland Police, along with the health and social agencies, were still reeling from the criticism they had received for their handling of a series of child sexual abuse cases. The accusations were that they had lacked co-ordination and had been too hasty in taking children from their parents and into care. The conclusions of the public inquiry, by Lady Justice Butler-Sloss, were very damaging, so much bridge-building was needed.

The situation itself was extremely sad. A number of children were deemed to have been sexually abused by their parents, and were taken into the care of the local authority. Many parents denied the charges and some were dropped, and their children were returned to them after a painful disruption in their lives. In other instances, the children were rescued by their removal from abusive homes. In a desire to understand more, I met the professionals concerned and visited some of the families and children affected. Whatever the truth of the matter, I recognised the pain and suffering some of those children had experienced. It is too awful to contemplate, but one girl had been subjected to sexual intercourse from the age of eighteen months, as had other siblings within the family. One must ask why the mothers did not intervene to protect their children. I know it is no excuse, but many of them had suffered the same fate at the hands of their fathers, and others simply buried their heads in the sand, as they felt they could not survive without their partners.

There are many misconceptions about the physical and sexual abuse of children, most of which is perpetrated by a member of the family or someone who has legitimate access to their lives. A test for the Cleveland children, some as young as five, was to draw pictures of themselves. The abused ones consistently drew portraits of children with either no lower body at all, or with a brick or other solid mass where the lower body should be.

Their statements were heart-rending. They talked of the love they had for the person who had abused them, but blocked out of their minds the pain they had experienced. I recognised these feelings, as I had suffered the same fate. I tried to help by sharing my own secret with other groups of damaged people, some my age, who were so scarred that they had been unable to forge any meaningful relationship in their lives.

In 1990 there was a lingering sense of blame in Cleveland between the various agencies concerned, and this had to be eliminated if we were to make progress. I formed closer working relationships with the Chief Executive of the council, the Director of Social Services, the Director of Education, the Chief Probation Officer, and the Chief Executive of the Health Authority. We met monthly to determine how we could improve our joint service, and bring about change for the good. Our work became the blueprint for inter-agency action, which had never occurred in this country before. Joint teams were deployed in the county's most deprived communities, with the common aim of improving our services and the quality of life for the people who lived there.

Another productive alliance was with the chief fire and ambulance officers. We were all in various stages of gearing-up our computerised command and control systems, and it seemed sensible to join forces. This liaison brought about some exciting joint ventures. I became a non-executive director of the newly-formed Ambulance Trust (which incidentally got me into hot water with leading Labour politicians, as the trusts were a Conservative Government initiative). My police colleagues also took the mickey out of me, asking if I had arrived at work by ambulance. The media were less friendly, suggesting that taking the fee for the post was greed on my part – which was annoying, as I directed the money to the National Society for the Prevention of Cruelty to Children.

Our ambition was to develop a joint control centre, which would immeasurably improve our emergency response to the public and save substantial amounts of public money. We received £50,000 from the Department of Health and the Home Office to pay for research, which proved it could be done. We set the necessary change in motion to achieve our objective, but never saw it come to fruition, as all three of us – fire, ambulance and police chiefs – left Cleveland for various reasons. I was heartened to learn later that our work was not in vain: the control centre is now up and running successfully, one of only two within the United Kingdom.

Our police command and control system was old and inefficient, and I jumped at the opportunity to update it. We chose an unproven American system which was revolutionary at that time, and our initiative sent ripples through the computing world. There was speculation within police circles about the wisdom of our choice; but morale lifted when my officers realised the system's potential and saw that it was the most advanced in the world. Jim Medlock, the billionaire owner of Intergraph, the company which supplied the system, came to visit the force and confided in me that he had tendered for the contract far below cost, as he wished to break into the European market.

When linked to a satellite, the computer was capable of plotting the movement of vehicles, and it could pass encrypted messages to and from them, automatically adding operational information for the officers in charge. This might include details of whether the person being visited held a firearms licence, or had convictions for violence or a warrant outstanding against his name. It could also tell the police officer if there had been previous crimes or incidents at any particular location, and how they had been resolved. At that time, 1991, Cleveland was the only police area in the United Kingdom which had all its Ordnance Survey maps converted to digital form and held a complete set of aerial photographs of the county. In short, the system gave us capabilities that no one else in England possessed.

For me, the contract with Intergraph brought a significant personal side issue, when Jim Medlock offered me a vice-presidency of the company. He did this at his home on Jupiter Island, in Florida, to which I had been flown in one of his private jets. From my suite on the top floor of the luxuriously furnished house the sea views were magnificent, and Jim and his wife Nancy proved delightful hosts, with very interesting backgrounds. He was the leading mathematician in the American Apollo space programme, and it was his calculations which helped to put men on the moon.

Leaving NASA, he set up his own company, and by the time I met him, after only eleven years, it had grown to 30,000 employees. Most of his team had gone with him and had traded their salaries for equity in the early years, and so had all become millionaires. Nancy, then recovering from a serious illness, was involved in the financial aspects of the business, and could bring up details of every one of their employees around the world on the computer screen in her study.

I could happily have spent days listening to Jim's stories about the space programme. Recognising my interest, he took me to see space rockets and the Apollo capsule, which was so tiny that it was impossible to believe that three men could fit into such cramped space, let alone survive re-entry through the earth's atmosphere. The burn marks on the heat-shield were evidence of the ferocious temperatures they had endured. Jim likened the mental attitude of the astronauts to that of our airmen during the Battle of Britain: they knew there was a high likelihood of death, but they were prepared to put their lives on the line for their country.

As for commerce – Jim said he needed someone with credibility to market his systems worldwide, a person with the ability to get close to major clients and ascertain the future needs of their businesses. He offered me the job, as he had a 'gut feeling' about me. I was flattered, and agreeably surprised by the package of rewards he offered, not least a salary at least four times what I was earning.

Naturally I was tempted, and I told him I would need to talk things over with Bren. By pure coincidence, I had just been offered a job with Unisys, another American computer company, who sought my services to market a system designed to solve murders, which I had helped develop after the Ripper inquiry. On a lecture tour to the States later that same year I was also invited to become a professor at the University of Southern Florida. After careful consideration we decided against accepting any of these offers, which I have never regretted.

Another West Yorkshire colleague also had an unusual offer about this time. Millionaire Robert Maxwell visited Bradford after the tragic fire at the football ground there. Maxwell asked to see all the directors of local agencies, and offered help in the form of money and resources, providing they didn't disclose his contribution. He asked if he could visit the scene of the fire with my friend – who described him as the most powerful man he had ever met. During the journey, Maxwell passed him a brown envelope in which were details of his career, his financial status and a list of indiscretions. The tycoon told him that he didn't think he would go any further in the police, then offered him a job and instructed him to call within seven days.

They next met on the roof garden above the Fetter Lane offices of the *Daily Mirror*. Maxwell said he had singled my friend out because he could trust him, as he himself had much to lose. He asked him to troubleshoot on his behalf around the world, insisting on complete loyalty and obedience. The benefits were substantial: a flat in London, whatever car he wished, and a salary which dwarfed his own. He turned the offer down.

During my two and a half years in Cleveland, I was also asked to consider applying for other posts within the police service – the newly-created job of Director General of the National Criminal Intelligence Service, and the post of Chief Constable in Northumbria, both of which I refused.

Local politicians were crucial to successful change, and I intended to use Police Authority meetings as the main axis for innovation. This proved impossible, as their deliberations lasted for less than ten minutes, the chairman, Ian Jeffries, believing that the Authority was unconstitutional, since it was outside the direct control of the Labour Council. Jeffries was also chairman of the Cleveland Labour Party, and he agreed to meet on a more informal basis. I found him guarded at first, one quirky reason being that his son was a police officer in London, and he didn't wish that to be known, as he feared it might undermine his credibility with other members. I thought this a strange attitude for the chairman of a police body – but later sessions proved very productive, and became a regular feature of our relationship

This was progress of a kind, but as there a lot of antipathy towards the police, I wished to influence the politicians on a broader front. Having addressed both the Liberal and Conservative Associations in the county, I asked the ruling Labour Party if I could do the same. The meeting took place at their sparse headquarters in Middlesbrough on a cold, windy, winter Saturday afternoon. It was one of those moments at which I questioned what I was doing with my life. I could feel the hostility of the gathered throng when Ian Jeffries opened proceedings by saying, 'I never thought I would see the day when a police officer attended one of our meetings, let alone a Chief Constable. However, he's asked to come and I've promised him ten minutes.'

He sat down and looked in my direction. The room came to a hush. After I had introduced myself and thanked the organisers for inviting me, a woman interrupted and said, 'I'm not going to stay to listen to you. I've no time for any of you any more.' When I asked her why, she replied, 'Even before the miners' strike, I never thought much of the police, but that was the last straw. I'll never trust any of you again.'

When I asked her how often she had visited a coal mine, she replied, 'I've been a lot closer than you have,' so I explained my mining credentials – five years underground. She was visibly taken aback, and she sat down. At the end of this little scene I took off my jacket in a very theatrical manner, rolled up my shirt sleeves and said, 'If that's the sort of meeting it's going to be, I'd better get ready.' This seemed to go down well, and there were cries of 'Give the lad a chance.' More than two hours later, the chairman intervened to end my 'ten-minute' session, on all manner of questions about police and policing.

I left feeling that I had won some friends and supporters, including someone called Peter Mandelson, whom I later described to Bren as 'a callow young man who's obviously very bright'. He accompanied me out of the building, and, after complimenting me on the way I handled the meeting, said that I would not know him, but he was running Neil Kinnock's election campaign, and was the prospective Labour MP for Hartlepool. He asked if he could come and see me, because he wished to help. I told him to ring my secretary to arrange an appointment. We continued our conversation over lunch in my office a couple of weeks later.

Peter pursued the idea of my going into politics, saying, 'You're

a very marketable commodity, and I could help you exploit that.'
He also suggested that I meet a young politician called Tony Blair.
'You won't have heard of him,' he told me, 'but I'm grooming him
for greatness. You'd get on well together.' His intuition was good
in all respects: in due course Tony Blair became the Labour leader
and Prime Minister, and when he and I met, we quickly hit it off.

One of my concerns was the lack of involvement of the local MPs
and MEPs, whom I only met at social events and corresponded with
over complaints from constituents. I needed to draw them in. I
had a good relationship with Roy Hattersley, the shadow Home
Secretary, whom I used to help frame questions about the police.
(Immediately before the General Election of 1992 he visited me in
my office, to ask if I would like to become the Commissioner of
the Metropolitan Police, 'when we're elected' – which of course
they were not until five years later.) I arranged meetings with all
these political figures to discuss both my and their agendas. One
of the first to visit was Marjorie (Mo) Mowlam, the Labour representative for Redcar. My impression was of a very bright, personable young woman who was determined to make a difference. She
was well-regarded and liked by her constituents, and always made
my secretaries laugh. During my time in Cleveland we built up a
sufficient degree of trust for her to seek my advice about a very
delicate matter concerning one of my senior officers, who had made
inappropriate advances. I developed a good rapport with all these
committed people, who helped me put my work in perspective.

My predecessor and the senior management team advised me
that the force was 'in good order' and needed little change. I had
some reservations, as our performance lagged behind others, and
my impression was endorsed by the advice I received from local
and national politicians who considered that change was necessary.
I set about finding out the views of police officers on the ground
and other employees. They all told much the same story: a great
deal needed to be done. Their principal worries were low morale,
high levels of sickness, high levels of assaults upon them, and the
number of complaints against them.

My belief was, and is, that one of the most important tasks of a Chief Constable is to meet and listen to ordinary people, as they are the ones who need satisfying. I therefore attended public meetings, visited old people's centres, young mother and baby groups, schools and factories. These outings complemented my regular walks on the beat, where I spoke to as many people as possible. Through these perambulations I learned of the substantial mistrust and lack of confidence the public had in us. This was partly due to the child-abuse case, but it went much deeper, with many people feeling that we just didn't care.

Cleveland had some of the most deprived areas in the United Kingdom, with high unemployment, low life-expectancy and the physical appearance of a war zone, with graffiti, damage, boarded-up buildings and shops defended like fortresses. The law-abiding people who lived in these dismal surroundings considered that they had been written off. Crime levels were sky-high, with very low detection-rates. Residents were angry, particularly as they knew who the offenders were, and believed that 'your lot do nothing even when we tell you'. A stark sign of these people's lack of self-worth – and perhaps a factor contributing to child abuse – was the fact, revealed by our research, that women accepted the frequent beatings they received from their male partners as 'part of family life'.

There was also real fear among them. One old lady told me that she had lived on her particular estate for seventy years, but that it had deteriorated so much that she rarely left her house. She *had* gone out before Christmas – and returned to find all her presents and even her Christmas tree had been stolen. She knew who the criminals were, as they had bragged about the theft, but she alleged that the police had done nothing, and, for her trouble, the offenders had thrown a stone through her window, and embedded an axe in her door with a threatening note pinned to it. I heard many such distressing stories. Shopkeepers told me they had armed themselves with baseball bats to ward off youngsters who acted like locusts and stripped their shelves bare.

These were lawless places, controlled by a relatively small number of criminals who considered themselves free to do as they liked. When we cross-checked the names of a hundred young male offenders with entries on the education and social service files, we discovered that both agencies had problems with more than sixty per cent of the families on my list. To deal with the ten most serious trouble-makers was costing us jointly £100,000 worth of resources for each family every year.

Police officers at street level accepted the communities' assessment of the situation. They had identified a dozen or so fifteen- to seventeen-year-old lads in each area as being responsible for most of the lawlessness, but claimed they were powerless to deal with them for a number of reasons. First, the community would not give evidence against them – even when two young girls suffered multiple rape – and although this was clearly due to fear of reprisal, that was no help. Second, they criticised the force policy of cautioning: they complained that even when they arrested someone, the likelihood was the person would merely be cautioned for the offence and released within hours – which added to the community's lack of confidence in the system and increased the criminal's feeling of invincibility. (Cautioning is a facility employed by the police as an alternative to court. During the eighties there was strong governmental support for its use, and criminals were often cautioned five or six times before being put before court.)

The officers' third complaint was the leniency of the courts when criminals eventually appeared before them. Although recognising that the courts' powers were limited by rules covering first-time offenders, the lack of adequate sentences compounded the community's feeling of powerlessness.

My officers found it difficult even to penetrate some areas in response to calls for assistance, as they would be ambushed on the way. The ambulance, the fire service, social services and midwives were similarly attacked, and often refused to go in without police protection.

Cleveland had the highest rate in the country of theft of and from vehicles, and one of the lowest recovery rates. Young criminals were so confident that they would bait officers by revving up stolen vehicles outside police stations, or driving alongside a police vehicle shouting to its driver that they had stolen the car they were driving.

When my officers gave chase, they were often lured into a dead-end street, and another stolen vehicle would be driven up behind them to block their exit. They would then be physically attacked with sticks and stones, which along with snooker balls were hurled at our cars. During my early days more than 50 per cent of our vehicles were off the road for repair through such attacks.

We began to address these issues one by one. We knew we could not win the public's confidence overnight, so we tasked the joint groups to help us. Research indicated that children were extremely vulnerable in the high-crime areas, particularly after school and during school holidays. Many of them were being lured or bullied into anti-social acts such as riding in stolen vehicles. We offered police stations for use as crèches – an initiative not taken up because local authorities introduced facilities first. We persuaded head teachers to allow their school playgrounds and other recreational facilities to be used by children outside normal school hours. Church and industrial land was made available for young people to ride bicycles and motor cycles – something for which they had previously been prosecuted. Initiatives by teachers, police officers, priests and many other individuals were financially supported, for example to teach young people to build and repair vehicles, and ride them safely. Street furniture and public buildings were repaired, and graffiti removed.

We also changed our cautioning policy: young people were given one chance, and only then if the arresting officer believed in their contrition. We gained the support of the Crown Prosecution Service (CPS) to fast-track cases to the court, and engaged the magistrates and judiciary, through seminars and visits to the worst communities, so that they would recognise the plight of law-abiding citizens and use appropriate powers to help. I wrote to politicians both locally and nationally, encouraging them to bring about a change in the law, and went public to suggest that prolific criminality would only be stopped if we introduced some certainty into the system. I recommended a 'three strikes and you're out' policy, years before President Clinton adopted the phrase.

Police operations targeted the small groups of criminals in each community. They were followed, harried and questioned whenever they left their homes, and their friends and associates were dealt with in a similar manner. When arrested, they were questioned at length about other offences they might have committed, changing the practice which had grown up of asking them only about the offence for which their liberty had been removed.

Our initiatives made a huge difference to the confidence of the police and the deprived communities, and the two fed from each other. The public could see that something positive was happening: more criminals were arrested and – more importantly – imprisoned, so people began to confide in the police. With their support and the courts my officers could see they were making an impact on criminality. Crime fell dramatically, and in some areas halved within twelve months, reversing years of increases. Detection rates of the crimes which were committed improved measurably, and we moved off the bottom of the performance tables.

I would like to believe that I was beginning to build up some personal credibility within the force. I saw all retiring officers and asked them how they thought I might bring about improvements. Much of what they said was helpful, but some of their revelations were disturbing. One after the other two retiring detectives suggested that I might usefully examine our register of informants.

On the first occasion Jack Ord the Deputy Chief Constable tried to reassure me that everything was above board, and when I insisted that he inquire further, he again reported that everything was in order. Yet my unease increased when I spoke to the second detective, and I arranged for an officer from another force to investigate. Jack was unhappy, suggesting that I had questioned his judgement, and the head of the CID was similarly put out.

In addition to dealing with the communities' problems, we needed to put our own house in order. As the number of assaults on police dropped, sickness began to reduce, but my officers were still taking more days' sick leave in a year than those of any other force, and there was no identifiable reason, except that the practice was embedded in the culture of the organisation. My suspicions were confirmed when one officer boasted to me that he 'never took all his sick days' – as if there was an allocation, which of course there was not.

Examination of our procedures indicated that there was no control: when officers reported in sick by telephone, they were merely asked when they thought they would return, and provided they came back on time, nothing more was done. I introduced much stricter controls. Anyone who fell ill was required to furnish precise information, which was logged, and he or she was visited by a supervisory officer on the first day of absence. This change threw up some very interesting cases – officers playing golf or football on the beach, looking after their children to 'give the wife a rest', or just staying at home doing nothing.

Lax management benefits no one other than scroungers. Officers who wish to work become disillusioned when they see their colleagues getting away with it, especially when their absence imposes an additional burden, and morale suffers. To reduce operational pressures, I also altered the working patterns of the force so that more officers were available at times of peak demand. This may seem like commonsense, but shifts are very difficult to tamper with, as the more anti-social they are, the more they affect family life. The consequential increase in the number of officers available to deal with calls for service, and the considerable reductions in sickness and injuries on duty, further boosted the public's confidence in us, and this in turn raised our morale.

Running a police force has its own peculiar demands. Much of the time is devoted to driving a multi-million-pound organisation in order to improve the service, but a Chief also has to devote his attention to individual incidents. In the north-east the early 1990s was a time of strife. Outbreaks of public disorder by disaffected young men became common throughout the region, which added to our burden. Every day shops had their windows put through; fire bombs were placed through letter boxes; and two or three cars were stolen and torched, to destroy fingerprints.

In the summer of 1991, routine criminality boiled over into large-scale riots in Northumbria and Cleveland, where gangs of youths barricaded streets and threw missiles at the police, striking terror into local communities. Poor housing and employment were used as justification for this riotous behaviour, but many criminals – who had no intention of ever working – simply seized the opportunity to settle old scores by targeting particular individuals and premises. Peace was restored after a number of days, but the media were less than helpful, encouraging, and on more than one occasion paying, youths to commit crimes in order to get action photographs.

Another contrasting case involved the death of an unarmed black man, who had launched himself at the front of an ambulance, punching and head-butting its windscreen. He refused to stop even when restrained by both ambulance and police crews. During the mêlée one police officer held him in a headlock, from which he suffocated to death.

It didn't add up. The deceased came from Birmingham, and had no known reason to be in Middlesbrough: he had no history of mental illness, and no traces of drink or drugs were found at the postmortem. I spoke to his parents, who were as perplexed as we were, but they accepted my sympathy and explanation of their son's death.

Any tragic case like this is used by anti-police activists to further their cause. In this instance we were branded as murderers and racists, by a small group who picketed police headquarters. To no avail I had acquainted them with the full circumstances at meetings supervised by the Police Complaints Authority. This group gained maximum publicity from the case, knowing we could not comment until the inquiry was complete. Eventually the report exonerated the individual officers, but recommended the introduction of new restraint training, which was subsequently adopted by the service.

Satisfaction within my professional career was not matched by my health. For many years I had suffered from back problems, and these were getting progressively worse. I reached the stage at which I was unable to move from a sitting or lying position without help, and I didn't enjoy a single night's continuous sleep, due to the pain. I am sure the deterioration was partly caused by the distance I drove (130,000 miles in thirty months), a personal choice, as I thought it inappropriate to employ a driver in such a poor county.

When I sought medical advice, I was told that my spine had

been broken many years previously, damaging three vertebrae in the lumbar region. The bones had fused together, putting pressure on my spinal cord. The only incident which could account for this had occurred twenty years previously, when a car knocked me from my Lambretta scooter into a telegraph pole. The specialist said that there was little he could do other than operate, which he did not recommend. It was lucky that I paid to consult this surgeon, as he informed me that, were I a National Health patient, he would have had to contact my employers and advise dismissal, as I was 60 per cent disabled. If I had required any information on how the medical retirement system operated, I was experiencing it first-hand. Other than injuries caused by sport or an accident, my back had not necessitated my losing one day's work in thirty years. I was now being told that had I not paid to see the consultant, he would have effectively ended my police career, whether I wished it or not. I pondered how many other officers had found themselves in this position – and at what cost to the service. Thankfully, I discovered a wonderful naturopath in York, Atul Shah, who did wonders in relieving my pain by manipulation and has kept me going ever since. Without him, I would now be on sticks.

On the domestic front, our living arrangements had become unsatisfactory. My job kept me apart from Bren for a great deal of the time, and if Charles had not still been at home at the farm, loneliness would have driven Bren crazy.

At weekends Bren and the family would come and stay in the flat, or I would go home. The A1 was being upgraded at that time, and although the distance between the two properties was only about 100 miles, the journey often took four or five hours, which was exceedingly tedious. Sometimes it seemed more relaxing to stay in Saltburn. We all loved the rugged coastline, and when my back permitted, we would take long walks there.

Some of my critics have said that by retaining our home in West Yorkshire I displayed a lack of commitment to my job in Cleveland. In fact, the opposite was true. The additional cost, and the years of separation from my wife and family, amounted to a sacrifice which I would not advise anyone to make.

There were fewer official functions in Cleveland than in more affluent counties, and most of the occasions we attended were to do with the Lord Lieutenant, the High Sheriff and royal visits. These led to many enjoyable encounters, as we both found it fascinating to spend time with people from entirely different backgrounds. The 'County Set' – as many of them would define themselves – consisted largely of families who had been in the community for generations – land owners, titled people and senior members of the clergy – but their ranks were supplemented by successful industrialists and entrepreneurs who had made good more recently.

The Chief Executive and Chief Constable of any county are invited to join this exclusive club for their time in office – due in part to the fact that, until recently, their positions were traditionally occupied by people from the County Set. Some of my fellow Chief Constables believed that their membership would continue after they left office, but they were deluding themselves – unless they were enrolled as Deputy Lord Lieutenants, which secured their continuance.

Lord Lieutenants hold the most prestigious office in any county: they are appointed by the Queen as her representatives in the area, and they may remain in office until they are seventy-five. They officiate at royal visits and give out honours and awards, wearing impressive, quasi-military uniform and carrying a sword. This is a difficult piece of equipment to deal with, particularly if its owner has to jump in and out of cars to be ahead of a royal personage. A previous Lord Lieutenant in Humberside had an artificial leg, which made it doubly difficult for him to manoeuvre his sword. He was a real character who joked about his disability, and once said that when visiting the dentist he did his best to impress the pretty young receptionist, but failed miserably, because when he stood up, his leg fell off.

In my time Lord Guisborough was Lord Lieutenant of Cleveland; both he and his wife were delightful people, if a little out of touch with ordinary life. At our first meeting he gave me forthright advice on how to stop crime: 'Hand the criminals over to me, and I'll put them to work on the land. I'll feed them if they're good, and beat them if they're not.' Many people regarded Guisborough as eccentric. He had been to the public school patronised by his family for generations, and had old-fashioned courtesy. His dog was called 'Fiver', because that was what he paid for him, and he hunted and fished with boundless enthusiasm. I liked him very much. Not only did he and his family provide work for many people: they also created stability – something of which there is very little in our society today.

The ancient office of High Sheriff is taken up by an individual in each county for one year only. In Cleveland the nobleman in office immediately before my arrival had only just moved out of his family home, bought by Sir Richard Branson for conversion into a luxury hotel. The original responsibility of the office was for keeping law and order, but in modern times this is little exercised. Today's High Sheriffs play a large part in entertaining the judges who visit their county on circuit; they can, and many do, sit with a judge in court to hear cases. They wear a uniform which includes a frilly shirt, a velvet jacket complete with silver buttons, black tights and buckled slippers, and their hospitality often matches the extravagance of their dress: one night a visiting judge became so fuddled that he addressed Brenda as 'Sandy', and me as 'Eric', throughout the evening, even though repeatedly offered polite corrections. But every High Sheriff I have known offered whatever assistance he or she could, visiting the force, raising money for police charities and giving help in many other ways.

A Chief Constable spends a fair amount of social time in the company of these people. Bren and I were surprised to find that at the end of a meal the women were expected to leave the men 'to talk'. With the ladies gone, we would shuffle down the table to form a tight group at one end and drink brandy and port, accompanied by cigars. I have never smoked, and was completely teetotal all the time I was in Cleveland, so this part of the evening held little attraction for me, especially as I found the habit of banishing the ladies rather sexist.

The male conversation was largely harmless, although on one occasion, in another county, the men began to talk about 'blacks' and 'niggers'. I let them go on for a moment, then told them that I found it offensive and asked them to change the subject – to which one of them replied, 'It's all right. You're among friends. You can tell us what you really think about the black bastards.' At that I got up to leave the room – which broke up the gathering. Our host, tactfully changing the subject, invited us to 'use the facilities' before we rejoined the ladies, 'the facilities' being the rose bushes outside his front door. This was an exceptional incident, as most of the Sheriffs and their friends were (and, I am sure, are) good people, genuine in their desire to help the community through advice and charitable work.

I couldn't help but smile at some of the antics of people during VIP visits. We normally had a dress-rehearsal to check timings and familiarise ourselves with locations and routes. Often the people due to be introduced would be present, and insist that either I or the Lord Lieutenant walked the line as if we were the real thing. Although there was strict protocol, arguments – and even jostling – occasionally broke out over who should take precedence. Local mayors were particularly pushy, some suggesting that they should supplant the Lord Lieutenant in their own town. If there was more than one mayor, they would argue as to which of them should come first. Very often the people who really deserved to be presented were frozen out by the 'Chain Gang', and so were denied an intro- duction. During the visits proper individuals sometimes lost their heads, abandoned pride and dignity and pushed their way to the front. There was no small irony in all this, as in other circumstances these very people would make a point of refusing to stand for the national anthem or a loyal toast.

Cleveland was insular in many ways. Local politicians on Teesside had chips on their shoulders because they thought they ought to have been given the status of Metropolitan County, as had Tyneside. They were unwilling to involve themselves outside their district, and forbade officers of the County Council to do so. Newcomers to the county were regarded with suspicion, and I was one of these.

I think Cleveland's geographic location helped foster its isolation. People who lived any distance from their place of work were regarded as odd. Once, after an evening talk, I was offered overnight accommodation in Hartlepool, and when my hosts learned that I would have to travel more than twenty miles home, this became the subject of much discussion.

The local government reorganisation hadn't helped, as there was little or no affinity between Middlesbrough, Hartlepool and the rural tracts which were formerly part of North Yorkshire. Whenever the representatives from these districts came together, they had difficulty being civil with each other, and rarely missed an opportunity of point-scoring. On more than one occasion the animosity flared up into fighting. One member of the Police Authority had the whip withdrawn (his voting power was taken away from him) because he assaulted another member in the library.

People tended to hold extreme left-wing views, and would do all they could to frustrate the initiatives of the Conservative central Government. Their hostility extended to refusing to introduce changes in schools, in the health service and in support services such as catering and cleaning. This embarrassed some of their officers, who were instructed to act in an unconstitutional way which sometimes bordered on the illegal. The tension came to a head towards the end of my stay in the county, when chief officers were directed to make speeches against planned local government reorganisation because it threatened to curtail their powers. As I was neutral, a number of these officers confided in me, telling me they were virtually being blackmailed: if they didn't do as they were bid, they would lose their jobs – and it was the same with new appointments. If candidates would not agree to bend to the will of those in power locally, they would not gain employment.

All this, I know, is politics, but its application adversely affects people's lives. In Middlesbrough, for example, the authorities refused to let some children use their sporting facilities because they attended a new type of technical school which had been forced upon the council by the Government.

CHAPTER TWENTY

HOME AGAIN

In the late summer of 1992 Peter Nobes, the Chief Constable of West Yorkshire, announced his retirement to take up an appointment as an adviser to the British Secret Service. With Bren's blessing I decided to apply for his job.

As luck would have it, a few days before this announcement Lord Ferris, the Home Office minister responsible for the police, had spent a full day with me in Cleveland visiting some of our successful initiatives. As he was leaving, he asked if I was happy in Cleveland, and when I answered 'Yes', he said I was being wasted and ought to be in a larger force. Next morning one of his senior staff telephoned to repeat that message on his behalf. I thought this a good omen, as Ferris was the minister responsible for approving the short-lists for senior police appointments.

I told the chairman of the Cleveland Police Authority of my intention. He said he was sorry, as he didn't wish me to go, and neither would his colleagues. He recalled that on appointment I had told him that the West Yorkshire Chief was the only other job I would ever apply for, so reluctantly he gave me his support.

The vacancy was advertised for serving Chief Constables only. This was unusual, although not unique. The Police Authority had decided to appoint someone with experience in the rank, as theirs was the fourth largest force in the United Kingdom, employing

8,000 police and civilian staff and serving two and a quarter million citizens. I applied and was short-listed, along with four other serving Chiefs.

Communication between West Yorkshire and the candidates was very carefully controlled: written information was passed by hand, and conversations were conducted by telephone or in face-to-face meetings, as the Authority wished to keep the names of the applicants secret – an attempt which led to much speculation in the local newspapers.

In the middle of this process, a story appeared in the *Yorkshire Post* outlining my work with the Yorkshire Ripper and speculating on my candidacy. This was the first time anything had appeared in public about my relationship with Sutcliffe, and as the story contained details of the times I had visited Broadmoor, I was convinced that it was leaked from within the police service. Why? I could only think that it had been done in an attempt to undermine me, as it raised my profile at the very time I wished to remain low-key. The exposure was extremely distracting: I was pursued by the national and international media to talk about my encounters with Sutcliffe, and I knew that publicity would damage my relationship with him. Ironically, one of the other candidates, entirely misunderstanding the situation, accused me of orchestrating the story myself to help me get the job. I anticipated a call from West Yorkshire asking me to withdraw from the short-list, but none came.

The interviews – preceded, unusually, by a full medical examination – took place over two days. The interview process began in earnest with a reception and musical-chairs dinner, and concluded with a presentation and lengthy interview, after verbal and written exercises in between.

Halfway through, one of the candidates asked me how much influence the HMI, Colin Smith, would have on the decision of the Police Authority. I told him I had no idea, but if previous experience was to go by, the answer was 'little'. I was convinced the Authority would make up its own mind. He held out his hand to shake mine and congratulated me on getting the job.

In another curious incident Colin Smith asked one of the candidates if he still owned his donkeys. When the man said he did, Smith replied, 'You ought to have sent them in your place. They'd have done better than you.' The donkey-owner put on a brave face, but I know he was hurt by the remark, which was not said jokingly.

Our final test was to present our existing force's annual report, in the same way as we had to our own Police Authority. I was the last candidate, and it was late in the day. I sensed some of the panel had lost interest, which I read as a bad sign, thinking that they had made up their mind for someone else and were going through the motions to be polite.

During the twenty minutes we had to wait for the members to make up their minds, I wrote myself off, employing the sort of defensive mechanism which most people adopt to deal with failure. Then I was called back in. The chairman of the panel, Tom Brennan, said, 'We would like to offer you the job of Chief Constable of West Yorkshire. Are you prepared to accept?'

I was so overcome with emotion that tears came into my eyes, and for a moment I couldn't answer. When I composed myself, I said I would be delighted. This was everything I could have wished for in my career. Tom asked if I would like to ring my wife and tell her the news. I jumped at the opportunity, and called Bren from the Chief Constable's chair, in the office that was to be mine. I cannot explain how moved I was when I entered it – it was the proudest moment of my professional career. Bren was overcome with joy and congratulated me on my success.

When I returned to the members, Tom told me that the committee's decision had been unanimous, and they were pleased to have me on board. He outlined my first priorities – sort out the force's finances, which were in a very bad state, and improve the organisation's image by 'putting West Yorkshire back on the map'. He then sought two favours of me: 'First, please buy a new Jaguar staff car, as the current one gives the wrong impression, and second, join the International Association of Chief Police Officers [IACP]' – an American organisation which held its conferences in the USA. I told the members that I would be more than pleased to do as they asked. What a change in tone from the penny-pinching, introverted attitude in Cleveland!

After I had shaken hands and exchanged pleasantries with every member of the panel, the meeting broke up. One of them then drew me aside and asked, 'Why is the HMI working against you?' When I couldn't produce an answer, he told me that Smith had been pushing the candidate who congratulated me halfway through, and had been knocking me 'from the off'. 'I got very cross with him,' said my ally, 'because every time someone said something in your favour, he would chime in and be as negative as he could.'

At home I received a wonderful welcome. Bren and the children were waiting for me and greeted me with applause, hugs and kisses. My appointment had been announced on the local radio, and we received a succession of telephone calls from well-wishers. One was from the reporter at the *Yorkshire Post* who had leaked the Ripper story – now he was seeking a photograph. We have always kept our private life out of the public eye, but we were so overjoyed on this occasion that we agreed to pose. This picture of us both, sitting in front of the fire, still holds pride of place in our home.

The other candidates excelled in their careers. Two became Inspectors of Constabulary, one of whom was knighted and appointed Chief Inspector; the third rose to be Commissioner of the New South Wales Police in Australia; and the last retired shortly afterwards. Before I took up my new post, my predecessor gave me a comprehensive briefing on the state of the force. I had not realised how bad it was. Peter described the organisation as bankrupt: we couldn't meet the wages bill, and consequently we were 500 officers below establishment, making us the most under-staffed force in the country. The vehicle fleet was old; the building and refurbishing programme had almost come to a halt; and no technological development had taken place for years. As a result, the force languished close to the bottom of the national performance indicator tables; crime was rising, detections were falling, and sickness and ill-health retirements were almost off the scale. In 1992, 83 per cent of West Yorkshire officers left before their time, compared with 13 per cent nationally. Peter apologised for having to hand things over in such a bad state, and offered little encouragement for the future. He stated frankly that it was virtually impossible to turn the force round.

The HMI's briefing was equally depressing. He advised me that sexual discrimination was rife in the force: there were instances of female officers being sexually assaulted and even raped by their male colleagues. Due to the male-dominant culture, these crimes went unreported, as women had no confidence in the system and believed they would be ostracised if they told tales. He asked if I would address this issue as a matter of urgency.

During the few weeks between Peter's departure and my arrival, Paul Whitehouse, my new deputy, acted up. I called to see him once or twice to discuss matters, but sensed that he did not welcome my visits. I had some sympathy for him, as he had served the force as its deputy for a number of years and was naturally disappointed at not being allowed to compete for the top job.

I took up my appointment in West Yorkshire on 4 January 1993, the thirty-first anniversary of my joining the police service. After thirty challenging months in the north-east, during which I had driven myself, it was a treat to sink into the back seat of the dark-blue, chauffeur-driven, stretch Jaguar – automatic and air-conditioned, with built-in telephone – which drew up to my front door on that first morning. I felt a twinge of guilt at the decadence of sitting in such luxurious surroundings, reading *The Times* and the *Yorkshire Post*, which had been carefully placed on the back seat. My driver, an old colleague from Huddersfield who was about to retire, said he would stay on until I found a replacement. The thought of him going saddened me, as I liked him.

My new secretary had worked for me before in the Discipline and Complaints Department. She was extremely efficient, and I was pleased she had achieved the position, as I had recommended her to Colin Sampson when he was Chief. Unfortunately she had difficulty in adapting to my style of working, telling me, 'Mr Nobes wouldn't do it like this.' Peter had check-read all her work, which comforted her. I simply did not have the time or, to be frank, the inclination to be a check-reader, and insisted this was her job. This distressed her, and began to get her down. We had a number of quite amicable discussions, after which part of her work-load was farmed out to other members of the office. Yet she was never really happy, and asked if she could move: reluctantly I let her transfer to another position within the force, on the same salary.

Her move made me realise how important the working relationship is between a secretary and a boss: you get so used to each other's ways that when either leaves it is difficult to create a new bond. I advertised within the force, and after a few false starts recruited an outstanding woman, Margaret.

On the first morning I invited my deputy, the assistants and the senior administrator to meet me. After introductions and niceties, I asked them, 'Why are we here?' and 'What are our problems?' There was no consistency in their answers to either question, and as I talked to them, it became clear that they were operating as individuals, not as a team. They viewed issues from the perspective of their own portfolios, not from that of the force. I told them that if we, as the senior team, had no corporate approach to our problems and our future, how could we expect those who worked for us to have one? We needed clarity and vision, and we must work together to achieve it. These were all highly professional people who wished to do their best, but due to shortage of resources, they were in open competition with each other for money for their departments, which was highly disruptive.

At our first team meeting I found Paul hard to engage in conversation, and I noticed that two of the assistants looked to him for a lead. Moreover, he was always 'engaged on duties outside the force', having more than twenty national commitments, and he rarely attended meetings. I was determined that there would be no division between us, as I knew how damaging that would be, so I encouraged and supported Paul when he tried for other posts, and in due course he became Chief Constable of Sussex.

Retirements helped me create a new team. When Paul left, one ACC retired. Tom Cooke, another of the existing ACCs, took Paul's place as deputy: Greg Wilkinson, a chief superintendent within the force and Norman Bettison, a very young officer from

South Yorkshire with outstanding prospects, were appointed ACCs. Norman fulfilled his promise, becoming Chief Constable of Merseyside.

We set about building a new team. We spent days away together, sometimes with facilitators, to develop a joint vision of the future and a programme to reach our goals. We faced huge management problems, which had to be dealt with in real time: crime and public disorder did not abate while we were reorganising, and the supply of money did not increase.

Just as we needed to get the rest of the organisation on our side, so we had to reassure the public and satisfy the Police Authority that we were on the right track. During the first few months I repeated what I had done in Cleveland: arranged seminars for the Authority, staged open meetings with all ranks, walked the beat with street officers and held open meetings for members of the public, some of which were volatile affairs, because people were angry at the effect that crime was having on their lives. I wrote articles for local newspapers and appeared on television and radio programmes.

I saw all my superintendents individually, seeking their views on the future of the force and the problems we faced. I told them of my plans and asked how these fitted with their own. A number confessed they were not prepared to change habits at their stage of service and would leave, so I accepted their resignations. Others said that although they didn't wish to change, they would see their time out. I told them that was unacceptable: I needed them to be fully committed to the future of the force, or to leave it, giving them twelve months to reconsider. I was more than happy for senior officers to leave, as our plan was to reduce the cost of management. Within two years West Yorkshire had the lowest supervisor-to-staff ratio, and the money we saved was used to increase the number of police working directly with the public.

One or two superintendents gave me the key to reducing the high level of ill-health retirements. One whose personal record suggested that he was perfectly fit told me he had a bad back, 'and that's good enough to get out with'. Another declared he would leave on a date eighteen months ahead because of his 'bad knees'. Again, he had no record of sickness, and he admitted, 'You store these things up in the bank. Everybody does it. When you've twenty-six years in, you cash them.' Such remarks set off a train of measures which reduced the percentage of personnel retiring for health reasons from the highest to one of the lowest in the service.

There is no police pension fund: officers are required to contribute 11 per cent of their pay, but when it comes to paying its pensioners, the force has to top up this amount from the annual revenue budget. When I returned to West Yorkshire this deficit soaked up 13 per cent of my total budget (£270 million) and was increasing year on year. Nationally the gap was four per cent lower than mine. Our reforms in this area reduced ill-health retirement below the national average, which effectively meant we had an additional £10 million per year to spend on policing.

There was a further twist to the ill-health scenario. If an officer could prove he was retiring as the result of an injury on duty, he received an enhanced pension, in the form of a lump sum and annual payments of several thousand pounds for the rest of his life, all of which were tax-free. More and more officers were taking advantage of this rule: compared with others, my force had the largest percentages of officers receiving enhanced payments. The superintendent who claimed to have bad knees as a result of an injury on duty took me to court over this issue, and lost.

At our first meeting the Force Medical Officer (FMO) told me of several cases of female officers being sexually assaulted by their male colleagues, and went into detail about one particular case of rape. He said these were not isolated incidents, 'but the tip of the iceberg'. He believed the whole culture of the force was at fault, and would have to undergo radical change before we could make any real impact on the problem.

Then I moved on to the high level of premature retirements on ill-health grounds. If patients were unfit to do their job, he said, they ought to leave. I agreed, and asked him why he thought we had been losing so many more than anywhere else in the service. He didn't have an answer to this.

When I spoke to the Police Federation and the Superintendents' Association about this conversation, they both endorsed their support for the system and cautioned me against 'interfering with something which works well'. The superintendents' representative agreed that too many officers were leaving before their time, but added, 'That's the system, and you can't blame people for taking advantage of it.' The Federation representative said, 'Well – the bosses use the system. What's good for the goose is good for the gander.'

I then asked an ACC to review every case of ill-health retirement and claim for injury-on-duty award. The Police Federation took umbrage at my decision and threatened me with legal action. The ACC acquainted me with some of the more bizarre reasons proffered by officers for leaving the service early with an injury-on-duty award. 'They've changed my shifts and I can't work the new ones,' claimed one officer. Another lodged a claim because he'd failed his examination for promotion to the next rank, and the failure was weighing on his mind, so that he couldn't do the job any more. A third said he couldn't work in uniform any longer, as he felt 'exposed and self-conscious'. (Had he suffered a serious assault, this might have been justified – but he had not.) These people were in stark contrast to the many officers who were genuinely ill or injured; ironically, the majority of these had a strong desire to recover and get back to work. I visited police men and women who had contracted cancer; suffered heart attacks and serious injuries through road accidents who were determined to beat their ailments. Unfortunately, in 1993 this group was vastly outnumbered by the scroungers.

Our widely publicised change in attitude began to take effect, and the number of people presenting themselves under the ill-health scheme began to fall. We also introduced a follow-up mechanism for those reporting sick (as I had done in Cleveland), which further set the tone.

Our next stage was to review those who had already left on grounds of ill health and were in receipt of handsome pensions. It was clear that a large number would not have got them under the new regime. I asked for a list of the most blatant cases. Within the Police Pension Regulations is a rarely used provision which empowers a force to re-examine officers drawing an ill-health pension, providing they would not have completed twenty-five years' service if they were still at work. If they refused, they could forfeit their pensions.

I gave the first fifty names to the local police stations nearest to where they lived, and asked them to make inquiries about the state of health of each individual. One who had gone off with 'a bad back' had secured employment as a drayman humping heavy barrels of beer. Another had become a police officer in Australia, even though he was drawing an ill-health pension from us. A former traffic officer, who had claimed he could no longer drive because of his back, was driving buses for a living. Many more were openly flouting the system, which made me cross and strengthened my resolve. The exercise also gained the support of working officers, who were disgusted at what some of their former colleagues were up to. The 'representative bodies' were in a dilemma: they had to concede the situation was untenable and support my next course of action, which was to write to each of these individuals and arrange for a suitable time and date for them to be medically re-examined.

This was not the only way we addressed the problem of premature retirement. For example, most women retiring through ill health left after twelve-and-a-half years' service, and we discovered through research that a major underlying motive was to look after their families. As a direct result of this finding, we were one of the first forces in the country to introduce a battery of measures that included child care, job sharing, part-time working and career breaks. These provisions attracted large numbers of female officers to return to duty without the threat of a health re-examination, and encouraged serving officers to stay. The 'twelve-and-a-half year syndrome' ended.

One essential for management is to have a clear understanding of the workforce, whose mood is often misread. Unless you get out there on the ground, your feedback comes from sources who themselves have an interest in making you believe one thing or the other. The unions will tell you everything is bad, and offer suggestions for improvement. Middle managers will assure you the opposite is the case, as they feel more comfortable with the status quo. The truth is usually between the two, but you have got to go out and discover it for yourself.

As regards absenteeism and retirements on ill health, serving officers were very vocal about the injustice of colleagues abusing the system; yet they were unwilling to bring it to the notice of management, as they regarded it as management's responsibility. They attributed part of their low morale to this single issue, 'Why should I step in and do her nights for her? She gets away with murder.' 'Why do I always have to clear up his mess? You can plot his sickness by the calendar. The bosses don't care, why should I? I'm going to take my statutory sick days and retire with stress. Everyone else does.'

Merely by acknowledging the problem and beginning to do something about it, we gained the full support of the majority of the workforce. Many senior managers, and representative bodies, devote too much attention to the vocal minority, mistakenly believing that if they keep them pacified, they will keep the workforce happy – but nothing can be further from the truth.

I shared my force's ill-health problem and the methods I adopted to solve it with my fellow Chief Constables, who were not particularly interested, as it was not a big issue for them, and took no remedial action. The result is that in the past decade police sickness and ill-health retirements have spiralled out of control, becoming a major drain on finances. Through the mid-nineties, while our numbers fell, I watched with frustration as they rose elsewhere: when I left West Yorkshire in 1998, we had one of the lowest levels of ill-health retirements in the country.

In order to reduce overheads we examined all our working practices. We were disappointed to find that many were restrictive and costly. We were told that many of them had been introduced to 'keep the lads happy'. One example related to an officer's 'place of duty': if he had to work anywhere else on a temporary basis, he was entitled to compensation for both travel and meals. If, however, he worked at the new place for more than sixty days, the benefit ceased. Peripatetic squads were abusing this regulation unmercifully, claiming for every day they worked, wherever they were. Their supervisors would arrange for them to spend the sixty-first day in a different location, so that the sixty-day clock might start to run again, and they could go on drawing benefit. Officers could claim reimbursement for travel, even if their temporary places of duty were closer to their home than their normal station.

Officers' travel to and from their normal places of duty was also costing us a fortune. During a certain period of time, those who had moved out of police houses and purchased their own were entitled to claim travel expenses for any distance over six miles each day – even if they had chosen to live some way from their work. This benefit continued even when they moved home again or were posted to different stations: many had been drawing substantial tax-free sums for years. Some officers even found ways of abusing this privilege: for example, two who lived together, and travelled in the same car together, to the same place of duty, each claimed for the daily, seventy-mile round trip (minus the basic six miles). On today's figures, that meant they were getting $58 \times 50p \times 2 =$ £58 per day, or £11,600 per year, tax-free.

There were many other less costly abuses, all of which I brought to the notice of the Police Federation. They were reluctant to support removal of benefits, but, faced with inconsistency bordering on fraud, they offered little resistance. They blamed weak management for allowing abuse to have developed and grown, which was a fair criticism. Ending these dubious practices saved us more than £3 million annually, money we ploughed back into policing the streets.

In attempts to win public support for an increase in resources, my predecessor had made shortage of money a big issue in the Press. He used it to explain the rise in crime and disorder, and the declining success of the force; but his efforts had unforeseen consequences on the officers and staff, many of whom became demoralized. They hated the jibes from colleagues in other forces about their Chief 'holding out the begging bowl'. Less scrupulous officers used lack of funds as an excuse for not doing their jobs properly. If they were slow to respond to an incident, they would say, 'You're lucky we got here at all, because there are so few of us.' Consequently the public were dissatisfied with the service we provided: the year before I arrived, the number of public complaints against the police was on the rise, and justifiably so, as, for example, the burglary rate per capita was the highest in the country.

The way we dealt with incidents had not changed for years, and it was inefficient and counter-productive. The pattern was invariably the same. A uniformed police officer responded to every crime, to obtain an initial report; the scene was then inspected by a scenes-of-crime officer, to obtain forensic evidence; finally a detective would visit, to decide whether to investigate the crime himself or allocate it to a uniformed officer. At least three officers were involved (usually four, as detectives rarely ventured out alone), each from a different department, with little co-ordination between them.

It could take hours or even days for all three agencies to visit the scene, causing disruption and distress to victims, particularly if they had to leave their house in its burgled state, sometimes with excreta daubed on the walls, awaiting fingerprint examination. Working parents had to take time off their jobs to await our convenience. Telephone calls to try and establish the precise time of a visit were met with, 'You'll just have to wait, love.' To add insult to injury, when the officers eventually arrived on the scene, their response to criticism was frequently off-hand. The chances of the criminals being detected were slight, and people justifiably complained.

On delving, I found that even when crimes were detected, we didn't tell the victims unless we had to, so they laboured under the misapprehension that we had failed. The reason given by my staff was, 'We can't afford to type the letters.'

All the community groups complained about the waste of manpower. Why, they asked, did it take three people to do the same job? 'Wouldn't the police be better off out on the streets, catching criminals, rather than messing us about, especially when they're so rude when they arrive?'

We set about changing the way we responded to calls for service. After intensive consultation within and without the force, we began to grade our reaction. The most serious incidents – for example, a burglary in progress or a motorway pile-up – would get an immediate response. At the other end of the spectrum, the theft of a milk bottle, with no suspect, would simply be recorded. These changes would not have been possible without the support of the Police Authority and the public: we went out and asked people, 'What do you wish us to do with the resources available to us?', and we based our priorities on their answers.

The officers in the departments were less easily convinced: being used to the system, they saw no reason to change it. The number of people involved in a crime investigation offered them a defence against failure, as no individual or department had sole responsibility for detecting crime. This kind of duplication is often the root cause of failure in any organisation: everyone can blame everyone else. I raised this and other issues during my first Annual Open Meeting of our local Police Federation at which the Chief Constable was invited to give a 'state of the union' address and answer questions from the floor. In outlining my agenda for change, I did not pull any punches. My remarks were badly received, and the questions indicated the strength of feeling against the measures I had already taken. Some of the comments were downright silly – for example, one task force officer, referring to the change in rules on his allowances, said, 'You've taken the bread out of my children's mouths.'

I decided to examine the working practices in the specialist departments, and I was unhappy when I found that they were operating as closed shops: once an officer was in, he never left unless he chose to do so. There were hundreds of qualified men and women waiting to get in, all of whom had a very limited chance of success. These departments were also disproportionately funded, the CID being the worst example: 80 per cent of the whole force's overtime budget went to the detectives, who comprised only 13 per cent of the establishment.

This department also had excessive overheads in the form of

supervisory staff, vehicles, buildings and equipment. There was one sergeant to every three constables, one inspector to every two sergeants, and they occupied almost one quarter of the superintending ranks. In the rest of the organisation the constable-to-sergeant ratio was twelve to one, the sergeant-to-inspector ratio five to one, and a superintendent had an average of over 200 officers working for him. CID officers took a disproportionate percentage of promotions, even though their performance in examinations was no better than that of their uniformed colleagues. This was largely due to them selecting their own, almost like a force within a force. Detectives could also be promoted 'back into uniform', which rarely occurred the other way about.

To exacerbate the situation further, their shift patterns did not reflect the demands on them. They largely worked 'bankers' hours', and not at the time of peak crime or arrests. The result was that people had to wait for them, or they passed work to uniformed colleagues, or they worked overtime.

To add to my frustration, except in the investigation of major crimes such as murders detectives did not regard themselves as being responsible for either the prevention or the detection of crime. One said, 'That's down to the wooden-tops', a derogatory term used of uniformed officers.

The final straw was that the detective department was principally a male preserve. When I asked why, I was told by one officer, 'You know what women are like, Sir. They're off every month with women's problems.' Another man said, 'They're a bloody pest. They blubber all over the place when things go wrong.'

I arranged a series of meetings with senior detectives to enlist their support for change, but my overtures met a stone wall. One man told me, 'You know what it's like, Boss – we're family.' This grated on me, as it almost smacked of the mafia. When I shared my views with uniformed senior officers, it became abundantly clear that the CID was not the most popular department in the force. Those with responsibility for all aspects of policing within the territorial areas were very scathing about the detectives. One described them as 'martinets', and another said, 'They need sorting out. They're a law unto themselves.' A third comment was, 'You can't find one when you need one, but when there's overtime at stake, they're there in droves.'

Given this general support, I decided to make sweeping changes. I abolished the role of Assistant Chief Constable, Crime, which was not very popular with the officer holding that position, as he had spent the most of his service as a detective. I took away the power of senior detectives to select and promote people from within their own ranks: henceforth those in the CID had to compete with other officers in the force. I gave responsibility for the detectives in the territorial divisions to the uniformed divisional commander. I reduced the number of detective supervisory ranks, and transferred the decision to allocate overtime to the uniformed officers, saying that I expected to see some tangible results from this spend. In all the specialist departments I introduced a system of limited tenure, which reduced the time officers could serve to seven years, after which they had to return to uniform. Although this process took almost twelve months to introduce, and came in only after lengthy consultation, it was strongly resisted, particularly by the detectives.

Their first reaction came at the second Federation Open Meeting, attended by nearly a thousand officers, the majority of whom were detectives, many under the influence of drink. The meeting, which took place after they had been provided with a free meal and copious amounts of alcohol, was held at the Queen's Hotel in the centre of Leeds. Many officers had been drinking all day, since free transport had also been provided to and from the event.

When I arrived I was openly jeered at by what I can only describe as drunken louts, shouting out insults such as 'Pillock!' and 'C—t!' in the foyer of the public building. Although the meeting was closed to the Press, several reporters had been smuggled in by the detectives 'to see the Chief get it'. I was told this by two newspapermen who were there for the first few minutes but left in disgust at the antics of their hosts.

During my speech I was bombarded with cat-calls, boos and foul language. The question session was worse. One officer called the CID the only professional outfit in the police service, describing the detectives as 'pearls amongst swine'. Another said I was introducing a 'charter for the criminals'. Someone else told me I was a 'pillock', and I was 'ripping the arse out of the service'.

It was a dreadful evening, but at least I had faced my critics. Over the next few days I was heartened by the substantial number of telephone calls and letters I received from other officers present, who wished to distance themselves from the behaviour of their colleagues. One reckoned 'they were like animals. If I'd seen them in a public place, I'd have arrested the lot of them.' This was a little compensation for the rough handling I had received.

I pressed ahead with the reforms, but at some personal cost. Within weeks of the meeting strange things began to happen at home. Bren started to receive anonymous telephone calls each time I was away overnight. When she answered the phone, there was no response other than sound of background music. After listening for a while she would put the receiver down. The caller must have left the phone off the hook, because when she tried to ring out, the line was engaged.

In addition to these nuisance calls we had two attempted burglaries on our house: our garage was broken into, the soft top of our sports car was slashed with garden shears and the radio was damaged – all within the period of one month. This was an abnormal pattern of crime, for two reasons: first, we are off the beaten track, approached by a drive almost a quarter of a mile long and surrounded by fields, which rules out the opportunist criminal, who would be exposed if he came near the house. Second, the nature of the acts excluded professionals, who would have planned their actions and obtained entry. No normal criminal would have put himself at risk three times, at such short intervals, without gaining more than the satisfaction of damaging a beautiful car.

The nocturnal activities remained a mystery until a detective inspector asked to see me, to 'advise me' on crime prevention. I offered him coffee, as we used to play rugby for the same team years before. He told me, 'You're not going to win this one, Boss. Give it up.' I was taken aback. I thought I knew what he was telling me, but I didn't want to believe it. When I asked him what he meant, he replied, 'These changes. Let them go. You know you won't beat us. I'm telling you as a friend.'

I told him it wasn't a battle. The changes were in the interest of the force, and he would see that in time. As he stood up to leave, he said, 'I've warned you. If you go ahead, we'll break you.' I felt a shiver down my spine, but I was so angry that I told him to get out immediately.

The conversation left me more determined than ever to make inroads into this arrogant, sexist group of people. Over time, new officers, including substantial numbers of women and men from ethnic backgrounds, were posted into the detective branch, and the dead wood was swept away.

The result of all the reforms I had put in place was a steady increase in the number of crimes detected and a substantial reduction in crimes committed. One regret I have is that my successor abolished the tenure period for detectives, and I only hope this reversal does not herald the beginning of a new negative cycle. It is fair to say that the changes I made met with resistance from Road Traffic and other specialist units, but this came in a much more professional and measured form.

With these changes set in motion, we looked at other ways in which we could improve our performance. Before my arrival, all decisions were made in headquarters (known as 'the Kremlin'). The territorial commanders had no control over their budgets, the number or nature of their staff, buildings, vehicles or equipment (even the replacement of a pair of gloves had to be authorised by an ACC). Consequently they didn't really manage, and had limited means of manoeuvre within the constraints laid down at the top. In my opinion the top team must determine the direction of the organisation, set targets and standards, monitor progress and above all provide the resources and the environment in which those who deliver, whatever the product or service is, can do so in the most effective and efficient way. The support staff in headquarters are there to facilitate the whole operation, and the field managers should be able to get on and manage. This was not so in West Yorkshire, which was a very centralised organisation.

We made the simple but fundamental decision to devolve virtu-ally all budgets on to the operational commanders, which met with their universal support, although some had reservations about their ability to manage multi-million-pound budgets. Those in head-quarters who had hitherto controlled the supply of money and resources were against the proposal, because it lessened their power and influence.

They had another reason to feel insecure: their jobs were at risk. We set about identifying those officers who provided a direct service to the public, those who didn't but required police powers and training to do their job, and those who required neither. We made it clear that unless jobs fell within the first two categories, there was no justification for the posts being filled by police officers, and the people concerned would be replaced by civilians. This exercise resulted in 300 officers moving back into operational duties, and a corresponding increase in the number of civilian employees.

Both these initiatives required retraining and time. I likened the managers to fleas in a matchbox. Under the centralised regime they had all been constrained inside the box. Those who wished for change jumped up and down to try and escape, but after one headache too many they gave up. Others felt secure within their confines, as their boundaries were clearly defined. When the box was opened, the first group jumped so high that they were in danger of falling over the edge. The second group felt exposed, and were reluctant to leave the safety and security of their old quarters. Both needed guidance, as did we: we all had to operate by the new rules, for we had lost our power to dictate spending. Yet in due course these reforms reduced the overheads of the force and increased the number of officers on the streets, which resulted in quicker response times, increased success in dealing with incidents, fewer assaults on police officers, and fewer complaints against them.

The level of complaints is an important barometer of the health of an organisation, and it is often overlooked as a management tool. By analysing where and when complaints are made, their nature and the people they are made against, one can see patterns emerging. In our case, particular stations, groups of officers and individuals were the cause of a disproportionate number of complaints from the public. Individuals were brought in to see the deputy to discuss why they attracted so much hostility. Some were prolific thief-takers, and the complaints against them were largely vexatious. In contrast, others exhibited a bad attitude, about which they were cautioned. We introduced anti-complaint training for the whole organisation, along with complaint-reduction targets for our managers. These measures contributed to the sharp decline in the total of complaints against our officers, at a time of substantial increases elsewhere in the country.

The number of officers on the beat is often a battle-cry of politicians, who use it as their litmus test for success. In reality, numbers are a very crude measure, and have little to do with the results of policing, which depend on a far more sophisticated approach. The current Home Secretary, David Blunkett, is no different from his predecessors in this regard: promising to increase the number of officers on the beat, he intends to go one step further and introduce Community Service Officers – a new breed of lightly trained, lesser-paid, uniformed personnel. It seems to me to be a gimmick to try to get policing on the cheap.

During my time in West Yorkshire we managed to achieve substantial increases in numbers on the ground, but unless we had motivated our officers to achieve the goals that both we and the community desired, we would have gained very little. We tried to look at the organisation through the eyes of the bobbies on the beat, asking them (for instance) about their rewards system. Would they like bonuses, merit badges or reward payments? They dismissed all these as gimmicks. What they wished was to be recognised for what they did, and listened to. They pointed out their painstaking work within the community prevented many thousands of crimes a year, but went unrecognised, whereas detectives were frequently commended for solving a single, high-profile crime. The bobbies gave many examples of things which had gone wrong because their views had been ignored.

To reflect their contribution, we changed our commendation procedures, introducing a ceremony to present them and their families with long-service awards, which in the past had usually been posted to them. I promoted every person in the organisation myself, so that I could personally congratulate each and every one on his or her achievement. I invited every retiring officer and civilian to come and see me with their families, in order that I could thank them for their contribution. But we did much more. We also placed uniformed officers at the heart of our rewards system: no one could be posted to a specialist department or promoted unless they had served a set period on uniformed patrol duties.

The increased resources we created allowed us to provide the staff with the equipment they required to do their job. Little things meant all the difference to them – for example, some operational officers asked for mobile telephones. There were only a handful in the force, and they were issued against signatures in much the same way as personal radios had been guarded by police forces when they first came into use in the mid-sixties. When I asked why phones were not freely available, I was told, 'We can't trust people not to make personal calls.'

I had refused a request to recruit a number of 'snoopers' and to purchase an expensive interception-machine to catch 'illicit' users of the telephone. When we renegotiated the supply of telephone services, and changed from a charge-per-call basis to an annual fixed amount, we not only saved ourselves more than £1 million each year, but were able to issue hundreds of mobile handsets. Officers were encouraged to make domestic calls if the need arose, and put on trust not to abuse the privilege. Spot checks thereafter indicated that the number of unauthorised calls had reduced considerably, proving once again that if you treat people like children, they will behave like children.

Lip service was and continues to be paid to the value of uniformed constables, without a great deal of action to back it up. I inherited a force in which it was they who carried all the vacancies and, as a consequence of being under-manned, suffered the highest rate of injury and assault on duty, since it was they who had to deal with violent incidents. They carried the highest crime load, since detectives regarded themselves as too busy to deal with trivia, yet they were not allowed to pursue any investigations, because they could not be spared the time. They were under the most pressure: they answered emergency and other service calls from the public and were on the receiving end of their complaints. They made the most arrests and conducted the most interviews, and had the least time to ponder their decisions; they were the ones who had to fill in the most forms and complete the most paperwork, and had the least time in which to do it. They had to work the most unsociable hours, and were subject of most change for 'operational contingencies'. They had to deal with the broadest range of issues, as they were first on the scene, whether it be a murder, a road accident or a pub fight. They were the lowest-paid and the least experienced, as quite understandably everyone worked to escape from the position of uniform constable. To top it all, they were usually blamed for everything which went wrong.

High on our agenda was the elimination of sexual discrimination (one of my predecessors would not allow women to wear trousers, as he liked to look at their legs. When pressed, he set up a working-party to examine the role of women within the force without a single woman representative on it.) We had all the proper procedures in place, clear reporting processes, trained counsellors and clear rules of guidance; in fact, an inspection by the Home Office had described us as having a 'Rolls-Royce system'. Yet female officers still told me of the horrors they faced, and their fear of recrimination if they spoke up about them.

With the support of my senior managers, I went public about my concerns. I knew this would not be well received within the organisation, and would open us up to criticism outside it. I confided in the Police Authority – as I always did on any sensitive issue – and I gained its full support. The leaders of the Federation and the Superintendents' Association were sceptical, claiming it was unjustified, as the Home Office report had given us a clean bill of health; nevertheless I went ahead. Surprisingly, the editorials in local newspapers were complimentary about our honesty, saying that they were aware of injustice within the force, and it was right and proper that we should do something about it.

Female officers gained confidence and began to use the system. We expected large numbers in the first instance, and we were not disappointed. In fact I introduced a force target, 'to increase the number of *reports* of sexist behaviour'. We introduced similar innovations in other sensitive areas, resulting in increased reporting of racially motivated incidents by the public. Oddly, the Press were less sympathetic to this target and accused me of trying to increase racial tension. Fine words are well enough, but they need backing up with action. Within a relatively short time I began to hear disciplinary cases against officers charged with sexual and racial discrimination.

In those days the Chief Constable alone presided over disciplinary cases. The proceedings, akin to criminal trials, would generally be prosecuted and defended by barristers of high standing, both of whom would be instructed by solicitors. Hearings could last weeks, as evidence was called and questioned by both sides, and it was the duty of the Chief to decide on guilt or innocence and pass sentence.

I disliked these hearings. Apart from the fact that they were time-consuming, and engaged me for almost a month each year, I hated having to take away an officer's livelihood, which was my duty if the circumstances required it. My powers were broad. I could fine an officer, reduce him in rank, reduce him in pay, require him to resign or dismiss him. The Director of Public Prosecutions often made use of the system to avoid taking a police officer to court for a criminal offence, remitting the case for a Chief Constable hear.

I took exception to this on one or two occasions, as I felt it would be more appropriate for the case to be heard in open court, particularly when there had been some publicity surrounding the event. This would have undermined the claim from less scrupulous commentators that the police had whitewashed the case.

In one case in which I was instructed, a constable had punched a sergeant and caused him substantial injury. The assault was witnessed by many other officers, but the sergeant refused to pursue the matter. I listened intently to his representatives as they pleaded with me not to hear the case. It seemed that the constable hit the sergeant because he had made derogatory sexual comments about a female officer and a civilian, and sexually assaulted one of them. The constable had told him to desist, and when he refused, he struck him.

This was the opportunity I had been waiting for. However, because I had been pre-briefed, I could not hear the case against the sergeant. I did hear the assault case, gave the constable a lenient sentence, and passed the sergeant's case to another Chief to hear. After the man had been found guilty, I dismissed him. The verdict was published in our Weekly Orders as a lesson to others. I made a similar decision in a case where male officers called a female colleague a 'slit-arse', which I considered particularly distasteful. In other cases, female officers were touched, leered at, taunted with sexual remarks and made to endure sexually explicit videos and nude female photographs on police station walls. I outlawed these practices, and over a period of months the mood began to change. Most things can be done if you set your mind to it.

When you implement a new system, you are bound to find abuses. One long-serving female officer felt impelled to go off sick because of an article she read in the force newspaper reporting the fate of 'Old Smokey', a Victorian restraining chair (modelled on an electric chair, without the power supply), which had been con-signed to the force museum from the cells underneath Leeds Town Hall. The female reporter who wrote the article had asked a matron to pose for a photograph, sitting bound in the chair, watched over by a male inspector. The aggrieved officer wrote to the newspaper, with a copy to me, saying that this smacked of male dominance, and I should not have allowed it to happen.

Every Chief Constable is vicariously liable for the acts of all of his officers. This fact is little known – but it came to the fore when the Taylor inquiry, which followed the deaths at Sheffield Wednesday's football ground at Hillsborough, opined that Chief Constables were responsible for the safety inside football stadiums. I took issue with Mr Justice Taylor (who later, before his untimely death, became Lord Chief Justice and a close friend), because foot-

The Chief Constable of West Yorkshire in his office, 1995.

LEFT: With Archbishop
Dr Babgod and Rev.
Cannon Stephen Oliver.

BELOW: With Bishop
Nigel of Wakefield,
receiving my honorary
doctorate from
Huddersfield University.

ABOVE: With John Major at No.10 Downing Street.

BELOW: At the launch of Educational Haverstock School, Chalk Farm, London, shortly after being appointed New Labour's Drug Tsar in 1998.

ABOVE: With military contingent in Peshawar, Pakistan,
during a tour of the heroin route, 1999.

BELOW: Smugglers crossing on foot from Afghanistan into Pakistan.

RIGHT:
Presenting the
World Drug
Report.

ow: Myself
ond from left)
Pino Arlacchi,
cutive Director
he United
ions Office for
g Control and
me Prevention
tre), 2000.

ABOVE: With Ton[y] Blair at the Turnaround proje[ct] for female drug offenders in Glasg[ow]

LEFT: Myself, To[ny] Blair and Joanna Carling, who designed the logo [for] the Drug and Cri[me] Initiative, 1998.

RIGHT: With [Mo] Mowlam at Cus[toms] House in Lon[don] and approxim[ately] £10 million wor[th of] drugs seize[d by] Customs and E[xcise]

LEFT: Daughters Samantha and Alexandra.

RIGHT: Bren and I on holiday in Monaco.

ABOVE: The Hellawell family at the farm.

RIGHT: Bren and I with our cat, Phoebe.

ball matches are commercial events, at which the police are invited and paid to keep order by the owners of the ground, and are not there as a matter of right. I contended that in such circumstances we had no control, and should not carry the responsibility. Our debate was short-lived, however, as clubs soon took up another of his recommendations – to train and employ their own stewards.

In the field of equal opportunities, things began to improve. Like the heads of other organisations, Chief Constables have difficulty in being open and honest about such matters. Their employees expect some support from the top, and wish to be defended. If the leader comes clean about the problems within the organisation, they often feel that he or she has let them down. If he or she is silent, the issues are rarely resolved.

Police Authorities have a big stake in any difficult issue facing the force. Although we didn't always agree, we talked through any matters of contention. In my early days in Yorkshire one or two members expressed doubts about my taking a high profile in some of these delicate issues. They were unhappy at me 'washing our dirty linen in public', but the majority supported my stance. We included them as much as possible through seminars and focused briefings, which were always well attended, and members' views were very influential in forming my own.

In the closed session of each Authority meeting, I apprised members of sensitive criminal and disciplinary inquiries in progress, and they never betrayed my confidence. After a time, one or two sought more information, in order that they could intervene, but I refused, as this was beyond their remit. Some of my Chief Constable colleagues criticised me for being so open. However, it was in these sessions that members took the opportunity to raise anything which bothered them. One member was concerned that I was charging a fee for speaking in public. I told her this was not so, but if an organisation offered a fee, it was informed that I would be more than happy if it made a donation to one of my charities. Once, after I had spoken to a group of old people in Keighley, the master of ceremonies produced a brown flat cap and said, 'Keith's done a decent job. I think he's worth a bob or two.' I explained to the audience that they should keep their money, and was greeted with a round of applause.

There were many very enjoyable occasions with Police Authority members, one of which was our annual trip to the United States to attend the IACP conference. This lasted a week; the chairman always went of right, and was accompanied by a couple of members whose names came out of the hat. One of the most beneficial outcomes of these visits was that I spent more time with members and got to know them better.

Over the years we visited various cities in America. On arrival, together with 11,000 other delegates, we were greeted with all the trappings of their conventions – sashes and rosettes of different colours. Each city had its own badge, with the year of the conference emblazoned upon it; many delegates attached badges from previous years to enhance their status, and wore this bizarre paraphernalia around their necks for the whole of the proceedings. The host cities were geared up for the occasion. Bars provided free beer, local transport was free, and there was nightly entertainment, the climax of which would be a concert by a superstar such as k.d. lang, Donny and Marie Osmond (who embarrassed one of my colleagues – or so he said – because Marie sat on his knee and sang to him), Kenny Rogers and Glen Campbell.

The conferences took place in some of the largest halls I had ever seen: except for the National Exhibition Centre, there is nothing to touch them in this country. Because the numbers of delegates were so large, there would be up to twenty different sessions going on at one time. Along with other colleagues from this country, I would usually run a session, and I learned a lot from the trips.

I already had some experience of policing in the USA, but hearing in detail about the Waco killings and the Oklahoma bombing, together with many serial murders and various police prevent-ative measures, from those who headed the inquiries, greatly extended my knowledge. I was particularly interested in the success of the crime-reduction measures introduced by Bill Bratton, Chief of the New York City Police, as they were based on British experience, and I had given him some advice during one of my visits as honorary professor to John Jay College in that city.

One of the most memorable experiences of my working life happened at one of the big IACP conferences. The President of the United States always inaugurated the event, in person if possible, otherwise by live tele-link from the White House. Bill Clinton opened the one in Denver, Colorado, and his entrance made the hairs on the back of my neck stand on end.

The lights in the auditorium were extinguished, and a slow drum beat began to play. Spotlights came on over the stage, picking out a diminutive white female Marine lieutenant, standing to attention facing eight 6' 6"-tall black Marines, who began performing rifle drill with fixed bayonets, the blades and tips of which were swinging and lunging within inches of her face. She stood like a statue and didn't flinch for the whole of the five-minute performance, even though the rhythm and speed increased in a crescendo. The drum beat continued as they marched off the stage and then a voice announced, 'Ladies and Gentlemen, the President of the United States!'

What an entrance! Clinton never lost the impetus: he spoke without notes and was thoroughly inspiring. A number of speakers and foreign officers were invited to join him for a reception before lunch, and I was lucky enough to be one of them. I found him a most sociable and charming person.

In West Yorkshire, as in Cleveland, there were a number of incidents which I felt required my personal attention, the most serious being the Bradford riots of 1995. Tensions had been rising, particularly within the Manningham districts of the city, for a number of reasons. First, the elders of the Muslim community were unhappy that the police would not tell them the whereabouts of their teenage daughters who had run away to avoid forced marriages. If they were eighteen or over when we found them, and they didn't wish us to disclose their whereabouts to their parents, we honoured their wishes. My mailbag on this issue was huge, and I was often criticised at community meetings.

One such, held at the Bradford football ground, had an unusual outcome. In the gathering was a lone Asian female who spoke up to defend me when I was called racist: she stunned her male audience by telling them they were sexist, as they wouldn't allow their women folk either to learn English, or to work and mix with the indigenous population. She told them they should get their own houses in order before accusing others, and she cautioned me against giving away the young women's addresses: if I did, she said, they would be taken home, imprisoned and beaten for their disobedience.

Manningham had long been the haunt of prostitutes, and the Muslim community at large was offended by them. People felt particularly slighted when sexual acts took place, or discarded sex objects were found, close to their places of worship. Tensions were so high that vigilante groups had begun to harass and on occasions badly assault prostitutes working within the area. The irony was that many of the women were run by Asian pimps, and a high proportion of the punters were Asian. Asian taxi-drivers would take clients to the area if asked. This issue continued to simmer, as, whatever we did, we could not really resolve the situation.

Irrespective of race, I had grave concerns about girls involved in this pernicious trade. Some as young as twelve were prostituting themselves, more often than not to feed a drug habit – in one case a £200-a-day crack addiction. My view, not shared by others at that time, was that this was a child-protection issue and had no place in the criminal arena. I pointed out to my detractors the duplicity of their thinking, as they supported the protection of children in their homes but labelled them criminals when they were molested several times a day on the street.

The paedophiles were having a field day. I visited the home of a young woman who had been murdered by a punter. Her dwelling comprised one room, for which she had been paying an exorbitant rent, furnished with a bed, a table and a chair. The only other piece of furniture in the room, a bedside cabinet, contained condoms, hypodermic needles, cotton wool and an empty box of cornflakes, which was all she ate.

I recommended that we legalise prostitution in our country. I advocated the licensing of brothels, and age restrictions and medical examinations for prostitutes. Prostitution outside these premises would remain unlawful. I felt that these provisions would protect the women working within the 'lawful' side of the industry and allow more police – and charitable organisations – to focus on the young girls who remained on the streets and the punters who preyed on them. I was ostracised for my views, not for the first or last time. This issue, like many others, is one which people would rather not speak about so long as it does not affect them directly. When it does, however, they become most vociferous.

Another reason for unrest among the Asian community was our positive policing, and a change of tactics from focusing on crimes to targeting the people committing them. We knew that a small number of Asian youths were active criminals in the area and were responsible for a disproportionate amount of crime. I went public saying that I would stop, search and harass them as much as I could within the law, to prevent their anti-social behaviour. This was a novel idea that I had pioneered in Cleveland, and it produced remarkable results.

The Manningham and Toller Lane areas of Bradford were part of a force-wide initiative in which we targeted about twenty young local males who, our intelligence indicated, were committing the bulk of local crimes. We followed them and harried them until they were caught, either in the act of criminality or with its proceeds. Once they were in custody, crime in that area alone fell by more than 50 per cent. We had enlisted the support of the CPS and the magistrates to fast-track the youths we brought before them, and many received prison sentences. None of these criminals liked being caught: in ethnic communities they 'played the racist card' as often as they could, claiming that the police were picking on them because of their racial backgrounds; this accusation was easy to refute, as the initiative was force-wide.

I spent a lot of time on the streets in racially sensitive areas. On the streets of Bradford one of my officers told me he considered Muslim fundamentalism to be one of the most pernicious things he had encountered among young Asians, something which he was afraid would take hold. After having my Special Branch officers prepare a file on this, I discussed it with our national intelligence agencies.

The tension finally boiled over one sunny afternoon in June when two officers on routine patrol remonstrated with a group of youths whose football went into the path of their vehicle. The officers, after being shouted and gesticulated at, chased the youths into a house, where an altercation took place. The official inquiry was never able to establish exactly what happened, and folk-lore has a life of its own. Suffice it to say that untrue stories got around that the police had 'misused' one of the older women in the house. The building was quickly surrounded by a hundred or so young men chanting anti-police slogans, and a substantial number of other officers had to attend to extricate the two, as the crowd had turned ugly and there were fears for their safety.

As time passed tensions grew rather than abated, and in the evening full-scale rioting broke out. Shops were set on fire and looted, cars were stolen and burnt, blazing barricades were assembled in the middle of roads, and people were dragged out of their cars, which were then used to fuel the fires.

We had learned over the years that this type of disturbance cannot be beaten by force alone; marauding groups of twenty or thirty youths are difficult to contain, especially in an urban area such as this, because when chased, they melt into friendly premises, only to emerge elsewhere. If several of these groups are running riot, the best the forces of law and order can do is contain the situation and prevent as much damage as possible. This is clearly difficult when you are in the middle of urban violence, especially as incidents of this nature attract anarchists, who will go anywhere to participate in public disorder.

That evening in Bradford, hundreds of police officers were sent in to contain the situation. Young Asian men were flooding into the area from other parts of the city, to vent their anger – which, interestingly enough, was to some degree controlled, as it was carefully targeted. Only white and non-Muslim Asian properties were damaged and fired. Streets with twenty or so shops would have one or two which were Muslim-owned left intact, while the others were destroyed. The idea that this was an Asian-versus-white contest was not correct: old scores were also being settled within racial groups.

The brave officers on the front line had to restrain themselves – something which is extremely difficult when you are facing petrol bombs and half bricks, and being called racist names – and it was especially frustrating for them to accept an order not to arrest people they witnessed committing criminal acts. They did as they were told, and stayed in formation. We had given these orders for good reason: officers acting alone, or even in twos or threes, would have been picked off and assaulted, and we were determined to minimise such possibilities. Instead, we deployed members of our photographic department to capture events on film – used, we believed, for the first time in our country in a riot of this magnitude – in order to defuse and control the situation on the ground, and to enable us to make arrests later.

The rioters thought my photographic staff were from the media, and accepted them, but the cameramen were on dangerous ground, in front of the police line, and would have been ripped to pieces had their identity been discovered. Their video and still films were later used to identify the offenders, who were arrested in the weeks after the event. More than seventy were dealt with by the courts, with very little negative reaction from the community.

The rioting went on until dawn the following morning. During the night millions of pounds' worth of damage was caused to property, and many people were injured. My officers became exhausted with the strain and the long stretch on duty.

In the course of the night, away from the stand-off, we made a concerted effort within the community, and held many meetings with different groups in an effort to defuse the situation. One of the problems highlighted was the chasm between different generations: the elders had lost control of their young – but when I said this at one of the many Press conferences I held during those dark hours, I was criticised for being racist, and making remarks 'likely to undermine the Asian community'.

Next morning, with the help of the local authority and the community elders, we did as much reparation work on the streets as we possibly could – for to leave visible signs of rioting undermines the confidence of everyone. We put as many community officers out on the streets as we could muster, and the meetings went on. Walking the streets that day, I was invited into one of the undamaged shops by a young articulate Asian man. He told me my remarks were justified. He said young people were frustrated by the lack of educational, housing and work opportunities. They had lost confidence in their elders, who did not put their case as forcefully as they should, and they believed that older people had 'sold out, to become accepted'. When I asked him how we could reach young people, he said, if I was genuine, he would see what he could do. True to his word, next day he arranged a meeting attended by thirty or forty young men, and although it was a very volatile affair, it was the beginning of a period of understanding which endured for a number of years.

The initiative was not enough to prevent further rioting on the second night, however. Although not as noisy or violent as before, it was frightening for the community at large, and particularly for my officers, who had to endure the violence.

The fire was fuelled by some local politicians, who accused me of using inappropriate words and blamed the police for the whole incident. To their eternal discredit, one or two of them later telephoned me to say that I had spoken the truth, but they could not support me publicly, as they relied on the Asian vote. The debate about my integrity lasted for forty-eight hours, until an editorial in *The Times* described me as 'a beleaguered Chief Constable' who was perhaps right in what he said and ought to be supported.

Whatever the facts of this or any other riot are, most people learn about them through media reports. I, together with my senior officers, remained on duty throughout the disturbances, and held hourly briefings to keep myself abreast of developments. As well as assuming Gold Command (the overall command) in turn with my ACPO colleagues, I had the particular responsibility of dealing with the media circus. We set specific times at which we would report progress. At the height of the rioting these were at four-hourly intervals and were attended by up to fifty journalists from all over the world.

I found those interviews some of the most taxing I had ever undertaken. Our aim was to restore peace, and I knew I could inflame the situation by one chance remark. I was torn a number of ways. If I made sympathetic noises about the lack of amenities for the ethnic groups in the city, this would enrage my officers and much of the white population. If I put the blame on the Asian youths, it would inflame the whole of that community, and in particular the non-Muslim section of it, which had been on the receiving end of the violence. If I made a distinction between different factions within the ethnic groups, it would only stir up more trouble between them. So I walked a tight-rope, which is difficult to do when you have had no sleep for forty-eight hours and you are fielding questions live on television which is being broadcast across the world. I learned a great deal about media handling during those hundreds of interviews, a lesson which stood me in good stead for the future.

There followed the usual postmortem: I had kept my Police Authority and the Home Secretary involved, but the Prime Minister, John Major, required a personal briefing on progress. None of the politicians expressed support for the police until the riots were over, hedging their bets to see what line they could take most advantageously. Their congratulations eventually came when they saw that our actions had been sound and justified.

I thought all my officers and their civilian colleagues had acted magnificently. I only wish their detractors could have stood beside them and seen what they endured with patience and fortitude. The senior officers also excelled: their true professionalism was apparent for all to see, and they instilled much confidence in the officers on the front line, with whom they stood.

The independent report on the riots was critical of the initial actions of the two police officers. I had publicly refused to bend to media pressure to sack or suspend them. I told the Press I would not allow them to be scapegoats: I would act on evidence, not emotion. We adopted the resulting recommendations for police community action, but unfortunately the recommended educational, housing and employment measures were not taken up in full. Deficiencies in these areas were cited as reasons for a recurrence of the riots in 2001, when there was little criticism of the police.

Back in the early 1980s, the Brixton riots had found most public bodies wanting in respect of racial issues, and these deficiencies were ably reported by Mr Justice Scarman in the inquiry which followed. The police took his remarks to heart and set about improving matters within their ranks. West Yorkshire was lucky, as it had pioneered many community-based initiatives in Afro-Caribbean communities as far back as the late sixties, and we already had in place much of what was recommended. When I returned to the force in the mid-nineties, I was very disappointed to find the situation had deteriorated: although the structures remained, police officers were virtually excluded from some black areas.

The police denied claims that there were any 'no-go' zones in the county, but that was not true. There were no foot patrols in Chapeltown, a district on the edge of Leeds; minor offences were ignored, and major crimes could be responded to only by large detachments of men. Hard-skinned Transit vans crewed by six or seven persons, and double-manned firearms vehicles, patrolled just outside the square mile of Chapeltown.

Even this weight of response often failed to achieve its objective. Within minutes of the police arriving, up to 100 young men would surround them and prevent them making any arrests. Officers would be physically pulled off prisoners and assaulted so violently they often had to retreat in order to protect themselves. Every incursion became a major public-order incident and was dubbed 'racist' by those who attacked the police.

Drug dealing, street robberies, car-jacking and theft were all out of control. In 1994 more than eighty per cent of the robberies in the whole force took place within this tiny area, committed by young black men. The police were afraid to make positive interventions, believing they would contravene the principles laid down by Scarman.

I was as unhappy as the officers, who felt powerless to act, so I held clandestine meetings with older community leaders with whom I had eaten, drunk and danced when I was previously in charge of Leeds. I discovered that they too were very discontented. They told me the young thugs were ruining their area, and were out of control. They favoured the stronger police methods I was advocating, but would not publicly say so, for fear of reprisal.

So another community was terrorised and effectively controlled by young men. They had become so confident that they had shot out a police surveillance camera and burnt down premises which had been made available for police surveillance.

It seemed to me that a personal initiative was needed. I invited a reporter from the *Yorkshire Post* to accompany me on a walkabout in the area, as the paper and its readers had been highly critical of the lawlessness, running lead stories about women having their cars stopped by hooded men and being forced to hand over their belongings at knife-point. The newspaper readily accepted my invitation, as did a volunteer constable from the local police station.

We were out and about for three or four hours, talking to local residents from diverse backgrounds. The eastern European community was aggrieved at an unprovoked murder of a visiting seventy-year-old man. The Vietnamese residents were angry at the constant break-ins and thefts. The Asian community were outraged by the racist chants, graffiti and damage they suffered at the hands of Caribbean youths. These people were highly charged, and told me that if the police continued to do nothing, they would take the law into their own hands. All the while we were followed by a group of about twenty fully hooded young black males, but when I approached them to try and speak with them, they melted away. I told the reporter that they were cowards, who dared not face their accusers and could only attack defenceless women. The paper reported me correctly, including one of my quotes, which said, 'I don't care whether Leeds criminals have black, brown, yellow or white skins: they will not be allowed to continue their criminal activities.' I told the reporter that they were constantly using the race card, but that did not impress me: as these young men had been born and educated in Leeds, the colour of their skin was immaterial. They were simply Leeds criminals, and their ethnic background should not shield them. Our visit, and the comments made by myself and members of the community, were faithfully reported in the front page story which followed.

At a meeting with the local officers and their commanders, seeking their suggestions as to how we ought to bring the streets back under our control, I found a strong movement in favour of reintroducing foot patrols, but reservations about the safety of those who undertook them. Again, I thought a personal example was needed, so when I left that meeting at around six o'clock in the evening, I asked my driver to take me into the centre of Chapeltown, where I left him in the car and walked off on my own.

I was wearing a pinstripe double-breasted suit, a fashionable silk tie, and had my usual, hand-bulled Oxford-fronted shoes on. I encountered several groups of the hooded young men I had seen on my previous visit, and this time, rather than melt away, they came and surrounded me, telling me they knew who I was and asking why I was there. I walked with them towards the Hayfield public house, a notorious meeting place for the criminal fraternity, which I entered. The pub was a seedy place, smelling strongly of stale cannabis, cigarettes and ale. I walked to the bar and asked for a half of bitter. The dozen or so people present stopped talking and watched my every move, as did the posse behind me. The licensee didn't appear to know how to treat me, but a young black woman at the bar moved off her stool and sidled up to me.

'You've got some balls, copper,' she said. 'I know who you are.'

'I just wanted to see this place for myself,' I told her. 'I've heard a lot about it' – to which the licensee said, 'I don't want any trouble with you. Why don't you just leave, and you'll be OK.'

'I'd like a beer,' I replied.

By this time the occupants of the pub had got from their seats and come to the bar by my side. I could sense tension, but the young woman relieved it by saying, 'I'll buy him one.'

This drew some light-hearted banter from the other customers. I was given a glass of beer, and many of the people returned to their seats. The girl stayed where she was and said, 'I like you. You've got bottle. Have you ever slept with a black girl?'

'I can't say I have,' I told her – and added that, attractive as she was, this might not be the best moment to start. She smiled, and took my remarks in the right way.

The pub began to fill. Forty or fifty of the hooded young men drifted in and stood around looking at me. 'He's all right,' the girl told them, and they seemed to settle down – until a uniformed sergeant and two constables poked their faces round the door.

'You OK, Sir?' the sergeant asked.

'I'm fine,' I told him.

'The lads are outside if you need us,' he said, and left.

By the time I finished my drink, the hoods had been removed to reveal boys of thirteen and fourteen, who acted their age, asking me about my job and putting many of the other questions that young people usually do. When I left, I felt like the Pied Piper, as a group of them followed me to my Jaguar under the watchful eyes of my sergeant and the drivers of two police Transit vans, which I waved away, as I was afraid they would spoil the mood. The boys were fascinated by the secreted blue lights, emergency horns, built-in fax machine and telephone communications equipment in the car. Several asked to sit in it and play with the equipment, which I let them do.

I left to smiles and waves all round. These were the criminals who were terrorising their community – young men who considered that street crime gave them the status and rewards society could not offer. I felt they were wasting their lives.

Within weeks, foot patrol officers, albeit in pairs, were back on the streets of Chapeltown, where they were welcomed with open arms by the community at large. My hooded youths hated them, as their freedom of activity was constrained, but street crime began to fall, and robberies were almost halved within one year.

I would like to report this initiative as a success story, but I am afraid it had a nasty twist. Older and more vicious criminals could no longer hide behind the activities of my young men, who were prevented from carrying and selling small amounts of drugs, and acting as a distraction when cars were stopped and their occupants robbed, and they resented the police reasserting control. Firearms became more widely used to frighten my officers: fortunately none of them was shot, but weapons were often discharged when they were dealing with incidents. Drive-by shootings began: cars and houses were peppered with bullets to warn off competition, and over the years this has developed into murders and serious injury by shootings, often endangering innocent bystanders.

Drugs turf-wars are largely the cause. The annual Chapeltown Festival, which mirrors the one in Notting Hill, London, is usually the occasion for at least one drug-related murder between opposing gangs. One year we received information that five drug-dealers from Manchester were coming to kill two Leeds dealers. They obtained permission from their gang leader in prison to draw Uzi machine guns from their arsenal: they fired more than a hundred rounds into the ceiling of the Chapeltown community centre, in order to terrorise the 300 innocent people enjoying the evening there, then stripped them of their jewellery, which they collected in a sack. They were never arrested for this crime, but we were told by an informant that they committed it to vent their frustration at not finding their intended victims, and as a warning to others.

The use of firearms by members of the criminal fraternity has several consequences for the British police. More officers now carry guns, and weapons are more in evidence at major operations and at planned arrests. Officers are issued with bullet-proof vests, and although they are nowhere near as vulnerable as their American counterparts, they wear them as standard uniform, which has, to my mind unnecessarily, changed their image. There is also more chance of police discharging weapons than there was even ten years ago.

During the years 1993 to 1998 West Yorkshire Police shot more people than any other force in the country – a record which subjected us to much criticism. It stands to reason that if officers have the necessary fire-power, they will use it to protect themselves in circumstances which previously they would have had to deal with in a different way. This was exactly what happened when British police officers were issued with CS sprays in the late nineties: although they were designated a 'last-resort weapon', in practice they are the first option for a young officer confronted with a situation of disorder: self-preservation is a powerful driver.

I have no intention of reliving each of those firearms incidents here. Suffice it to say that one man was shot and killed as he leaned out of his bedroom window aiming a broom-handle at police marksmen; a second was shot and killed because he threatened officers with a Western-style .38 revolver; and a third, an elderly Alzheimer's patient, was shot and remarkably survived after threatening his wife and police officers with a stick which had nails hammered through it.

Most commentators erroneously believe that the decision to arm the police is taken by the Home Secretary: in fact, it falls on Chief Constables. There are common guidelines, which are open to interpretation by each Chief Constable, with the consequence that in some forces it is now common for firearms to be carried openly on patrol, and issued at the drop of a hat for special operations, whereas in others they are rarely made available. I am unsure whether there is any justification for the divergence, or for the increased threat to members of the public which the more frequent arming of the police creates.

I was determined to use every means I could muster to beat the criminals. On one occasion in Bradford a young officer was threatened with a sawn-off shotgun when he gave chase to a youth who had committed a robbery at a club. Fortunately the man was caught, but not before shots had been discharged in an urban area. He stole to buy drugs, and told us of the 'tariff': in that area, addicts didn't even have to convert the goods they stole into money – they exchanged them directly for drugs. A domestic iron or toaster was worth one fix of heroin or two joints of cannabis; a good CD player, double. Dealers would order the make or type of goods they wished to have stolen for waiting customers.

To break into this market, I authorised the setting-up of second-hand shops. These were run by undercover police officers, for whom we provided new identities, and to all intents and purposes ran as ordinary businesses – although we didn't sell any goods we knew to be stolen. Every transaction was recorded on camera and tape, and we closed the shops down after a year, then arresting the majority of our clients. This was so successful that we did the same thing with a large van which toured the estates where the majority of criminals lived, buying up goods almost like old fashioned rag-and-bone men.

To catch car thieves, we installed a number of 'rat traps' – vehicles which you can get into but not out of. The windows are of strengthened glass, and the locks seize when a device is activated by watching officers. I was criticised for using these measures by the human-rights lobby, who said 'it wasn't cricket'. What nonsense! If people choose to commit crime, there is nothing wrong with increasing the odds of catching them.

Other more sensitive operations never came to the notice of the public, as officers worked under deep cover for months on end to obtain general evidence about crime and criminals. This is a ploy the service rarely uses, except to infiltrate a particular group or organisation for a specific purpose. We found it very beneficial in understanding more of the crime culture. We did intervene where necessary for public interest – to buy drugs or guns for example – but only when the intervention could not be linked back to our officers. They were only withdrawn when we felt they were at risk or the criminal tally was so high that arrests had to be made. These officers are very brave people who put their lives at risk, as we cannot provide them with the back-up and safeguards that normal undercover officers have.

Another anti-crime enterprise had to be abandoned because it became too successful, and the CPS thought it might get out of hand. Covertly, we set ourselves up as drug-dealers and quickly opened the door to purchasing hundreds of thousands of pounds worth of sub-stances. The normal police routine is to test-purchase small amounts through 'buy' operations: when we suspect a supplier, either we or one of our informants offer to buy, and we make the arrest when the drugs are handed over. We wished to go further up the chain and were prepared to buy larger amounts. I can understand the concerns of the prosecutors, but I believe it is only by unorthodox means that we will make a real impact on crime.

I got away with what I did because of the system of law under which we operate. In this country, unless there is a law against something, you can do it. In others the opposite is true: unless there is a law allowing you to do something, it is forbidden. Here, under the 'common law', made by the courts, your actions can be questioned, and if found to be unreasonable may be punished. New legislation may also be introduced to plug a gap. Until the law changed to involve the judiciary, Chief Constables used 'common law' powers to authorise the installation of bugging devices in vehicles and people's homes (telephone tapping is controlled centrally by the National Criminal Intelligence Service). This activity largely went unquestioned until the mid-nineties, when defence barristers realised they had the opportunity to undermine evidence collected by means of this equipment, saying it was unreasonably installed. I would authorise it whenever I could, although ACPO had agreed guidelines to follow. A Chief Constable had to be satisfied that a serious crime had been or was about to be committed, that all normal means of collecting evidence had been exhausted, that there were no other orthodox means available, and that there was a likelihood of success.

A few examples will illustrate the point. When drug-dealers were operating behind steel doors, in a windowless room in the centre of a block of flats within a close-knit ethnic community, a listening device planted by some subterfuge in the house enabled us to catch them purchasing drugs in another area. Other dealers, wary of in-house surveillance, made random use of many different vehicles in which to conduct their business, but devices fitted to their cars enabled us to catch them in possession of a large amount of drugs and money.

In the late eighties and early nineties, before European co-operation developed, the police used to operate beyond these shores on a very informal basis. I was the Secretary of the Number 3 region of the Crime Squad and responsible for authorising some of its actions. These included police officers acting undercover as lorry drivers to take vehicles to Spain to collect a consignment of cannabis; officers travelling incognito to Pakistan to negotiate the purchase of heroin; officers being given hundreds of thousands of pounds of 'flash money' to buy back stolen works of art.

We were acting *ultra vires*, as much of our action was sparked by tips from the 'old-boy' network – links with officers from other countries whom we had met on courses or through crime investigations. We were, however, putting the officers in jeopardy: they had no legal standing for what they were doing, and often the foreign country in which they operated was unaware of their action. If they were injured or killed, there was a question as to whether they or their families would be entitled to draw the relevant pension, because they were acting outside the law. I took my concerns on this score to the ACPO Crime Committee, and on to the Home Office, which we tried to make underwrite officers on such missions. Support was not forthcoming, and it took several years to put this kind of activity on a proper footing.

Due to some of the excesses of the police, it became more difficult to gain a conviction if evidence was uncorroborated, and more scientific methods had to be employed. Fingerprints have always been a boon, if limited in scope; but the discovery of DNA was an immense advance, which has exposed many killers and rapists who had escaped detection for years. I recognise the natural reluctance of the public to support wholesale DNA testing of communities, but I believe that in opposing it people are acting against their own interests. If samples were taken from us all at birth, the databank created would aid the police immeasurably in solving crime, without any particular inconvenience to anyone except wrongdoers. The public's attitude to DNA is difficult to reconcile with the support people have for the thousands of surveillance cameras planted in their midst, which are far more intrusive to normal life.

In Yorkshire lighter moments leavened the serious work. Mayor-making ceremonies were always fun, and I was privileged to speak when Peggy White, the Conservative leader of the Police Authority, was appointed Lord Mayor of the City of Leeds. Sometimes such an event was just the excuse for a booze-up. At one, the outgoing mayor said of his successor, 'Ah'm supposed to say summat good abaat tha, but Ah can't think of owt. So 'ere's tha chain.' The incomer replied, 'Ah've never thought a gret deal of thee, and ah think even less nar' – with which the assembled company stampeded for the bar, where pints of beer, whiskies and gin-and-tonics had been set up in lines, for them to down as many as they could before dinner.

Set around the country are sumptuous lodgings in which the judges stay when 'sitting' within the area. Strict protocol is observed within their walls, and bedrooms are allocated according to the status of the visiting judge: if a senior man arrives, the occupant of a particular room may have to move to another less grand. Dinners held in the lodgings were always splendid affairs, with the finest food and wine one can imagine.

Judges are great story-tellers, as they have seen and heard so much in court, but I found that some of them lacked the experience of normal life that others have. Few of them exhibited the arrogance of which they are often accused, although I must confess that Bren was annoyed on one occasion when the judge on her left would not stop squeezing her knee. Lord Lieutenants' and High Sheriffs' events were also usually very grand, and some of the individuals were great characters.

For the High Sheriffs, whose term of office lasted only a year, royal visits were particularly important. Some would buy new or high-quality old cars especially for the occasion; new or refurbished clothes were always in abundance, and good cheer and happiness were the order of the day. It was impossible not to be imbued with the joyous mood of the occasion, particularly when popular members of the royal family were involved. The enthusiasm of the crowds was infectious, and even I would be given kisses and flowers and invited to shake hands with dozens of happy people. Attempts to undermine the royal family over the last decade have not worked, for ordinary working men and women are still proud of their heritage and those who represent it – an attitude strikingly

demonstrated by the numbers of people who congregated in Westminster to pay their respects after the death of Queen Elizabeth
the Queen Mother, and the millions who came out onto the streets
to join in the Queen's Jubilee celebrations.

I have been privileged to visit Buckingham Palace on more than
one occasion. Bren and I have attended a number of garden parties
in the grounds, and we found them quaint affairs. People dress up
in their finery, but then all shapes and sizes rush for seats outside
the refreshment tent or jostle for position at the edge of the artificial
lines which form when the royal party arrives. Hats are cocked on
the backs of heads, bodies contorted in curtsies and bows, until the
scene resembles something from a Gilbert and Sullivan opera. The
regulars, senior politicians and the great and the good use the
opportunity to renew acquaintances, avoiding hoi polloi whenever
they can. More than once I spotted Margaret Thatcher with her
nose in the air. After one of these events, Bren and I were walking
through St James's Park on a lovely hot summer evening. I was in
uniform, and she was wearing a beautiful red dress, with hat to
match, but her new shoes had pinched her feet and she had taken
them off them as we strolled. We were stopped by a photographer
who asked to take our picture, as he thought Bren embodied the
phrase, 'When the party was over.' I wish he had sent us a copy.

A greater pleasure is to be invited to eat at the Palace. The first
time we did so, we were invited to dinner by Prince Philip and the
Princess Royal. It really was something to drive through the archway
at the front of the house, cross the quadrangle and park underneath
the carriage entrance. We were graciously received by liveried foot-
men, who escorted us up to one of the magnificent reception rooms,
and there the royals joined us. I was nervous, not knowing what
to expect, but they quickly put me and the other dozen or so guests
at ease. The Princess even linked my arm as we went into dinner,
saying, 'I've always wanted to arrest a Chief Constable.' The food
and wine were exquisite, each guest being individually served, the
host first. I found this unusual as I had long since adopted military
etiquette, insisting that as host I am served last. The Prince got
stuck into his food straight away, whereas again I had been taught

that you wait for everyone to be served before starting. When I mentioned this to him, he said that it was an old habit: in some of the castles he frequented, the kitchens were so far away from the dining room that if you didn't eat as soon as the food was served, it would be stone cold.

Prince Philip is a very individual person. Once, after the opening of a new building society in Leeds, at which he drank a couple of pints of Tetley's bitter in preference to champagne, he decided to pilot the royal plane home. I jokingly asked him if that was wise. 'You may be breathalysed, Sir,' I warned him. He looked at me as if to chew me off, but then smiled and said, 'If you can catch me, Chief Constable, you can do it yourself.' Months later, at Frogmore House, I saw Prince Philip drinking a glass of beer and asked, 'Tetley's, Sir?' 'No,' he said. The brewery used to provide him with his favourite ale, but for some reason had stopped doing so. As their headquarters was in Leeds, I relayed my conversation to the firm's chief executive, who was much taken aback and said that he would sort the matter out.

Our greatest thrill came in the summer of 2001, with an invitation to lunch with the Queen and Prince Philip at Buckingham Palace. I was received in the same manner as before, and was moved when the Queen, Prince Philip and two of their dogs joined us for a pre-lunch reception. Her Majesty's first remark to me was, 'I like your tie' – an 'Ichthys' from Monte Carlo, with a black background and red fish swimming all over it.

The royal couple are both extremely worldly; they converse in a most intelligent matter about almost any subject, and have a very easy way about them. The criticism about them being insular and out of touch is nonsense. At table I was seated on the Queen's left, with the conductor Sir Simon Rattle on her right. He and I had met on a number of previous occasions, the most recent of which was slightly embarrassing for him – he had spontaneously embraced a royal lady in a lift when she entered with a party which included myself. We told this story to the Queen, but declined to name her relation, despite her saying excitedly, 'Do tell! Do tell!' It would be improper for me to relate the views of either the Queen or the

Duke: suffice it to say they both know the subject well, and care deeply about the harm that drugs are causing.

The trooping of the colour that year had been blighted by a torrential downpour, and yet had gone ahead. I asked Prince Philip what it had been like, as he participated in full uniform, with a bearskin helmet. He said that the instruments were so filled with rain that he was surprised the bandsmen didn't blow bubbles rather than make music – but he said that although a bearskin looks heavy, hot and cumbersome, it is completely the reverse, being light, cool and a joy to wear.

During my years as a Chief Constable I averaged sixty-five working hours every week, held seven individual and three group meetings per day, and attended 200 public engagements annually, addressing at least half. I travelled an average of 45,000 miles by car each year, 10,000 by train and 100,000 by air, and I loved every minute of it. It was a privilege to be in a position to help others and work with some of the most dedicated and professional people possible. I am especially indebted to Christine, my secretary in Cleveland; to Margaret, my PA in West Yorkshire, who was the best; and my companion, Graham, who besides being a most able driver was one of the best marksmen in the police service and in whom I had the utmost confidence. I would also like to thank the public for all the personal support they gave me over those years.

When I left Cleveland, we returned to the farm at Kirkburton, where we still live.

The nineties were very eventful for our family. All three of our children got married and started families of their own. They chose to be married from home, and as a father I was privileged to have the last moment alone with my daughters before leaving for the church. They both looked radiant and beautiful, and I will never ever forget the last hug and kiss we shared before I gave them away to their husbands-to-be.

We now have ten grandchildren. Samantha, now a police inspector and part-time law lecturer, has five girls, including one set of twins; Alexandra, who works part time on cancer research at Liverpool University, has two girls and a boy (she lost twin boys at birth), and Charles has twin boys. We continue to see a great deal of each other; the cousins all get on together, and Georgia, Sam's eldest, takes the lead in playing games both outside and in. They love the swimming pool, although they make an enormous mess, and have taken over the old tennis pavilion as their own, eating meals and playing school within its walls.

I like creating new things, and we twice extended the house. However, Bren then said enough was enough, so I turned my attention to the land, where I spend hours in wellies, old trousers and a frayed jacket – garb in which I am not allowed to visit the village to get petrol for the mower. As we live about 800 feet above sea level and our land is quite exposed to the west winds, it is difficult for delicate plants to survive, so we are restricted to planting hardy perennials and late annual blooms. We both adore the place where we live, as it is so fresh and quiet. Many species of birds nest in our woods, and their chorus at first light on a summer morning is wonderful to hear. I stay up late and rise early, and spend many hours sitting somewhere in the garden in the dark, stirred by the sounds of owls and foxes. As dawn breaks, our two remaining dogs – Joshua, a Welsh Border Collie with an odd eye, and Heath, a teenage Jack Russell called Weenu by the grandchildren and sometimes known as Queen Anne because of the shape of his legs – snuffle and shuffle about in the undergrowth.

I promised myself I would make a special effort and create a garden for the millennium, but that will have to wait until I have more free time. One winter's evening at Castle Howard I heard about the joy of owning pot-bellied pigs from another dinner guest, and, deciding to surprise Bren, arranged for a piglet to be delivered to our door on Christmas Day. It was snowing when the bell rang, and I suggested that Bren answer. To her great surprise she was presented with this little mite nestling in straw in a shoe box, with a red ribbon round his neck. She wasn't sure whether to laugh or cry, but soon became fond of Oswald, our first black. He had a lovely nature, but he'd not been castrated and became rather fond of one piece of ancient farm equipment, the wheel of which was just the right height and size for him to embrace and make love to. He would walk with us and the dogs around the woods, and come to a call. One of his party-pieces was to spin round to the command of '*Twirly whirly!*' If he was close to you, he would run through your legs as he turned, and one day Bren, who was wearing a long skirt, was bowled off her feet and carried some distance, to much mirth, by his manoeuvre. He used to sleep in the stables with our horses, Oliver, Emma and William, our geese Frederick and Rosy, the mallards Sadie and Lionel and the Aylesbury, Chloe.

The birds grew so numerous that we built them a house, away from the horses, which they shared with our rabbits Jemima and Pandora. This menagerie was in addition to our dogs, who all lived quite happily with our four cats. Whenever one of these characters dies, we bury it on our land.

In the early days Oswald was the source of some embarrassment. He travelled miles seeking a sow – without any success, as far as we knew. We would receive calls from farmers to tell us where he was, and would have to collect him. One summer's evening we both were dressed ready to go to some official function, I complete with miniature medals, Bren in a long evening gown, when a call came from our Control Room. 'The Chief Constable's pig is rooting in the garden at ———, and the owner would like you to collect it.'

We had no alternative but to travel there in our finery, in the chauffeur-driven Jaguar. I jumped out, apologised to the poor householder, who was more amused than cross, ushered Oswald on to the pavement with my silver-topped walking cane, and chivvied him the mile or so back home. We must have looked a merry sight. When I got up to speak at the function, a couple of hours later, I began by saying, 'A funny thing happened to me on the way to the dinner . . .' but I feel certain no one believed me.

Once, within forty-eight hours I addressed a course in Leicestershire on equal opportunities, spoke about management change to a course at the Police College in Hampshire, and then went on to London to attend a dinner addressed by the Home Secretary.

Unfortunately, somewhere during the journey we lost the trousers of my dinner suit – a deficiency which I discovered only when I was dressing in my club in Eaton Terrace.

In my dressing gown, I asked the steward if anyone had handed a pair in. He said, 'No' – but one of the guests had remarked that there was a pair of trousers hanging on the metal railings outside. Together we ventured out into the street, but there were no trousers in sight, so we both walked about this very grand neighbourhood searching in dustbins and yards for the damned things, without success.

It was late-night opening at Harrods, and thither I went (having first dressed, of course) to see if they could help. They had no trousers to match, and the cheapest dinner suit cost about £400, which at that time I could not really afford – so I missed the dinner. The sequel to this story came the next evening, when I was addressing the Institute of Insurance Brokers in Leeds. I recalled the saga with one slight amendment. I told the audience that I had bought a new suit from Harrods at a cost of £500, and added, 'I am insured by the Royal Sun Alliance, and would appreciate meeting their representative after dinner in order that I may be reimbursed.' The audience went very quiet until they realised that I was joking.

At its peak, Bren's business of assembling printed circuit-boards was employing over fifty workers. During the early nineties she was so successful that she was asked if she would like to be nominated for Business Woman of the Year, but she refused without a second thought, always shunning the limelight. Her company assembled the first batch of remote meter-reading equipment, which Ferranti used to ferry to and from her workers day and night, as the units were in such demand. The company wished her to become involved in a much larger way, which would have entailed opening a factory, but she was against it, preferring her 'cottage industry'. Had she agreed, her business would probably have grown even more.

From 1985 to 1991 she earned far more than I did as a senior police officer. Then, in the mid-nineties, technology moved on: machines replaced much of the skilled work formerly the province of individuals; she was left with limited specialist work, and she gradually ran the firm down.

Over the years we have built up a wide circle of friends – artists, lawyers, bankers, builders, police officers and entrepreneurs. Our longest-standing friends are Stewart and Christine Calligan. He was a police cadet in Huddersfield when I joined, and we played rugby for the same team. He rose to the rank of chief superintendent, and is now a successful author of law books. We made our first trip to France in their company, we in our MGB and they in a Triumph Spitfire. We had planned the holiday for some time, but shortly before we left Stewart broke his leg in several places playing rugby. We all heard it crack, but told him it was nothing and he should continue the game. He did, in a great deal of pain, which was later deadened by five or six pints in the bar; only when this failed to relieve his agony did we take him to hospital. His leg was in pot until the day of our departure, and he drove all the way with this weakened limb.

We have visited France every year since, first under canvas, then towing a mobile caravan, hiring static ones, owning our own, and latterly staying in our own home there. The Côte d'Azur has a special place in our lives.

Our other closest friends include Michael and Helga Evans and their children. Michael's father laid the foundations of a lucrative property business in Leeds, which his son has developed into one of the most successful in the region. When he was forty Michael moved to Monaco, for tax purposes, and now describes himself as an exile. Martyn and Liz Oldroyd are other long-standing friends who left the country for tax reasons. Our sons attended the same school, and when we lived next door to each other we would, quite irresponsibly, race his Daimler Dart against my E-type through the country lanes around our homes. I am glad to say we were never caught.

When we first walked along the front at Cannes and St Tropez in the mid-sixties, and saw all the luxury vessels with their liveried crews, we never thought that one day we would be sitting on board one of them, looking out at the milling throng ashore. Now the

Evanses invite us every year to stay on their wonderful boat – and a magical experience it is.

Bren and I try, unsuccessfully, to keep fit by jogging and going to the local gym. Whenever the yacht is moored in one or other of its exotic berths, we go running. Once on shore, I feel exactly as I did before, outside looking in. Returning from one of these jogs in St Tropez, we learned of Princess Diana's tragic death – and we were again in France when Her Majesty Queen Elizabeth the Queen Mother passed away.

Another time we moored next to an exquisite boat, which moved off soon after we had arrived. On our morning jog we saw it again, moored around the bay, and I shouted to the British crew, 'Was it something we said?' A man leaned over the side and said in a whisper, 'No – the owners are Russians, and they recognised you.' It is remarkable how much of the cash being spent on boats and property in this region has been accrued from the proceeds of crime.

However wealthy you are, there is always someone richer than you. We have been very lucky in life. My police salary and Bren's earnings have allowed us to educate our children privately, live in comfortable surroundings, and drive some of the world's most beautiful cars; but this is nothing compared with the style that some of our friends can afford, most of which they have achieved during their own lifetimes.

Unlike many people we have met, neither of us is envious of these wealthy individuals. On the contrary, we are both pleased for them. One such person, Paul Sykes, told me that he was swimming in the Mediterranean when a thought came to him which he decided to share with his wife Valeria. As he climbed back on board his yacht, he said, 'We've lost it, lass.'

Puzzled, she asked what he was talking about.

'We've joined bloody champagne set,' he replied. 'Come on – we're off.' They returned home, for the last time in one of their two private jets, and Paul sold them, his yacht and his villa, to live as a humble being. It didn't last long.

We have met some wonderful people, mainly from Yorkshire, among them members of the Ogden family, who came from very humble beginnings. Sir Robert, one of the brothers, heads a property empire and is best known for his race horses, but through his charitable work has helped many thousands of disadvantaged children.

CHAPTER TWENTY-ONE

DRUGS

There is a great deal of ignorance about drugs. Many young people derive pleasure from them, and others make huge profits; but the very word raises fear in the minds of parents and uncertainty in politicians. It is difficult to have a sensible debate on the subject, as, by and large, national newspapers limit themselves to discussing the legalisation of cannabis on one side of their divide, and prohibition on the other – extreme positions emphasised by single-issue politicians, pressure groups and the chattering classes.

I first became interested in the subject in the early sixties, when I dealt with the death of a married couple of doctors who had overdosed on heroin. Looking at their emaciated bodies on the slab, I felt it was such an unnecessary waste. I had read of drug taking by the Beatles and other pop stars, but the deaths of the doctors brought home to me the full horror of substance abuse. I began to read more widely on the subject, and in the late sixties formed one of the first drug squads in the United Kingdom, in an attempt to do something about the problem.

Drugs have run like a thread through my career ever since. During my spell in Los Angeles I saw them in a racial context – there, the increased number of white addicts brought about a change in police tactics: they stopped shooting and began zapping by Taser those who were fighting mad while under their influence.

During the seventies and eighties I observed the huge rise in the number of deaths and injuries to young people through sniffing noxious, albeit legal, substances. I saw the tragic result of one eleven-year-old's 'flight' from a rail viaduct. In the late eighties and nineties I dealt with the explosion of crime committed to feed drug habits, and the violence – in one case an addict's fingers were axed off – towards people who could not pay their suppliers. In the past ten years I have been chilled by the willingness of drug dealers to use guns to eradicate opposition and maintain control within their areas, and the deathly consequences for many innocent bystanders.

During those early years there was little if any lead from Government, who largely denied that a problem existed, and acted only when faced with irrefutable evidence, by following other countries in increasing the powers of the criminal justice agencies. Politicians paid lip-service to education, prevention and treatment, and it was only by accident that the free hypodermic needle-exchange programme, introduced to prevent the spread of Aids, benefited injecting drug users.

By the late eighties, ordinary people were crying out for change. They saw their children becoming more attracted to drugs, and felt powerless to intervene. Whenever drugs took hold within a family, they had nowhere to turn: doctors didn't wish to know, and specialist clinics rejected victims because they were under-funded and over-worked. When children began stealing from their parents – and everyone else – families were faced with a dilemma no parent should have to countenance: should they turn their own son or daughter in to the police, or should they watch their children destroy themselves? Many partnerships foundered on this decision. People felt let down by the police and local authority agencies, who appeared to take no action against the peddlers in their midst. Even if dealers were arrested, they were back on the streets within hours or replaced by others. Parents grew angry with politicians for ignoring their plight, and with the media, who remained locked into their own meaningless campaigns and ignored the real issues.

The police had difficulty reconciling politicians' hard-line public pronouncements with the behind-the-scenes pressure exerted on them and the courts to reduce the number of people kept in custody or imprisoned. If the courts and the probation service tried to put prolific drug offenders into treatment, rather than send them to prison, they were hampered by lack of powers; if they were 'creative' with what powers they had, there were no funds to support them. Even those stalwarts who persuaded someone else to foot the bill were floored at the last hurdle, as there were so few treatment places to take their charges.

I found this situation totally unacceptable. By the early nineties, whenever I visited a community, drugs had become the first item for discussion. It was the same when I talked to my officers, spoke at public gatherings and met other agencies or local politicians – but we seemed to be getting nowhere.

I asked my colleagues on the Crime Committee of ACPO if they would consent to my setting up a separate drugs committee. They readily agreed, and through this platform I began to raise drugs issues in public. My honesty was welcomed by most people, although it caused some embarrassment for the Home Secretary, Michael Howard, as he and his department often wished I kept my thoughts to myself. He once called me to ask what I was going to do about Sir Paul Condon, the Metropolitan Commissioner, who had cautioned a pop star for possessing Ecstasy. I reminded him that he, the Home Secretary, was the Police Authority for London, and should approach Sir Paul directly if he wished to intervene.

The media regarded me as contentious. The *Panorama* documentary, *Needle Park*, in which I appeared, attracted their largest-ever audience, indicating the strength of public feeling on the subject. I concluded that we ought to be honest about the subject of drugs, and focus on trying to reduce the problems they cause. I could see children destroying their own lives and those of their families through their addictions. They bunked off school, and stole from family and friends. When this could not support their habit, some prostituted themselves, living in fear of violence from dealers and deteriorating into a half-life, only able to function when under the influence. The criminal justice system only exacerbated their problems, and the community suffered as a consequence. I was determined to stop this vicious cycle with education, treatment and counselling. I was inundated with requests to speak from people who until then had been unwilling even to talk to police officers. Non-governmental organizations (NGOs), many of which regarded themselves as ginger groups, sought my support. A Liverpool doctor who pioneered the prescription of diamorphine for heroin addicts, invited me on to his steering group. My mail increased enormously, most letters coming from ordinary people who thanked me for representing their views and speaking out.

This was a testing time. I faced searching questions from the media about the inconsistency of police action, which was often indefensible. I was pitted against drug experts in public debate. I was asked to comment on the effectiveness of current legislation, and my remarks offended the legal profession. I was ridiculed by the media for saying that the use of drugs had spread to 'our leafy communities', that drug dealing was 'a cottage industry undertaken by the boy next door', and that children in their early teens were committing crime or prostituting themselves to feed a habit.

I didn't always have the support of my police colleagues, some of whom considered I was stirring up a hornets' nest. Even some of our friends suggested that I ought to back off. I received threatening letters of a most unpleasant kind, and a fellow guest at a High Sheriff's dinner party said I was 'unfit to hold public office' – simply because I advocated telling our children about the dangers of drugs. 'A diet of Postman Pat is all they require when they're young,' she said smugly. In this she was expressing the views of the Government at the time, who opposed drugs education on the grounds that children told about drugs were more likely to try them – much the same view as that held by Victorians on sex education several generations before. Schoolteachers, seeing the problems first hand, firmly rejected this outdated perception, and welcomed my and other people's input to their students.

I tried to break down the prejudice against drug-users, assembling (with their consent) a montage of photographs of a police officer, a young woman, a Rastafarian, a down-and-out, an elderly lady, a man of the cloth and a businessman, and challenging audiences to identify 'the druggie' among them. The Rasta and the down-and-out were usually singled out, when in fact all seven were addicts – my point being that addiction was politically correct in every aspect.

Slowly, attitudes began to change. In 1995 I helped prepare *Tackling Drugs Together*, a document published by the Conservative Government which marked a significant policy change, as it discussed health and education in relation to drugs for the first time.

During the lead-up to the 1997 General Election I received a call at home from one of Tony Blair's personal aides, soon known as spin doctors. 'Tony's giving a speech on drugs in Aberdeen tomorrow,' she said. 'He's looking for a new angle, and would like to say that if he's elected he'll appoint a Drugs Tsar. What would be your response?'

I knew that the American experience of such an office was mixed, so I asked what the role would entail. 'Oh,' she replied, 'we haven't got that far yet. We just want to know if you'd support the idea or not.' I told her I would need more clarity before giving the proposal a green light, but, if asked, I would say that I would welcome any initiative which would help resolve the drugs problem.

The aide thanked me, Blair gave the speech, and Labour was elected in June that year with a huge majority. Bren and I stayed up all night and were excited by the mood, as victory after victory was announced. Two days later at the Rugby League Challenge Cup Final at Wembley, we shared the elation of a few senior politicians when we were both bearhugged by our old friends John and Pauline Prescott. The mood was so effervescent that John received a standing ovation from the capacity crowd when he entered the Royal Box.

Within weeks, together with half a dozen people from other backgrounds, I was invited to a meeting with Ann Taylor, the newly appointed Leader of the House of Commons, a Cabinet post. She told us she had been given the task of appointing a Drugs Tsar, and sought our views about the role. We had a lively debate, at the end of which she thanked us for our contributions, and jokingly added that she would give a prize to anyone who could come up with a better title, as she hated that one.

The post of Drugs Tsar – special adviser to the Prime Minister, with responsibility to develop and co-ordinate the United Kingdom's drugs policy – was advertised in the national Press in the autumn of 1997. After much heart-searching I, along with more than 250 others, applied for the job, and after a series of short-listings and interviews with the Home Secretary, the Secretary of State for Health, Ann Taylor and a moderator, I was appointed by the Prime Minister to start work on 4 January 1998, thirty-six years to the day since I became a police constable.

CHAPTER TWENTY-TWO

THE TSAR

The transition did have its complications, first over pay: my salary as a Chief Constable was higher than the pay of any other of the Government's special advisers, including Jonathan Powell, the Prime Minister's Chief of Staff, and Alistair Campbell, his Press Secretary. However, the Tsar's job carried a 'no detriment' clause, which the Government contractually had to honour, so that my remuneration could not be reduced. To my extreme discomfort, my salary was bandied about in the Press for my first two years in office – a form of harassment which strangely ceased when the pay of other special advisers leap-frogged mine significantly.

A second problem arose over the armed protection I had been receiving, after two criminals in the north had put out a contract to kill me (it was eventually foiled when they were arrested). The Government refused to continue this support, on the grounds that they knew of no precedent, even though the West Yorkshire Police Authority offered to pay for it.

When my appointment was announced, I received a large number of letters of congratulation and a few which expressed reservations. One old friend suggested that I was taking on a poisoned chalice: he said that drugs were an insoluble problem, and that if I won any success, ministers would claim credit for it. If I achieved nothing, I would have to carry the can. I replied in all honesty that I felt it a privilege to be given the opportunity to try and make a difference. Another friend said that the job was just 'Labour spin', and I wouldn't be given the wherewithal to complete my task. One colleague remarked that I had become political and sold out for my knighthood – but that was quite untrue, as I had stipulated on interview that I would not be interested if the job had any political bias.

My children were excited and happy, and perhaps a little proud of their dad. They made jokes about the Tsar. 'Is Mum now the Tsarina?' 'Are we Tsarettes?' They wished to know if I would meet the Prime Minister and other members of the Cabinet. Alexandra bought me a concrete pig, which she called Tsar, and which still resides in the courtyard of our home.

In the weeks before I took the job I spent time getting to know key ministers, civil servants and others in the field. I invited groups of interested people to join me in London and Wakefield to discuss their perception of the drugs problem and say what they would like done about it. Their responses were extremely encouraging, and generally endorsed my own views – I felt sure I was on the right track.

The Press conference held on my first day in office was startlingly large. The room, one used by the Church Synod, in the grounds of Westminster Abbey was overflowing with reporters and cameramen from all over the world. Ann Taylor chaired the event and fielded questions between herself, myself and Mike Trace, my deputy, who had been appointed after consultation with me.

I was surprised by the reporters' aggression. 'Is your appointment anything more than a cheap publicity exercise by the Government?', 'It's all spin and no substance,' 'Aren't you a tiger without teeth?', 'You won't get any power or funding,' 'Won't you be muzzled?', Aren't you too old for the job?', 'Have you ever taken illegal drugs?'

I explained the unusual constitutional position I held – although I had no direct power, I did have the backing of the Prime Minister and the Cabinet. I said I would be submitting a budget within weeks, and that would be the time to ask questions about funding. I explained that I would not have left the police service, had I considered this a superficial exercise. My job, I said, was to co-ordinate the work of others, and I had many years experience at doing that.

Then followed the one-to-one interviews, which meant being marshalled into different parts of the room and the yard outside to face TV cameras, tape-recorders and newsprint journalists. From there I was whisked around a number of studios for live outputs, and these continued for the rest of the day, ending with a live interview on *Newsnight* by Jeremy Paxman. In all I faced more than seventy individuals, all of whom had their own takes on the subject. When at last I fell into my London bed, some eighteen hours after I had risen, I was shattered – but I thought to myself, 'Now the real work has to begin.'

Next day's headlines were mixed. I was surprised to see how little of what we had said appeared in print. It was as if most journalists had written their copy before the event, and decided my fate before they met me.

The drugs problem in this country is so vast that one could easily be defeatist about it – one reason why some people would legalise all substances and let others deal with the problems they cause. I have never supported such a policy, because I believe that something *can* be done to reduce the danger and harm that drugs cause individuals, their families and the community at large – and I was encouraged by others from all walks of life who were similarly convinced.

In order to bring about change, I needed to identify exactly what was happening and establish how much money we were spending on the problem; but this proved more difficult than I expected, first because of the paucity of information, but principally due to obstruction from civil servants. In their view, merely by asking simple questions I was trespassing on hallowed ground.

Senior civil servants were annoyed by the fact that they had been excluded from my interview process. Sir Richard Wilson, Cabinet Secretary and head of the home civil service, chose to raise the matter at our first meeting. 'It would have been much better for you if we'd had a hand in your selection,' he said, and added patronisingly, 'I'm sure the outcome would have been the same.' Ann Taylor told me a different story – the Government didn't want to involve the civil servants in the selection, as 'they couldn't be trusted'.

Sir Richard is a tall, gangly man with prominent teeth, who peers at you over his large spectacles while scrunching his nose in Bugs Bunny fashion. I had been given Grade 1 status, the highest in the civil service, and he made me feel at home by instructing his personal staff to allow me access to him whenever I wished, telling them, 'This is one of the most important people in the country.' Again, I recognised I was being patronised. Sir Richard promised to visit me in my office, which he said would send a very strong signal about my status to his colleagues – but alas, his good intentions were never realised in the form of any practical support during the three-and-a-half years I occupied the post of Drugs Tsar.

I had an early disagreement with him over a personal matter. I had joined the board of Evans of Leeds, a publicly quoted property company, and he asked me to relinquish the post, as it would 'undermine my credibility with the public' and upset some of his colleagues, since, with the extra stipend, I would be earning much more than them. When I refused, he said he would have to put the matter before the Prime Minister – only to be completely wrong-footed when told that I had been granted permission to take the job by ministers and his own staff. When I added that I had asked Evans to pay my dues to the NSPCC, and that I would use part of my annual leave to attend meetings, he twisted uncomfortably about on his chair; but he was less than gracious and offered no apology for his officious blunder, merely saying that he would have to make further inquiries. I heard no more of it.

From the start, the civil service seemed determined to make my task difficult. I was never given enough staff to do the job properly, and could do nothing to remedy the deficiency, as I had no control over appointments. In three years I was allotted four different heads of unit (the first of whom was outstanding), seven different secretaries and eight different Press secretaries. Every other person in the office was changed at least once. At first I had only seven people to create and co-ordinate a new, UK-wide drugs strategy – a telling contrast with the massive resources directed at other commitments made in Labour's election manifesto. Additional difficulties arose because I had no control over the individuals within my office, their chain of command, their appraisal process or their line of reporting. Although on paper they were appointed to support me, in reality they took their lead from the senior civil servant in the department to which they were attached.

I don't know whether it was inefficiency or bloody-mindedness, but one secretary even expected me to book my own transport arrangements. This lack of support manifested itself in many ways: for example, when letters to me remained unanswered for months, I was told I could not deal with them myself, as they had to be cleared by other departments first. The justification for the delay was that I was not 'covered by the rules governing replies to correspondence'. Even in the latter days of the Tories, much had been made of 'joined-up government' – a phrase without substance. I was reminded of the response I received from Sir Robert Armstrong, former head of the civil service, at his annual meeting of senior staff, to which I was invited as an outsider. When I suggested that Government departments should adopt the same principle as local government agencies and work more closely together on major issues, my remark caused a sharp intake of breath from his colleagues, and a wry smile of satisfaction when he replied, 'What a charming idea!'

To be fair, the civil servants did show some willingness to join me in discussing strategy, but they absolutely refused to reveal how much money they had, or to account for how it was being spent. Control of money is one of the keys to civil servants' power, and they made strenuous efforts to prevent me even setting out to prepare a corporate budget. When they failed in that endeavour, they tried, unsuccessfully, to supplant me with a senior civil servant.

The fiscal systems at that time were departmentally based, in much the same way as those of the police service had been a decade before. Each unit within a department drew up its bid for money based on its individual needs; these bids were amalgamated into departmental claims, which were fought for by the Secretaries of State for each department, in front of a Cabinet Committee chaired by the Chancellor of the Exchequer, Gordon Brown.

Once the money had been allocated to a department, it was divided and given into the control of individual unit heads, who guarded it jealously, as it was the basis of their power and status. They had no interest in corporate policy – even within their own departments – or anything else which would interfere with the spending of 'their' money. Moreover, their accounting procedures were based on 'processes' – for example, reducing the waiting times for hospital beds – rather than on outcomes – the health of patients after treatment in hospital – and as such were meaningless measures of success.

My whole philosophy was to base budgets on achievement. This was how I had successfully run two police forces, and I sought to change the Government system, as I was determined to create a cross-Whitehall budget which identified the costs and benefits of each pound spent. I made no secret of my view that if there was no measurable improvement, the money should not be made available. In this regard I was fully supported by the Treasury, who saw me as an instrument of change, and by drugs workers, who were frustrated by the prevailing bureaucracy. Inside the civil service I was regarded as a threat to the system and the individuals in it – but I had been through the process of reform before, and knew that without radical change little progress would be made.

The tactics employed to frustrate me were often quite childish. Civil servants, particularly those in the Health Department, failed to turn up for meetings or to provide information on time, using sickness, annual leave, vacancies and even 'leaves on the line' as excuses. I found such tactics amusing, but they became damaging when I needed information in a hurry.

I recognised that I had no real power base. I was a hybrid, without the support mechanisms enjoyed by civil servants, politicians or traditional special advisers; but I had the advantage that my unusual constitutional position placed me outside their normal control and influence. My lack of 'belonging' was a feature of my time in

Government – and I was quite comfortable with it, as I am by nature a loner. I ruffled the feathers of many powerful people – not out of spite, but in order to bring about change. Tony Blair once remarked, 'This is what I expected you to do. I knew you'd have to tread on a few toes if things were to change.'

I did not realise how much I had breached protocol until I was told by one senior official of the strength of feeling against my attendance in front of Gordon Brown, the Chancellor of the Exchequer, to present and later report progress on my budget. The fact that I sat on a number of Cabinet committees also gave great offence. This was regarded as creating 'a very dangerous precedent', for two reasons. First, civil servants were precluded from membership, and second, I didn't rely on their advice in the same way as 'their' ministers did. Childishly, the minutes of these meetings never recorded that I had been present, even when I had acted as chairman.

The corporate budget I submitted in the spring of 1998 left a lot to be desired. I would not have accepted it as a Chief Constable, because a substantial part of it was based on supposition and conjecture. I had established some loose figures for the total expenditure on anti-drugs activities, but they were vague, and devoid of detailed financial information about current spending.

One or two examples will illustrate this. Money had been allocated to improve drugs education in schools, and a performance indicator established to identify the number of schools with drugs policies in place. The Department for Education did not know what educational programmes were in place and thus had no means of either costing them or evaluating their effectiveness. Similarly, money was allocated to increase the availability of drug treatment, but the Department of Health did not know how many people were being treated, what type of treatment they were receiving, how much it cost or what impact it was making. They didn't even know how many bed spaces were available for drug addicts. When I asked how many people died as a result of illegal drugs, they inquired 'Which set of figures do you want?'

In the final stages of my budget preparation I also came into conflict with ministers who saw that some of my recommendations would undermine their own departmental bids. Jack Straw, the Home Secretary, for example, sought additional funds for prisons to house a predicted increase in numbers of prisoners, whereas my report indicated that the numbers would be reduced by the provision of treatment. 'Let it ride this time, Keith,' he suggested, 'and I'll support your treatment programmes.'

Gordon Brown's PX committee, which assesses bids for money made by the Departments of State, was made up of other Treasury ministers and Cabinet ministers who did not have spending departments of their own, the Lord Chancellor and Ann Taylor being two examples. We met in one of the original Cabinet Rooms, which was full of history. I found it easy to let my mind wander as I imagined the discussions which had taken place there, and thought of all the Prime Ministers who had participated.

Before my first meeting, Gordon came to shake my hand and welcome me 'on board'. I was faced by a dozen politicians, the majority of whom quizzed me on the recommendations in my report, which ran to fifty pages, as it covered the combined budgets of every major Department of State. The questions were very wide-ranging, and I was glad to be well prepared. I was honest about the difficulties I had experienced in obtaining information (without pointing the finger at any particular department). When I asked the company to trust me, Gordon responded, 'That's my line.' The fairly good-humoured process lasted just shy of an hour.

The Government announced its decision on drugs in the three-year spending plan published in July 1998. They accepted my principal recommendation that we make a fundamental change, from spending the bulk of our money (63 per cent) on the criminal justice system, which I described as dealing with the consequence of drugs, to preventing the problems in the first place, by investing more in education and treatment, on which, respectively, only 12 and 13 per cent had been spent in the past. (In my presentation I had commented that any company which spent two-thirds of its money on reparation work would soon be out of business.) The Government voted all the money I had requested to bring about the changes, and gave additional sums for other areas of work.

Although the budget was generally hailed as a success, the conditions it imposed inflamed civil servants, as they were unable to spend the new money without my consent. They were instructed by the Treasury to satisfy the 'anti-drugs co-ordinator' – myself – that expenditure was in line with the new drugs strategy (published at the same time), was likely to achieve the targets I set, and represented good value for money. I was also put in charge of monitoring progress, and had to report directly to the Treasury committee. I had not been consulted about this responsibility and had a number of reservations, as I didn't have the staff to cope with the administrative burden this imposed – so the Treasury promised some help.

The aim of the four-part strategy, *Tackling Drugs to Build a Better Britain*, was – and is – to lessen the danger and harm drugs cause to individuals, their families and the community as a whole, through education, treatment, community action and the reduction of drug availability on the streets.

My supervisory role was unacceptable to many civil servants, who focused their anger on my staff. 'Who the hell does he think he is?' they demanded. 'If he thinks we're going to report to him, he's going to have a rude awakening,' 'I'm not working for him,' 'I've only got one boss and it's not him,' 'You can get lost if you think we're going to take any notice of this,' were some of the remarks made, with the bad language removed.

The mandarins were as good as their word. They consistently ignored the Treasury's directive, and undermined every initiative we took to monitor progress. Such was my frustration that I asked the Prime Minister's Policy and Innovation Unit if they would look into what was happening. They reported that my position was untenable – I had been given responsibility without power. They outlined a number of options, all of which would give me the power to direct. The report was leaked to the Press by 'an unknown source inside Government', erroneously suggesting that it was critical of me, and the media used it as an example of how I was failing to cope with the job. Later, when the report was made public, we asked editors to publish a true version of its contents, but they declined, saying that it was water under the bridge.

I learnt to anticipate the tactics of the civil servants. They supposed that once they had overcome the initial blush of my appointment, I would be marginalised, and things could get back to normal. Unfortunately for them, I had had too much experience in managing change to allow this to happen; I had also seen how they operated in the run-up to the 1997 election, when I helped them prepare a brief for both main political parties, the rule being that they matched each of the parties' manifestos but retained the status quo. I had also embodied a number of devices to help me deliver the new ten-year strategy. These included a set of performance indicators by which each department and agency would be judged, key milestones for them to achieve, publication of my Annual Plan of Action for each of them, and my Annual Report on the progress they were making.

My first office was just around the corner from No. 10 Downing Street. I had been allocated a room on the second 'ministerial' floor at the back of the Treasury, overlooking St James's Park. There, directly above the Cabinet War Rooms, my spacious office had previously been occupied by Michael Heseltine, a former contender for the leadership of the Conservative Party, but more interestingly by Lady Churchill, wife of the Prime Minister, as a changing-room and occasional bedroom during the war.

With a deal of effort I managed to furnish the room with period furniture, but I had to beg, steal and borrow, as the requisitioning process was turgid. I found a partner's desk, conference table and twenty chairs already in situ, and I managed to scrounge two sofa tables and four chairs from No. 10 Downing Street, and two standard and two table lamps from the Cabinet Office. The paintings, supplemented by my Yorkshire scenes painted by my friend Ashley Jackson, came from the Government's Art Service. I was initially told I would have to wait six months to make a choice, as 'the new lot' needed looking after first; but when the art experts realised that I had taken over what they described as a 'minister's office' I was bounced to the front of the queue.

I was quite happy to be five minutes' walk away from the Cabinet

Office, as it gave me a degree of space – although, except for the Cabinet Committee meetings which would be arranged around my diary, and an hour's 'one-to-one' with Ann Taylor each week, I was left to my own devices.

Each day differed. I would try to spend Monday and Tuesday in the office, to deal with administrative matters and meetings. I had set this pattern many years before as a Chief Constable and found it suited my working habits. My days in London began at about 6 a.m. with a half-hour run around Hyde Park. After a shower and breakfast of grapefruit juice, toast and coffee, I walked the twenty-minute journey to the Treasury, arriving at about eight, taking in both Green and St James's Parks, which reminded me of my home in Yorkshire. I always got a buzz when approaching the magnificent array of white stone Government buildings on Horse Guards Parade, and enjoyed banter with the security staff on the door, one of whom was a former constable of mine from West Yorkshire.

My day would include at least nine meetings with people from all walks of life, from ministers to drug addicts, Church luminaries to industry, local politicians to foreign dignitaries. I didn't have lunch, and usually finished around seven in the evening, taking the same return route home. I ate dinner alone in one of a small number of favourite restaurants within walking distance of base, the meal accompanied by a glass or two of sparkling water. I invariably watched the ten o'clock news before reading the contents of my lead-lined 'Box' – black, rather than ministerial red – which I carried with me everywhere. I retired to bed around one in the morning. Bren would sometimes accompany me to London to do a little shopping but she much preferred being at home on the farm.

The remainder of my week I spent travelling around the United Kingdom. I used trains whenever possible; otherwise I flew or was driven in the car provided me. On arrival at a rendezvous I would hold a Press conference, organised either by my own Press office or by the Central Office of Information, visit a number of venues, one of which I might officially open, eat with people who had been organised into groups for my convenience, give at least one talk, hold private meetings with local officials who were answerable to me, and appear on an evening's live television or radio programme before returning to base around nine or ten o'clock in the evening. If I could, I would begin and end these journeys in Yorkshire, which enabled me to sleep at home, and Bren could accompany me on my visit.

This was impossible when I visited more than one region in a day. For example, after a full day in the office I might travel to Devon for an overnight stay before a 7.30 a.m. television interview, followed by engagements later in the morning, then a car journey to Bristol for an afternoon meeting, then on by train and car to Oxford to speak at a Union debate, then by car to Manchester, arriving at some ungodly hour in order to be available for engagements early next day, then back to London by air.

This hectic schedule continued for the whole of my time as a special adviser, and stretched my personal staff, one of whom spent a large proportion of her time making the necessary arrangements. Bren worried, telling me I was going to kill myself, but I have always felt that hard work never killed anyone. As the Drugs Tsar, I travelled some 40,000 miles by car, 50,000 miles by rail and, including my later work for the Home Secretary, 100,000 miles by air every year. Besides this I read and prepared reports at weekends, and often had to leave home on a Sunday.

For pleasure I gardened at least six hours on a weekend, and devoted Sundays to the whole family's visits. We are very fortunate in that at least two of our children live close by and regularly visit us at home. All our children and ten grandchildren choose to bring their families to holiday with us in France.

The Strategic Communications unit in No. 10 Downing Street, led by Alastair Campbell, scheduled the time-scale for publication of the new strategy and the financial plan. I was surprised at how little ministers were interested in the performance targets, particularly as they were determined to introduce objectivity into their performance as a Government.

This was an issue raised by the Prime Minister at one of my

early meetings with him to discuss my draft strategy before it went to Cabinet Ministers. We met in one of No. 10's small drawing rooms, which was furnished with chintzy, floral-covered furniture. Tony Blair, dressed in casual light-coloured trousers and a blue, open-necked shirt, sat in one of the chairs eating an orange and bade me sit beside him. I found him very personable and pleasant, and he made me feel completely at ease.

After asking if I had settled in, he discussed my paper. I could tell that he had read and digested it, as he was able to put quite detailed and intelligent questions without reference to the document. He asked me what I had left out, and I told him I had been unable to include all the performance targets that I would have liked to bring in, because, as I put it, 'the system isn't ready for them'. This aroused his interest, and he asked me why. I explained that as we had not had such controls before in drugs policy, certain people needed a lot of convincing of their worth. He said he understood, adding that if I had any problems in that direction, I should go back to him. (The reality was that civil servants from every department were unwilling to commit themselves to detailed outcome targets.) The Prime Minister gave his full support to my report, asking when we could make an announcement. I explained that the paper had to go through the usual process, and he said he would like it done sooner rather than later.

That was my first business meeting with the Prime Minister, and I was impressed – more so than at the social events which Bren and I had attended in No. 10, where I thought he was too accommodating to the star personalities he had invited. These affairs are really large bun fights, full of celebrities who like to be photographed by the paparazzi at the entrance gate to Downing Street and then be noticed in the reception room. Some, particularly pop stars and radio DJs, act like children: they create a lot of noise and make big licks about either smoking where they are not allowed to or being deprived of a particular type of alcohol.

The more mature celebrities stand quietly and talk sensibly, but politicians seem to be drawn irresistibly to the glitterati. Once Bren and I were having a long discussion with the late John Thaw and his wife Sheila Hancock about real and fictional policing when Tony Blair joined in the conversation, only to be rudely interrupted by Liz Dawn, alias Vera Duckworth from *Coronation Street*, who shouted across the room, 'Tony! Tony! I want a photo!' When he started to apologise and excuse himself, I said, 'You don't have to go, if you don't wish to.'

'I'd better,' he said.

'No you don't. You're the Prime Minister, and this is your home.'

He went – whereupon 'Vera' threw her arms around him in a bearhug and kissed him as if he was a long lost friend, even though this was their first meeting. Others were less demonstrative. The 'two fat ladies', the elderly, charming women who hosted a travel and cooking television series, were more interested in the furniture and the paintings than being noticed. Cabinet ministers are expected to attend these soirées, but some clearly dislike them and escape as soon as is decently possible.

No. 10 Downing Street is a wonderful house, with all its rooms beautifully furnished and steeped in history. The main reception rooms are approached by a winding staircase with portraits of previous Prime Ministers on the wall in date order – so that the latest occupier of the office is right at the top of the stairs.

I was first invited to a reception there by John Major, who explained jovially that when he left office his picture would go on the top step, and all the rest would be relegated downwards, which meant that the one at the bottom would have to been removed altogether. Major went on jokingly to explain that the deposed portraits were put in a tea-chest in the cellar, and that one day he intended to switch them about to see if anyone would notice. So much for him being a 'grey man'.

The Foreign Office is another historic building which I had to visit at least monthly to see the minister with responsibility for drugs overseas. At first this was the late Derek Thatchett, and he was succeeded by John Battle, both from Leeds and well known to me. Their office was very ornate, with a fireplace at either end and two matching doors side by side, to enable foreign dignitaries of equal standing to enter the room at the same time. I also had occasional meetings with the Foreign Secretary, Robin Cook, whom I found charming and well-informed. Once when discussing foreign travel, I remarked, 'I don't know how you put up with it. I enjoy the work when I get there, but I hate the travel' – to which he replied, 'I like the travel but dislike the bit when I get there.' We agreed we ought to share jobs.

Once the strategy had been reviewed and a final version agreed (a summary appears at the end of this chapter), the next step was its public launch. The strategy was formally presented at a glitzy Soho theatre by myself and Frank Dobson, standing in for Ann Taylor, who was simultaneously making the announcement in the House of Commons. Afterwards we moved to one of the formal rooms in No. 10 Downing Street, where Press launches and conferences take place, and it was there that 200 people from all walks of life were gathered to celebrate the strategy. Most of them had contributed to the document's preparation, and I was amazed at the way they acted in the plush environment of the Prime Minister's office. After Tony Blair and I had made a few remarks, drinks and nibbles were served, and within minutes he and I had been hustled into a corner by these normally very conservative people demanding autographs. I felt acutely embarrassed, particularly when some of the requests came from former colleagues, and said so to the Prime Minister. He let on that at first it had come as a surprise to him, but I had to get used to it and regard it as part of the job.

The strategy was well received by other key ministers. Ann Taylor had been involved in its evolution, and I had discussed it with Jack Straw and Frank Dobson, the Secretary of State for Health, at our monthly meetings. Frank struck me as a real character. He would always receive me alone at the door of his office, which at one end resembled a front parlour, complete with sideboard and television, which was often on. He invariably greeted me with a joke, and we would part in the same way. I suspect that he was such a nice person that he was manipulated by his civil servants, who seldom if ever delivered what he promised.

Jack Straw I found more serious and businesslike. We would meet either in his office in the House of Commons or in the Home Office, the first being smaller, and furnished with better taste. He was always accompanied by at least four civil servants and advisers, a posse whose numbers rose to double figures as time went by – though whether this was due to his or their insecurity, I was never sure.

So, by the summer of 1998 the stage was set: a new, ten-year drugs strategy was in place, with new money to fund it. I thought that the announcement would be well received, and would answer some of the journalists who had said that I would be given neither the power nor the money to do the job. Not a bit of it. Their ruminations centred largely on whether there really was any new money, and whether the strategy was not merely an exercise in spin.

At the time I was going round the editors of the national newspapers, trying to convince them of the honesty of the launch, and one or two of them told me that, whatever I did, they could not support me, as I worked for the Government. I protested that I was non-political, and told them that I had insisted that I would take the job only on condition that I had the freedom to consult and brief all parties, as I firmly believed that drugs must not become a political issue. The friendlier journalists said, 'There's nothing personal, Keith, but you're a political figure now, whether you like it or not, and we'll treat you as such.'

Having spent some time at the heart of New Labour, I can understand the media's scepticism. At that time the Strategic Communications unit in No. 10 really did control all announcements and appearances on the major news programmes, and they naturally looked for key messages, to show themselves in a good light; but when I was asked to single out the headlines in the new drugs strategy, I said there were none, as we would have to work hard on a number of areas, for years to come, in order to make a difference. I suggested that this ought to be the message, for the public realised there was no quick fix, and would appreciate it if the Government was honest about it.

In contrast with many ministers, I had no problems with the communications set-up in Government. I was given first one, then eventually three, Press secretaries, who worked in the Cabinet Press Office, dealing with the enormous number of media requests that came to us. When I sought the advice of Alastair Campbell on how I should deal with the media in Government, he told me to be honest, keep the message simple and control interviews.

I was in an unusual position, perhaps even a unique one, in that I had to speak on behalf of Government. I know of no other special adviser who is the lead spokesperson on an aspect of Government policy so broad as drugs. Campbell, and later the Prime Minister, impressed upon me that I was the person they wanted out front to represent them on drugs issues. 'Drugs need branding, and you're the brand,' they said.

I formed a good relationship with Alastair. Even though I am six feet two inches tall, he towers over me. His office is reached by passing through a number of other rooms which form the nerve-centre of public relations for Government, although from the windows there is a view out into Downing Street itself. He can usually be found sitting with his feet on a desk covered with paper: he greets you warmly and invites you to join him in a cup of tea at the large, round table in the middle of the room, whose walls are adorned with various pictures and drawings without any theme or period. Any meeting is liable to be punctuated by his staff, or even by the Prime Minister, coming through his open door to discuss some issue of the day which necessitates his immediate response.

I have always found his advice sound. He told me that the public 'don't like smart-arses', and that it is not a bad thing to show vulnerability on occasion, but added, 'Don't do it too often.' He told me how to react if I was door-stepped by the media with a question, the truthful answer to which would be embarrassing in either a personal or a professional way. His golden rule was, 'Never lie, or deny it if it's true. Play for time. Tell them you need to think it over, and you'll get back to them. Then ring me, or the duty Press officer.' In view of the fiasco over Robin Cook's private life, I found this particularly interesting, but it was good advice all the same.

In the first few weeks I had also re-established contact with Peter Mandelson, who was then Cabinet Minister without Portfolio, and variously described by the media as 'the Fixer', 'the Black Prince' and 'the Prince of Darkness'. I asked him what he thought of these titles, and, like others I have known who loved power, he smiled and shrugged, as if they were of no consequence. He said that I had a difficult task ahead of me, and advised me to keep the issues simple for public consumption. He also offered help and support, but I found him difficult to take at face value. Maybe I am being unfair, as he has never to my knowledge caused me anyharm; but he seemed so deep that I couldn't help wondering whether the charm was just a gloss, and questioning what lay beneath.

One thing that surprised me was the importance that politicians place on having their names in print. A photograph or an interview means a ridiculous amount to them, and many crave a high-profile radio or television appearance. My appointment cornered the publicity market on drugs issues, which until then had been a fruitful source of exposure, particularly for the ambitious ministers who had held the drugs brief within their department, and they didn't like losing it.

Happily for me, the minister responsible for drugs in the Home Office was George Howarth, with whom I had worked as a Chief Constable, and when we discussed the subject, he said that he was more than happy for me to take the lead, as 'You know a damned sight more about it than I do.' Others took a different stance and saw me as a threat.

The launch strategy was designed to cover a period of several weeks following the main release, and included a series of announcements specifically related to Health, Education, the Home Office, the Foreign Office, Scotland, Northern Ireland and Wales. These were to be co-ordinated by my staff, and to include myself and the relevant minister at each smaller launch.

Nothing was ever said to me, but the feedback was that the

ministers wouldn't do it – and so it proved. Sometimes they refused to accept a brief which had been prepared in consultation with their own officials; sometimes they made the announcement alone, without consulting us, or they refused to turn up and had the announcement cancelled.

The grapevine told me that they didn't like 'appearing with the Tsar', as they thought I took their limelight. I found this approach very childish and counter-productive, especially as the individuals concerned refused to discuss it with me. I told them that I was just carrying out the Prime Minister's brief, emphasising that there was nothing in media appearances for me: I was not out to win votes, and I would be more than happy for them to take the stage.

The civil servants were not happy with my cornering the media market on drugs, either, because they saw it as the shop window for their work: by preparing endless briefs in advance of ministers' speeches and Press interviews, they could control the agenda. The special advisers disliked my arrival just as much, because their only concern was to develop and foster the image of their ministers, without whom they would have no jobs.

My earliest specimen of a special adviser was a man who clearly resented my appointment, which rubbed him up the wrong way so much that he made derogatory comments about my salary, and the fact I had a contract and was not tied to a particular minister. My pension, he said, would allow me to go and 'sun myself in the South of France if it didn't work out'. When I referred to the Prime Minister as such, he remarked, 'Oh—you mean Tony. If he starts putting on airs and graces, I'll soon put him right.'

Under the guise of looking after ministers, off his own bat he interfered in the production of an hour-long *Panorama* special on drug issues, instructing them that I must not be asked any direct questions by either viewers or the audience. Since he did this only a few minutes before we went on air, he put the presenter, Kirsty Wark, in an impossible position, and created the impression that I was very difficult and should not be invited onto the programme again.

He also interfered with a BBC crew who were filming a

documentary on my work for which they had received approval from everyone and his aunt, after bidding against seven other film makers in a contest which lasted six months. They were so offended by his actions that they withdrew, and the film was never made.

Such need to control may be fuelled by a genuine desire to get things right; but this man had nothing at all to do with me. He should not have been interfering. Had I been aware of his antics when they were going on, I would have taken steps to counteract them; but, as with many things, it was months before I discovered what he had been up to.

In other words, media appearances were an issue from the word 'go', and continued so right throughout my stay in Government.

THE STRATEGY

Tackling Drugs to Build a Better Britain was an amalgam of the views of ordinary people, drug users, drug offenders, drug victims, relatives of drug users, teachers, the police, social services, treatment agencies, health workers, probation officers, magistrates, prison officers, academics, politicians and civil servants. It laid down the principles by which the Government would operate in this area of our lives. It was essentially a long-term project, built on evidence, which aimed at reducing the damage and danger that drugs cause to individuals, families and the communities in which they live. The document was short, and available either from the Stationery Office or on the Internet.

Most of my time was spent in the heart of the British community, listening to and helping ordinary people, who were facing the havoc wrought by illegal drugs on a daily basis. Sharing the pain with parents who had lost sons or daughters strengthened my resolve. Most of them felt guilt for not preventing the tragedy, even though they had been powerless when drugs took control of their children's lives. They admitted their own ignorance had prevented them discussing the subject with their offspring, and they pleaded for better information to be made available. We therefore published a number of guides for parents and distributed them free through commercial outlets.

Many young addicts told me that they had not dared seek medical help because they knew that, if they did, the doctor would have to tell their parents. Without exception, parents said that they wanted their children to receive treatment at all costs: if this constraint on doctors led to a child's health being damaged, they would prefer not to know about it. Doctors still have a duty to report cases of addiction, and I believe that this ethical dilemma must be addressed, to encourage young people to seek the support they need. Many people were still reluctant to recognise the drugs threat so I shocked them by relaying some of the most moving cases I had encountered – like a crack girl who was abused and neglected in childhood to such an extent that when she escaped on to the streets at eleven she was so affected by her trauma that she stopped speaking. Six years later, in the middle of a remedial programme, she uttered her first words: 'Help me.' Today the ever-increasing occurrence of such tragedies is creating a greater acceptance of the dangers of drugs in most households, and this in part is helping to resolve the problem.

Education

Everyone I spoke to felt that education was the key to the future. The young people told me they didn't know enough about drugs. They admitted they knew more than their parents and teachers, but their knowledge was still sketchy. They wanted to be told the truth, and to be told it earlier. They didn't buy all the horror stories about drugs, but neither were they fooled by people who pronounced them harmless. They were critical of the double standards taught in some schools – that is, all illegal drugs are bad and all legal drugs good – many of them had witnessed the dire consequences of tobacco and alcohol in their homes.

Teachers supported the need for change. At that time only about half of our secondary schools and a quarter of the junior ones included any mention of drugs in their curriculum, as the subject had been discouraged in the naive belief that if children knew about drugs, they would be more likely to try them, and if they were ignorant, they would abstain. Even where anti-drug teaching took place, there were no standards or clear guidance, and it formed no part of the Ofsted inspection process.

As a consequence, coverage was very patchy and inconsistent. In some schools the subject had been handed over to the police, to former addicts or to voluntary bodies. Few teachers had been trained in drugs issues, and of those who had, many admitted that their only experience had been smoking a joint at university. Of course, there were some highly motivated individuals who dealt with the subject extremely well.

The same disparity was apparent in the way schools dealt with offenders. At one extreme was automatic expulsion for possession of any illegal substance – a rule most prevalent in public schools. At the other end was the laissez-faire approach: 'We know you're going to do it. Just take care of yourself.' I challenged these extremes each time I addressed teachers' conferences, as I did with the public school parents who were reassured by hard-line measures. To counter the old tactics, which were not working, we set common standards, introduced guidance on the best-known teaching methods, and provided money for teacher training. The launch of one of these documents nearly met with disaster, as on its eve a minor text change caused tens of thousands of the offending booklets to be reprinted during the night.

All this was – and is – aimed at reducing experimentation and the use of drugs by our young. The teaching methods employed differ from school to school, but all now work to a common agenda, which begins with children from the age of five. We introduce them to the drugs and medicines they would normally find in their homes, and explain the dangers if they are used out of context. We go on to tell them about the dangers of solvents – such as glue and lighter fuel – from which eighty British children die every year. We then progress to cigarettes and tobacco, the greatest killers of all, and illegal substances, especially cannabis. This is not preaching: young people are told quite honestly about the medical, social and legal consequences of their actions. By the time children reach early teens, they learn about the effects of the most dangerous drugs.

Research has shown that a young person who regularly smokes cigarettes is sixty times more likely to smoke cannabis than one who resists tobacco: furthermore, a person who smokes cannabis at least once a week is sixty times more likely to indulge in more harmful drugs. This does not mean that it is inevitable that smokers of cigarettes and cannabis will go further, but statistics suggest it dramatically increases the likelihood.

More than 90 per cent of our secondary schools and two-thirds of our junior schools now have teaching programmes of some kind, and these are increasing month by month, welcomed by pupils, parents and teachers alike. It will take at least a generation to establish whether or not this initiative will deflect children from taking noxious substances, but early research into their habits is encouraging. Within two years of our intervention, the largest schools survey in the UK, undertaken by Exeter University, commended our work for bringing about the first fall in drug experimentation by early teenagers for more than a decade.

One of the most damaging aspects of the debate over the legalisation of cannabis is that it confuses young people, some of whom try the drug just to show that they are 'cool', particularly when they perceive they have been given the green light by politicians and public figures in positions of authority.

Treatment

One addict within a family will destroy it. Most parents simply will not believe their child could become involved with drugs – and so, if one does, they either keep the secret to themselves, or ignore it, trying to explain away the child's strange behaviour and the fact that money and valuables are missing from their home. When they finally pluck up courage to face the child, it is with much trepidation, as they fear the consequences if their suspicions prove well founded. When they are – and this may be after a number of denials – they are at a loss what to do. Do they seek help by exposing their child's problem and face the social stigma? Do they send the child away, to save the rest of the family? Or do they, as some at the end of their tether have done, buy drugs for their child?

Whatever parents decide, they need an infrastructure to support them, and the strategy aims to provide this. We set about training a large number of GPs to offer first-line help, recruited more treatment workers and specialist doctors and increased the number of treatment places. Over the three-year spending period 2001–2004 these measures will cost an additional £1 billion; but this amount will be offset by a reduction in the cost that drug-addiction adds to the accident, emergency and social services bill – and the pain and suffering in families it will alleviate are incalculable.

To be obstructive, Department of Health officials questioned why there was so much fuss about drugs, when they formed only a tiny part of their work. All the pressure from their politicians was to reduce hospital waiting times and achieve other Government high priorities for which performance indicators had been set. I introduced similar indicators of success or failure in the drug sphere into their annual plan of action, and questioned them on progress. This put me at odds with them, since they saw my inquiries as an irritant they could do without. I needed the support of a Health Minister, but after Alan Milburn replaced Frank Dobson, this was rarely forthcoming. Alan was far less receptive to our initiatives, and the Department of Health reduced the financial commitment it had given.

Some of the money allocated by Government for drugs treatment in my first budget had not reached the streets, as it had been 'lost' in the system. I was determined this would not happen again, so my second budget report, in 2000, recommended the creation of a 'corporate budget', in which more than one agency would be involved in providing an anti-drugs service – a device aimed at taking control away from Health. Civil servants, backed by ministers, were totally against this proposal, but misread my tactic. When I hinted that I wished to control the funds myself, their objections were marshalled against me; but my proposal was accepted by

Gordon Brown's PX committee, and the objectors were faced with fighting a rearguard action.

The Drugs National Treatment Agency was created in 2001 to manage the new corporate health fund. Although this has the status of a Special Health Authority, I am sceptical about its effectiveness, particularly when I hear that Alan Milburn is reluctant to fund it up to the level promised in that budget, and when I learn of the cost of staff drafted in to run it.

Community Action

The strategy not only considers the cost of drugs to the individual: it also focuses on the effect they have on the community at large. Driving or working under the influence of drugs poses dangers which had received little attention until I addressed them. Now they are incorporated into the Government's programme: all the relevant agencies and institutions have been recruited to support our initiatives, which I hope will reduce the number of injuries and deaths in factories and on roads. Anyone who doubts the dangers involved need only read the results of recent research. Postmortem examination of all the people killed on our roads over a three-year period at the end of the nineties into 2000 indicated that almost a fifth had illegal drugs in their bodies, cannabis being the most common – a four-fold increase on a similar survey a decade earlier.

One effect of cannabis is to slow down a person's reactions, and some of its stronger strains are hallucinogenic. Even the most ardent supporters of legalisation advise people not to drive, use machinery or take examinations when under its influence. The softer approach the Government is taking is likely to increase the danger to us all. I also anticipate a rise in the use of drugs. Many would have us believe that most young people already use illegal drugs, which is untrue. Experimenting with substances is a part of growing-up, and although many youngsters try them, a very small percentage go on to regular use.

Research into the consequences of drugs in the work place is more limited, although one study undertaken in Northern Ireland showed that Ecstasy affected the actions of a user for up to three days. The possible consequences for a bus or heavy goods vehicle driver, or even an airline pilot, are unthinkable, yet there are no mandatory or voluntary testing regimes in place in these professions. I addressed more than 2,000 business leaders on this subject, encouraging them to take a more active approach to combat drugs in the work place, with limited success. I hope it doesn't take a disaster before they act in a responsible manner.

The main thrust of our intervention in the community was in the criminal justice system. Not only do drugs increase gun warfare between dealers protecting their territories: a third of all property crime is committed as a direct result of drug-taking. Eighty per cent of the people arrested by police have drugs in their system – a similar proportion to those who enter prison. We set about providing what will become one of the most comprehensive treatment intervention programmes in the world. A person can now enter a treatment programme via a police station, through courts or while serving a prison sentence. The first results from this radical innovation have been amazing: up to eighty per cent reduction in repeat offending. This initiative is likely to prove the most effective crime-prevention measure for many decades.

The effect within prisons has also been encouraging. When the new strategy was introduced, about a quarter of all prisoners tested positive for drugs. Within three years the figure had been halved, and it continues to fall. New rules introduced at the same time to penalise those who attempt to bring drugs into prison, allied with stronger penalties for their intended recipients, are also proving effective. To avoid the high relapse rate on release, we have introduced a support programme to help prisoners reintegrate within the community. Tens of thousands of crimes have been saved by these innovations, the cost of which is a tiny proportion of the crimes they prevent.

Prisoners deserve some credit in bringing about improvement. Many performed plays, made videos and gave talks in schools, to help deter young people from getting involved with drugs. Others sought atonement for the damage they had caused to others by volunteering to help in prevention and treatment programmes.

We were determined to ensure that our community-based programmes were co-ordinated and delivered adequately at local level. Drugs Action Teams (DATs) had been created for this purpose under the previous Conservative Government, and now they came under my responsibility. They comprised the heads of the local police, health, education, social services, prisons and the local authorities. My initial impression was that they were little more than talking-shops: although highly committed people, they admitted they had little direction and were uncertain what they were supposed to do. This was a huge waste of potential, as no other country in the world had this local action mechanism in place at that time.

Together, we developed a much more focused agenda, which included setting performance indicators, targets, annual plans and reports, which mirrored my own at national level. DATs were also given more control over spending, an initiative resisted by civil servants in Whitehall. These groups of people are now a powerful link in implementing the drugs strategy in the UK, and have been copied in several other countries.

Reduction of Drug Availability

The other major area of our strategy was to reduce the availability of the drugs which caused severe harm. The switch away from cannabis to concentrate on heroin and cocaine, coupled with a closer focus on the sources of supply, had consequences for all the law-enforcement agencies. Customs officers lost their posts, as it was quickly recognised that a physical presence at ports was far less effective than precisely targeted, intelligence-based operations. Some aggrieved officers leaked negative stories to the Press, suggesting that we were 'opening up our shores to drug dealers'.

The police faced a more difficult task, as there was much less heroin and cocaine in circulation than cannabis, and the change of emphasis onto the two more harmful drugs naturally reduced their arrest figures. In my early days I had to counter scepticism from all quarters, including Jack Straw, who asked me if I was seriously suggesting that he should be the first Home Secretary for a decade to preside over a fall in drug-arrest figures. I told him I was, as this was the only way to make a real impact on the problem. Further initiatives were introduced to make a greater impact on medium-size drug dealers and to be more effective in dismantling drug dealing at street level.

These measures have not been as successful as I had hoped, partly because of lack of conviction within the police, who had gained comfort from increasing the number of arrests of drug offenders – largely cannabis users – year on year. I am struck by the duplicity of some of my former colleagues, who argue they would save police time if the law on cannabis was softened: they would have achieved this aim within the existing law if they had adhered to the strategy.

The main thrust of the 1998 strategy, however, was to prevent drugs ever reaching our shores, by greater use of intelligence, and by influencing governments in countries which grew or processed drugs, or were used as conduits for them. This initiative has resulted in the seizure of many tons of cocaine destined for this and other countries in western Europe. Most of this success cannot be described, for fear of exposing our sources. Publicity might also undermine our relationships with other countries and the agencies within them, where we have exposed inefficiencies and possible corruption. In such cases we have resorted to high-level political intervention, and offered training and assistance.

We have been much more successful with cocaine than with heroin, partly due to our closeness to the Americans and our constitutional ties with various Caribbean nations, which are used as staging-posts on the supply routes west. The last phase of my work in Government was to try to replicate this success in eastern and central Europe.

The need for more and different intelligence became obvious soon after the introduction of the new strategy. Hitherto all the intelligence agencies – the National Criminal Intelligence Service (NCIS), the Secret Intelligence Service (SIS, which operates overseas), the Security Service (SS, which operates within the UK),

GCHQ (the Government's monitoring centre in Cheltenham) and to a lesser extent military intelligence – contributed operational intelligence when requested by either the police or Customs. In effect this meant they collected information on particular individuals who were thought to be involved in drug-trafficking, in this country or abroad.

I recognised that if we were to make a real impact we would require information of a more strategic nature which spanned organisations, institutions, political and terrorist groups, and which was much more long-term. The heads of all the intelligence agencies supported me, as did the Prime Minister, and in 2000 a new joint unit was created within the Cabinet Office to fulfil this function. This facility, unique in the world, is proving extremely effective in increasing our understanding of drug-trafficking, and it proved a very useful tool in predicating our actions after the 11 September 2001. One sting in the tail was that I had to find half a million pounds out of my budget to pay for its initial running costs.

CHAPTER TWENTY-THREE

MINISTERS IN A MUDDLE

Ann Taylor featured in the Prime Minister's first Cabinet reshuffle, becoming Chief Whip. Dr Jack Cunningham was appointed to the newly created post of Minister for the Cabinet Office, and dubbed by the media 'the Cabinet Enforcer'. At the same time my unit was moved into the control of the Cabinet Office. Although I was not consulted, I had no particular problem with this, as it didn't change my terms or conditions of service. I still worked for the Prime Minister, to whom I had direct access.

Within an hour of taking up office, Jack Cunningham invited me across to see him. I found him warm, friendly and quite open. He told me he was pleased to be given the post, as he had thought that his ministerial days were over. (Few people outside Government realise that on the day before a Prime Minister's announcement, all ministers vacate their offices, collect their personal belongings and leave. They then wait by the telephone for 'the call' from the PM. If it doesn't come, they are backbenchers again.)

Jack told me that he knew little about drugs, and was happy for me to continue with the work I was doing, but would welcome regular updates on progress. I told him I had spoken to Ann every week, but as he considered this too frequent, we agreed on a monthly meeting, with discussion between if that proved necessary.

In among their mischief-making, some newspapers commented

on his new role, which included the drugs portfolio. It was suggested variously that he had replaced me – that he had become the 'Drugs Enforcer', and that I had been downgraded. I asked that we put out a Press release to clarify the relationship between us, but Jack considered this unnecessary, and advised me to continue in exactly the same way as I had operated with Ann. In retrospect this was a mistake, as the lack of clarity blurred the boundaries, and gave civil servants and the media an opportunity to play one side off against the other, to the detriment of our personal relationship.

The first manifestation of this came over media interviews. Until then, requests had reached me directly through my Press secretaries, whose recommendations I usually accepted. These staff worked to the senior civil servant within the Cabinet Office, and Jack was their minister. At our next meeting he confided in me that there was little in his new role to get his teeth into, other than drugs, and he would like to take a more active part. We therefore agreed on a number of areas to which he could contribute.

The next thing I learned was that his office had insisted that all media requests for information about drugs be routed through them before they came to me. I thought this a little strange, but when I asked Jack, he said he only wished to know what level of media interest there was, and the arrangement would not interfere with my work. I accepted his explanation, until the requests gradually began to dry up. When one did arrive, it was often too late for me to take it up. A typical example was a bid for me to appear live on the BBC one o'clock news: made at 09.30, it reached my office at 13.40, when the programme was over. Journalists started trying to bypass the Cabinet Press office and ring me directly, but I played by the rules and told them to follow the proper procedure. After a few months these tactics began to be noticed by No. 10; at one of our meetings Alastair Campbell asked why I was not as visible as I had been, so I told him what was going on, and he said, 'We like having you out there. Keep the profile.'

Just about this time I was invited to lunch by one of the editors of the *Mail on Sunday* and Chester Stern, the crime writer. Chester and I had known each other for many years, and he is one of the journalists I trust. He told me that I was being gagged, and suggested that I ought to do something about it, as it was destroying my reputation with his journalistic colleagues. They were beginning to believe that I was getting too big for my boots, since requests for me were regularly being turned down without explanation, or totally ignored, or replied to after their deadlines had passed. Often, he said, the Cabinet Office Press office was offering Dr Cunningham in my place.

These squabbles may seem minor, but they typified the difficult position I was in. The civil servants could quite correctly follow their natural inclination and work to a minister, excluding me entirely. One of my Press secretaries told me to my face that she didn't work for me, and I had no influence over her. On the other hand, one of her colleagues kept telling me to watch my back, saying things like 'They're gunning for you', and 'Be careful.'

My civil servant head of unit, the excellent Stephen Rimmer, had been replaced by a more junior civil servant brought in from the Home Office, who was not of his calibre. She began to attend the weekly meetings held by Cunningham to discuss policy across his portfolio, which left me unsighted. She also went to other meetings with one of Sir Richard Wilson's deputies, at which decisions were made without consulting me. In retrospect, I recognise that this was the beginning of the rot.

Cunningham's special advisers saw me as a threat, because I was an obstacle to their minister's progress. I was not at all surprised to find that they were the ones who had orchestrated the media block. Jack himself was under threat from a number of sources, and because he seemed to mistrust everyone, our relationship deteriorated. The media campaigned against him from the start, dubbing him 'Junket Jack' because of his alleged excesses in self-provision and reports that he was 'lazy' and 'not a detail man'. That was certainly not my experience of him. Some of the leaked information obviously came from within.

He had committed a cardinal sin by requisitioning an office for himself – a move which displaced, and embittered, a number of senior civil servants. According to him, Sir Richard Wilson tried to intervene on their behalf, but backed off when Jack threatened to take his office from him as an alternative. Civil servants bandied stories about his incompetence in dealing with his boxes, and would regularly joke about 'today's excuse'. Jack also felt excluded by his Cabinet colleagues, especially the Prime Minister. More than once, when we discussed a policy issue, he said to me, 'You'll have to talk it over with Tony. He never speaks to me.' He also suspected that some of the negative briefing emanated from No. 10.

Feeling sorry for him, I offered help several times. After a particularly offensive article about him had appeared in one of the tabloids, I visited him and asked if the constant media tirade got him down. Clearly it did, but he was macho about it.

By the summer of 1999 the situation between us was becoming untenable. The media were being briefed against me. Some articles were trivial, suggesting (for instance) that I was driving around London in a black Porsche and living a millionaire lifestyle, in contrast to my deputy, who drove a motorcycle. This was quite untrue – but so what? Other stories questioned my intellectual capacity to cope with the job.

My second annual plan and first report were due to be published in the summer of 1999, and their preparation caused further aggravation. I have always been in the habit of writing the foreword and much of the rest of my own reports. When my senior civil servant said that she would do this for me, I agreed, providing she showed me a draft. The deadline for submission came and went, but still she insisted that she was going to do the work herself. The renewed deadline, in order to fit in with the public launch date I had been given by No. 10, was the week before I flew to Australia on an official visit. Every day the draft was promised, but it did not materialise. In the end I told her that she must e-mail it to me in Australia, so that I could work on it before I submitted it to the ministerial committee of which I was a member.

When I spoke to her three days into my visit, she coolly told me that she had already submitted the report to Dr Cunningham. I was livid. I pointed out to her that this was *my* report, and I had given her explicit instructions how it should be dealt with. She told me I was wrong. It was *not* my report: it was a Government report, and as such should be dealt with by ministers. I explained to her that the whole purpose of the exercise was public accountability and open government: the status of the report was important, because of its degree of neutrality. I threatened to take her actions up with Sir Richard Wilson if she did not send me a copy immediately – which she did with the utmost reluctance.

I have to add that her report was very poor, and I spent whatever time I could spare from a busy schedule rewriting it. When I spoke to Jack on the telephone and told him what I was doing, he replied, 'Thank God! This thing I've got is bloody awful.' As an aside he told me he had no confidence in 'this woman', and instructed her boss that she had to be replaced, which she was within weeks. I suspect she believes I was the cause of her move.

My visit to Australia was made at the Canberra Government's behest, and paid for by them. Before accepting the invitation, I had sought approval from the Prime Minister, routing the request through Jack, who had written on it, 'Insist you go at least Club.' Even so, while I was down under, a scurrilous newspaper story appeared in England, with a headline claiming that I was 'Out of Control'. The piece urged the Prime Minister to bring me into line, but went on to claim that 'insiders close to Dr Cunningham' had said that he was 'powerless to do it'. The article suggested that my frequent trips around the world were more irresponsible than anything Jack had done in what it called his 'junketing'.

This was ridiculous, as during my first three years in office I spent fewer than twenty nights out of this country. Nevertheless, the newspaper had been well briefed, for it gave a detailed account of my itinerary, which was quite worrying. The Australian police had provided armed protection for me, believing I was under threat from one of their citizens who had published some malicious and threatening articles about me. Back home, I anticipated a rebuttal from Jack, but none came.

During the time leading up to the launch of my report, tensions grew even worse, not least because Jack insisted that he should present the report to the House of Commons, and the Speaker was having difficulty in finding the time to fit it in. This meant that the original date and time had to be altered, which ruffled feathers at No. 10. There was much debate about who should speak to the media. Jack's advisers insisted that he should do the major news programmes such as *Today* and *The World at One*, whereas I should brief the regional media and 'sweep up' later in the day.

I was not happy with this, and neither was Alastair Campbell. For the first time I expressed my frustration at the way I was being manipulated; Alastair altered the schedule, and I completed most of the interviews, to the annoyance of Jack and his staff. Alastair assured me that I wouldn't have to put up with the situation for much longer, as Jack's days were numbered. What irony! I was not being allowed to undertake the duties I had been encouraged to perform, because of the actions of a minister who was about to be sacked. No. 10 were reluctant to take direct action, lest they be accused of openly undermining Cunningham. I had become a political pawn.

In October that year the reshuffle finally came, and Jack went out. There had been intense speculation as to who would replace him, and I was very pleased when Mo Mowlam's name came out of the hat. We had enjoyed a cordial relationship while she was Secretary for Northern Ireland, and I had stayed at her official residence in Hillsborough Castle, where we had many a laugh, even though she was under intense pressure.

On the morning of her first day in office she invited me to go over and see her. After the usual pleasantries, and her telling me that she didn't wish to be there, she asked, 'Why are you doing this job?'

I thought this rather strange, but I told her it was because I believed in it, and felt privileged to be able to make a contribution. 'That's good enough for me,' she responded. Then she asked, 'Are you aware that Tony has given Jack [Straw] the drugs brief?' I was not. She revealed that Jack had tried on previous occasions to get it, but had been told that nothing could be done while Jack Cunningham was in post. However, the previous night, the Prime Minister had told Straw he could have it.

Mo had an appointment with the PM later that morning, and

was prepared to fight for the brief herself. That meeting resulted in her wresting it back, much to the annoyance of Straw. Mo was helped in her plea by a rare gaffe by Alastair, who told the morning Press briefing that *she* would be responsible for drugs, in response to a correspondent's allegation that she had been downgraded.

I sensed, although nothing had been said, that this decision did not help my relationship with Jack Straw, who later insisted that, had he been successful in his bid, 'it wouldn't have affected you, Keith'. I am not so sure, as I kept hearing that a stream of negative briefing against me was emanating from the Home Office, where Justin Russell, an able young man, had replaced Norman Warner (now Lord Warner) as Jack Straw's special adviser.

Russell was determined to make a name for himself. He, like all the spin doctors I have met, was constantly on the look out for opportunities to issue announcements which would propel his minister to the fore, and he, like many others, saw drugs as an ideal medium. He was not helped by No. 10's directive that I should lead on the subject, or by the comprehensive nature of the drugs strategy, which left little room for manoeuvre. I know he found me less than helpful when I vetoed announcements which merely repackaged the strategy.

His frustrations were compounded when he did manage to bypass me in preparing the Prime Minister's speech to the Labour Party Conference that autumn, only to find that the speech went badly wrong. One mistake was that it made no mention of the strategy, but a much worse blunder was that it heralded the introduction of hard-line measures against drug-addicted criminals – a measure which was criticised by the police and the judiciary as both unworkable and unlawful. No minister can commit a worse *faux pas* than to compromise the Prime Minister, and there were rumours that Jack Straw had fallen out of favour with Tony Blair. But time and political necessity are great healers. Jack was determined to get the drugs brief from that moment on.

When Charles Clarke replaced George Howarth as minister responsible for drugs, the landscape in the Home Office changed considerably. Charles, a large, blustering fellow whose grizzled growth of white, stubbly beard compensates for the lack of hair on his scalp, was determined to make a name for himself, and he forcibly expressed his frustration at the lack of opportunity he had in the drugs field. His initial reaction was to disclaim any connection with the strategy, remarking, 'That's *your* strategy, Keith.' He hated not being in control, and the fact that he did not sit on the relevant Cabinet committees rankled. He told me quite frankly, 'I will not support any policy which I have not had a hand in making,' and I heard from former colleagues that on occasions he actively sab-otaged my efforts.

I found this lack of subtlety faintly amusing. The *Daily Mail*, whose editor was a long-time friend of Jack Straw, took every opportunity of undermining my credibility, and once went so far as to announce that I had been sacked, congratulating the Govern-ment on appointing 'the impressive Charles Clarke' in my place.

Shortly after this fiasco the Prime Minister sent a note to his Cabinet colleagues, warning them off. Ironically, within a month of this directive an article appeared in the *Financial Times* ridiculing me for recommending that we should buy the poppy crop in Afghanistan from the Taleban. It went on to say that ministers had dismissed the idea out of hand. This was a complete misrepresen-tation of the truth. In a memorandum I had advised that the world powers needed to be more radical in dealing with the drugs issue, and one of my suggestions was that we should buy the poppy harvest from the Afghan *farmers*, to cut off the drug supply at source. There had been no rejection by ministers, as the memo was merely a discussion document (the idea is now being actively considered by the international community in its support of Afghanistan).

On the morning the story broke I was twice called out of meet-ings in the West Country to take 'urgent' phone calls. The first was from Charles Clarke, who promised, 'It was nothing to do with me.' The second was from John Battle, who admitted responsi-bility and protested his innocence by saying he had been duped by the reporter over lunch. What a tangled web they weave!

*   *   *

At first, working with Mo Mowlam was most refreshing. She was open and honest about her feelings and the problems we faced. She thought we needed to give a lift to the drugs strategy, to prove something to 'Tony'. Like all other politicians she was looking for a new angle, but unlike others she did read my strategy document and asked probing questions about its limitations and failings. I told her the strategy was sound, well received by all the practitioners, and needed to be supported. I explained about the negative spin, the lack of commitment from some departments within Government and the infighting over the media. I told her the Government had been given credit for the long-term nature of the strategy, and counselled against the desire of ministers and the spin machine to make short-term announcements, which would erode its credibility.

Mo's first action was to tell the Cabinet Press office to allow me free access to the media, which was a big help. With the approval of Tony Blair she restructured the Cabinet committees, creating a smaller, more powerful team of ministers. Her intention was that this group – comprising the Secretaries of State for Health, Education and Home Affairs, the First Secretary in the Treasury, myself and herself – should be relatively informal. But the civil service could not allow this, and within two meetings our deliberations became formal, as civil servants insisted on controlling the agenda. Even an attempt by Mo to have a preliminary meeting was scuppered by civil servants insisting they must make a record of the proceedings.

The meetings were far from dull. Tensions surfaced between ministers, and slanging matches took place. I am precluded from disclosing the business of the sessions, but not the actions of those present. A Secretary of State (still in the Cabinet), annoyed at a derogatory remark I made about 'his' officials, squared up to me for a fight, physically pushing me and warning that it was dangerous to 'get on my wrong side'. I told him, 'Grow up and go away.'

I found it fascinating to observe the dynamics of power at such close quarters. It was soon patently obvious to me that the post of Minister for the Cabinet Office had little clout. The two incumbents had both been on their way out, for one reason or another. In her autobiography, published in 2002, Mo wrote about her own downgrading: even the seat she occupied in the Cabinet meeting room was further away from the Prime Minister. It was clear she had little or no influence over her colleagues, most of whom openly indicated their lack of respect for her.

My job was to co-ordinate all the Government's anti-drug activity, which I could only do with the support of ministers. When Ann Taylor was in charge, this had not been a problem, as she encouraged me to communicate directly with all ministers. There was much benefit in this, as, not being a political rival, I was not seen as a threat. But when Jack and Mo directed me to operate through them, I was seen as their agent, and thus lost my neutrality. Both of them were extremely insecure, and reluctant to press a case against more powerful Cabinet colleagues. In consequence the drugs agenda began to fragment. The civil servants took advantage of this and reverted to type, briefing their ministers from a departmental rather than a corporate Government perspective, and I was powerless to do anything about it.

A large part of Mo's frustration was due to the fact that she had no meaningful job to do. The role of Minister for the Cabinet Office was more that of an administrator, someone who tidied up and kept a finger in a wide range of corporate policy matters, without having any measure of control over them. For someone who had come from a high-profile, hands-on job in Northern Ireland, this must have been very difficult to cope with. Drugs would have offered her a real opportunity, but her options were limited because of me.

The change of emphasis I had introduced, distinguishing between the different types of drugs and effectively switching attention away from cannabis, caused her a problem, as it limited her ability to appear to be radical and make a name for herself. She had made no secret of the fact that she had smoked cannabis (although she came out only in response to a newspaper exposé), or that friends who visited her house did the same. (I warned her about the foolishness of this, particularly as at that time she was living in Government accommodation.)

We argued about the subject more than once, but she consistently failed to put forward any empirical evidence in support of her view that cannabis is harmless, relying on the populist arguments of freedom of choice and the level of usage. I could see no justification for her stance, other than its appeal to the chattering classes. She rarely studied the research, which all pointed to the dangers of cannabis, and instead relied on the flimsiest of arguments – 'Lots of people smoke it, so we ought to listen.' She dismissed out of hand the conclusions of the lengthy inquiry by the House of Lords into the subject.

She was kept under some degree of control both by the strength of the argument against her, and by the fact that her personal views did not accord with Government policy. Although she was mischievous, and would answer questions about her views on legalisation by clasping her hand over her mouth as if she was gagged, to my knowledge she did not put over her views in public.

What she did do was talk to journalists about her frustrations. Stories began to appear about the split between 'Mo, the people's favourite', and myself, 'the hard-line ex-copper', over the cannabis debate.

Journalists announced their support for Mo, who was 'battling against stiff opposition within Government' to distinguish between cannabis and other more harmful drugs. But this distinction was Government policy. Every time it was reported in the Press that Mo was 'for' the distinction while I was 'against' it, I asked Mo to issue a corrective statement, but for obvious reasons she never did.

The matter came to a head after the publication of the Police Foundation Report on the law surrounding cannabis. I had helped set up this independent inquiry, which made about eighty recommendations for change in drugs policy. During the two years in which the inquiry sat, much had already been achieved through the new strategy, for which the report gave some credit. The headline-grabbing proposals, however, were those which recommended the downgrading of cannabis and Ecstasy, which had been leaked in advance of the report.

I was asked by No. 10 to handle the Press on publication, which didn't please Mo. I took the deluge of Press inquiries and appeared on all the news programmes. Many of the questions were not about the report, but about the differing views of Mo, myself and Jack Straw. Reporters quoted statements, allegedly from people close to Mo, which supported legalisation. I asked her what on earth was going on, and told her that the matter had to be resolved: 'I'm out there representing the agreed policy of your Government which you, as the minister responsible, are undermining by your words and actions, and this is untenable.'

I sought a meeting with the Prime Minister, and got one within a few days. Tony Blair first asked Mo for her views, which were in support of decriminalisation. He then sought Jack's views, which were for maintaining the status quo. Then he asked mine. After listening carefully he pronounced that we would maintain the Government line on cannabis. Mo's body language indicated that she was not pleased with this, and the PM asked her, 'Mo, are you happy with my decision?'

'Tony,' she replied, 'you know I'm a loyal supporter.'

'Mo,' said the Prime Minister urgently, 'this is Government policy, and when you leave this room, I'll need your assurance that this is what you will abide by.'

She was clearly uncomfortable and garbled some incoherent response, to which he retorted, 'I need your word on this issue.' She then nodded in a very resigned manner, saying, 'I knew you'd go with Jack and Keith on this.'

The Prime Minister indicated that the meeting was at an end, but as we got up to leave, he asked Mo if she would remain behind. My immediate thought was that she was in for a rousting.

I left the room with Jack, to find Gordon Brown half-sitting on a table outside in the corridor, waiting to go in. 'What mood's he in?' he asked. Jack and I looked at each other, and I remarked that he was in 'headmaster mode', having asked Mo to stay behind.

I waited for Mo, who emerged about ten minutes later completely dejected. Her shoulders were slouched, her head was down and she shuffled along the corridor at a very slow gait. In the north we would have said she was 'sloughened'. I fell in beside her, inquiring what was the matter, but she didn't want to talk about it. I felt sorry for her, believing that she had received a dressing-down, and that I was the cause of it, so I walked a way with her, offering my support. She later disclosed that 'Tony' had pressed her to replace Frank Dobson as the official Labour candidate for Mayor of London. This astounded me, as, a few days later, No. 10 denied Press allegations that they had made such an approach.

My meetings with the Prime Minister always created a problem for other ministers. At one summit, arranged to discuss anti-drugs initiatives in schools, Mo, who apparently had not been invited, came bustling in at the last moment, directing anger at me, implying that I had 'left her out of the loop'. In fact, I had had nothing to do with the arrangements for that particular meeting, but normally I always provided her, and indeed all relevant ministers, with an advance copy of my engagements – a courtesy which neither they nor the senior civil servants returned.

This was the first meeting I had attended in the main Cabinet Room, and I found the experience quite moving. At one moment Tony Blair and I were there alone, he in his seat and I on his right hand. He must have noticed something, because he asked me if I was feeling all right. I told him that this was a moment I would not forget, and when he asked me why, I said, 'I am sitting on the right hand of the Prime Minister of the United Kingdom, in the Cabinet Room, and I am moved.'

'But it's me,' he replied. 'Tony.'

'Yes,' I agreed. 'I know. But you are the Prime Minister.'

He said that he knew what I meant, and that it was all too easy to take things for granted. Thereafter, every time we were in that room together he would either say something personal to me, or touch my arm, in recognition of that conversation.

At a meeting with the President of Colombia, Mo turned up unexpectedly (we thought she was in Germany). As always at such events, strict protocol prevailed. The President and his staff sat opposite our Prime Minister, who had his Foreign Secretary and officials on his right. I was on Tony Blair's left. Mo placed herself on the seat closest to the door, next to the Foreign Office officials.

In the run-up to the meeting No. 10 had announced I would be visiting Colombia on behalf of the Prime Minister to offer assistance in developing the country's drug policy. After formal introductions, the President outlined his desire for co-operation, and his support for our programme of action. The PM thanked him and said that he was pleased that he had accepted our offer of assistance. He then asked me if I wished to say anything – at which Mo interrupted and said, 'Tony I'd like to say a few words on this subject.' He had little alternative but to give her the floor.

She talked and talked and talked. Most of what she said was valuable, as she drew upon her experience in Northern Ireland, which she said would be of value to the Colombians in trying to achieve some *rapprochement* with the terrorist organisation which controlled part of their country and the drugs trade. However, it seemed to me that she was unashamedly pushing herself on to the President, saying she would be prepared to make a contribution herself, and even suggesting that she would be willing to do this when she left Government.

I felt acutely embarrassed by her performance. More than once Tony Blair tried to stop her, without success. She was still talking at the time the meeting was scheduled to end, and she suggested to the PM that she should continue the discussion on her own. The gathering broke up, and the PM escorted the President out of No. 10.

There was a significant follow-up to this minor fiasco. All the diplomatic and domestic arrangements had been made for my visit to Colombia, and they appeared in my forward diary a week or two later. Mo had not raised the subject again in the meantime, so I thought she had made her point at the meeting, and that was that.

Not so. One morning she rang to ask if she could come and see me straight away. A meeting was arranged within two hours, and she arrived in high spirits with one of her senior civil servants. She told me she wanted to do something meaningful and wished to take an interest in drugs foreign policy. What did I think of that?

I advised her that this would be a political decision, not mine, and suggested she ask the Foreign Secretary. 'I've been to see Tony,' she replied, 'and he says that if I can clear it with you, he wouldn't stop me. So if you agree, I'll sort it out with Robin [Cook, the Foreign Secretary].'

This approach smelt to me like many I had received in the police service from people who wanted to do something but told me only part of the story. When I asked her what, in particular, she wished to do, she replied, 'I want to go to Colombia.' I said I saw no problem from my point of view: she was a Minister of State, and if the PM agreed, it could do no harm. But then she said, 'I want to go instead of you.'

I pointed out the arrangements had already been made and my visit announced in both countries. She said she could take over my programme. I said that was not practical, as I would be speaking to gatherings of experts about technical matters with which she was not acquainted, and in any event it would cause confusion.

'We could split the world,' she suggested. 'You take heroin, and I'll take cocaine. Then it'll be clear to everyone where we stand.'

I told her this was completely impractical. We needed consistency in our policies, the international nature of the drug problem would not allow it to be partitioned in this way. I told her that she and I performed different functions: we were complementary, not interchangeable. When she persisted, I said, 'Look, Mo, if you want to visit South America and you have the blessing of the PM, then go. I'd be happy for you. But please don't confuse matters.'

She seemed to accept this, but added, 'Look – I want to go soon. Will you rearrange your visit to allow me to go?'

There was always pressure on my diary, and Mo was really desperate to do something, so I agreed to stand down. She visited the South American region a number of times and visited some Caribbean countries on another occasion. Under the drugs banner she also made separate visits to the United States, which were tolerated by No. 10, as by that time she was on her way out.

I felt all along that Mo and before her Jack Cunningham saw me as obstructive. This was because *their* role in relation to drugs was never clearly defined. They were given the drugs portfolio without any terms of reference, and along with it a sitting tenant in the form of myself, who worked for the Prime Minister with the precisely delineated terms of reference 'to develop and co-ordinate and monitor the United Kingdom's drugs policy'. The result was that both were constantly seeking a role for themselves.

The tension this created grew more and more unmanageable as it became clear that their future was limited and they tried even harder to prove themselves. In these circumstances it was quite natural for them to see me as competition, inhibiting them in their quest to 'do something'. Their position was weakened by my hearing from both senior civil servants and special advisers in No. 10 that their time was short, and I would only have to survive until the next reshuffle. I was encouraged to 'keep my head down and put up with it', as it wouldn't be for long.

In spite of the tensions, I was always very supportive and respectful to them personally, but I could not bring myself to back announcements by which they sought to restate policy as a means of raising their profile. Novelty is the life blood of ministers, and with nothing new to announce, they looked covetously at my role, and decided to take on some of the public relations work. The results were mixed, as they had to cancel a fair proportion of visits at short notice due to pressure of other work. The real contribution they could have made – the very reason why my role had been created – would have been to drive the drugs agenda forward within Whitehall; this was not a role that either of them relished, and in the event neither of them was prepared to risk offending heavy-weight Cabinet Ministers.

I felt particularly bad about the disintegration of my relationship with Mo. I liked and trusted her, and naively felt that I could provide her with some support and stability, but this was never possible. She once described me as 'too Chief Constably for her liking' – which may have reflected our past, as she once remarked, 'I used to have to make an appointment to see you. How things change!'

Her frustration with me nearly boiled over several times when I refused to go along with her proposals because they were not in the interests of the drugs agenda. One such incident came immediately after her visit to a cannabis farm where the crop was being grown under licence to establish whether the plant's derivatives relieved pain for people suffering from multiple sclerosis. She wished to make greater progress than was possible under the international rules governing the development of a medicine, and asked me if we had any money to allow a substantial increase in the number of people participating in the experiment.

I explained that the enterprise was a commercial one, and Treasury rules would prohibit any increase in funds. I added that the Government was already being criticised for restricting the use of an approved drug to treat MS patients on the grounds of cost, and to spend more under these circumstances would be illogical. Mo was not happy, and accused me of always blocking her ideas.

'I'll get my doctors to issue cannabis to their patients, and that'll do it,' she said. I asked where they would get the cannabis from, and which doctors would do this: a House of Lords report recommended this course of action, which had been rejected by the Government and the British Medical Association. Mo responded by saying, 'I've got some doctors who would do it, and I can always get hold of cannabis.' I left her office, and the matter went no further.

I was sad to witness Mo's demise. By the summer of 2000, rumours were abounding that she would be out at the next election, but she made her own decision to go. During those last months it was almost as if she set out to destroy herself. I know not where the negative spin came from, but it seemed to me that she played into the hands of those who wished to get rid of her. I shared a public platform with her on a few occasions towards the end, and she made her displeasure towards Government plain.

She opened one drugs conference by telling the audience that she was an icon, and then asked them to imagine how this felt. She said that she had once been the pin-up of the City, and could have had any man she wished. She claimed that wherever she went she was mobbed by children seeking her autograph, almost like the

Pied Piper. It was very sad that such a warm and talented individual felt so insecure that she had to present herself in such an embarrassing manner.

Much has been leaked about her inability to hold a brief. I never saw this. She could always identify the critical issues in a document and ask the most pertinent questions; however, ever-growing criticism undermined her confidence, and instead of acting spontaneously she began looking over her shoulder to see if someone was waiting to knife her in the back. I once raised the issue of politicians' insecurity with the Prime Minister, who said, 'That's the nature of politics, and we're all subject to it.'

'Not you, Prime Minister,' I said.

'Me too,' he replied. 'We all are.'

I had, and still have, difficulty in deciding whether Mo's determination to make an impact reflected her desire to improve the drugs situation, or whether she simply wanted to make a name for herself. Towards the end of her political career her media appearances became more risqué, and some of her statements more outrageous. Having said that, I was sorry when she told me she had decided not to seek re-election in June 2001. She is a kind-hearted woman, a talented and committed politician who became an embarrassment to New Labour and paid the price. I do wish her and her husband, John, much health and happiness in their future life.

CHAPTER TWENTY-FOUR

ON THE HEROIN TRAIL

My experience has led me to be critical of the international community's lack of support for effective anti-drugs measures. Every country agrees to an agenda set by the United Nations, but ignores it if convenient. Some UN decisions defy logic. Although Pakistan was penalised for allowing the growth of poppies, for example, India is encouraged to cultivate the flowers for medicinal qualities, and in the late 1990s the Delhi Government was put under pressure to increase production to meet global demand. The UN permits the flowers to be harvested in the traditional way, by lancing each of the millions of pregnant poppy pods, a system wide open to abuse, because the thick juice can easily be misappropriated.

A more secure method of harvesting is practised in Turkey and Tasmania to service the legitimate diamorphine market. In what is known as the 'straw' method, the plant is allowed to die back, so that the contents of the pod become unusable except through an industrial process. I recommended the Foreign Office put pressure on India to change its methods.

When I visited Islamabad in 1999, America was considering a resumption of trade with Pakistan, as the country had proved it had virtually eradicated poppy-growing within its borders. The final obstacle to agreement was the Pakistan Government's reluctance to publish a new anti-drugs strategy. During my meetings with senior politicians and officials, I urged them to go ahead; the document was ready, but national pride made them reluctant to be seen to bring it out under duress. In the event, a compromise was reached, and publication went ahead, to everyone's satisfaction.

To me this was a somewhat hollow success, for although Pakistan had closed down poppy-production, it was left with the fastest-growing addiction problem in the world, and it is now estimated to have more than two million addicts. The international community has virtually walked away from this disaster, even though it knows that the Pakistanis are without the means of resolving a terrible amount of human suffering.

Drugs often take second place to other political considerations, not least in the Caribbean. There, the banana crop is regarded as an alternative to drugs – one of the reasons why growers were granted favourable trading conditions, until the American banana-growers persuaded President Clinton to freeze them out. He did this against the advice of his officials, but his election campaign was indebted to the American growers to the tune of half a million dollars, and they called in their marker.

In the first half of 2001, with help from the Iranian Government, we were making progress in Afghanistan. In return for international recognition, the Taleban had imposed a ban on poppy cultivation. We were sceptical about their motives, and knew they had stock-piled at least a year's supply of heroin; nevertheless, the ban was real and America was prepared to support the initiative. Then, the events of 11 September changed everything. Without Taleban control, a new crop was planted which will, without intervention, be harvested. How much pressure can other governments put on the new regime in Afghanistan, bearing in mind all the other problems it faces? I smile when I hear that one of the favoured solutions is to purchase the crop from the farmers.

Very few countries in the world regard drugs as more than a domestic issue. Britain is one whose policies approach drugs on a strategic level, and I recognised that little would be achieved if this inconsistency remained. Moreover, I saw little evidence of other countries taking seriously the commitment they made at the United

Nations Special Assembly in New York in 1998, where they agreed to eradicate the production of illegal drugs.

To encourage others to take a more forceful approach to the subject, I recommended a series of actions, which Tony Blair pursued. The first approach was to our European Union partners, who accepted our proposals to raise the status of anti-drug activity, introduce tighter targets, set more stringent standards and introduce more objective protocols for the EU candidate countries in central and eastern Europe. The Prime Minister offered assistance and advice to these latter nations, which I would spearhead. The second set of proposals, to raise the issue of drugs to a strategic level and examine their impact on the global economy, was accepted in full by the G8 group of nations.

For me, the consequence of these international agreements was greatly increased travel. In the last twelve months of my time with Government I travelled the whole of the heroin route, from the borders of Afghanistan through Pakistan and Iran, and across the width of Turkey. I then followed the different routes through eastern and central Europe and visited Russia at the behest of President Putin, advising politicians, heads of agencies and non-governmental organisations as I went.

It would take a whole book to describe my experiences on those trips and give credit to the many courageous people I met; but a few sketches must suffice. The road journey from Islamabad to Peshawar in northern Pakistan, and on through the Khyber Pass to the borders with Afghanistan, is one I will never forget. The hordes of people, the brilliantly painted lorries and the raucous blasts of their horns were all electrifying – and so, in a different way, was the state of the road and the nature of the driving. The A2, as it is euphemistically called, is known as the most dangerous stretch of highway on the planet, and, having been on it, I would not challenge the description.

In Peshawar, travelling under the protection of a thirty-strong Pakistani army bodyguard, I stopped for an arranged meeting with an informant who told me about a consignment of heroin destined for Eastern Europe. The liaison officer who accompanied me insisted the man's bodyguard remove the clutch of weapons from around his waist and leave his automatic rifle outside our covert rendezvous. That contact was typical of the informants we cultivate throughout the world, many of whom are deeply involved in criminality themselves. Few help us for altruistic reasons: money, retribution against competitors, and exemption from prosecution are common incentives. Whatever their motives, the information they provide is very valuable in seizing drugs and dismantling trafficking organisations (the Peshawar source led to the seizure of a substantial amount of heroin).

The morality of using such people is questionable, as is the amount of money we have to pay them for their information; however, without them more drugs would reach our streets. It is all a matter of balance. Look at it this way. A single payment of £20,000 could help us seize more drugs in one consignment than all the law-enforcement agencies can achieve in a whole year.

Through such contacts we are now intercepting drugs in larger quantities than ever in the past – though we can rarely take credit, as to do so might compromise the safety of our informants and the agents who run them. We have a network of very brave officers fighting this war on our behalf throughout the world; many live in constant fear for their lives, and we owe them a debt of gratitude.

Peshawar is one of the most vibrant places I have ever visited. It is home to more than a million Afghani refugees from the Russian war. Most live in roughly constructed mud buildings with walls thick enough to protect them from the ravages of the harsh winters. The streets resemble those of biblical times: people clad in flowing robes and turbans sit around open fires on the roadside, eating, smoking and talking. Others sell wares of every kind. You could buy anything in that town: craftsmen were fashioning exhaust pipes from old tin cans and everything is recycled. Refuse of almost any nature has a value, being picked over and over by assorted entrepreneurs until it disappears. There is an enormous buzz about the place, as it is throbbing with people.

Immediately behind the main street are little shops, no more than ten feet square, which sell everything. 'You can buy anything from a duck egg to a tank in this town,' I was told by the captain of my bodyguard, and I believed him. Against his advice I decided to walk about and take in the flavour of the place. Our convoy of two hard-skinned Range Rovers, flanked by army vehicles containing soldiers with rifles, caused great interest as it drove slowly through the main street, and crowds gathered round us when we came to a halt.

I went into the nearest shop which sold guns and found everything on display, from a single-shot pen gun to a Kalashnikov. Prices ranged from about $1 for the pen to $100 for the automatic weapon. The special offer of the day was a block of hashish with every purchase. Within minutes the captain asked me to leave, as he was worried for our safety. Two hundred agitated people had surrounded our vehicles, and he wished me to leave – without any purchase I might add.

I learned a day or two later that during the short time we were in town, two women had been beaten to death because they had broken the strict rules of the Taleban regime by displaying parts of their bodies in public. The local newspaper's report of the incident praised the actions of their murderers.

After Peshawar, progress became still more difficult. The roads were appalling, with much of the surface unmade and severe adverse cambers, winding between precipitous vertical drops on either hand. Every few yards we came on a broken-down vehicle or a wreck lying on its side. The countryside was barren and hostile, with rocky outcrops rising to mountain summits on which many a British serviceman spent his last days. Painted on the rocks were the numbers and designations of British soldiers who served and died there.

On the northern outskirts of Peshawar were a number of large, fortress-type houses, each surrounded by high walls of red mud, almost all of which had been breached in one place or another during 'neighbourly disputes'. It seemed that the local sport was to fire Stinger missiles at rival compounds to settle any minor grievance such as the theft of a chicken. We knew that the occupants of these outposts were some of the biggest drug dealers in the world: they controlled the routes between Pakistan and Afghanistan, and were immune to the forces of law, which they would not hesitate to eliminate with superior weapons if the occasion arose. We drove in silence through their midst.

On our left as we headed north I noticed a solid ribbon of people carrying various types of goods over tracks traversing the foothills of the mountains. They reminded me of pack-mules, travelling sure-footed at a fast pace over undulating, dangerous and rocky ground. Some were bent double with the weight of their burden, carrying car bonnets, tyres and even fridge-freezers on their backs. I asked my guide who all these people were, and he replied, 'Smugglers.' Later, guards on the Afghan border told me they simply ignored them, as they were the 'poor people' – who also carried drugs and firearms. Our journey was broken by a visit to the home of some Whirling Dervishes, who entertained us to a meal and an exhibition of dancing which was most colourful.

At the border I stood on a mountain post gazing at the majestic Himalayas. Under a clear blue sky and bright sun, the gleaming snow summits were a most beautiful sight; but below us at the border post itself I could see thousands of people waiting to cross into Pakistan, and there were armed lookout posts on the tops of the mountains, each with a large number painted beneath it in white, reminding one that this is a hostile land. This is one of the paths by which drugs come to pollute our society.

The actual crossing was no more than twelve feet wide and resembled the entrance to a mansion, with high, wrought-iron gates hung on stone pillars surrounded on both sides by vehicles, animals and a mass of humanity. Cyclists had three or four other bicycles hung on the frames of the ones they rode. The machines were made in China and smuggled out into Afghanistan: the couriers rode them from the frontier to Peshawar, where they were paid, and returned by bus to pick up new consignments. These must have been some of the toughest cyclists in the world, as many completed the return trip two or three times daily. I could not have covered that terrain on one bicycle, let alone carrying two or three others. I remarked they ought to enter the Tour de France, as I felt sure they would win.

The guards on both sides of the border were very friendly. I was invited to go across and join the Afghanis for a drink of tea, which I did. I was surprised how young the men looked once they removed their hooded robes and I could see the features their beards did not hide. One English speaker gave me a glowing account of the Taleban regime, which included a justification of the way in which they treated their women folk. My unofficial visit ended when I chose not to accept their invitation to go further into their country, as I was unsure if I would ever return.

Equally fascinating was my visit to the Afghan border with Iran. In Tehran I was advised it would be too dangerous to visit the frontier region by helicopter, because of the likelihood of being shot down, so I travelled in a Toyota 4 × 4. Not that I felt that was any safer – especially when I learned that more than 3,000 border guards had been killed by drug traffickers. The Iranians' willingness to prevent drugs being transported through their country is not altogether altruistic, for they have a fast-growing addiction problem among their own population. A senior official admitted that in the early days after the revolution of 1979 they actively supported the drug trade, in the belief that it would help undermine the decadent West; but now their policy has come back to haunt them.

In spite of the risks, I had some memorable helicopter rides. One was during a visit to Turkey with a UN delegation, when we flew over the mountains to Burgalac, the eastern border post with Iran, in an ageing Chinook. On the return trip night began to fall, and the colour drained from the face of our guide, a senior military officer, who was clearly frightened and told us afterwards that neither our pilot nor the aircraft was suitable for such an excursion. I got the same message on return from a six-hour flight in snow and sub-zero temperatures in a small military helicopter from Poland into Belarus – although I am unsure if the crew's fear was about the journey or what might happen to us when we arrived.

Many of my journeys, however, were very comfortable. Being whisked through the VIP channel at airports takes much of the aggravation out of travel, as does staying in our ambassadorial residences by kind invitation of their occupants. This was a rare privilege, for Britain owns wonderful buildings in the major cities of the world. The house in New York, on the banks of the Hudson River, once belonged to Greta Garbo, and there was an amusing moment at dinner when the outgoing Ambassador upset John Prescott, our Deputy Prime Minister. Becoming mischievous, John asked me, 'What do you think of these digs, Keith?' I told him they were splendid, and he retorted, in the Ambassador's hearing, 'I don't think they need a spot like this, do you? I reckon they'd be all right in an hotel. I'll have a word with Gordon Brown about it.' The Ambassador's face was a picture. (I should add here that none of the ambassadors I met bore any resemblance to the caricatures of popular imagination. On the contrary, I found them all down-to-earth, hard-working champions of our country, often operating in very difficult circumstances.)

The residence in Tehran is very oriental, and has been guarded like a fortress ever since the troubles in the early 1980s. Our Moscow residence, across the river from the Kremlin, was built by a salt magnate, and is dark and forbidding, in complete contrast with the High Commissioner's house in Canberra, which resembles a miniature White House. In Athens we took over a mansion built by a rich Greek to woo his fiancée; when the man became Prime Minister, he thought the place too grand for his position, and we bought it at a knock-down price.

My travels took me to all the borders on the heroin routes between Afghanistan and our shores. In every country I gave advice to ministers and officials on matters in the drugs arena. I received one or two strange requests: the Deputy Minister of the Interior in Iran asked me if I would help his country reorganise its police force, whereas a Chief of Police in Russia wished to know 'the truth' about Margaret Thatcher. I also received many strange gifts and some odd offers. After I had nearly choked on some non-alcoholic beer the Iranians served up, my guide and security officer asked if I would like some whisky, failing to mention that in his country drinking alcohol can be punished by death.

One of the saddest stories was told to me by a soldier on their borders, who said that camels were the principle means by which drugs are smuggled across the mountainous terrain. The more unscrupulous traffickers removed a baby from its mother's womb in Iran and forced the mother over the border into Afghanistan, where they filled the womb with drugs and let the camel go. Its maternal instincts would lead it back to its baby unaccompanied by people, thus making its burden impossible to detect.

Greater use of intelligence is the key to making a real impact on the drugs problem. This is the only way to beat a well-resourced and organised network of traffickers, many of whom have their roots in terrorist or political activity. The international community must use all the resources available to it: satellite monitoring, listening devices, human agents and military might must all be assembled against the threat. There is a degree of sensitivity about the subject of spying, particularly in the former Soviet bloc countries because of their history. Even within the EU there is very limited co-operation between the intelligence and law-enforcement agencies on drugs, in part due to governments being slow to recognise the strategic nature of the subject.

During my travels I met the heads of the many national intelligence agencies, sometimes after elaborate switches of vehicles and other diversionary manoeuvres resembling those in a 007 movie. I often reflected that only a few years ago these people were our sworn enemies. It felt strange, for example, to address senior Russian politicians at the Moscow School of Politics. The Communist regimes of central and eastern Europe used to support drug-trafficking to the West because they hoped it would destabilise our society. The challenge they now face is therefore all the greater, because much of the support structure remains, and the trade is highly lucrative to the people involved, some of whom retain powerful positions within their establishment. As a consequence they are very difficult to get at, and they spawn corruption throughout the system. The new regimes also face growing drug problems among their populations, and have limited means with which to counter them. Britain has been very helpful in this humanitarian cause: we are one of the largest donors of money, equipment and expertise, and our generosity is much appreciated by national states.

My experiences have increased my understanding of different peoples. Most of us are looking for the same things for ourselves and our children. We all value life largely in the same way, and, taken one on one, are very much alike. We are all manipulated by politics and religion.

CHAPTER TWENTY-FIVE

DEATH BY A THOUSAND CUTS

The call from No. 10 Downing Street on Friday, 8 June 2001, was answered by Bren. I took hold of the telephone. The caller asked me to confirm that I was Keith Hellawell, then said, 'I have Sir Richard Wilson for you.' After a moment's pause Sir Richard said, 'Keith, this is a courtesy call. The Prime Minister has asked me to tell you that your unit is going to the Home Office.'

'Where does that leave me?' I asked.

There was a second's hesitation before he repeated, 'This is just a courtesy call. We're sorting out the new ministers, and you can imagine it's very busy in there. But the Prime Minister wanted you to know before you read it in tomorrow morning's papers.'

The following Monday morning my senior civil servant telephoned me with the news that on Saturday she had attended a briefing by the Home Secretary, who hoped to arrange an early meeting with me. Next day I learned that a reporter from the *Financial Times* had spoken to David Blunkett, and the paper was to publish a story of my demise. I relayed this information to John Gieve, Permanent Secretary in the Home Office, and asked him what was going on.

He didn't seem particularly surprised, but reassured me they would 'rebut the story'. I was unhappy, and insisted they take pre-emptive action. He hesitated, so I asked him if there was something he knew which I didn't. He said it was 'difficult', and we ought to discuss it when we met later in the week. I could not accept this, and insisted that I must know if any changes were proposed. He told me the Home Secretary wished to take a more hands-on approach, and my position would have to change. I asked him point-blank if that meant the Government would like me to go – which I was more than ready to do. He was adamant this was not so, but asked if I had any views about the future.

I explained I had intended to leave when my initial three-year contract ran out, in January 2001, but that after a special request from the Prime Minister in the spring of 2000 I had agreed to stay on for three additional years. (Senior civil servants in the Cabinet Office were furious when the PM announced this, and did all in their power to prevent it being borne out, taking nine months to draw up my new contract. One told me, 'He [the Prime Minister] cannot make these decisions without consulting us.')

Two days before the election, discussing the role of the Drugs Tsar with Lord Falconer at No. 10, I had said that, without change, the post would lose credibility altogether, for throughout my term of office I had been put in the classic position of having responsibility without power, and others were exploiting this weakness. On the other hand, ministers had the power to deliver but were failing to accept their responsibility. I made a number of suggestions as to how the situation could be resolved, beginning with my resignation, to which Charlie Falconer replied, 'God forbid! Tony wouldn't accept that.' He thanked me for my views, which he said were very useful, as the PM intended to make radical changes in the role of the Cabinet Office.

Now, on the Monday, I told John Gieve that as Blunkett had assumed the responsibility for drugs – which had been one of my suggestions to Charlie – I would be happy to take a different role, but only on a part-time basis. He seemed relieved, and jumped at the idea. I still had an unfinished agenda in Europe, so we agreed I would limit my activity to international affairs and intelligence, and would make a joint announcement to that effect. We put one out later the same afternoon, but to no avail, as the *FT*'s story of my sacking appeared in their next edition.

Late in the evening of that day a well-respected journalist on a newspaper that supported Labour telephoned to ask, 'Have you seen tomorrow's papers? They've screwed you.'

I asked him to elaborate.

'All the Murdoch newspapers have crucified you.'

'Why?'

'You must have trodden on some important toes. This stuff is so bad, it has to have been pushed from an authoritative source high in Government.'

He went on to tell me that over the previous few months there had been a stream of negative spin emanating from the Home Office in particular, and asked if the name Justin Russell meant anything to me. I told him it most certainly did – he was, of course, Jack Straw's spin doctor at the Home Office.

When I read the papers next morning, it was clear they were falling over themselves to quote anonymous Government sources who were prepared to damn me. They were like jackals round a kill, feasting on my remains.

Later that day David Blunkett telephoned me at home to apologise for what had occurred; he sought to distance himself from the barrage of negative media spin, assuring me he did not operate in that way. He added he was pleased I was staying, and welcomed my expertise, as neither he nor any of his new ministers knew much about drugs. I learned much later that at the Saturday meeting after the election he had said he didn't like high-profile special advisers, and wished to get rid of me, but was persuaded against doing so. Immediately after the election, Justin Russell was promoted to become Tony Blair's spin doctor on drugs. Not one word was spoken in my defence from No. 10 or any other department of Government, either on that day or since.

I was understandably upset at the treatment I had received, but determined not to be beaten. It was clear they wished me to go, and were using the media to achieve their ends. I was resolute. In the ensuing days the media made dozens of requests for me to answer my critics. I countered by asking who they were – suggesting that if these cowardly people were prepared to come out and face me, I would be more than happy to answer them. I also recommended that the papers should print the facts, and outlined what had been achieved over my period in office; but, as I had noticed in the past, this was not to the media's taste. I also recognised the traps being set for me: had I made any accusations without evidence, I would have been castigated. Moreover, I had no intention of becoming a pawn in the hands of newspapers, whose only real interest was to stir up controversy. I kept my counsel, as I knew my moment would come.

In time media interest waned – until a strange article appeared in the *Sunday Times* suggesting that I had changed my mind on cannabis. It claimed, erroneously, that I no longer considered cannabis led on to harder drugs. I was perplexed, and asked the Home Office Press office to refute the article (I had no Press support of my own by this time). Nothing happened, and other stories began to circulate, using my alleged change of view as justification for amending the law on cannabis. I pressed the office for a reaction, which was promised but never came, and I later learned that the Home Office blocked many requests for me to appear on media programmes.

I asked a senior civil servant in the department what on earth was going on. She told me that Blunkett didn't want anyone to say anything about cannabis, 'as he may have a change of mind'. I asked if there was any evidence to support this. 'No,' she said. 'I think it's political.' Had Blunkett consulted the Prime Minister, who, I knew, was firm in his view about cannabis? No – he had not.

I became very concerned about the damage being done to drug policy. By failing to react to the issue, or to counter claims put forward by the increasingly active 'legalisation lobby', the Government was being seen to support a softening of drug policy. I sought an early meeting with Blunkett, but none was forthcoming, so I had to resort to writing him a note, which I copied to Tony Blair.

I received no acknowledgement, but my *cri de coeur* did have some effect: within forty-eight hours a very strong statement was issued by No. 10, followed by a firm, unequivocal briefing to the Press, which reaffirmed that the Government had no intention of

changing its policy on cannabis. This was a breach of normal protocol, as any statement on this subject would normally have come
from the Home Office – a point noticed by one or two newspapers,
which described the announcement as a 'slap in the face' for the
Home Secretary, which it clearly was. Mission accomplished, or so
I thought.

I had agreed that I would complete my Annual Report on the
work of Government for the year 2000–2001. John Gieve told me
this was what Blunkett wanted, and that the Home Secretary would
be present at the report's launch, to 'say something positive about
you'. Then, he said 'we'll be able to draw a line under your work,
give it time, and make new announcements'. He told me he would
be happy for me to be critical of Government, as it would give
them more opportunity to show how the 'new regime' was going
to improve matters. It was no surprise to find that when my report
was published, Blunkett was 'unavailable', and no recognition of
my work was expressed.

Even though I was supposed to be his expert adviser, I had only
one audience with Blunkett – and that not until almost four months
after the election. It was a very amicable meeting, and he clearly
had one purpose in mind – to sound me out about cannabis. I
believe he had little option but to speak to me, because we were
both scheduled to give evidence before the Home Affairs Select
Committee, which was considering the subject.

He told me he intended to announce his views on reclassification
of the drug to the committee, but before making any decision he
would seek advice from the Advisory Council on the Misuse of
Drugs (ACMD). When I asked if he had consulted the Prime
Minister, he said he had gained his support. (I have been told –
although I am sure it will be denied – that the meeting between
the two of them took place on 12 September 2001, the day after
the terrorist attacks in New York, when the outrage was claiming
everyone's attention.) Immediately afterwards I was approached by
a senior civil servant in the Home Office who was surprised that
the meeting had taken place. 'I didn't think he would speak to
you,' I was told. 'Our advice was against it.'

I duly appeared before the Home Affairs Select Committee, flanked by a number of civil servants who were anxious to answer questions on my behalf. Interestingly, I was not asked for my views on the legalisation of cannabis. The Home Secretary subsequently made his announcement, backing the reclassification of cannabis from a Class B drug to a Class C drug.

The ACMD, which reports to the Home Secretary, announced its support for his views when it reported to him in March 2002. The document is worthy of attention, because it outlines the danger cannabis poses. I was a little disappointed its authors chose not to discuss the increased danger to users of the strains containing the high content of Tetrahydrocannabinol (THC) favoured by users today, or to comment on the consequences of reclassification for the police, who now take virtually no action against Class C drugs. By then, however, the damage had been done.

Without any credible opposition to these proposals, the law will change. It is ironic that new medical evidence points to the dangers of cannabis. The argument that change is necessary to save police time is equally fallacious, as economies can be achieved under current policy. When the police commander in Brixton ordered his staff not to enforce the old law, he created a safe haven for drug-users in that part of the capital, and led the Commissioner, Sir John Stevens, to declare that the 'experiment' will not be repeated elsewhere in London. He will have little option if the law changes.

It is true changes are taking place in other parts of Europe. However, these must be seen in context of the various countries' legal systems. Their police officers have no power to caution offenders, as do ours, and they have had to change the nature of the offence of drug possession to achieve the results which are possible here.

The bottom line is this: *Tackling Drugs to Build a Better Britain* identifies the major problems drugs cause to individuals, their families and the community. It outlines the way in which these need to be tackled, and its provisions are beginning to take effect. It tasks police and Customs with addressing the most dangerous drugs – heroin and cocaine – and advises them to deal with personal possession by way of warning or caution. They do, however, retain the power to arrest people if that is justified by the amount of drugs in their possession, or by the circumstances in which they possess them (for example when children may access them), or when they refuse to acknowledge their offence, or for repeat offending.

I became increasingly disillusioned by this aspect of official policy, and by the Government's failure to defend its own drugs strategy. When commentators suggested we educate our children against the danger of drugs, provide treatment for addicts, look for alternatives for those who grow the crops, focus more on heroin and cocaine, and try and stop them coming into this country, all such sensible proposals went unanswered.

I was desperate to leave, but had committed myself to organising and chairing a European Union conference at which all the candidate countries would be invited to share experiences and set an agenda for the future. I therefore continued to act as the Government's international adviser on drugs, and the conference took place in June 2002, after which I submitted my letter of resignation, *under private and confidential cover*, to John Gieve.

Nothing is sacrosanct in Government – not even personal matters. Within twenty-four hours the female head of the drugs unit telephoned me to ask why I wished to leave. I told her I had stated my reasons in my resignation letter. To my surprise and chagrin – because she obviously had the letter in her possession – she said, 'We can probably accommodate the first part, but we will have difficulty with cannabis.'

She went on to ask, 'What do you want, Keith?'

I told her there was nothing.

'What do you want?' she repeated. 'They'll give you anything.'

I repeated I sought nothing.

A second call came, from another civil servant in the Home Office, who told me my letter had caused mayhem. They were frightened to death that I would approach the Press, and Gieve had instructed my first caller to do whatever she could to pacify me.

I had no intention of going public then, but as my letter was bandied about the Home Office, I will divulge its contents here.

I hereby give notice to terminate my contract as an expert adviser to the Home Secretary. I am unhappy to continue under present circumstances. My last day in office will be 7 August 2002 [I had to give a statutory period of notice].

You told me that the Home Secretary wished to 'draw a line' under my time in office, but I didn't expect a rewrite of history. Over the last few weeks I have been appalled at the way in which Government has failed to answer criticisms about drug policy. An uninformed observer would believe none was in place, when nothing is further from the truth. Under the provisions of *Tackling Drugs to Build a Better Britain* more children are being educated, more drug addicts treated, more criminals deflected from anti-social behaviour by treatment intervention within the criminal justice system, and more drugs seized, particularly before they reach our shores.

I can only surmise this omission is contrived to create a vacuum, which will be filled by the impending 're-launch' of the Strategy. This subterfuge undermines the confidence of people working in the anti-drugs field, gives the wrong message to those who are deeply concerned about the subject, and brings discredit on its architects.

Neither can I support the decision to soften the law on cannabis, which gives completely the wrong message to young people, who will be more inclined to experiment with this drug, and creates more difficulties for parents in guiding them. I have seen no evidence to support this change in Government policy, which – if the power of arrest for personal possession is taken from the police – will *de facto* decriminalise this dangerous substance. No other country has gone this far. I can see no justification for meddling in this way, other than political popularity, and I hope and pray this does not have to be paid for by the pain and misery of others.

Keith Hellawell

Thus ended more than forty years of public service, during which I would like to believe I made a small contribution. I was Chief

Constable of two forces both of which, during my stewardship, achieved substantial reductions in crime and in complaints by the public, increases in detection rates, reductions in the levels of sickness and ill-health retirements, and improved financial stability. These successes were all the more praiseworthy because of the unique problems each force faced. I would like to thank all my colleagues for their dedication and commitment in bringing this about. My work afforded me the opportunity of meeting some wonderful people from all walks of life across the world, and others I would choose to forget.

I found the interaction between politicians and civil servants fascinating. On my arrival almost all the ministers I met told me how they mistrusted civil servants, and outlined how they were going to sort them out. Within months they had become so reliant on their *bêtes noires* that very little change was made. Over the last decade, when successive governments have pledged to reduce the numbers of administrators, the number of civil servants in Whitehall has grown. When challenged, they give you information about reductions, but when you check, you find that all economies have been made away from headquarters, at community level, where cuts have a negative effect on services.

This Government has shown its determination to reduce the rewards to fat cats in industry, but during the same period the pay of senior civil servants has considerably exceeded inflation and put many of their salaries on a par with those in industry. The performance-related pay system of the highest in the service – which was shown to me by accident – is inefficient by industrial standards, and is measured by those at that level themselves. The civil service is the most powerful closed shop I have ever witnessed, and I can see no way in which it will ever be changed.

CHAPTER TWENTY-SIX

LOOKING AHEAD

POLICE

If Home Secretaries are serious about improving the police service, there is much they could do; merely adding to the numbers of front-line officers, without resolving their problems, will have at best a neutral effect and at worst a negative one. Only a percentage of crime and anti-social behaviour is reported to the police. This is in part due to the public belief that the police are so busy that they don't want to be troubled with trivial problems; another reason is loss of confidence in them, and a perception that they don't care. Yet another is withdrawal of cover by insurance companies. Why report a theft to the police if there is no chance of recompense? When police numbers and efficiency are increased, public confidence returns and more reports are made, with a consequential increase in workload.

It is time for politicians and police leaders to be more radical. First, they should reduce the number of police ranks, which were introduced more than a century ago by the military leaders who helped shape the service. The modern organisation is community-based, not quasi-military, and should recognise itself as such. Constables do not act on orders from their superior officers, but at their own discretion, as they hold a unique office under the law. A police force is by-and-large territorially based, and does not need the same number of ranks in command as does a military unit. Everyone joins as a constable: there are no 'officers and other ranks', and therefore no need for the number of ranks to maintain the distinction. The badges of rank are also an anachronism: they mean nothing to those outside the service, most people believing that a detective is of higher rank than all the rest.

It is the principle of rank which creates the greatest difficulty, as most people who join the service do so to make their way up the ladder of promotion. In this they are encouraged by recruiting campaigns, which point to rank as the criterion of success: with it comes money, status and other benefits, and to remain a constable is considered a failure. However, when one analyses what the ranks contribute, their value is in reverse order to their perceived importance: the higher the rank, the less involvement in the job you are recruited to do. How many Chief Constables do you hear of dealing with operational matters? When I interviewed the Yorkshire Ripper, I was the only Chief Constable in the country who had been directly involved in a murder investigation for many years. Would society tolerate a doctor, a nurse or a teacher doing work for which they were expensively trained for only four or five years? I think not. Yet this is what the police are set up to do.

There is another aspect to this. Because power and its rewards lie with the ranks, those in the organisation always try to create more senior posts, eroding the number of front-line officers. If you visit any police station in this country during the day, you will find almost as many people of rank on duty as constables out on the streets. What would your reaction be if that were so in schools or hospitals? (This of course does not apply at night, as most ranks above that of inspector work bankers' hours.) It is time that the rewards system is changed to reflect the value of those officers who directly police our streets. We need a much flatter structure in which promotion is not the primary reward.

We must also examine what we expect our constables to do and the conditions under which they have to operate. The burdens of human rights, equal opportunities and racial discrimination are carried on their shoulders. Politicians and senior officers pontificate about these legitimate issues, but they don't have to grapple with them in practice: they don't face the bricks and missiles and endure the racist chants; they don't stand in police charge-rooms handcuffed to someone with whom they have struggled or by whom they have been assaulted, to answer questions about the precise words they used at the moment of the arrest. They don't get spat at or have excreta thrown over them by HIV-positive prisoners, 'just for the hell of it'. Nor do they face being questioned in the witness-box at Crown Court about the legal niceties of an action they took in the heat of a disturbance a year before.

These same senior figures are the ones who burden front-line officers with administrative work and then chastise them for taking time to complete it. In Huddersfield in the 1960s we prosecuted on one sheet of paper completed by the officer after an arrest; only if the person pleaded not guilty were further inquiries made and witnesses' statements obtained, usually by beat officers during the course of their duties. When the Crown Prosecution Service took on the responsibility for police prosecutions, complete files had to be prepared and submitted in every case, so that the authorities had 'the full facts to decide whether or not to prosecute'. Eventually, they even had to collect information which might be of value to the defence.

Who had to prepare all this material? The officers on the beat. Were they given any more time to do it? Of course not. Is the reader aware that an officer is charged with completing his or her inquiries into an incident before he or she goes off duty, but the rest of those involved have weeks to add their contribution? The constable is seen as 'serving' everyone else, rather than they being his or her support.

When stop-and-search powers were being abused in the Metropolitan Police area, the system had to change. New forms and report-back procedures were introduced for, you guessed it, the uniformed officer to complete without additional resources.

Over the last two decades individual rights have become a political issue in this country, with the emphasis on race, gender and sexual preference. Who has to carry the can if the police service is found wanting in this area? The uniformed officers. They have also had to shoulder the responsibility of a person's mental or physical state at the time of arrest, and any mistake subjects them to severe criticism.

What contribution have the politicians made, apart from criticising those who could not answer back, and dreaming up ways in which they could work harder? They have passed obscure laws such as those relating to dogs, for the police to grapple with, because they were too weak to resist media pressure. (I was once asked to adjudicate on the type of dog we had impounded in one of my police stations when it had been found without a muzzle. After months of deliberation, two white-coated experts still could not agree on the breed. The irate owner was present, so I took the lead and handed the dog back to him.)

If politicians are really serious about improving policing in this country, they should at least recognise these issues. They must also remember that, even without added burdens, the work-load of the service has increased with the advent of better communications. If all you have to do to report a crime is lift a telephone, rather than take a bus or car journey to a police station, you are more likely to do it. You only need to sit in a police control room for an hour or so to see how much time is taken up by well-meaning mobile-phone users reporting this or that on motorways. Each call has to be answered in a professional and courteous manner, even though the three or four hundred which may follow are nothing but a nuisance.

The full weight of public accountability also falls on the uniformed officer, as he or she is the visible police presence on the streets, and the majority of public complaints are made against this section of the service. It is easy to be righteous when you are not in the firing line. Police officers are human: they sometimes snap and respond in a less than professional way, and they are penalised for it. The growth in the complaints industry has reduced numbers of officers on the streets and increased those of the senior ranks. Because of the dictates of politicians in Britain today, a complaint against a police officer will be more thoroughly investigated than a crime of burglary. I do not think this is what the public really wants. The time wasted by street officers preparing their defence and being interviewed under caution, let alone the worry that it causes, is immeasurable.

So what is the reality of policing today? Those we entrust with the most exacting duty are the most lowly paid and junior in rank and experience. They are the most accountable and carry the heaviest administrative load. They feel isolated and unsupported by their senior officers, whom they regard as remote, and by politicians who, they believe, lack any understanding of their work. They have to abide by rules which effectively tie one if not both of their hands behind their backs. The completion of reports is a stronger imperative than dealing with incidents in the first place. As far back as 1982 I examined the time the service expended on recording a crime compared with the time spent investigating it; except for major crimes, the recording cost twice as much as the investigation – one reason being that you would be disciplined for not recording a crime correctly, but there was no penalty for not solving it.

The case of Stephen Lawrence and the Metropolitan Police brought the race issue into the limelight. The Commissioner and all the other Chief police officers were put on the spot about racism within their own forces, and they gave various replies. I had many years before publicly pronounced my own fears: I had been brutally honest about the situation in West Yorkshire, and I believe this allowed us to tackle racial problems before other forces. At the time, however, I felt alone, and I was criticised within the force for running it down. Some of my colleagues thought I should have kept my mouth shut, as I might be stirring up a hornets' nest.

The hornets they have to face in the twenty-first century are larger and more abundant than they were when I addressed them. I knew I didn't have the total support of the Police Authority in the way I approached this issue, and that of sexual harassment: I had been asked to tackle them, but my way of doing it caused some of them concern.

The work of the police service is set within a quasi-political environment. A Chief Constable is part of a triumvirate, of which the Home Secretary and the Police Authority are the other members. Since the Police Act of 1964 this three-headed body has had a very uneasy existence, since each agency within it has fought for power and supremacy. In the early days the Police Authority was to the fore, as it hired, fired and promoted everyone within a police force and also controlled the purse strings. During the local government reorganisation in the late 1960s and 1970s the balance of power shifted to Chief Constables, as politicians at local level took their eye off the police, being more concerned with establishing power-bases within their newly created boundaries.

The current Blair Government is trying hard to erode the authority of Chief officers. The police in Britain are not (yet) politically controlled. As I have said, Margaret Thatcher, used to getting her own way, was extremely cross when she was refused access to the co-ordination centre set up by Chief Constables in response to the miners' strike of 1984. What a later conservative government did succeed in doing, through different pieces of legislation, was to clarify and balance the roles between the three.

Chief Constables kept their operational independence and were given power and control over the resources to run their forces, being made accountable to their Police Authorities for the way they did it. The Authorities were given new powers to publish annual policing plans, of which the Chief Constable had to take cognisance. The Home Secretary continued to oversee the whole system through reports and inspections, taking on to himself more supervisory powers over the Authorities and additional powers in regard to disciplinary proceedings against senior officers.

During the last five years, however, the balance of power has moved away from Chief Constables, largely to the benefit of others. This has partly been due to the reluctance of some Chiefs to grasp the power they were given to control resources: some refused to take the opportunity, perhaps because they felt uncomfortable or incompetent to deal with multimillion-pound budgets. Others bent to the wishes of their Authorities, who were reluctant to lose fiscal control. Authorities have now begun to abuse their influence when selecting Chief officers by asking them if they are prepared to 'share' some of their powers – and even be subject to appraisal by them – if they are appointed. Few refuse, as they know that to do so would mean certain rejection.

Home Secretaries seem more willing to throw their weight about and threaten Chief officers with dismissal if they don't toe the line. David Blunkett has set up a 'Standards Unit', headed by a £200,000-a-year, part-time appointee, to 'sort out police forces which are not up to scratch'.

Another controlling influence on a modern Chief Constable is the length of his appointment, which is now set by politicians. This system is far removed from that of my generation, when Chief Constables could serve until age sixty-five. When your career and income depend on others, you are effectively under their control and more likely to bend to their will. I believe that Chief Constables are quickly losing their independence. Perhaps this is why they rarely speak in public, and why we more often have to listen to national politicians pontificating on policing issues.

The service needs leadership from individuals who are accessible and visible. Control from London in reality means control by the civil service – which is what civil servants have dreamed of for a long time. They never liked the independence of the police, but they had to wait for a long time for a Home Secretary to give them the power they desired. Now it appears as if David Blunkett is their champion.

True leadership is required of a senior police officer. He or she is expected by both the force and the community to take command – however the speed at which people are achieving supervisory rank today means that experience is in short supply, and they find themselves incapable of leading in the true sense. More and more training is geared towards managing rather than leading, which is fundamentally changing their relationship with officers on the front line, many of whom believe they are having to 'carry' their bosses.

This is not inconsistent with the wish of some people. If the reformers can remove all the operational element from a senior police officer's role, this would open the door to management by the civil service – but at what cost?

I have always proudly proclaimed that the British police service was the best in the world. Its strength has lain not in its equipment, its buildings or its resources, but in the fact that it has always been answerable to the general public, through Chief officers who were not controlled by politicians and bureaucrats. Within a very short time this will no longer be the case, and our service will sink to the level of mediocrity.

DRUGS

There is no short-term solution to the problem, and politicians must recognise this. Political activity must be focused on colleagues in other countries, to encourage them to recognise the strategic nature of the problem. International institutions must realise this is an issue for them: NATO, for example, has taken years even to accept drugs as an agenda item, yet terrorist organisations are funded by them, and drugs feature in most of the military hot-spots on the globe. The cost of illegal drugs to health, crime, the social services, industry and our families is incalculable.

The environmental consequences of illicit drug production are rarely discussed, but rivers are being polluted and deforestation is rife. The billions fed into the pockets of drugs racketeers, and the consequent corruption, reach every sector of our society and need routing out. The ineffectiveness of professionals in the banking, legal and accountancy sectors – their failure to take decisive action – is worthy of closer scrutiny.

When no real attempt is being made to address the major issues, minor alterations of domestic laws are a distraction, an insult to our intelligence, and an indictment of those who contemplate them. There is so much to be done I beg the politicians to get on and do it.

LIAR

On the afternoon of 9 July 2002 I received a request to contribute to the BBC's *Today* programme next morning, on an item about the reclassification of cannabis. I decided to take the opportunity to speak out against something about which I felt so strongly.

At 07.30 on the tenth James Naughtie came on the line, asking what I thought of the Home Secretary's intention to soften his approach on cannabis. I replied that I could not support him. Why, then, he asked, was Blunkett making these changes? I told him they must represent a personal initiative by the Home Secretary, and Naughtie should ask *him*.

After a number of other questions, he remaked, 'You're still an adviser on drugs policy to the Government. How can you continue in that role if this is your view?'

'With respect, James,' I replied, 'I'm no longer. I've put in my resignation.'

'You've resigned?'

'Yes. I've resigned over this issue, and over the issue of spin, because I understand – although I've been kept out of the discussions – that today there's also going to be a relaunch of the drugs strategy. There's already a ten-year strategy in place, which is educating more children, treating more addicts, and intervening in the criminal justice system. But over the last couple of months

I've become more and more concerned about the Government's lack of response to criticism that these things are not happening. And I think there is just a repackaging, a re-spinning of the issue, to make it appear that something has been done. And this is causing great problems on the streets – a great deal of problems for parents who just don't know where they are.'

I did not realise what an effect my remarks would have. For the next seven days I was constantly hounded by journalists from newspapers, radio and television, from this and other countries. My comments caught the Government's spin doctors by surprise.

More than an hour passed before they managed to crank out a first response, expressing 'surprise' at what I had said; but as the morning developed, the spin machine went into full swing against me. Number Ten claimed to be 'bemused' by my remarks. The Home Office released a statement which alleged that I had *changed my mind three times* on the subject, that 'they had evidence to prove it', and that they were under the impression that I was in favour of reclassification. They also began briefing journalists, off the record, to the effect that the only reason I had spoken out on *Today* was to increase the value of my book to potential buyers. This was complete nonsense, as my agreement with HarperCollins had been made more than two years earlier.

By lunch-time the Government's spin machine had managed to do what it often does when in trouble – muddy the waters and shift the emphasis. Interviewers began to ask why I had changed my views, rather than why the Government had changed its policy. I was surprised by the naivety of journalists who fell for this tactic, but I managed to bring the story back to the substantive issue. I did, however, challenge the Home Office to produce evidence of my alleged change of mind. My chance came during an interview on the BBC's *World at One*. The alleged three changes of mind related to statements I had made over the past two years: they were all about different issues, and not inconsistent with each other. When I said so, I received no reply.

The 'evidence' proving that I supported the reclassification of cannabis was a note of a meeting I had had with David Blunkett on 17 October 2001 – described on page 358 – at which, it was alleged, I agreed with him about reclassifying the drug. It is significant that I have never seen a copy of this document – but I do have a very clear recollection of the meeting, as it was the only one I had with the Home Secretary after the 2001 election.

To recap, we discussed a number of issues, including the police service, and Blunkett told me he intended to 'seek the views on reclassification of cannabis' of the Advisory Council on the Misuse of Drugs (ACMD). He said he would make these views public when he gave evidence to the Home Affairs Select Committee a few weeks later. I saw no objection to this, and said so, as I believed the ACMD would advise him against any down grading of the drug.

On 30 October I gave evidence to the same Home Affairs Select Committee, who, to my surprise, did not ask about my view on reclassification. It was, however, sought by waiting journalists at the end of the session, and my objections to reclassification duly appeared in the national Press next day – for example in the *Daily Mail*:

> Former Drugs Tsar Keith Hellawell yesterday condemned David Blunkett's move to soften the law on cannabis. Speaking for the first time since the plans were announced, Mr Hellawell said his advice to ministers had always been to maintain existing tough laws. He added that he had seen no evidence to change his mind.

I have to question why I was not taken to task for my views, which – if the Home Office is to be believed – totally contradicted their evidence.

There are other factors which undermine the Government's allegations that I changed my mind. First, the strong note I sent to Blunkett and the Prime Minister; second, the meeting I had with John Gieve, Permanent Secretary at the Home Office, in March 2002, when I expressed my reservations after discovering that the ACMD had reported in favour of reclassification; third, my resignation letter of 23 June, in which I took a further opportunity of outlining my objections to any softening of the law.

These factors did not stop Blunkett pursuing the line against me in interviews he gave during the late afternoon and evening of 10 July. 'I have changed my mind only once on this subject,' he said, 'and he [Hellawell] has changed his three times.' He added that he had come to favour reclassification only when he received the advice of the experts (ACMD). This was in March 2002 – so, if he is to be believed, he had been against the downgrading when we met the previous October. In other words, my alleged support for change was contrary to his own views at that time!

Next day the *Sun* picked up his words and called me 'a liar'. I have not lied on this subject. Even if I had changed my mind – which I have not – it would not make me a liar, and Blunkett had no justification for publicly denouncing me merely because my views did not match his.

What an ending, after more than forty years of dedicated service to law and order in this country! The final act of a 'caring' Government was to brand me a liar. What a reward!

POLICE RANKS

The rank structure of the police service is a mystery to many. All officers join at the rank of **constable**. Unlike in the military, there is no officer entry level. There is a fast track for graduates, who are allowed to complete the Special Course interviews before they join the service, but they still have to join as constables and take the promotion exam with everyone else. If they fail – and a high proportion do – they remain on the bottom rung of the ladder.

The first promotion is to the rank of **sergeant**. About 11,000 constables take their promotion examination for it each year, with a pass-rate in the teens of per cent. Once you have passed, unless you gain a place on the Special Course, you have to qualify by experience and through promotion boards before you are promoted further.

This process is mirrored for the next rank of **inspector**. Officers qualify for the ranks of **chief inspector**, **superintendent** and **chief superintendent** through experience and by passing successful promotion boards, although few achieve the rank of superintendent without completion of the appropriate course at the college. Completion of the Special Course gives you a head start in the form of automatic promotion to the next rank, always providing you have proved yourself back on the streets.

The most senior ranks – **Assistant Chief Constable** and **Chief**

Constable, of which there are only 200 in a service of 130,000, are appointed by Police Authorities, with the approval of the Home Secretary.

Her Majesty's Inspectors of Constabulary (HMIs) are appointed by the Queen to undertake inspections of police forces on behalf of the Home Secretary. Their original role was to satisfy him that the 51 per cent of money paid by Central Government to fund the police service was being spent with due diligence. They now, additionally, undertake inspections on any subject that touches on the effectiveness and efficiency of the service. They are mostly recruited from the ranks of Chief Constables, and serve for a period of five years. One of their number is appointed to the role of Chief Inspector (HMCI).

The **Police Authorities** are local bodies, appointed in every police force area in England and Wales. They consist of elected politicians, magistrates and a third group of members approved by the Home Secretary. Their most important responsibilities are to appoint the chief police officers in each force (with the approval of the Home Secretary), to prepare an annual policing plan for their area, in consultation with the Chief Constable, and to oversee the Chief Constable in his or her management of the force.

INDEX